Content Moderation in the Age of AI

Siddhartha Paul Tiwari
Google Asia Pacific, Singapore

Adi Fahrudin
Faculty of Psychology, Universitas Bhayangkara Jakarta Raya, Indonesia

IGI Global
Scientific Publishing
Publishing Tomorrow's Research Today

Published in the United States of America by
IGI Global Scientific Publishing
701 East Chocolate Avenue
Hershey, PA, 17033, USA
Tel: 717-533-8845
Fax: 717-533-7115
Website: https://www.igi-global.com E-mail: cust@igi-global.com

Library of Congress Cataloging-in-Publication Data

Names: Tiwari, Siddhartha Paul, 1979- editor | Adi Fahrudin editor
Title: Content moderation in the age of AI / edited by Siddhartha Paul Tiwari, Adi Fahrudin.
Description: Hershey, PA : IGI Global Scientific Publishing, [2025] | Includes bibliographical references and index. | Summary: "Artificial intelligence allows organizations, platforms, regulators and even users to analyze massive amounts of data in real time, flagging and filtering offensive and inappropriate content that violates user expectations, community guidelines or can harm users. With the use of artificial intelligence, we are able to manage content in a way that is more effective and scalable than manual moderation, which has its limitations"-- Provided by publisher.
Identifiers: LCCN 2025000177 (print) | LCCN 2025000178 (ebook) | ISBN 9798337303352 hardcover | ISBN 9798337303369 paperback | ISBN 9798337303376 ebook
Subjects: LCSH: Content moderation (Social media)--Technological innovations | Artificial intelligence | LCGFT: Essays
Classification: LCC PN4565.C66 C66 2025 (print) | LCC PN4565.C66 (ebook) | DDC 302.23--dc23/eng/20250312
LC record available at https://lccn.loc.gov/2025000177
LC ebook record available at https://lccn.loc.gov/2025000178

British Cataloguing in Publication Data
A Cataloguing in Publication record for this book is available from the British Library.

Table of Contents

Detailed Table of Contents

In the digital age, multi layered AI content moderation systems are necessary to balance free and secure. To focus on the ethical, legal, and technological implications of automated content moderation this manuscript seeks to explore this challenge. The research examines hybrid models that leverage the top performance of AI but with the added oversight of having humans, and proposes a way to improve the accuracy, accountability and transparency of decisions machines make. To make digital platforms safer, more equitable, and a more level playing field by leveraging data that reflects the diverse realities of the world – we recommend designing, promoting, and deploying ethical AI frameworks; improving the data ecosystem; and bringing users up to speed on the technology and encouraging global regulatory collaboration.

The challenges of moderating flammable content in online spaces are discussed in this paper, which explores the impact of global digital connectivity and the innovation of technologies. AI-driven tools today suffer from the messy issues of covert harassment, deepfakes and misinformation. Prototypical adaptive AI systems that combine reinforcement learning and contextual analysis prove promising in filling these gaps. However, some hybrid models that combine AI automation with human oversight are more culturally sensitive but raise ethical issues of bias, amplification of outrage, etc. Diverse datasets, explainable AI, and collaborative frameworks from case studies of platforms such as Twitter and TikTok are highlighted. In the era of digital platforms, with an increasing number of integrated disciplines and novel technology, it's imperative. Finally, the paper calls for adaptive moderation systems that balance innovation with ethics to make internet space safer, inclusive, and trustworthy.

The rapid expansion of content, omnicommerce platforms have encountered significant challenges when it comes to maintaining stringent quality standards, regulatory compliance, and ensuring the safety and trust of users. The sheer volume of content uploaded on a daily basis poses significant moderation challenges, necessitating the detection and management of listings that might be irrelevant, inappropriate, obscene, illegal, harmful, or defamatory in nature. As the content volume on omnicommerce platforms grows exponentially, manual moderation becomes increasingly inefficient, prone to errors, and overly time consuming, which is why it has become imperative to develop a robust, scalable moderation solution. For omnicommerce platforms to be able to address these critical challenges, advanced technologies need to be utilized in order to design and implement a premoderation framework that is innovative and adaptive.

Although online social platforms are vulnerable to private information leakage, third parties can still do want with your data easily and consent. With Indeed the rapid spread of information today and changed role for social media, people more commonly worry over privacy. India's Digital Personal Data Protection Act 2023 seeks to cope with this risk by strengthening data protection. The legal framework must evolve constantly to guarantee the privacy and dignity of its recipients, permitting properly informed control over personal information in a world increasingly digital all the time.

Misinformation poses a significant challenge in the digital age, affecting public opinion and societal trust. The advent of artificial intelligence (AI) provides promising solutions for identifying, countering, and preventing the spread of false information. This study investigates the effectiveness and perceptions of AI applications in combating misinformation among students from two universities with distinct socio-cultural backgrounds. Our research objectives are threefold: to assess the awareness and understanding of AI tools among university students, to evaluate the effectiveness of specific AI applications in identifying and reducing misinformation, and to compare the perceptions and attitudes towards these AI tools among students from both countries. This exploratory study employed a survey method of (n=80) student. This study contributes to the understanding of how AI can be effectively deployed to combat misinformation and provides insights for educators, policymakers, and technology developers on enhancing the adoption and trust in AI solutions across diverse educational settings.

This chapter explores the psychological effects of AI-driven content moderation on users, content creators, and human moderators. While AI enables efficient, large-scale moderation of digital content, its opaque, automated processes often introduce emotional and behavioral challenges. Users may experience frustration and distrust due to AI's lack of transparency, potentially leading to self-censorship or disengagement. Content creators, especially those monetizing their work, face stress and anxiety from unpredictable AI decisions, impacting their creativity and autonomy. Human moderators also encounter psychological strain, caught between AI efficiency and empathy. Addressing algorithmic bias and promoting transparency, fairness, and human oversight are crucial for mitigating these impacts and fostering a healthier digital environment.

Preface

INTRODUCTION

Artificial Intelligence (AI) has revolutionized numerous industries, offering unprecedented possibilities for innovation, efficiency, and scalability. However, as AI becomes increasingly accessible, it also empowers malicious actors and content abusers with the ability to generate inappropriate, harmful, or deceptive content with ease. This dual-edged nature of AI necessitates a careful and strategic approach to content moderation, ensuring user trust and safety in digital spaces.

Traditional content moderation tools, frameworks and methods are struggling to keep pace with the rapid evolution of AI-generated content. To address this, organizations must move beyond a singular solution and instead implement multi-layered moderation systems. AI itself plays a crucial role in content moderation, allowing organizations, platforms, regulators, and users to analyze vast amounts of data in real time. By leveraging AI-driven moderation tools and frameworks, we can identify, flag, and filter offensive or inappropriate content efficiently, ensuring compliance with user expectations and community guidelines. Unlike manual moderation, which is often limited in scope and scalability, AI-powered solutions provide a dynamic, adaptive, and efficient means to manage digital content responsibly.

This book aims to comprehensively explore all aspects of content moderation in the AI era, with a particular focus on the moderation of AI-generated content. It delves into both the challenges and opportunities complexities, challenges, opportunities and advantages, presented by AI-driven content moderation, providing industry use cases and case studies that illustrate real-world applications.

The challenges addressed include:

- AI-generated harmful content, such as inappropriate material, deepfakes, hate speech, and disinformation.

- Content moderation frameworks that are outdated, specifically their inability to adapt to rapidly evolving threats from content abusers.
- Media content moderation and analysis that needs to be rapid and agile, with real-time assessment capabilities and fast identification, classification, and mitigation of harmful content

The opportunities explored include:

- AI-powered moderation tools and their effectiveness in detecting and removing harmful content.
- The development of new frameworks for content moderation that emphasize proactive detection, content filtering strategies, and scalable enforcement.
- The development of strategies for supporting the psychological well-being and wellness of human moderators, including interventions aimed at reducing mental fatigue, stress management practices, and supportive workplace frameworks.
- Comparing current methodologies and the efficiency of artificial intelligence applications to combat inappropriate content.

By examining these topics in depth, this book contributes to ongoing research and offers valuable insights to a diverse audience, including researchers, academics, corporate professionals, students, entrepreneurs, policymakers, industry leaders, investors, and regulators.

We hope this book serves as a vital resource for understanding and advancing content moderation strategies in an increasingly AI-driven world.

ORGANIZATION OF THE BOOK

In our ever-evolving digital landscape, the tension between freedom of expression and the necessity of safeguarding online spaces has become more pronounced. This volume begins with **Chapter 1**, *Balancing Freedom and Security: Multi-Layered AI Content Moderation in a Rapidly Evolving Digital Landscape*, which sets the tone by examining the critical need for ethical, legal, and technologically sound AI moderation systems. The authors propose hybrid models that unite the precision of artificial intelligence with the discernment of human oversight, advocating for inclusive data ecosystems, transparent decision-making, and international regulatory collaboration.

Chapter 2, *Adapting AI Moderation: Navigating Emerging Online Trends and Mitigating Evolving Harmful Content*, continues this discussion by focusing on the adaptive capabilities of AI in the face of shifting digital behaviors and threats such as deepfakes and covert harassment. Through reinforcement learning and culturally sensitive hybrid frameworks, the chapter emphasizes the importance of explainable AI and collaborative strategies, drawing on lessons from global platforms like Twitter and TikTok.

Shifting toward commercial applications, **Chapter 3**, *Building a Content Moderation Framework to Provide a Safe & Secure Experience for Omnichannel Commerce*, delves into the challenges of maintaining trust and safety across rapidly growing omnicommerce platforms. The chapter outlines the development of scalable, premoderation frameworks powered by advanced technology to address the surge in harmful and non-compliant content while preserving consumer confidence.

Chapter 4, *Data Privacy Law in the Age of Social Media*, presents a legal perspective on the governance of personal data within social platforms. Focusing on India's 2023 Digital Personal Data Protection Act, the authors highlight the pressing need for evolving legal frameworks to uphold digital dignity, informed consent, and meaningful user control over data in an increasingly interconnected world.

In a more applied context, **Chapter 5**, *Full Stack Powered Documentary Review App to Foster Documentary Enthusiasts*, showcases a user-focused, full-stack application built to support community engagement with documentaries. Through the integration of technologies such as React, Spring Boot, and MongoDB, this chapter illustrates how personalized experiences and scalable systems can create vibrant digital ecosystems around content sharing and discussion.

As the prevalence of AI-generated harmful content rises, **Chapter 6**, *Human-AI Collaboration in Moderating AI-Generated Harmful Content*, emphasizes the need for a hybrid approach to digital governance. Combining AI capabilities with human judgment, this chapter argues for proactive moderation, user empowerment, and the advancement of forensic AI to mitigate emerging threats while preserving ethical integrity.

From a cross-cultural perspective, **Chapter 7**, *Leveraging AI Applications to Combat Misinformation: A Comparative Analysis of University Students in Malaysia and Egypt*, explores how young adults perceive and interact with AI-driven misinformation tools. The comparative study provides valuable insights into trust, awareness, and adoption of AI tools, offering guidance for policymakers and educators aiming to enhance digital literacy in diverse environments.

Chapter 8, *Psychological Impact of AI Moderation*, shifts the focus to the emotional consequences of automated moderation systems. The authors examine the psychological toll on users, content creators, and moderators, advocating for transparency, fairness, and human oversight to reduce the unintended harms caused by opaque algorithmic decisions.

Extending the conversation on well-being, **Chapter 9**, *Psychological Well-Being of Human Content Moderators and Wellness Strategies in AI Driven Content Moderation Organizations*, identifies the organizational and cultural shifts needed to support the mental health of human moderators. Drawing on psychosocial research, the chapter calls for sustainable workplace practices, mental health programs, and ongoing training to protect the emotional resilience of those who stand at the front lines of digital content moderation.

Finally, **Chapter 10**, *Reducing the Workload: AI as a Support Tool for Human Content Moderators*, synthesizes the promise and pitfalls of integrating AI into the moderation pipeline. By analyzing real-world practices from platforms like Meta, Reddit, and YouTube, the authors underscore the importance of transparency, fairness, and hybrid systems that support—not replace—human judgment in complex ethical scenarios.

Together, these chapters offer a comprehensive exploration of AI-driven content moderation across legal, technological, psychological, and social domains. The contributions reflect a shared commitment to fostering safer, more inclusive, and ethically guided digital ecosystems for the future.

CONCLUSION

As we navigate the complexities of AI-powered content moderation, it is clear that innovation must be accompanied by responsibility. The insights, case studies, and research presented in this book highlight both the immense potential and the critical challenges of leveraging AI in this domain. While AI provides powerful tools for detecting and mitigating harmful content, its deployment must be continuously refined to align with ethical standards, legal frameworks, and user trust.

Our hope is that this book inspires further exploration and collaboration among researchers, industry professionals, and policymakers to develop robust, transparent, and effective content moderation strategies. By fostering a shared commitment to responsible AI use, we can create a safer and more trustworthy digital environment for all.

We thank our contributors for their invaluable research and perspectives and our readers for engaging with this crucial discourse. May this book serve as a stepping stone toward more ethical and effective content moderation practices in the age of AI.

Chapter 1
Balancing Freedom and Security:
Multi-Layered AI Content Moderation in a Rapidly Evolving Digital Landscape

Rashid Hashmi
https://orcid.org/0009-0006-3232-0705
SSMFE, Sharda University, India

Hemlata Parmar
https://orcid.org/0009-0009-1438-5427
Manipal University Jaipur, India

ABSTRACT

In the digital age, multi layered AI content moderation systems are necessary to balance free and secure. To focus on the ethical, legal, and technological implications of automated content moderation this manuscript seeks to explore this challenge. The research examines hybrid models that leverage the top performance of AI but with the added oversight of having humans, and proposes a way to improve the accuracy, accountability and transparency of decisions machines make. To make digital platforms safer, more equitable, and a more level playing field by leveraging data that reflects the diverse realities of the world – we recommend designing, promoting, and deploying ethical AI frameworks; improving the data ecosystem; and bringing users up to speed on the technology and encouraging global regulatory collaboration.

DOI: 10.4018/979-8-3373-0335-2.ch001

1. INTRODUCTION

The intersection of artificial intelligence (AI) and content moderation represents a critical dialogue in the digital era, as society grapples with issues of online safety, freedom of expression, and platform accountability. As online content exponentially increases, fuelled by social media platforms, video-sharing websites, blogs, and e-commerce, the task of moderating digital interactions to remove harmful, offensive, or unlawful content while maintaining user freedoms becomes both crucial and complex (Gorwa, Binns, & Katzenbach, 2020). At the forefront of this effort lies AI-driven multi-layered content moderation systems that offer automated, scalable solutions to address this mounting challenge. However, the ethical, legal, and technological implications of such systems must be critically examined in order to strike a delicate balance between freedom and security in the digital landscape.

Over the last decade, the reliance on AI to tackle content moderation has grown in parallel with the increase in toxic behaviours such as hate speech, misinformation, cyberbullying, and extremist propaganda on digital platforms (Vidgen, Harris, & Lemon, 2021). Manual moderation methods that rely entirely on human agents have proven unsustainable at scale due to the sheer volume of content produced daily (Douek, 2020). AI tools, such as machine learning algorithms, natural language processing (NLP), and computer vision technologies, have thus emerged as essential tools to automate large portions of moderation processes (Gillespie, 2018). Yet, AI moderation systems have limitations, as they are prone to both false positives, where benign content is mistakenly flagged as harmful, and false negatives, where harmful content bypasses detection (Binns, Veale, Van Kleek, & Shadbolt, 2018). This introduces risks to users' rights to free expression and the integrity of public discourse online (Raschke, Esau, & Meinel, 2019).

Also in the discourse around the AI based content moderation systems is also accountability of the platform. Using AI powered algorithm alongside human moderators, many leading digital platforms such as Facebook, Twitter, YouTube, and TikTok have adopted what is known as a multi-tiered moderation strategy (Gorwa et al., 2020). While AI solutions improve the efficiency of spam identification, graphic content detection, and misinformation, stakeholders raise concerns about their fairness and transparency. Because AI models lack an intrinsic moral compass, content classification and enforcement needs to be thoroughly calibrated against predefined ethical parameters, community standards and legal frameworks (Brundage et al., 2018). There are also more concerns about automatic systems' systemic bias and discrimination hinge on their black-box reliance on algorithms and the lack of explanation for moderation decisions (Noble, 2018; Taddei, 2021).

Therefore, based on three core principles such as accuracy, accountability, and transparency (Prates, Avelar, and Lamb, 2020), the ethical discourse in AI content moderation is based on. Accuracy thus means that AI moderation tools do an effective and dependable job of separating between harmful and nonharmful material. In general, this requires large amounts of robust training datasets that reflect cultural, linguistic, and contextual nuances. While accountability addresses the legal and ethical consequences when AI models carry editorial control of errors, whether they mistake legitimate speech or allow harmful content to stay online (Citron, 2019). Depending on platform openness, transparency demands that markets be more transparent about their algorithms during the decision making processes and the implementation of ethical best practises.

Critics of using AI for content moderation consider this from an ethical perspective, specifically that this way of content moderation may involve an over removal of content and violate users' freedom of expression even further if the AI's has biases in the training dataset which allow for its unequal enforcement across groups (Gorwa et al., 2020; Gillespie, 2018). Current studies suggest that automated moderation has and will continue to disproportionately impact marginalised voices who are outside of the dominant linguistic or cultural group out of which AI tools learn (West et al., 2019). Additionally, the deployment of automated moderation methods raises concerns of unchecked algorithmic power in policing online behaviours.

Also, security has to remain central in the discussion of content moderation technology. As AI systems have developed to track, target, and respond to the accelerated evolution of harmful online activities (such as extremist propaganda, child exploitation content, disinformation campaigns, and hate speech) there is an urgent need to deploy fast, proactive measures (Wardle & Derakhshan, 2017). As we address these harmful activities, security becomes concerned with user safety, content authenticity, and platform resilience to digital harms. Due to being able to process very large data sets on the spot, with the ability to identify these early trends and have a feedback loop, AI is just now firing on all cylinders in these security applications. As an example, sentiment analysis and other manners to detect and analyse misinformation via NLP and fact-checking approaches work with natural language models such as GPT (Chen et al., 2020).

While artificial intelligence is important for making security better, such systems don't work in a bubble. More and more, researchers and technologists have called for multi layered moderation frameworks leveraging hybrid human and AI interventions to optimise content moderation (Gorwa et al. 2020; Douek 2020). By using human in the loop systems, the humans add accountability and precision to nuanced cases, where satire or sarcasm would be easily mistaken for human intent, for example in regards to political discourse, or even just sarcasm.

Policy frameworks at international and national levels shape how multi-tiered content moderation models address these ethical and security challenges. Regulatory developments such as the *European Union's Digital Services Act*, India's *Information Technology Rules*, and U.S. debates around Section 230 of the *Communications Decency Act* have placed increased emphasis on requiring platforms to adopt responsible AI moderation systems (Barrett, 2021; Klonick, 2021). These legal instruments attempt to regulate intermediaries' liability and enforce moderation transparency while protecting fundamental freedoms.

Consequently, empirical recommendations for a sustainable drone between freedom and security include developing ethical AI models, enhancing the algorithmic transparency, adopting policies to advance privacy and stand for digital rights, and creating governance policies to protect platforms. Integrating user feedback and community-based moderation could also somewhat help to restore agency and accountability to online governance processes (Suzor et al., 2019). Looking ahead, this chapter places multi-layered AI content moderation as a tactic to moderate between democratic freedoms and security imperatives in a developing digital media environment.

The ensuing discussion will cover five core areas: This research paper describes the historical evolution and technological background of AI driven content moderation systems; the main challenges of balancing security and freedom in AI deployments; practical solutions to improve accuracy, ethics and fairness of moderation systems; and directions of future research. Second, this inquiry demonstrates that AI moderation is a necessary solution to addressing digital harms, but also highlights that ethical and responsible deployment of AI moderation must be a collaborative effort between researchers, policymakers, platforms, and the users they serve.

1.1 Evolution of Digital Communication Platforms

Since the prehistoric days of the internet, the digital communication landscape has seen rapid change. Consequently, in the early 1990s most interaction was via the likes of Usenet, early bulletin boards, and internet relay chats (IRC). Users used these platforms to share text based messages, and these platforms had rudimentary content moderation, relying upon users to self-regulate. The tools we use to create and share content evolved and changed as the internet transformed from an interlinked global network to something more global (Gillespie, 2018). From the 2000's mid onwards the advent of social media major platforms such as Facebook, Twitter, Instagram and YouTube has dramatically changed the scope and scale of digital communication, offering real time sharing and interaction with millions of users or even billions of them.

With the growing effects of social media, content moderation came to our immediate attention. Moderation at the start was basic on these platforms, with humans boring through explicit content and further filtering it according to guidelines – such as determining if an image is hate speech, for example. But such manual system proved ineffective as user bases exploded. And, to a greater degree, content regulation on these platforms has become an exercise of algorithm and automated moderation. They offer tools for the deluge of daily generated data such as tweets, videos, discussions and posts (Brundage et al., 2018).

But some of these platforms have grown so fast that new challenges emerge that require sophisticated, subtle content moderation systems. This involves everything from the propagation of misinformation to the difficulties but of course the difficulties of content moderation across various cultural nuances. Digital platforms are serving a local audience as well as global one and their content should be free to combine broad guidelines with respect to local regulations, especially since the content that is allowed in one jurisdiction could be considered illegal or culturally offensive in another (Napoli, 2019).

1.2 Content Moderation Challenges in a Globalized Environment

Now with the digital communication platforms have grown and have become more important in global discourse the challenges of the content moderation have been altered. Now they are managing millions, and sometimes billions, of user generated posts each day on social media platforms. For instance, as written by Zeng et al. (2021), an estimated 300 hours of video content are uploaded on YouTube every minute. But as a result of this overwhelming amount of data, platforms are forced to deploy conversation algorithmic and AI based systems to automatically detect and philtre out inappropriate content. But because digital platforms are by definition large in scale, human only moderators are simply not feasible, which makes AI tools a necessary feature.

But the ballooning size of the content generation took a heavy toll on the platforms striving for safety and accuracy of the information that users see. In the presence of this massive amount of content, AI tools (Natural Language Processing (NLP), computer vision, sentiment analysis, etc.) have been crucial for quick and large amount of inappropriate, violent and harmful content detection. These automated systems are helpful, but fall short when the ambiguous or nuanced content. For example, a post intended for satire or humour that an AI system without contextual understanding can easily be misinterpreted as hate speech (Barrett, 2021). This creates a very high risk of false positives where content that doesn't violate the guidelines is removed.

The wider challenge of the moderation process is also complicated by the fact that the ways that misinformation and extremism are spread online are continually becoming more sophisticated and complicated. For example, they've been criticised for doing nothing about the spread of fake news or extremist ideologies with their social media platforms. First studies have revealed that misinformation spreads faster and further on social media than fact (Zuckerberg, 2021). Automated systems designed to identify fake news or extremist content must adapt continually to detect these evolving tactics, which often exploit social media's viral nature.

Ordering of sorts, geopolitical and cultural differences also present a significant hurdle for content moderation work. With their presence across multiple countries and cultures digital platforms have troubles balancing the rules and regulations of localization and their commitment to maintaining a uniform level of moderation. In global governance, a content that may be offensive is received well by one country but rejected by another country. Yet consider what may be hateful speech in one political context may be perceived as a matter of free speech in another, creating tension between platform rules and both national and cultural standards (Douek, 2020). The cultural and legal requirements of multiple regions require platforms to adjust their content moderation policies so that they remain in line with this global coherence, while still absorbing the specificities of different regions. But this endeavour is dauntingly complex, when considering how regulatory frameworks are murky in many countries, even more so in the context of global political reorientation.

The dilemma of content moderation involving free speech vs security complicates matters even further. Many democratic societies have a core value of free speech and this is built into the fabric of many digital platforms which encourage open communication (Wardle & Derakhshan, 2017). But unrestricted freedom of speech online can still yield harmful content — hateful speech, harassment and harmful misinformation — that then, in turn, prompts greater regulation. The main challenge in this area is to ensure that content moderation systems protect user both without stifling legitimate expression (Gorwa et al., 2020). This means that when presented with polarising political content or disinformation, platform providers must decide at what point in between intervening and not intervening do they intervene under the constraints of respecting users' right to voice their opinions.

Now, the intersection between content moderation and privacy is almost always about AI powered tools. Running the risk of overstepping user privacy and becoming victim of laws such as GDPR (General Data Protection Regulation) in Europe, it's a monitoring contingently. The challenge then is how to implement systems that maintain transparency and respect individual privacy rights but allow us to effectively monitor (West et al. 2019).

This debate of automation and human intervention and their ethical considerations in AI moderation helps to further the debate. In the shifting tempo of online communities around the globe, a more nuanced and still blanket approach of utilising both machine driven moderation, and human review is becoming more and more necessary. This hybrid model addresses the possibility of bias in algorithms by allowing human moderators to provide contextual understanding of errors and therefore increasing fairness — a system which may help to mitigate the potential harm that can be caused by this bias.

In these challenges, we try to recommend and attempt to explore a series of technological improvements, such as improving AI models that can better understand nuances of human communication. It goes beyond merely developing better machine learning (ML) tools and maintaining a proper balance between AI systems and human moderators ready to ensure the fair and effective regulation of content.

Finally, digital platforms are developed with a holistic approach that combines AI tools and the dependency on human moderation input. It is a challenge at the intersection between freedom of expression and digital and interconnected, globalised users' capability to limit harmful, inappropriate, and harmful content (Gillespie, 2018).

2. THE ROLE OF AI IN CONTENT MODERATION

Content moderation is becoming a more and more difficult task to manage in the scale, and Artificial Intelligence (AI) has been already fast becoming a vital tool to do the job. As billions of daily posts, images, videos, and messages are shared all over the world across global platforms, you simply have to use AI systems to be able to detect harmful, illegal or inappropriate material. With AI, social media sites can automatically process large swathes of the moderation process in real time as they analyze millions of pieces of content (Gorwa et al., 2020). Tools driven by AI provide the speed and scale human moderators alone cannot deliver, they are essential ingredients to content governance on platforms such as Facebook, Twitter and YouTube.

2.1 Machine Learning Models in Content Moderation

Machine Learning (ML) and content moderation automation is one of the most important subset of AI. To detect offensive speech, hate speech, graphic violence etc. ML algorithms are powered by large volumes of labelled content for their training to learn. Platforms also use supervised, unsupervised and deep learning models to find a pattern and categorise the content (Binns et al., 2018).

As an arm of Artificial Intelligence, Natural Language Processing (NLP) or Natural Language Processing focuses on how to understand human language, to interpret textual content. For instance, AI tools such as sentiment analysis and keyword detection let platforms flag hate speech, harassment, and misinformation (Chen et al., 2020). A critical component for NLP is contextualising language given the fact that this is more sensitive to an AI system's intent, tone, and emotional subtext that then produces more accurate classification in real time. However, language nuances- sardonic comments, cultural idioms- are too much for any AI to parse without human guidance, so this requires a hybrid approach of speed and scale (of AI) and then ethical alignment.

2.2 AI-Enhanced Image and Video Moderation

Textual content continues to be the dominant focus of content moderation, but images and videos are a very serious challenge. There are computer vision techniques that platforms use to scan visual content for any violent imagery, hate symbols, nudity, or other harmful images. With the increase of video content, platforms have had to put in place automated systems which identify potentially harmful videos and images. Convolutional neural networks (CNNs) have improved the accuracy of image and video moderation by being good at detecting visual patterns, such as being specific (Zeng et al., 2021). Yet, the problem is that AI-based moderation tools may find it challenging to tell the difference between contextual images, including artistic, educational content, from those with explicit, harmful visual materials. So, refining these AI models to understand better, and with cultural nuance, is important to avoiding unfair censorship.

With the integration of AI and deep learning, more sophisticated image detection is now possible: hate symbols, for instance, or abusive or extremism related content (Zuckerberg, 2021). While videos have come a long way, it is more complex to moderate video content because it has a contextual meaning of how you interpret the multimedia material. An AI may be able to correctly label violence in a video but cannot understand what this violence means, in the context it is in: a conflict documentary, for example. Human moderators are still necessary, though, in some edge cases' content, to better ensure a higher level of accuracy and accountability (Brundage et al., 2018).

2.3 AI and Misinformation Detection

The accelerated spread of misinformation on social media platforms has increased the use of AI in the moderation of not only explicit harm, but also the unintended consequences of misinformation, fake news and conspiracy theories. Using network analysis and pattern recognition (West et al., 2019), the existing AI tools help platforms determine if the content being posted has been manipulated using a technique such as a deep fake or overly clickbait in its headline. The way AI algorithms flag content is by looking at behavioural patterns or content discrepancies that, given past performances, yield high confidence that the content is misleading or false, but especially in real-time or when the content has spread online within first few hours.

Traditional methods are no longer effective in detecting minor manipulations in multimedia content like facial modifications in videos and artificially generated images, which have been bought up by deep learning models to identify. These models are regularly trained on new datasets to stay current with evolving strategies used by malicious actors online. For example, identifying deep fakes—hyper-realistic but entirely synthetic videos that can spread misinformation—requires advanced machine learning algorithms capable of detecting anomalies at a pixel level (Zuckerberg, 2021). These AI-powered tools have made it more possible to combat harmful content before it spreads virally, though it is important to note that no model is infallible.

2.4 Challenges and Limitations of AI Moderation

But while AI is not without challenges. Machine learning systems are as advanced as they can be, but they still suffer from data quality, unjust algorithmic bias, and the inability to grasp context. Being trained on with data, AI models are naturally dependent on the data. For instance, if the training data predominantly consists of one group's website, the algorithm could end up biassing the predictions, performing poorly on other contexts or other groups (Gillespie, 2018). That's more of a problem when AI systems disproportionately censor particular perspectives or groups, or miss certain harmful speech due to the heavily skewed nature of the data that the system was trained on. AI based moderation systems have been shown to inadvertently reinforce bias, such as racial, gender, and cultural prejudice (West et al. 2019).

Another major limitation is a lack of understanding of context. For example, while AI systems can relatively easily spot certain kinds of hate speech or abuse, they are much less successful when faced with more complex situations like satire or jokes or coded language (Brundage et al., 2018). To detect context, you can't discount the words or images alone, but the intent, the wider conversation, the traditional or political biases that determine how something might be read. Yet, many forms of controversial or harmful content run in ways that AI still cannot fully comprehend enough to know what it's seeing or to have it do what's best. That means human intervention is still required for a clear judgement.

However, to solve these challenges, a hybrid moderation model based on a combination of AI technologies and human moderators is now essential to guarantee fairness, transparency and an even higher level of content moderation accuracy.

2.5 Balancing Free Speech and Security in Digital Platforms

One of the thorniest ethical problems in content moderation is: how do we strike the right balance of upholding the value of free speech while safeguarding user safety and security? One of the bedrock rights in democratic societies is freedom of expression, but how it plays out in the digital world is become murkier by the day due to the rapid spread of increasingly harmful content: hate speech, extremism, misinformation. While platforms like Facebook and Twitter have implemented stricter policies around content moderation, they have faced both pushback from free speech advocates who view such policies as censorship, and critiques that they are not doing enough to curtail harmful behavior (Napoli, 2019).

2.6 The Case for Free Speech

Platforms such as Facebook, Twitter, and Reddit were originally designed to foster open discussions and freedom of expression. Free speech proponents argue that digital platforms provide a much-needed outlet for diverse voices, especially marginalized or minority groups who traditionally had less access to mass communication channels. Without the availability of platforms to voice their concerns, individuals may find it harder to communicate and advocate for change.

The ethical value of free speech requires that people should not fear persecution or retribution for expressing their thoughts, regardless of how controversial or unpopular they may be. However, given the potential harms associated with allowing unfiltered content—such as the propagation of hateful, discriminatory, or violent speech—many platforms find themselves walking a delicate line between curbing harmful speech and protecting individual freedoms (Gillespie, 2018).

2.7 The Importance of Security

However, the explosion of the internet and social media platforms has also allowed for the expansion of extremist content, cyberbully, disinformation and hate speech that can have real world impact. There is also the concern that unchecked hate speech, and violent rhetoric, can lead to real world violence, influence election outcomes and intrude on social cohesion. In response to such high profile incidents as x violent extremism on livestreaming platforms or the role of social media in political destabilisation (Vidgen et al., 2021), governments and advocacy groups have increasingly pressed for governments and companies to improve their content moderation practises.

That challenge, then, becomes systems in which the free expression does not unduly intrude and the harmful activities do not undermine public safety and social trust. Balancing freedom of speech with content moderation is especially complicated with hundreds of billions of users ranging from many to zero languages featuring diverse cultures and expectations. For instance, policies that work in one region do not unavoidably carry over to others: a demonstration of this is the divergence among European, Asian and North American reactions to hate speech laws and government regulations (Douek, 2020).

3. THE ROLE OF ALGORITHMIC MODERATION IN BALANCING FREEDOM AND SECURITY

The notion of automated content moderation is one of the key ways on which platforms monitor the number of posts a user is posting and keeps the threshold with respect to content guidelines. But what makes the AI tool so advantageous is that unlike humans, it can search and process so much content much faster than humans, and even flag this content for further review (West et al., 2019). Delving into these, these AI-powered systems use top learn patterns indicating harmful content, such as racial slurs, graphic violence, or false narratives.

Though these tools can act swiftly, they fail to perform well when the content is ambiguous or entwined with contextual subtleties. For example, taking political speech related to protests out of context could be interpreted as incendiary and violent when heard alone, however it may, in fact, be legitimate opinion. For this reason, AI needs to maintain a particular balance between its speed and the contextual understanding that human moderators deliver. However, these automated systems can help flag content, serving as an initial step in this process, but human judgement should continue to guide more difficult cases.

However, there is no room for AI here, as the volume of user generated content on digital platforms is huge, and neither AI nor nothing can effectively handle it, and there is an urgency to integrate AI and human oversight in moderation. These platforms struggle to balance free speech and security in digital spaces, all while designing robust content moderation systems. Researching what makes it stronger, safer and still fair, as well as research into moderation models that respect diverse cultural norms will inform the future of the digital governance.

4. SOLUTIONS AND RECOMMENDATIONS

In the age of digital platforms, moderation of content is bigger than just service moderation. And they must account for the fluidity in content, the worldwide array of users, and the mesh between technology, human freedom, and legal frameworks. In this chapter, a comprehensive set of solutions and recommendations that overcome these challenges are explored using ethical, inclusive, and scalable approaches.

4.1 Technological Solutions: Advancing AI for Content Moderation

4.1.1 Enhancing AI Algorithms for Nuanced Moderation

Due to its capability to analyse huge sets of data, Artificial Intelligence (AI) is a spine of content moderation. AI systems however miss out on the cultural nuances and regional contexts; or, emerging content, forms that we, humans, create every day. In order to improve AI, we have to broaden datasets by cleaning cultures, linguistic and social contexts. Training AI on this broad foundation reduces inherent biases and allows platforms to deal with content that is sensitive (Binns et al., 2018).

Context aware AI systems must be created for better decision making. By using AI to resort cutting edge neural network models like transformers and context dependent language structure, it can learn out of the box subtler Stuff like sarcasm, irony or layered meanings (Chen et al., 2020). Real world user feedback can be a source of adaptive AI algorithms, which are able to learn and become more and more accurate with time — in fact the more new content categories you tackle the more AoT (top of the funnel) you'll need to get to.

Some of the other innovations are in proactive AI action to flag harmful content before it is spread far and wide. AI developed to decode potentially dangerous patterns in social media trends — for example, virally spreading misinformation or coordinated harassment campaigns — can operate automatically, tailoring output accordingly. That's why, by noticing these risks earlier, the platforms can intervene with preemptive measures like rallying for higher scrutiny on flagged posts.

4.1.2 Employing Hybrid Moderation Models

AI gives scale; human monitoring is needed to solve ambiguity. Combining automated systems with skilled moderators allows for contextual and culturally assertive evaluation of sensitive or borderline cases (Gillespie, 2018). High volume tasks like spam detection or repetitive hate speech patterns can be handled by AI while human moderators determine the content that needs to be determined with nuance.

By developing user friendly dashboards with sentiment analysis and real time detection tools, moderators now have better decision making power. The tools that have to be implemented must ensure there are transparency reports of the system's decision path including the ability for moderators to review flagged content, validating or overruling AI decisions. Early examples of this collaborative process are the platforms such as Facebook's Oversight Board, but scalability remains an open challenge.

For this approaches to be strengthened, platforms need to be enabled with workflows that combine the power of human and AI. Before you even think about humans handling anything, putting low risk cases (e.g. spam) entirely in automation boosts potential for them to do no harm, while making sure humans handle high risk cases (e.g. cyber bullying) prevents humans from being an attack vector.

4.2 Human-Centered Moderation Strategies

4.2.1 Scaling Human Moderation Teams with Regional Expertise

To moderate effectively in a globalised internet ecosystem, platforms require human moderators who know the broad intellects of regional cultures, languages, and political systems. The teams that have to be made up of people from different cultural backgrounds in terms of their geographic and socio-economic background. There is diversity in this that ensures locally sensitive topics get treated fairly and reduce the risk of ethnocentric application of content rules.

A robust hiring policy that emphasises diversity and inclusion helps overall effectiveness by better understanding local context, and avoiding harmful subtext missed by automated systems using regional experts. The examples include picking up culturally ambiguous hate speech that the AI might miss as literal translation errors. Moreover, platforms can allow regional moderators to alert the platforms of politically charged terminology, or symbols common to that region.

Moderators need specialised training, so that they should be able to cope with emotional stress and ethical dilemmas of work (Barrett, 2021). Moreover, moderators are provided with refresher courses on technological developments in content regulation, and on legal precedents in order to keep them up to date with the fluidity of their duties. By means of such programmes, moderators could further obtain how to interpret and handle internationally sensitive issues successfully.

4.2.2 Supporting Mental Health for Moderators

The exposure to disturbing or harmful content can cause mental health issues such as secondary trauma and chronic stress among moderators. Platforms must prioritize mental health by offering professional counseling services, setting limits on the amount of distressing content reviewed daily, and alternating challenging tasks with less taxing activities. Peer-support networks and wellness workshops specifically designed for moderation teams are vital in sustaining their morale and well-being.

A preventive care approach, using technology to rotate assignments or pre-screen harmful images with "blurring" mechanisms before moderator exposure, reduces the immediate impact of traumatic material. Offering compensation packages that account for the psychological strain of such work also encourages greater job retention and mental wellness.

4.3 Collaborative Regulatory Frameworks

4.3.1 Establishing Harmonized Global Content Standards

The reality is that this is a regulatory process functioning within a fragmented regulatory environment, which often hampers the implementation of effective content moderation processes. We need to standardise, so nations and platforms should agree on minimum standards of what is acceptable yet retain freedom to adapt for local tastes. Educational institutions can collaborate through multilateral institutions like the United Nations, OECD, and regional bodies to create guidelines that balance the two principles of free speech and the need to fight harmful content (Napoli, 2019). The Digital Services Act proposed by the European Union's in itself a pioneering model, by which the convening of the platform obligations and the users' rights in the fight against the risks online.

By building universal ethical frameworks based on human rights laws, like the Universal Declaration of Human Rights (UDHR), platforms can be given a guiding hand in dealing with morally ambiguous scenarios. With that, we must also put an emphasis on transparency on takedown requests from governments, that these actions in no way deprive from the right of people to express their dissent and that the possibility do not compromise the ability of democracy to progress in this or other ways.

Formal institutions are not the only way to bridge the chasm between regulators and the tech industry; civic and academic collaborations can also assist. Regional think tanks that focus on locally relevant internet governance policies can offer more complex frameworks that account for the international best practises while taking into consideration regional differences.

4.3.2 Enforcing Transparency Mechanisms

To rebuild public trust in enforcement, platforms must be more transparent about how they practise it. These bi-annual transparency reports detailing algorithmic decisions and policy enforcement metrics as well as government takedown requests give users and regulators an account of what took place (West et al. 2019). By using Explainable AI (XAI), your users won't have to wonder why their content was flagged and removed — they can simply understand the reasoning behind the algorithmic process.

4.4 Empowering Users

4.4.1 Simplifying Content Reporting Systems

Engaging users as proactive stakeholders in moderation involves creating user-friendly reporting interfaces that facilitate complaints about offensive, illegal, or harmful content. Enhanced reporting mechanisms should allow for multilingual accessibility, simplified options for categorizing complaints, and a transparent mechanism for users to track their submissions. Providing feedback loops that inform users of the final outcome boosts transparency and user engagement.

4.4.2 Promoting Digital Literacy and Media Awareness

A digitally literate user base is crucial to reducing the prevalence of misinformation, hate speech, and harmful behaviors. Media literacy programs must be scaled globally through partnerships between platforms, governments, and NGOs, focusing on user awareness about misinformation detection and content authenticity checks (Vidgen et al., 2021). Incorporating digital literacy modules in school and university curricula ensures that future generations engage responsibly with digital platforms.

For vulnerable user groups, particularly older adults prone to misinformation consumption, customized outreach programs should teach critical evaluation of online news sources and techniques for verifying information. Campaigns using gamified learning approaches—such as simulations—can make educational programs engaging while increasing impact. Community-oriented efforts where citizens collaboratively fact-check popular stories on local forums may create positive civic reinforcement for trustworthy content.

4.5 Addressing Emerging Challenges

4.5.1 Tackling Deepfake Content

A deepfake is a significant threat to the credibility of digital information. Deepfakes are a manifestation of this phenomenon, and AI models trained for deepfake detection can, and hopefully will, play an integral role in its eradication. Video and audio content should be watermarked for deployment by platforms and authenticity tracking based on metadata (Gillespie, 2018). Journalists, civic groups and platforms could start collaboration to develop stronger ways of verifying manipulated media with each other.

As for authentication, there is a pathway through on the recent thrusts of blockchain technology. With blockchain-backed timestamps or certificates attached to media upload, creators and platforms can authenticate the unaltered media more efficiently, and at least some of the public can trust the material without being suspicious. Public led verification tools might be provided by platforms that will allow for a broader participation in maintaining online integrity.

4.5.2 Countering Misinformation with Collaborative Fact-Checking

Partnerships between digital platforms and independent fact-checking organizations can identify false or misleading information at scale. Incorporating these fact-checks into platform AI can speed up the moderation process. However, transparent communication about the sources and processes of fact-checking must be provided to prevent skepticism about bias in content takedowns. Platforms must go a step further by implementing mechanisms to redirect users exposed to false claims toward verified sources.

In addition, empowering local communities as verification hubs—inspired by Wikipedia-style collaboration—can enhance vigilance against misleading content and increase community accountability. Extending fact-checking partnerships to citizen advocacy groups operating within rural or semi-digitalized regions bridges digital literacy divides.

4.6 Ethical Considerations in Moderation

4.6.1 Mitigating Algorithmic Bias

Training data and/or flawed algorithmic assumptions often leads to exclusionary biases to algorithmic systems. The moderation process should incorporate audit mechanisms by which algorithms will identify and prevent discriminatory enforcement patterns. Bias bounties create welcome crowdsourced reviews of moderation algorithms, providing diverse input and feedback to help ensure implementation equity (Brundage et al., 2018).

Steps to avoid unnecessary bias bootstraps include proactive measures to begin diversifying algorithm training team. Long term solutions include academic and industry collaborations that set shared protocols for equitable data collection. Another form of systemic safeguards against future incurrence is the further investment in algorithm ethics training in engineering curricula.

4.6.2 Establishing Independent Oversight Bodies

By introducing content governance councils with ethicists, social scientists and reps of marginalized communities on the moderation policy, we ensure we are weaving ethical considerations into moderation policies. On the other hand, these councils can look at complex cases, establish standards for fair dispute resolution or fairness in political dissent, satire, or the art. Systemic imbalances must also be addressed by oversight bodies, for example, corporate platforms must be checked to meet socio cultural obligations beyond metrics of profitability. This strengthened public accountability can be achieved if grievance mechanisms for appeals are monitored and the results are published transparently in dispute resolutions.

4.7 Encouraging Long-Term Innovation and Research

To keep up with digital innovation, platforms must continue investment in research to improve their moderation systems. Research grants for universities or public institutions looking to study decentralised platforms, or the use of such platforms in moderation mechanisms that avoid text, like augmented and virtual reality (Duok, 2020).

Further, experimental pilot programmes incorporating the use of decentralised moderation systems, including committees of user driven governance or communities moderating spaces, offer the opportunity to diversify decision making frameworks as a means for promoting platform accountability. Given that digital spaces are evolving so rapidly to immersive formats, it's important to continue expanding efforts in augmented reality (AR) and the metaverse so that we will be as prepared as possible for new content moderation challenges that may arise.

Dynamic communication across sectors is needed to solve content moderation challenges by combining advanced technological solutions and human centred approaches with robust regulatory systems. Given transparent governance structures that empower them, and ethical imperatives guiding them in taking up fundamental freedoms and responsibilities to safeguard user safety, these platforms are in a position to fulfil their roles. In these transformative solutions, the broader digital community is an integral partner in the user education and proactive engagement.

5. FUTURE RESEARCH AND DIRECTIONS

Ensuring public trust in online spaces requires that content moderation grapples with the challenges presented by ever evolving digital landscapes to the deepest extent possible, and with the greatest strategic innovation, as we struggle to keep up with the latest technological developments. Contemporary globalised digital platforms are complex in different ways, from misinformation and hate speech, to cultural sensitivities, and even deepfake technologies—which make it necessary for sustained academic and practical efforts to understand received and plausible paths forward. This chapter argues for future research in these areas and furnishes strategic directions emphasising interdisciplinary collaboration, ethical governance, and integration of emerging technologies.

5.1 Making AI Capabilities Even More Useful for Content Moderation

While Artificial Intelligence (AI) remains a key pillar of content moderation, there remain clear gaps in what it does and does not effectively do, namely in its efficacy, transparency and scalability. Algorithmic capability in processing nuanced contexts must be reined and efforts have to be made in research to refine this. For instance, such as transformer based AI will have been advancing in context aware AI, which will be able to spot inferences like sarcasm, double entendres or even regional dialects. Yet, as Chen, Wong, and Jiang point out, such models struggle with limitations of datasets and bias, preventing their use equitatively.

5.1.1 Mechanisms for reduction of algorithmic bias: This is one area of exploration for reduction of algorithmic bias which is one critical area to explore. Today's algorithms tend to reflect the narrow views of their training datasets, enforcing moderation policies unfairly. Future studies should focus on gathering representative and inclusive datasets of the global culture, language and user interactions. Alongside transparency in AI decision making, facilitated by Explainable AI (XAI) technologies, it will also boost user trust and create a channel for oversight by moderators and regulators.

5.1.2 Leveraging Multimodal AI: Exciting opportunities for holistic content analysis come with AI models that are able to integrate text, imagery, audio and video modalities, as seen in paper 1.2. For example, multimodal approaches can improve detection accuracy, or at least improve the identification of deepfakes, coordinated misinformation campaigns, and visual hate symbols. Future research should investigate scalable real time multimodal processing for balancing technological advancement with the ethics (Vidgen, Braun, Hayes).

5.2 Human-Centered Approaches to Moderation

While technology plays a central role, human involvement remains indispensable for addressing complex and contextually sensitive cases. Research is needed to explore methods for optimizing human-AI collaboration in moderation workflows and ensuring the welfare of human moderators exposed to harmful content.

5.2.1 Exploring Hybrid Models Hybrid content moderation models that integrate AI and human judgment require careful optimization. Future studies must analyze how to effectively allocate tasks between AI systems and moderators based on the severity or complexity of flagged content. Case studies from platforms like Facebook and YouTube can provide insights into the efficiencies and ethical implications of such frameworks.

5.2.2 Mental Health of Moderators Moderation work can exact significant emotional tolls on individuals due to prolonged exposure to graphic or disturbing content. Barrett's work underscores the urgent need for longitudinal studies examining the mental health impacts on moderators and the efficacy of interventions like counseling services, wellness programs, and task-rotation mechanisms. Incorporating neuroscience and psychology expertise into moderation research will help develop tools that prioritize emotional resilience and mental well-being.

5.3 Regulatory Evolution and Policy Frameworks

The policy landscape surrounding digital platforms remains fragmented and reactive. Regulatory challenges are compounded by differences in regional norms, governance philosophies, and legislative frameworks. Future research should explore how global collaboration and adaptive policies can promote harmonization without undermining localized values or freedoms.

5.3.1 Ethical Governance Models Developing universal governance models that prioritize ethical content moderation is a pressing need. Research efforts can draw from human rights law, such as the Universal Declaration of Human Rights, to inform policies that balance free expression and harm prevention.

Emphasis should be placed on ensuring that governance structures are independent, participatory, and transparent (Napoli).

5.3.2 Regulatory Sandboxes for Innovation Emerging technologies often outpace regulatory frameworks, creating enforcement challenges. To address this gap, policymakers and platforms can establish "regulatory sandboxes"—controlled environments for testing novel technologies or content governance strategies without fully implemented legal obligations. Future research should evaluate the feasibility, impact, and scalability of such experimental models in both developed and developing contexts.

5.4 Combating Emerging Threats

And now, new frontier of challenges: rise of deepfake technologies, coordinated disinformation campaigns, and augmented reality (AR) content. These issues need anticipatory research that stays ahead of technology.

5.4.1 Deep Fakes Detection: Deep fake threats to societal trust: Political destabilization; Reputational harm; 4:1 The development of AI that can pinpoint manipulated media with strict detail must be a priority in the research of this field, and blockchain solutions for confirming authenticity via metadata (Gillespie).

5.4.2 Content Moderation in the Metaverse: If digital interaction begins to show up in immersive formats, such as the metaverse, existing moderation strategies may become obsolete. There should be research into how decentralized, community driven moderation models can work in AR and VR environments. Immersive behavioral norms, and augmented ethics studies could likely mature into best practices when it comes to ethics and safety in virtual spaces.

5.5 Ways Companies Empower Users through Digital Literacy

Even if this can't completely eliminate the need for moderation systems yet, educating users on how to surf in the digital spaces responsibly could dramatically lessen the load on moderation systems. To build digital literacy, particularly among underserved and vulnerable populations, research needs to find effective ways.

5.5.1 Developing Scalable Programs For developing scalable, culturally relevant digital literacy programs, such initiative require collaborate of academic expertise, governmental support, and platform engagement. Future research can consider whether gamified tools, augmented reality training simulation, etc. can be used to make literacy education more accessible and more retains (Brundage et al.).

5.5.2 Studying the Impact of Civic Fact-Checking: Promising area for exploration is studying the impact of civic fact checking, which involves involving users in community driven verification initiatives where people work together to fight misleading information. Researchers can assess their impact on trust dynamics, user engagement and the amount of misinformation seen on those platforms by studying platforms that have piloted these systems.

5.6 Research Initiatives that are Interdisciplinary and Collaborative

Interdisciplinary approaches to content moderation that require the combining of technology, law, ethics, and sociology are necessary precisely because of the complexities of it. Holistic pathways exist through collaborative frameworks: a balance of governments, academia and tech industries.

5.6.1 Academic-Industry Partnerships Future research should examine the structure and outputs of academic-industry collaborations; such as grants for moderation-focused studies or co-authored policy recommendations. These partnerships can promote the equitable sharing of knowledge while accelerating progress in challenging areas like algorithmic fairness or privacy-preserving moderation.

5.6.2 Open-Source Platforms for Research Building open-source platforms where researchers can access anonymized datasets and standardized moderation tools will help advance the field collectively. Studies must investigate the practicalities and risks of this approach, focusing on preserving user privacy while fostering collaborative problem-solving.

The future of content moderation research rests on a collective commitment to address persistent challenges, anticipate emerging threats, and build equitable solutions. By emphasizing technological innovation, human welfare, regulatory evolution, and user empowerment, researchers can help shape digital environments that are safer, more inclusive, and ethically governed. However, this ambition depends on robust interdisciplinary cooperation and sustained investment in knowledge-sharing mechanisms.

6. SUMMARIZING THE COMPLEX LANDSCAPE OF CONTENT MODERATION

Digital platform content moderation is one of the most complex, contentious issues of the digital age. The complexity comes from the need to balance users' rights to safety against the spread of harmful content while still protecting freedoms of expression. As the scale and breadth of internet users expand, and new forms of harmful content arrive at increasing speed – including deepfakes and misinformation – it makes this already complicated struggle even more so. Where content moderation decisions are not technical acts, but deeply political acts with consequences for what is, and isn't sayable within public discourse, Gillespie points out.

Technological, regulatory, human centred, as well as ethical strategies for creating a holistic road map for overcoming these problems. So with these artificial intelligence advancements, these transformers based models, this explainable AI, we can do much better at finding and doing something about harmful content at scale. Human moderation with the correct cultural competence and mental health is still something you will need, but also moderation teams. Automation is not deemed to be at odds with human oversight, Brundage repeated as the AI does not have the power to comprehend the subjective and contextual aspects of speech and images. For instance, the European Union's Digital Services Act and parallels like it highlight the importance of harmonised regulation — that is principles emerging from other contexts adapted to a given local context. These initiatives of platforms' accountability and transparency must be accompanied by investments in user empowerment, both in terms of accessible reporting mechanisms as well as media literacy. And so it was with such multi layered solutions that we reconfirmed what we've always known — moderation won't be effective when it's not systematic, when it's not done in coordination by different stakeholders, i.e. governments, platform tech companies and finally users themselves.

6.1 Challenges and Gaps in Current Approaches

Despite the proposed solutions, the advancements in technology and governance, many challenges remain. Insights into AI's struggle with cultural nuances, language barriers and contextual ambiguities suggest automation alone is not a reliable substitute. But Brundage thought it was important to warn the dangers of feeding bias or introducing new forms of it by using a flawed algorithm, and that we should have diverse datasets and multidisciplinary teams of developers to keep the algorithm 'right.'

Harmonisation is also a challenge to regulatory efforts. According to Napoli, asymmetrical treatment of speech and privacy across nations poses a difficult challenge for consensus. The United States may have stronger protection for free speech than, say, areas of the Middle East or Asia, where stricter content controls prevail. It further heightens the requirement for adaptable architectures that uphold baseline global standards while permitting local interpretation.

User engagement is another critical area of concern. Despite the availability of digital literacy programmes and user friendly reporting systems, barriers such as low awareness, absence of resources in rural areas and entrenched social behaviours discourage full application of these programmes. According to vidgen et al.'s research, populations that are digitally underserved are still very susceptible to the negative effects of misinformation and hate speech. There are also sustained attention requirements around human moderators psychological toll. Barrett's highlighting of mental health support and workload management initiatives do offer helpful insight, however there is little to no consistency on implementation and their measures are particularly inconsistent among smaller companies with smaller resources to even begin implementing.

6.2 Long-Term Implications and Ethical Considerations

There can be no thinking about the future of content moderation without reference to the substantive ethical problems the digital platforms pose. Questions surrounding who decides what is considered "harmful" or "inappropriate" remain critical. The centralised decision making by tech giants invites fears of power consolidations and ideological hegemonies. Brundage's call for bias audits and algorithmic transparency is an excellent start that should be buttressed by the democratisation of moderation policies. And there may be user driven governance models and independent oversight boards where one can include multiple voices in moderation decision making processes.

Deepfake detection and blockchain based content verification have ethical dilemma overlaps. These technologies aren't perfect, yet they offer strong tools against what morphs into poor information, which comes with its own privacy, surveillance, and use concerns. As an example, such deepfake detection algorithms may also violate privacy rights by analysing biometrics, where there is no consent. Our approach to these risks demands integration of ethical considerations into every stage of policy development and technology creation, so that our solutions aren't only effective but also equitable.

6.3 Path Forward: Collaborative Solutions for a Safer Digital Space

Innovation and collaboration are the future of content moderation. The first is for platforms to build broad partnerships with governments, civil society organisations, academia, and independent fact checkers in order to develop more coherent solutions. Particularly in situations involving digital literacy programmes or regional moderation teams, public private partnerships can easily help bridge resource gaps. This collaborative approach is consistent with Napol's focus on bringing diverse stakeholders aboard the governance ecosystem.

Second, funding for long long term research must be continuing. Douek speculates that content moderation systems must evolve hand in hand with the development of new formats used in the coming years, such as augmented and virtual reality, which will bring their own issues to moderation. Alongside traditional strategies we must pay attention to pilot programmes for decentralised content management, blockchain authentication tools, and immersive reality frameworks.

Third, user trust must always be a cornerstone. By publishing regular enforcement reports, explaining AI driven decisions and whether machines learn from human mistakes, platforms can increase their legitimacy and make their accountability explicit. Moderation policies tend to remain responsive to community needs by providing more opportunities for user feedback. Furthermore, the scaling of literacy programmes in local languages can lead to digital empowerment across geographies, of which the underserved communities remain farthest.

Finally, all strategies must be underpinned by philosophical and ethical frameworks that can be used as a moral foundation for a programme. The Universal Declaration of Human Rights and principles of inclusive internet governance must be encouraged to be drawn upon by both policymakers and platforms alike, in pursuit of values such as equality, fairness and respect. A way to promoting trust, while reducing harm includes strengthening mechanisms of appeal and oversight that reduce algorithmic and institutional biases.

7. CONCLUSION

The task of effective content moderation is neither static nor singular; it is an evolving challenge that must adapt to the ever-changing dynamics of digital spaces. By combining technological innovation, human expertise, regulatory collaboration, and user participation, content moderation can be transformed into a more equitable and sustainable system. This holistic approach aligns the goals of protecting users, preserving freedom of speech, and promoting societal well-being.

As platforms and societies navigate this intricate terrain, they must remain committed to fostering inclusive and ethical digital ecosystems. The onus lies not just on technology companies but on all stakeholders to work collectively in building a safer and more accountable internet. This collaborative effort reflects a shared responsibility for shaping a digital future that respects both the richness of human diversity and the values of shared humanity.

REFERENCES

Barrett, P. M. (2021). *Who moderates the social media giants?* NYU Stern School of Business, Center for Business and Human Rights.

Binns, R., Veale, M., Van Kleek, M., & Shadbolt, N. (2018). "It's reducing a human being to a percentage": Perceptions of justice in algorithmic decisions. Proceedings of the 2018 CHI Conference on Human Factors in Computing Systems, 1–14. https://doi.org/DOI: 10.1145/3173574.3173951

Brundage, M., Avin, S., Clark, J., Eckersley, P., Garfinkel, B., & Amodei, D. (2018). *The malicious use of artificial intelligence: Forecasting, prevention, and mitigation*. ArXiv Preprint.

Brundage, M., Avin, S., Clark, J., Eckersley, P., Garfinkel, B., & Amodei, D. (2018). *The malicious use of artificial intelligence: Forecasting, prevention, and mitigation*. ArXiv Preprint.

Chen, L., Wong, C., & Jiang, Z. (2020). Textual analysis of sentiment-based content regulation for hate speech moderation. *Social Media + Society*, *6*(3), 1–14. DOI: 10.1177/2056305120930846

Citron, D. K. (2019). *Hate crimes in cyberspace*. Harvard University Press.

Douek, E. (2020). The rise of content cartels. Knight First Amendment Institute. https://knightcolumbia.org

Gillespie, T. (2018). *Custodians of the Internet: Platforms, content moderation, and the hidden decisions that shape social media*. Yale University Press.

Gorwa, R., Binns, R., & Katzenbach, C. (2020). Algorithmic content moderation: Technical and political challenges in the automation of platform governance. *Big Data & Society*, *7*(1), 1–15. DOI: 10.1177/2053951719897945

Klonic, K. (2021). The new governors: The people, rules, and processes governing online speech. *Harvard Law Review*, *131*(6), 1598–1670.

Napoli, P. M. (2019). *Social media and the public interest: Media regulation in the disinformation age*. Columbia University Press. DOI: 10.7312/napo18454

Newton, C., & Witt, C. (2020). *The trauma floor: The secret lives of Facebook moderators*. The Verge.

Noble, S. U. (2018). *Algorithms of oppression: How search engines reinforce racism*. NYU Press. DOI: 10.18574/nyu/9781479833641.001.0001

Prates, M. O. R., Avelar, P. H., & Lamb, L. C. (2020). Assessing gender bias in machine translation. NeurIPS 2020.

Raschke, P., Esau, K., & Meinel, C. (2019). Measuring the potential of online deliberation processes: Automated content analysis of argumentative quality. *Policy and Internet*, *11*(2), 208–227.

Richards, N. M., & Hartzog, W. (2019). The pathologies of digital consent. *Washington University Law Review*, *96*(2), 1003–1071.

Suzor, N. P., West, S. M., Quodling, A., & York, J. (2019). What do we mean when we talk about transparency? *International Journal of Communication*, *13*, 1526–1543.

Taddei, S. (2021). AI and its ethical challenges. *AI & Society*, *36*(1), 101–115.

Vidgen, B., Braun, R., & Hayes, G. (2021). Designing for digital governance: Challenges in automation and scaling content moderation at large platforms. *Communications of the ACM*, *64*(4), 24–27. DOI: 10.1145/3411789

Wardle, C., & Derakhshan, H. (2017). *Information disorder: Toward an interdisciplinary framework for research and policy making*. Council of Europe.

West, S. M., Whittaker, M., & Crawford, K. (2019). *Discriminating systems: Gender, race, and power in AI*. AI Now Institute.

Yeung, K., & Lodge, M. (2019). Algorithmic regulation: A critical interrogation. *Regulation & Governance*, *13*(1), 1–16.

Zeng, J., Chan, C. H., & Fu, K. W. (2021). How false information spreads on social media: A systematic review. *Social Media + Society*, *7*(2), 1–13.

Zuckerberg, M. (2021). The challenges of governing content on digital platforms. *Journal of Digital Ethics*, *5*(3), 67–81.

KEY TERMS AND DEFINITIONS

Algorithmic Bias: Refers to systematic and unfair discrimination in the outputs of machine learning algorithms, often caused by biased training data or flawed design assumptions. It affects how content is flagged or moderated on digital platforms.

Artificial Intelligence (AI): A branch of computer science focused on creating systems capable of performing tasks that require human intelligence, such as content recognition, decision-making, and natural language processing. AI is a cornerstone technology in automated content moderation.

Content Moderation: The process by which digital platforms monitor, evaluate, and manage user-generated content to ensure compliance with their policies and reduce harm, such as misinformation, hate speech, or harassment.

Deepfake: Highly realistic and manipulated video, audio, or images generated using AI techniques, often used to spread misinformation or deceive viewers by creating fake content that appears authentic.

Digital Literacy: The ability to navigate, evaluate, and create information in digital environments. This includes skills necessary for identifying misinformation, engaging responsibly online, and contributing positively to digital discourse.

Explainable AI (XAI): A subset of AI designed to make its decision-making processes transparent and understandable to human users. XAI is essential for ensuring trust and accountability in automated content moderation systems.

Harmful Content: Material that may cause psychological, societal, or reputational harm to individuals or groups. Examples include hate speech, cyberbullying, or extremist propaganda.

Hybrid Moderation: A model that combines AI-driven tools with human moderators to address the challenges of automated moderation, such as contextual ambiguities and cultural nuances in content.

Transparency Reports: Documents published by digital platforms to detail their moderation practices, enforcement actions, and government content removal requests, thereby increasing accountability and user trust.

Universal Declaration of Human Rights (UDHR): A landmark document adopted by the United Nations that provides a global framework for human rights, including freedoms related to expression and access to information. It is often used as a guiding principle for ethical content moderation.

Media Governance: The set of policies, standards, and frameworks that regulate the operation and management of media, including digital platforms, to ensure they serve the public interest responsibly.

Misinformation: False or misleading information spread unintentionally. It differs from disinformation, which is deliberately disseminated with the intent to deceive or harm.

Moderation Fatigue: The psychological toll experienced by human moderators due to prolonged exposure to distressing content, resulting in mental health issues like stress and secondary trauma.

User-Driven Moderation: A content moderation approach where users actively participate in identifying, flagging, and assessing potentially harmful content. Examples include content flagging tools and peer moderation systems.

Digital Services Act (DSA): A regulatory framework by the European Union aimed at creating a safer and more accountable digital ecosystem by defining the responsibilities of online platforms in content moderation.

Chapter 2
Adapting AI Moderation:
Navigating Emerging Online Trends and Mitigating Evolving Harmful Content

Hemlata Parmar
https://orcid.org/0009-0009-1438-5427
Manipal University Jaipur, India

Utsav Krishan Murari
https://orcid.org/0009-0007-1606-6775
Sharda University, India

ABSTRACT

The challenges of moderating flammable content in online spaces are discussed in this paper, which explores the impact of global digital connectivity and the innovation of technologies. AI-driven tools today suffer from the messy issues of covert harassment, deepfakes and misinformation. Prototypical adaptive AI systems that combine reinforcement learning and contextual analysis prove promising in filling these gaps. However, some hybrid models that combine AI automation with human oversight are more culturally sensitive but raise ethical issues of bias, amplification of outrage, etc. Diverse datasets, explainable AI, and collaborative frameworks from case studies of platforms such as Twitter and TikTok are highlighted. In the era of digital platforms, with an increasing number of integrated disciplines and novel technology, it's imperative. Finally, the paper calls for adaptive moderation systems that balance innovation with ethics to make internet space safer, inclusive, and trustworthy.

DOI: 10.4018/979-8-3373-0335-2.ch002

1. INTRODUCTION

The digital age has revolutionized how people communicate, share ideas and build a community. Social media, online forums, and messaging applications have come to play increasingly essential roles in the lives of people around the globe in ways that enable unprecedented connectivity and innovation. At the same time, there has been an explosion in digital space, causing new management and mitigation challenges regarding the presence and dissemination of harmful content. The phenomenon is dynamic at once, given the pace of online interactions and on a global scale, as the internet operates anonymously, which has led to an increased frequency of negative behavior: harassment, false information, and manipulative content (Adapting AI Moderation, 2024). Such content requires an ever more sophisticated solution, as harmful content evolves faster than traditional moderation mechanisms can catch up with.

1.1 The Rise of Harmful Online Content

While harmful online content is a broad spectrum that includes explicit materials (graphic violence, hate speech) and insidious ones (covert harassment, deepfake media, AI-generated misinformation), it ranges from significant pervasiveness (pornography, cyberbullying) to extreme marginalization (free speech). For example, deepfake technologies permit the manufacture of hyperrealistic but fabricated videos and photos to misguide watchers or slur somebody's name (Chesney & Citron, 2019). Similarly, AI-generated misinformation can spread massive amounts of misinformation, influencing public opinion by spreading false narratives. These forms of content are hazardous because they harness technological advances to erode trust in digital media and kick against traditional moderation methods.

Moderation systems for covert harassment also have unique challenges in itself. Covert harassment, however, is far from explicit threats or abuse – it is more of something subtle and context-dependent, like tone policing, gaslighting, or veiled insults that make it hard for AI to parse what is going on. Moderation approaches that such interactions require can analyze the content and the social and cultural subtleties surrounding it (Gillespie, 2018). Thus, there has been a considerable gap between the proliferation of harmful behaviors that are both complex and complex and the development of practical moderation tools, resulting in the online safety mechanisms featuring a significant catch-up.

1.2 The Role of AI in Content Moderation

Artificial intelligence has become a powerful weapon in the war on harmful content. Since AI moderation systems can process large amounts of data at high speeds, they are particularly good at identifying explicit material like nudity, graphic violence or hate speech (Binns et al., 2018). For example, YouTube and social media platform Facebook use machine learning algorithms to automatically flag or remove content that violates the community standard, offloading some of the work away from human moderators. In these systems, problematic content is identified by utilizing techniques like natural language processing (NLP) and computer vision against prescribed criteria (Schroeder et al., 2021).

While AI has been good at least some harmful content, it cannot deal with nuanced behavior or content that needs context. For example, such a phrase might not be offensive in some contexts but simply offensive in others. Sarcasm is challenging for AI systems to recognize, or they over-content or fail to detect dangerous behaviors (Crawford, 2021). This, therefore, underscores the requirement for AI moderation systems to outgrow a rule-based approach and adapt to context, intent and dynamic norms of harmful behavior in AI moderation systems.

Table 1. Comparing static and adaptive AI moderation

Aspect	Static AI Moderation	Adaptive AI Moderation
Data Dependency	Relies on pre-trained datasets.	Continuously updates with real-world interactions.
Flexibility	Rigid and unable to adapt to new threats quickly.	Dynamically adapts to emerging threats and contexts.
Context Understanding	Limited or no understanding of context.	Uses real-time contextual analysis for nuanced content.
Effectiveness	Effective for predefined harmful content.	Effective for evolving and complex content.
Resource Requirements	Requires moderate computational resources.	High computational demand for real-time processing.

1.3 Challenges in Balancing Safety and Expression

Keeping users safe alongside freedom of expression is one of the most significant problems in content moderation. Suppose we are overly aggressive in moderating the discussion. In that case, we might be censoring/suppressing legitimate discourse, and if we are too lenient, we could expose the users to harmful content. This task is challenging inÂ multicultural and multilingual platforms, where the norms and expectations are pretty diverse with different user groups (Suzor, 2019). A trivial example is a comment that may be offensive to one culture but tolerated in another; in this case, moderation systems must balance diverse worldviews without adopting a mono-cultural regime.

However, AI moderation systems encounter an extra hurdle regarding borderline content—stuff that creeps around the edges of platform policies without breaking them. Much of this type of content exploits moderation algorithm loopholes to the point where complex issues arise in trying to do something about it. You might face losing valuable expression while trying to keep things reasonably safe. In addition, platforms face stricter moderation, increasing concern over AI systems' transparency and liability. Most users know nearly nothing about the process by which decisions are made on what is allowed, which often leads to frustration and a sense of bias or unfair treatment (Noble, 2018).

1.4 Adaptive Measures for AI Moderation

For context-aware AI moderation systems, you must be adaptable to the evolving landscape of harmful content. Typically, this means using cutting-edge machine learning techniques, including deep learning and neural networks, to learn to detect dangerous behavior in real-time. Sentiment analysis tools can, for example, detect covert harassment with the help of tone and intent analysis and multimodal approaches that combine text, image, and video analysis, enabling the detection of sophisticated content such as deepfakes (Kim et al., 2020).

Using human-in-the-loop (HITL) systems is another promising direction: these systems blend the velocity of AI with the backing of human assessors and market perspective. HITL systems enable us to let AI moderate routine tasks and escalate complex or ambiguous ones to human reviewers. This hybrid approach improves moderation decisions' accuracy and benefits training AI systems to learn better to practically understand contextual and nuanced content (Schmidt & Wiegand, 2017).

Platform platforms, political decision-makers, and researchers also need a collaborative effort to build a more efficient moderation framework. Shared resources and best practices to address harmful content are beginning to be demonstrated with industry-wide initiatives like the Global Internet Forum to Counter Terrorism (GIFCT). Stakeholders can leverage pooling data and expertise to build more robust yet transparent AI tools that allow moderation to reflect ethics and user expectations (GIFCT, 2022).

While harmful content continues to develop, AI moderation's future will only be successful due to the incorporation of emerging technologies and a firm resolve to ethical practices. Explainable AI (XAI), while still in its infancy, may soon become the technology through which moderation decisions by tools shed some transparency and accountability for users (Miller, 2019). This opens up a similar space for innovation in federated learning to allow platforms to better moderate without sacrificing privacy, mitigating one of the major ethical concerns in the deployment of AI (Bonawitz et al., 2019).

It is also essential to understand that people are generally quite good at identifying inappropriate content and that content moderation is, after all, a human activity. AI systems are imperfect and must be constantly refined to the newest harmful behavior. Stakeholders can, therefore, encourage a culture of collaboration and never-ending innovation, thereby allowing moderator practices to evolve in tandem with the challenges they face.

2. UNDERSTANDING THE LIMITATIONS OF CURRENT AI MODERATION SYSTEMS

Online content moderation is contingent upon artificial intelligence (AI) in social media platforms, forums, and digital communities. AI moderation systems are meant to use algorithms to do the dirty work—automate the detection and removal of offensive or harmful material—to keep online spaces safer. However, even with a great deal of technological progress, these systems are ineffective in dealing with the intricacies of online content. The inherent challenges of an AI moderation system are explored in this section — specifically, their shortcomings when dealing with the nuances in content form, the consequences of omission when dealing with context deficit, and the scalability of digital landscapes operating in a globalized manner.

Keyword detection and pattern recognition have proven how AI moderation systems identify explicit, offensive material, such as hate speech and graphic content. However, those systems are not up for nuanced stuff like satire, humor, or cultural references. An example is satirical posts, which use irony or exaggeration to criticize or entertain, but AI algorithms might tag them as offensive because AI misinterprets their underlying intent (Floridi et al., 2018).

Moreover, this problem is aggravated by cultural and linguistic differences. Some phrases and symbols might be considered offensive in some cultures and benign or even positive in others. To provide one example, the swastika is found on many sites in the West as the mark of hate but is sacred in Hinduism, Buddhism, and Jainism. This may be to say that AI systems trained on data sets from Western contexts may not have a cultural nuance to distinguish between these uses (Noble, 2018). Such contextual misunderstandings inherently demand that we build much stronger and more universally representative training sets that recognize the variety of cultural and linguistic contexts they need to understand.

In addition, AI systems often miss the insidious forms of harm, coded language or dog whistles. They are indirect messages designed to express offensive ideas to a particular audience without angering those policies. For instance, words or phrases may evolve to run a step ahead of moderation algorithms and may also indicate the reactive nature of many of the AI systems (Chesney & Citron, 2019). While these gaps can be addressed using AI, we are still very much stuck in the pre-clinical understanding era, which is an ongoing challenge.

However, global platforms like Facebook, YouTube, and Twitter generate so much content: trillion tweets, videos, images, games, GIFs, comments, remixes, and photoshops. It is a monumental task. Moderators have found it virtually impossible to identify and approve all content shared daily: billions of posts, images, and videos. With a scalable solution like AI, effectiveness decreases the more content there is.

The main problem is the computational cost of real-time content moderation. Such complex models of AI that can not only understand the big picture but also understand nuances are incredibly computationally resource-intensive and often are not available at scale (Manyika et al., 2017). However, platforms must also fittingly balance the trade-offs between accuracy versus speed, sometimes at the cost of OK-grained detection in favor of quicker processing. Consequently, harmful content may be left online for a long while or inaccurately taken off, resulting in user dissatisfaction and the platform's reputation risk.

The multilingual nature of global platforms further compounds the otherwise scalability challenges. Moderation systems trained with AI are usually only trained on one primary language, such as English or Mandarin, and leave other languages exposed to unmoderated harmful content. Therefore, when Facebook made no effort to effectively filter out hate speech in Burmese during the Myanmar crisis, Facebook's AI could not deal with specific content (Mozur, 2018). This incident reminds us that for multilingual AI models to effectively moderate content in different linguistic contexts, we need threaded content moderation models.

The datasets used to train AI moderation systems are responsible for system bias. However, these datasets reflect their parent or creator's social, cultural and linguistic biases, which may perpetuate unfair outcomes. For example, AI algorithms have knowingly flagged more content from marginalized communities as harmful versus less harmful material that further promotes systemic discrimination (Noble, 2018).

Again, it is compounded by the lack of transparency in the AI decision-making process. Most content creators who get their posts flagged or removed do not understand what has happened to their content, and often, there is no explanation whatsoever, which makes it very difficult to appeal a ruling or even know what has been against the criteria in the first place. Moreover, this lack of accountability can erode trust in the platform and stifle legitimate ways of expression.

In addition, enforcing content moderation policies accordingly is vulnerable to relying on biased datasets. To illustrate, Davidson et al. (2019) report that benign content would be flagged as offensive more frequently when a user uses (for example) African American English (AAE) rather than standard American English. The disparities on such accounts point to the pressing need for equitable and transparent practices of AI moderation.

What are the limits of AI moderation systems, and what are they raised in terms of ethics and law? Moreover, platforms walk a tightrope between protecting users from being harmed and protecting free speech. However, overenthusiastic AI moderation can have the opposite effect, producing censorship and stifling open discussion on, for instance, politics, religion, or social justice. However, under moderation, there is a risk for platforms to allow harmful content to proliferate, endangering vulnerable users and undermining trust in the platform.

These concerns are being addressed by the European Union's General Data Protection Regulation (GDPR), the Digital Services Act (DSA) and other regulatory frameworks, which force greater transparency and some level of accountability in content moderation practice (European Commission, 2018). However, AI development must be significantly invested in human overview to comply with these laws, which could be a complex undertaking for smaller platforms.

Ethical considerations also include the intense well-being of human moderators collaboratively with AI systems. Many of these moderators look at the most flagged content — content flagged by AI — which is psychologically traumatic. While it is hoped that AI will mitigate this burden, the limits of AI prevent human oversight for more nuanced cases, leaving moderators more emotionally burned by their responsibilities (Barrett, 2020).

Many advancements are required to overcome the limitations of the existing AI moderation systems. The first important thing to do is to develop context-aware AI models. To understand some of the more nuanced content that you see, these models should be able to be combined with very semantic, very sensitive to culture, very flexible over time, and able to actually -- by unconsciously being there, by allowing people to learn, being successful, continue to adapt, and ultimately evolve. An example of this is the integration of Natural Language Processing (NLP) techniques with state-of-the-art contextual glosses to improve the accuracy of the satire and humor classifiers (Florida et al., 2018).

Second, it encourages cooperation between AI developers, policymakers, and multiple communities to control moderation systems' biases. Involving stakeholders from underrepresented groups can help create more inclusive training datasets with comprehensive perspectives and experiences (Noble, 2018).

Finally, a promising solution lies in hybrid moderation models, AI-automated but managed by humans. Moderation jobs range from simple, high-volume cases to complex, ambiguous cases. Human moderators can take on the complex content, while AI steps in for the easy cases. By following this approach, there is some balance between efficiency and accuracy to prevent over/moderation as much as under/moderation.

However, existing AI moderation regimes are poorly equipped to handle ambiguous content, suffer scalability issues, and are ethically problematic. These shortcomings bring to light that AI technologies need to come further to understand the context well, reduce the biases of AI, and make it more transparent. If platforms apply inclusive and collaborative ways, they can maximize the effectiveness of the AI moderation systems, maintain ethical standards, and run alongside users' trust. These limitations will be essential to address as the platforms become digital.

Table 2. Challenges in AI content moderation

Challenge	Description	Example
Algorithmic Bias	Training datasets may perpetuate systemic biases.	Minority communities' content was flagged disproportionately.
Transparency	Lack of explicit explanations for moderation decisions.	Users are unable to understand why content was removed or flagged.
Scalability	Difficulty managing the sheer volume of global content.	Billions of posts, images, and videos are uploaded daily across platforms.
Cultural Sensitivity	Inability to account for cultural or linguistic differences.	Misinterpreting symbols like the swastika holds different meanings in Western and Eastern contexts.
Evasion Techniques	Malicious actors use coded language or multimedia to bypass detection.	Harmful content disguised in memes or images.

3. EMERGING THREATS: NEW FORMS OF INAPPROPRIATE AND HARMFUL CONTENT

Artificial intelligence (AI) technology development has become rapid, offering almost unprecedented opportunities for creating and disseminating media. While those advancements are emerging, so too are significant risks — in the form of inappropriate, harmful content. While existing content moderation systems are failing to keep up with the pace and scale of novel threats like deepfakes, AI-generated misinformation, and covert cyberbullying, these systems are not designed to handle these challenges. This section addresses these emerging threats, their implications for personal and societal well-being, and the necessity for more robust detection and mitigation techniques.

1. Deepfakes: Threats to Reality and Trust

AI-generated videos, images, or audio recordings that closely mimic real people. With techniques such as Generative Adversarial Networks (GANs), these synthetic media creations can reproduce voices, faces, and other person-identifying information. Deepfake technology offers us great opportunities in entertainment and education, but this enables the creation of false narratives to be weaponized in a way that harms people's reputations and breaks public trust (Chesney & Citron, 2019). Deepfakes have more than an individual impact. They have been used to spread propaganda, to influence elections, and to skew the opinion of a public. For example, forged videos mutating public figures purportedly saying incendiary things have circulated virally, eroding confidence and democratic institutions. The challenge with deepfakes is that they are so real that they are almost impossible to detect, even with advanced detection tools. Because the arms race between creation and detection persists unabated (Huang et al., 2022), researchers have developed algorithms to identify pixel patterns and audio syncing inconsistencies.

2. AI-Generated Misinformation: Scaling False Narratives

AI tools have automated the spread of misinformation and driven it onto digital platforms. Unlike traditional disinformation, AI-generated disinformation targets scale, generating any number of different variations of fake content for the mission of escaping detection. While created for creative and informative purposes, language models have been misappropriated for creating news articles, conspiracy theories, and social media posts that read far too human to be anything else. By generating misinformation using artificial intelligence, AI helps to form an “information fog”, a fog of content that obscures the truth and undercuts public discourse. For example, during the COVID-19 pandemic, AI tools generated and spread false health advice, misleading millions and compounding efforts to respond to the health crisis (Zhou et al., 2023). On top of this is the amplification effect of social media algorithms to engage rather than accuracy. This means that sensational AI-generated content likely spreads faster than verified content, making it more challenging for users to sort fact and fiction (Pennycook & Rand, 2018).

3. Covert Cyberbullying: The Development of Online Harassment.

As direct cyberbullying has been a problem for a long while, AI has brought more covert kinds of harassment. This type of cyberbullying uses coded language, memes and AI content to bully individuals or groups with much difficulty. Unlike overt discrimination or harassment, covert tactics could use, say, cultural references, implicitly targeting minorities and typically cannot be detected by current filters. For instance, coded language, where usually harmless words or signs are used to express negative intention, is now widely used by harassers. These codes constantly change and can be developed faster than AI moderation can recognize. Targets of covert cyberbullying are at a disadvantage because the emotional damage done by these methods is often severe. However, it is difficult to prove in court or a complaint (Adapting AI Moderation, 2024). AI content has also been used to launch hate campaigns, and such tactics as doxing and faux images meant to shame or coerce have been employed. Due to the anonymity and large-scale applicability of AI tools, the offenders are encouraged, whereas the affected become exposed to situations when responsibility is minimal. These existing detection systems cannot capture the context or the finer details of coercive harassment, which is why further and more elaborate techniques are required.

4. Implications and the Call for Strong Interventions

The appearance of deepfakes, AI-based fake news or information, and stealthy cyberbullying is a new form of threat. These threats are much more sophisticated than spam and obscenity currently dealt with by keyword filters and human moderators. This deficiency severely affects individuals' lives, the public's credibility, and society's coherence. A significant consequence is the loss of confidence in the digital information. As deepfakes and other AI-created fake news spread, people's suspicion of the content they consume from the internet increases. This skepticism can result in what is known as the 'liar's dividend', where even the actual content is considered fake, further adding to the division of opinions (Chesney & Citron, 2019). For covert cyberbullying, the absence of such interventions implies that the victim is left alone, and therefore, the psychological impact of cyber harassment is amplified. To address these threats, enhanced AI moderation systems are required. These systems are not enough to identify and prevent only the overt forms of harm because algorithms that recognize more subtle forms of harm should be applied. Technological companies, researchers, and policymakers should collaborate to create ethical AI usage rules in content moderation. Furthermore, public awareness campaigns can teach users how to recognize and respond to harmful content while preventing its adverse impact. This is because new generation AI-based threats such as deepfakes, fake news and hidden cyberbullying call for new ways of addressing content moderation. Such emerging categories of malicious content take advantage of gaps in the existing architectures and present challenges that call for a preventive and integrated effort. Since AI tools are considered future threats that can threaten society, context-aware AI tools should be developed, collaboration should be encouraged, and users should be empowered to work effectively and safely alongside these emerging threats to turn them into opportunities for positive change.

4. Adaptive AI Moderation: A Necessity for Digital Platforms

With the rise of social media and user contributions, there is a lack of appropriate and adaptive moderation mechanisms to foster safe and quality participation. As the digital environment grows, the problems of controlling adverse content – from hidden harassment and deepfakes to propaganda – become more acute. Modern-day traditional AI moderation systems can detect and remove numerous categories of obscene content but cannot adapt to new threats and contexts. Static AI systems are trained and powered by prior data sets and cannot quickly learn new patterns of abuse, including coded language or new forms of disinformation. Due to these challenges, new adaptive AI moderation systems that use reinforcement learning, real-time context analysis, and multimodal data processing have been created. These systems are designed to solve the limitations of the static models by providing a more potent way of dealing with the dynamic nature of HOC.

Table 3. Features of adaptive AI systems

Feature	Description	Benefit
Reinforcement Learning	Improves through real-world feedback loops.	Continuously adapts to new patterns of harmful behavior.
Real-Time Contextual Analysis	Considers tone, intent, and broader conversational patterns.	Reduces false positives and ensures nuanced moderation.
Multimodal Data Processing	Analyses text, images, and videos simultaneously.	Effectively detects harmful content across multiple formats.

4.1 The Limitations of Static AI Moderation Models

Static AI moderation is based on datasets generated during AI training and is used to identify the patterns of the described content. Although these models perform relatively well in detecting documented types of harmful content, they are essentially reactive and cannot cope with emerging threats. For example, hate speech, disinformation techniques, and coded language are challenging to detect due to these systems' static nature. Waseem and Hovy (2014) discovered that even the slight modification of toxic language by using euphemisms or specific platform language only worsens the problem. Moreover, the time gap between detecting new adverse behavior and retraining the static models opens the platforms to being exploited. While the adversaries are constantly developing new ways of outviting the detection systems, the static models are exposed to their flaws more than ever.

Dynamic AI moderation models are meant to solve the problem of rigid models that do not adapt to new situations through learning. These systems' main characteristic is reinforcement learning, which enables them to learn from the processes occurring in the real world. With feedback mechanisms, adaptive models improve their algorithms based on the occasions they correctly identify prohibited content or on the occasions that they fail to do so. This cyclic approach was designed to guarantee that the system is relevant and adequately equipped to prevent new risks (Sutton & Barto, 2018).

A fourth aspect that characterizes adaptive moderation is contextual analysis in real-time. As opposed to the static models, which examine individual content, adaptive systems consider the context of content usage. Various features, including the users' intent, past behavior, and platform characteristics, are employed to judge better the existence of material that may be detrimental to the user. For example, the adaptive models learn the distinction between the positive and negative connotations of the same term based on the context, including the tone, targeted groups, and overall conversation patterns (Dinakar et al., 2012). This capability is used to minimize the amount of false positives and make sure that none of the actual content is being banned.

The use of multimodal data processing further improves the functionality of the adaptive systems. With the help of text, image, and video data, these systems can recognize the multi-type content that may include the harmful one. This approach is instrumental in fighting against evasion techniques where the villains employ non-text formats to get around text-based filters (Gao et al., 2022). This approach allows the platform to effectively mitigate the risk of missing the moderator's attention due to using many data types.

Table 4. Solutions for AI moderation challenges

Challenge	Solution	Implementation Example
Algorithmic Bias	Use diverse, representative datasets and continuous auditing.	Collaboration with underrepresented communities for dataset development.
Transparency	Develop explainable AI (XAI) models that clarify decision-making processes.	Facebook's Oversight Board provides transparency on content moderation decisions.
Scalability	Implement hybrid models combining AI automation and human oversight.	TikTok uses AI for high-volume tasks and human moderators for complex cases.

continued on following page

Table 4. Continued

Challenge	Solution	Implementation Example
Cultural Sensitivity	Train AI models with multilingual and culturally diverse datasets.	Addressing hate speech in Burmese during the Myanmar crisis.
Evasion Techniques	Employ multimodal learning to analyse text, images, and videos simultaneously.	Algorithms detect harmful memes by analysing associated metadata and content.

4.2 Applications of Adaptive AI Moderation

Adaptive AI moderation systems have many uses and can be applied to solving some of the main problems of content moderation.

1. Preventing the Access to New and Potential Dangerous Content.

Adaptive systems are well suited for the new threats becoming increasingly prevalent in today's society, including disinformation operations and stealth radicalization. Due to the processing of real-time data and the ability to track the development of trends, such systems can recognize and eliminate such content before it gains momentum. For instance, the adaptive AI models were helpful during the COVID-19 pandemic by identifying patterns of information pollution and offering interventions at the right time (Cinelli et al., 2020). This is crucial for protecting the credibility and safety of the digital platforms.

2. Combatting Evasion Techniques

Cybercriminals can easily circumvent static moderation systems as they are unchangeable and use coded language, altered images or even embed unwanted content into videos. Adaptive systems with the feature of multimodal learning can process the content in different formats and forms to detect harmful content. For instance, these systems can identify the wrong content in images or videos by matching the photo or video with text since the system contains text appropriate to the image or video in question (Gao et al., 2022). This capability prevents the users from taking advantage of the weaknesses of static systems to a large extent.

3. Tailor-Made Moderation Techniques

Adaptive systems of AI moderation allow the platforms to adopt moderation approaches that fit them best and the audiences they serve. For instance, an educational platform may have rules to detect cyberbullying and explicit content, while a professional network may set rules to detect harassment and fake news. Comprehending each platform's specific objectives and values makes it possible to create moderation techniques that correspond with users' expectations and help improve the conditions of the online environment (Gillespie, 2018).

Table 5. Applications of adaptive AI moderation

Application	Description	Example
Detecting Emerging Threats	Identifies and mitigates new harmful trends like disinformation or radicalization.	Adaptive AI models countering COVID-19 misinformation in real-time.
Combating Evasion	Addresses malicious techniques such as coded language and multimedia manipulation.	Identifying harmful content embedded in memes or videos.
Personalized Moderation	Tailors moderation to platform-specific needs and user expectations.	Educational platforms prioritize cyberbullying detection over misinformation.

4.3 Challenges and Ethical Considerations

Adaptive AI moderation systems may have advanced capabilities, but work must be done. Significant hurdles to human-based testing remain: ethical concerns, issues of bias and fairness, and resource demands.

1. Bias and Fairness

All AI models – including adaptive systems – can follow through biases present in training data. Discriminatory outcomes can still result from historical biases due to disproportionate 'harmful' content flagging in some designated groups. For instance, results have been obtained that demonstrate that an AI system trained on a biased dataset can unfairly target specific minority communities where; by doing so, they perpetuate a systemic inequality (Noble, 2018). To address these biases, one needs diverse training datasets, ongoing auditing, and incorporating ethical AI design into it. Transparency, as well as Accountability. Despite their advanced capabilities, adaptive AI moderation systems are not without challenges. Ethical concerns, issues of bias and fairness, and resource demands remain significant hurdles.

2. Transparency and Accountability

The complexity of adaptive AI systems often creates a "black box" effect, where users and moderators cannot fully understand how decisions are made. This lack of transparency raises concerns about accountability, particularly in cases where moderation decisions have significant consequences, such as de-platforming or content removal. To build trust and ensure accountability, explainable AI models that provide clear justifications for their choices are essential (Lipton, 2018).

3. Scalability and Resource Requirements

Adaptive moderation systems need quite some computational resources to analyze and process data in real-time. This is financially prohibitive for smaller platforms with limited budgets. However, this gap can be bridged through collaborative solutions—whether shared AI frameworks or partnerships with larger technology companies—which can democratize access to advanced moderation technologies (Marra et al., 2019).

5. ETHICAL AND PRIVACY CONSIDERATIONS IN AI MODERATION

The introduction of AI moderation systems into digital platforms has changed the event of content regulation, only to include some vital ethical and privacy concerns at the table. However, these challenges stem from how AI technologies are developed, trained, and deployed in their technical performance and broader societal implications.

1. Algorithmic Bias and marginalization

Algorithmic bias is the most pressing ethical agenda in AI moderation. Training datasets that lack diverse populations can lead models to perpetuate or neglect stereotypes and constitute a source of bias. For instance, Noble (2018), Noble finds that search engine algorithms that are biased are amplifying narratives towards women and people of color in dangerous ways. Regarding content moderation, the problem can be biased in favor of too much policing of specific communities while taking little action against those committing harmful behavior. An imbalance erodes moderation systems' trust and worsens things for existing social imbalances.

2. Risks to Freedom of Speech

These AI moderation systems that provide harmful or inappropriate content can sometimes delete legitimate discourse. A phenomenon known also as overmoderation — where AI systems flag and remove content that should not be — can stifle free expression and curtail public dialogue. Moreover, automated filters, often with limited nuance, cannot usually distinguish between harmful speech and satire, activism, or debate. For instance, hateful speech about hate groups or governments may be flagged as harmful content, disrupting users' rights to say what they think. As a result, the relevance of the introduction of human oversight to AI moderation highlights the dangers of over-censorship.

3. Privacy Concerns About Data Usage

Because AI moderation is so data-intensive, it relies on vast amounts of user-generated data for training. It uses them in real-time to moderate what they see. The European Union's General Data Protection Regulation (GDPR) is extremely prescriptive regarding user rights and strictly limits user information collection, storage, and processing (European Commission, 2018). However, most moderation systems function in legal grey areas that involve using users' data without explicit user consent. Not only are they violating privacy laws, but they are also damaging users' trust in digital platforms. Fostering ethical AI practices requires appropriately balancing the need for effective moderation with the law.

Table 6. Ethical considerations

Aspect	**Concern**	**Proposed Solution**
Algorithmic Bias	AI systems perpetuating societal stereotypes.	Continuous auditing and diverse datasets.
Freedom of Speech	Risk of over-moderation leading to censorship.	Hybrid models with human oversight for nuanced cases.
Privacy	Excessive reliance on user data for training and operation.	Compliance with data protection regulations like GDPR.

5.1 Leveraging Human-AI Collaboration in Moderation

As the complexities of moderation of content outweigh its simplicity, hybrid approaches anchored in the application of AI automation and human oversight are adopted. As automated systems become more powerful, human-AI collaboration is increasingly recognized as taking advantage of fully automated systems' strengths and compensating for their weaknesses.

1. Contextual Judgment and Cultural Sensitivity

They are good at processing lots of data quickly but not as good with nuance and cultural differences. The skill set humans bring to the table when moderating the comments is essential and includes, at least, the ability to comprehend local contexts, capture subtle cues, and make value-based decisions. For cases of ambiguous or context-dependent content, such as political or religious speech, where AI systems may not be sensitive or precise, this combination is essential.

2. Hybrid Moderation Models

For many leading platforms, hybrid moderation models have become the industry standard. On the other hand, these systems assign high-volume tasks, say detecting spam or explicit imagery, to AI and leave the more complicated or edge cases to human moderators. Take YouTube, for example: Despite deploying AI to flag potentially harmful videos automatically, they still need human review to, for example, account suspension. Like Facebook, hate speech and misinformation on the Facebook platform are monitored using the same model, rated to have found content flagged for contextual appropriateness (Adapting AI Moderation, 2024).

3. Benefits and Challenges

Moderation using a collaborative approach is more accurate and efficient. AI systems help remove the repetitive tasks that load on human moderators, allowing for more content review that requires critical thinking. Nevertheless, this model also faces hurdles of moderator fatigue, exposure to tempting content, and lots of training necessary for human reviewers to line up with platform rules. The success of hybrid systems relies heavily on ensuring that human moderators are looked after and on transparency in the decision-making process.

5.2 Case Studies: Successes and Failures in Modern AI Moderation

Analyzing real-world implementations of AI moderation provides valuable insights into the strengths and weaknesses of current approaches. Case studies from platforms like Twitter and TikTok highlight the diverse strategies and outcomes of deploying AI for content regulation.

1. AI-Driven Hate Speech Detection on Twitter

Twitter has been under fire for years for its missteps in moderating hate speech and harmful content. The key contribution we have noticed is that the platform's AI-driven moderation system has significantly diminished the prevalence of hate speech, automatically detecting offensive language and behavioral patterns. Internal reports claimed the system flagged millions of tweets to review, meaning user exposure to harmful content plummets. However, the system has also been criticized for being inconsistent in its enforcement and algorithmically biased. For instance, tweets from minorities advocating for social justice were flagged much more than others, showing the limits to which AI systems can read context and intent (Adapting AI Moderation, 2024).

2. Adaptive Moderation Techniques on TikTok

TikTok takes a real-time adaptive and dynamic model update approach to AI moderation. Advanced machine learning models are applied to the platform, which can detect newly emerging threats, such as new kinds of misinformation or harmful manners. TikTok has improved its moderation accuracy by incorporating user feedback and constantly retraining its models. Its one notable success was in being able to identify and contain a spread of harmful challenges that endangered user safety. Though these improvements have been made, some traditional content has been flagged inappropriately by TikTok because it lacked localized training data (Adapting AI Moderation, 2024).

5.3 Recommendations for Ethical and Effective AI Moderation

To address AI moderation's ethical and practical challenges, platforms must adopt comprehensive strategies prioritizing fairness, transparency, and user privacy. Key recommendations include:

1. **Improving Dataset Diversity:** Using AI to moderate can be easier if AI systems are trained to look at a wide range of datasets that mirror as many cultural, linguistic and social factors of the world as possible to reduce algorithmic bias and increase moderation accuracy.
2. **Enhancing Transparency:** Users should know how decisions are made on a platform, with platforms communicating their moderation policies in a manner that platforms are making decisions using AI systems.
3. **Prioritizing Privacy Compliance:** Respecting data protection regulations such as GDPR encourages moderation systems to build trust.

4. **Supporting Human Moderators:** Can hybrid systems be mitigated with sufficient psychological support, training, and proper compensation from human moderators?
5. **Continuous Model Updates:** AI systems are updated regularly on the feedback from the users and the rise of threats to be relevant and practical.

AI moderation is a powerful weapon in the fight against online content at scale, but only on the condition that it is rooted in a strong ethical foundation. To address challenges like algorithmic bias, over-moderation, and privacy concerns, the work must be done with an AI automation/oversight tug-of-war. From platforms like Twitter and TikTok, case studies show what is possible and what is not with these systems and how constant improvement and agility are key. Transparency, fairness and respect for user rights will help us build moderation systems that protect individuals and communities in the digital age.

6. THE FUTURE OF AI MODERATION: ANTICIPATING EMERGING TRENDS

As digital ecosystems continue to grow and diversify, the future of AI moderation is becoming increasingly critical: shaping how content management and ethical governing are managed within digital ecosystems. However, even AI moderation has been shown to identify and eliminate such hazardous content, spam and misinformation. At the same time, future systems will need to adapt to a more complex structure of online interactions. The area of focus, in particular, is explainable AI (xai), which aims to make algorithms more transparent and understandable. The importance of this approach in building user trust and regulatory compliance lies in enabling users and auditors to know the reasons for AI-driven decisions (Florida et al., 2018). For example, Facebook's Oversight Board has recognized the importance of explainability in enabling accountability and boosting public confidence in content moderation systems (Rosen, 2020). However, XAI has a potential tradeoff between system performance and transparency in such complex tasks as identifying subtle hate speech and misinformation. Transparency is equally important in building AI moderation systems that are culturally and contextually aware and must be built alongside collaboration across disciplinary lines. Timed with the launch of the Common European Framework of Reference for Languages (CEFR), input from linguists, sociologists, and legal experts will help AI understand complex cultural references, sarcasm and slang and the way that are often misread by traditional algorithms (Taddeo & Floridi, 2018). This promise of collaboration helps to ensure that moderation practices respect human rights and oppose over-censorship and cultural insensitivity. Promising democratizing direction for AI moderation comes from open-source initiatives. Through its open source projects such as Jigsaw's Perspective API, open source projects are making advanced moderation tools accessible for smaller organizations and non-profits, making those resource-constrained platforms adopt the bleeding edge of moderation technologies (Jigsaw, 2021). Additionally, open-source models allow for collective innovation since developers worldwide can work on their improvement, even though guidelines should be set up to avoid misuse. Moreover, another critical trend is the need to collaborate globally as moderation standards are increasingly fractured. In collaboration, such as the Global Internet Forum to Counter Terrorism (GIFCT), the value of shared databases and unified strategies becomes clear in helping to remove harmful content more effectively (GIFCT, 2021). Smaller platforms can leverage pooled resources through these partnerships, but these partnerships must be created to retain competition and innovation in a digital landscape. Governance on the web requires new abilities to cope with emerging threats, such as deepfakes or coordinated disinformation campaigns, that are new to online governance. In traditional static models, these dynamic issues remain inadequately addressed. We need self-learning algorithms that learn in real time and update based on any new patterns of harmful content. For instance, predictive analytics can study user behavior patterns to detect when certain threats may take off, eventually moderating proactively (Chesney & Citron, 2019). This adaptability has to be traded against the ethical consideration that predictive systems can be over and false positive. Ethical and legal frameworks regulating AI moderation must also change with technology. Unlike GDPR in data protection, which provides clear guidelines and internationally recognized standards, it ensures regulation and accountability for services across international borders (Florida et al., 2018). Algorithmic biases can also be based on ethical concerns and limit the ability of a group of people to use or feel belonging. Ensuring fairness and inclusivity in AI-moderated systems depends on minimizing bias through diverse data sets for training and transparent deployment practices. Technological innovation gives us hope and engenders online content management using AI but with public skepticism. We need to address this skepticism through user education and engagement. AI platforms have to make users aware of the capabilities and limitations of AI and establish a collaborative relationship with them where the users can participate actively in moderation processes. Fast forward, and while it takes longer to moderate and AI is not perfect, new technologies like quantum computing might make the process fast and accurate, able to handle real-time processing of vast amounts of data. AI's vulnerabilities will, however, attract adversaries; cybersecurity and system resilience will need to remain at the forefront. How AI moderates will influence the direction AI moderation will take: towards innovation or ethical responsibility. The systems that will become effective and trustworthy will need to be developed using explainable AI, interdisciplinary collaboration, open-source initiatives, and cross-platform partnerships. Adapting and predicting as we approach new threats and ensuring our fundamental rights are secure will become increasingly essential. By encouraging openness and broadening the diversity that defines online spaces, AI moderation should bring safer, more equitable spaces where technological progress is attuned to cultural values and choices.

7. CONCLUSION: BUILDING SAFE AND INCLUSIVE ONLINE SPACES

The value of creating safe and inclusive digital spaces cannot be overstated in the fast-moving digital landscape. With the emergence of adaptive AI moderation systems, these challenges have become one of the key problems online spaces face and have compelled the designers of such systems to seek solutions. Dynamic Risk identification and Mitigation are enabled by these systems using advancements in natural language processing, machine learning and sentiment analysis. However, while innovative technology is necessary for their effectiveness, so is a commitment to ethical development and transparency.

Trust in AI moderation systems is based on transparency. A straightforward, easy-to-access moderation process makes users more likely to accept and trust AI interventions. To foster ever greater accountability and transparency, platforms must clearly and transparently describe the use of their algorithms, where that data comes from, and what steps are taken to address potential biases. Without that transparency, users can link moderation efforts to arbitrary or biased, and the platforms themselves could be undermined in credibility.

Free expression must not be sacrificed for safety in the ethical development of the AI moderation system development. While reliance on automated systems can reduce the 'noise' and facilitate engagement as well as reduce costs and delays, if automated systems are over-reliant on themselves without the input of humans, errors can occur, such as the removal of legitimate content or a lack of proper response to nuanced cases of harmful speech (Florida et al., 2018). Our moderation technology collaborations with community members, policy experts, and civil rights advocates are essential to fostering culturally sensitive moderation technologies in line with human rights principles.

In addition, adaptive AI systems must also continuously adapt to new threats and challenges. However, the fast nature of online discourse means that moderation technologies need to be able to learn and adapt in real-time. Nevertheless, we must guide this evolution through ongoing stakeholder engagement to keep the systems in tune with ever-changing needs and expectations from online communities.

In summary, for online spaces to be safe and inclusive, the solution requires a multichannel approach where the utmost is invested in cutting-edge AI technology, together with practices that are ethical and whose stakeholders are involved. While there is no shortage of platforms establishing AI moderation systems to help protect users from harm, those that invest in adaptive AI moderation systems and place precedence on transparency and inclusivity will be key to the development of digital communities that both safeguard users from harm and allow for open, meaningful interactions. By getting this balance right, platforms will help retain the online space's vibrancy, equity and resilience in the face of new challenges.

REFERENCES

Barrett, P. M. (2020). *Who moderates the moderators? The case for greater oversight of content moderation systems*. NYU Stern Center for Business and Human Rights.

Binns, R., Veale, M., Van Kleek, M., & Shadbolt, N. (2018). 'It is reducing a human being to a percentage': Perceptions of justice in algorithmic decisions. *Proceedings of the 2018 CHI Conference on Human Factors in Computing Systems*. DOI: 10.1145/3173574.3173951

Bonawitz, K.. (2019). *Towards federated learning at scale: System design. Proceedings of Machine Learning Systems*. MLSYS.

Chesney, R., & Citron, D. (2019). Deepfakes and the new disinformation war: The coming age of post-truth geopolitics. *Foreign Affairs, 98*(1), 147–155.

Cinelli, M., Quattrociocchi, W., Galeazzi, A., Valensise, C. M., Brugnoli, E., Schmidt, A. L., Zola, P., Zollo, F., & Scala, A. (2020). The COVID-19 social media infodemic. *Scientific Reports, 10*(1), 1–10. DOI: 10.1038/s41598-020-73510-5 PMID: 33024152

Crawford, K. (2021). *Atlas of AI: Power, Politics, and the Planetary Costs of Artificial Intelligence*. Yale University Press.

Davidson, T., Bhattacharya, D., & Weber, I. (2019). Racial bias in hate speech detection. *Proceedings of the 2019 Workshop on Online Abuse and Harms,* 25–35.

Dinakar, K., Reichart, R., & Lieberman, H. (2012). Modelling the detection of textual cyberbullying. *The Workshop on Computational Approaches to Subjectivity and Sentiment Analysis*, 11-17.

European Commission. (2018). General Data Protection Regulation (GDPR). Retrieved from https://gdpr-info.eu

Floridi, L., Cowls, J., Beltrametti, M., Chatila, R., Chazerand, P., Dignum, V., Luetge, C., Madelin, R., Pagallo, U., Rossi, F., Schafer, B., Valcke, P., & Vayena, E. (2018). AI4People—An ethical framework for a good AI society. *Minds and Machines, 28*(4), 689–707. DOI: 10.1007/s11023-018-9482-5 PMID: 30930541

Gao, L., Hao, J., & Huang, X. (2022). Multimodal AI for enhanced moderation systems. *Journal of AI Research, 45*(3), 345–360.

Gillespie, T. (2018). *Custodians of the internet: Platforms, content moderation, and the hidden decisions that shape social media*. Yale University Press.

Global Internet Forum to Counter Terrorism (GIFCT). (2021). *About GIFCT*. Retrieved from https://gifct.org

Huang, Z., Wang, Y., & Zhang, L. (2023). Detecting deepfakes using AI: Challenges and advancements. *Journal of Artificial Intelligence Research*, *67*(4), 1123–1142.

Jigsaw. (2021). Perspective API: Technology to counter online toxicity. Retrieved from https://jigsaw.google.com

Kim, J., Kim, J., & Oh, A. (2020). Detecting deepfake images in online spaces. *IEEE Transactions on Neural Networks and Learning Systems*.

Lipton, Z. C. (2018). The mythos of model interpretability. *Communications of the ACM*, *61*(10), 36–43. DOI: 10.1145/3233231

Manyika, J., Chui, M., Bughin, J., et al. (2017). Jobs lost, jobs gained: Workforce transitions in a time of automation. *McKinsey Global Institute Report.*

Marra, A., Righi, R., & Baletti, R. (2019). Collaborative frameworks for AI moderation. *Journal of Internet Policy*, *5*(2), 89–112.

Miller, T. (2019). Explanation in artificial intelligence: Insights from the social sciences. *Artificial Intelligence*, *267*, 1–38. DOI: 10.1016/j.artint.2018.07.007

Mozur, P. (2018). A genocide was incited on Facebook, with posts from Myanmar's military. *The New York Times.* Retrieved from https://www.nytimes.com

Noble, S. U. (2018). *Algorithms of oppression: How search engines reinforce racism.* NYU Press. DOI: 10.18574/nyu/9781479833641.001.0001

Pennycook, G., & Rand, D. G. (2018). The Implied Truth Effect: Attaching warnings to a subset of fake news stories increases the perceived accuracy of stories without warnings. *Management Science*, *66*(11), 4944–4957. DOI: 10.1287/mnsc.2019.3478

Report, T. T. (2023). *AI-driven content moderation: Challenges and achievements.* Retrieved from https://twitter.com/transparency

Rosen, G. (2020). Building transparency and oversight for Facebook's content decisions. *Facebook Newsroom.* Retrieved from https://about.fb.com/news

Schmidt, A., & Wiegand, M. (2017). A survey on hate speech detection using natural language processing. *Proceedings of the 5th International Workshop on Natural Language Processing for Social Media*. DOI: 10.18653/v1/W17-1101

Schroeder, R., Gurevych, I., & Eckert, K. (2021). *Multimodal approaches to content moderation*. Digital Platforms and Society Journal.

Sutton, R. S., & Barto, A. G. (2018). *Reinforcement learning: An introduction.* MIT Press.

Suzor, N. (2019). *Lawless: The Secret Rules That Govern Our Digital Lives.* Cambridge University Press. DOI: 10.1017/9781108666428

Taddeo, M., & Floridi, L. (2018). How AI can be a force for good. *Science, 361*(6404), 751–752. DOI: 10.1126/science.aat5991 PMID: 30139858

TikTok Safety Center. (2023). *Adapting AI moderation for dynamic content.* Retrieved from https://www.tiktok.com/safety

Waseem, Z., & Hovy, D. (2016). Hateful symbols or hateful people? Predictive features for hate speech detection on Twitter. *Proceedings of the NAACL Student Research Workshop*, 88–93. DOI: 10.18653/v1/N16-2013

Yang, Q., Liu, Y., Chen, T., & Tong, Y. (2019). Federated machine learning: Concept and applications. *ACM Transactions on Intelligent Systems and Technology, 10*(2), 1–19. DOI: 10.1145/3298981

Zhou, W., Zhao, H., & Tang, J. (2022). AI in the pandemic: Misinformation and its implications. *Computers in Human Behavior, 135*(C), 107635.

Chapter 3
Building a Content Moderation Framework to Provide a Safe and Secure Experience for Omnichannel Commerce

Siddhartha Paul Tiwari
https://orcid.org/0000-0003-1596-1501
Google Asia Pacific, Singapore

ABSTRACT

The rapid expansion of content, omnicommerce platforms have encountered significant challenges when it comes to maintaining stringent quality standards, regulatory compliance, and ensuring the safety and trust of users. The sheer volume of content uploaded on a daily basis poses significant moderation challenges, necessitating the detection and management of listings that might be irrelevant, inappropriate, obscene, illegal, harmful, or defamatory in nature. As the content volume on omnicommerce platforms grows exponentially, manual moderation becomes increasingly inefficient, prone to errors, and overly time consuming, which is why it has become imperative to develop a robust, scalable moderation solution. For omnicommerce platforms to be able to address these critical challenges, advanced technologies need to be utilized in order to design and implement a premoderation framework that is innovative and adaptive.

DOI: 10.4018/979-8-3373-0335-2.ch003

INTRODUCTION

Omnicommerce platforms, also known as omnichannel commerce, provide customers with a unified and seamless experience across a variety of channels (web-based, in-store/offline transactions, mobile web and apps, etc.) by integrating sales, marketing, and customer service functions. Integrated platforms are becoming increasingly popular across the globe as they have revolutionized the digital retail landscape in a significant way. By providing a comprehensive omnicommerce platforms marketplace, an enormous chunk of potential consumer spending can be addressed in an efficient manner. A variety of products can be accessed through this omnichannel platform, such as food and groceries, home furniture, fashion items, electronics, and much more. To add daily necessities such as food and groceries. Combined with the extremely broad range of products that omnicommerce platforms offer, as well as their extensive global reach, the result has been a high volume of merchant-generated content being uploaded daily for leading omni-channel platforms, including hundreds of thousands of new products. The rapid expansion of content, omnicommerce platforms have encountered significant challenges when it comes to maintaining stringent quality standards, regulatory compliance, and ensuring the safety and trust of users. The sheer volume of content uploaded on a daily basis poses significant moderation challenges, necessitating the detection and management of listings that might be irrelevant, inappropriate, obscene, illegal, harmful, or defamatory in nature. The performance of AI models on benchmark datasets is generally strong, but they remain susceptible to errors, particularly when inputs are not distributed. Such imperfect systems raise ongoing questions regarding how they can be effectively integrated into human workflows. AI research has primarily focused on supporting high-stakes individual decision-making, which may not scale effectively to situations involving high volumes of low-stakes judgments, such as managing social media content (Lai et al., 2022). As the content volume on omnicommerce platforms grows exponentially, manual moderation becomes increasingly inefficient, prone to errors, and overly time consuming, which is why it has become imperative to develop a robust, scalable moderation solution. For omnicommerce platforms to be able to address these critical challenges, advanced technologies need to be utilized in order to design and implement a premoderation framework that is innovative and adaptive. The use of artificial intelligence (AI) systems is increasingly affecting our environment and our ability to access and exclude opportunities and resources, thus making it necessary to establish some form of AI oversight. Providing such oversight is essential to the maintenance of the rule of law, to the protection of individual rights, and to the protection of our core democratic values (Nahmias & Perel, 2021). By combining the efforts of AI and humans to simplify and enhance content moderation processes, this strategic collaboration will result in improved accuracy, efficiency, and an overall reduction in the amount of time needed to moderate. By adopting automated moderation filters, the omnicommerce platforms will be able to proactively identify problematic content, thus significantly reducing the need for exhaustive manual reviews of content within their platform.

AI CONTENT MODERATION IN OMNICHANNEL COMMERCE PLATFORMS: KEY CONSIDERATIONS FOR EFFECTIVE IMPLEMENTATION

Managing complex global digital ecosystems effectively requires the adoption of AI-driven content moderation strategies that are comprehensive, adaptive, and context-aware so as to provide a comprehensive, adaptive, and context-sensitive moderation approach. Incorporating these principles into the moderation frameworks of platforms that manage omnichannel commerce not only improve the safety and trust of their users, but also promote a more inclusive, equitably, and robust digital community, etc., in addition to enhancing user safety. There has been an increase in the use of digital interactions, user-generated content, and the integration of AI into omnichannel commerce platforms as a result of the increasing use of digital technologies. This is to ensure the safety of users, the compliance of the law, and the freedom of speech are all balanced. There are several factors that need to be considered in order to ensure that omnichannel commerce platforms are trustworthy, compliant, and user-friendly.

Figure 1. AI content moderation in omnichannel commerce platforms: Key considerations for effective implementation

As shown in Figure 1, there are a number of key considerations that should be taken into account when implementing AI-driven content moderation in omnichannel commerce platforms so as to ensure an effective implementation. In order to implement AI-driven content moderation, a variety of factors need to be considered including adaptability, fairness, trust, transparency, and effectiveness. For global omnichannel commerce platforms to be successful, it is critical that AI-driven moderation strategies are adapted to meet local laws and cultural norms, as a necessary element of ensuring their success. The rapid advancement of omnichannel commerce platforms has resulted in content moderation becoming one of the most significant components to manage the vast amount of user and merchant generated content in today's rapidly evolving digital marketplace. Moderation of content provides many benefits, including safeguarding user experiences, ensuring compliance with regional legal requirements, thereby reducing the risk associated with legal and reputational issues.

As omnichannel commerce platforms become increasingly globalized, it becomes more and more important to understand and integrate diverse cultural, legal, and ethical norms from different geographies in order to effectively operate. There are a number of guidelines for the moderation of content that are used by omnichannel commerce platforms that might be acceptable in one region and inappropriate in another. The right to freedom of speech may be defined differently in different countries. For instance, freedom of speech in terms of political views against the incumbent government, which may be regarded as free speech in one country, may be considered inflammatory in another country or legally problematic in another. This requires the use of regionally specific data, norms, and regulations when training AI algorithms for moderation purposes. To ensure that AI systems are compliant with local legal frameworks, they must take into account regional sensitivities. A geographic-sensitive approach promotes compliance, allowing platforms to effectively navigate the complexities associated with international digital regulations. To reduce biases and adjust swiftly to evolving content trends, AI moderation systems used in omnichannel commerce platforms need to be trained regularly and retrained as new trends emerge in the industry. When AI is used in the moderation process, it heavily depends on training datasets. If the training datasets are outdated or biased for omnichannel commerce platforms, the AI system may unwittingly perpetuate harmful stereotypes, misinformation, or outdated norms. It is therefore imperative that AI training sets are continuously updated. There are severe limitations to the existing machine learning content moderation methods in terms of keeping up with and staying ahead of hateful language on the Internet (Udupa, Maronikolakis, & Wisiorek, 2023).

Moderating systems can learn new slang, symbolism, and societal norms by incorporating diverse and representative datasets. The ability to adapt to the dynamic nature of digital communication enables AI moderation to remain relevant and responsive, actively detecting harmful or inappropriate content before it escalates to a serious problem. In addition to playing a fundamental role in AI moderation, it plays a crucial role in protecting users from harmful content, such as explicit images, hate speech, or bullying. This is shown in figure 1.

The use of effective artificial intelligence (AI) for moderation in omnichannel commerce platforms is critical to maintaining a safer digital environment, improving user well-being, retention, and enhancing overall platform trustworthiness. The assumption that unnecessary data collection will be minimized will further strengthen the trust that users have in digital platforms. Moderation systems using artificial intelligence (AI) must be able to walk a fine line between their need to collect data as part of moderation purposes and their users' legitimate expectation of privacy. When a company collects excessive or invasive amounts of personal data, it can seriously undermine the trust and loyalty of its users. As platforms begin to implement moderation strategies, they should ensure that what data is collected is as minimal as possible, collecting no more than what is essential for an accurate evaluation of the content. There are several practices that reinforce trust and confidence in the company, including transparency in terms of data use, a clear policy regarding privacy, and empowering users to maintain control over their data. A number of proactive measures have been discussed in recent discussions regarding the regulation of vast quantities of online content, including the use of upload filters and automated detection tools for detecting potentially unlawful material. The policymakers and industry stakeholders frequently position artificial intelligence as a near-future solution to a variety of content moderation challenges, including hate speech, harassment, and the dissemination of extremist materials. The ability of artificial intelligence to resolve such complex issues comprehensively persists despite persistent limitations (Llansó, 2020). There is a marked improvement in the engagement and comfort level of users when they understand precisely what data is collected, how it will be used, and their rights regarding this information. The inclusion of diverse datasets and systematic audits are critical tools for countering the biases that are introduced by artificial intelligence. The talent of artificial intelligence systems is undoubtedly amazing, but the bias arising from unrepresentative training data or algorithmic flaws is still prevalent. The identification, analysis, and correction of biases within AI moderation systems requires regular and thorough audits to identify, analyze, and correct those biases. Diversity of datasets, covering a wide range of languages, dialects, cultures, demographics, and regions, increases the fairness and inclusivity of AI systems. Diverse perspectives ensure fair moderation outcomes and provide protection from discriminatory practices, resulting in an inclusive and respectful online community that fosters a sense of community and inclusivity.

Developing user trust in omnichannel commerce platforms is crucial to making sure there is a clear moderation process, as shown in figure 1, and robust appeal mechanisms for users to appeal. A number of factors contribute to building trust and reducing misunderstandings when it comes to the moderation process, including transparency regarding moderation criteria, communication of moderation decisions, and accessible appeal options. There should be a clear explanation accompanying AI-driven moderation decisions so they can be understood by both users and moderators alike. The perception of fairness and transparency is enhanced if users are given clear explanations for the removal or warning of content. Having an efficient and fair appeal process when it comes to omnichannel commerce platforms allows users to react quickly to errors in moderation and therefore improves the level of trust their users have in the moderation practices on the platform as well as the integrity of the platform as a whole.

A further advancement in AI moderation involves improving decisions through nuanced judgment, which shows that nuanced judgment is a significant advancement in the field. While AI is highly efficient, there are still situations in which a human judgment is still required, especially when there is ambiguous or context-dependent content to consider. Using AI-driven moderation skills in combination with the expertise of humans allows platforms to take advantage of the strengths of both approaches. Using AI systems, we can identify potential moderation problems effectively, while human moderators can assess the content's broader context and intent, ensuring fairness and accuracy of the content. The objective of this balanced approach is to ensure that the outcomes of moderation are both just and effective, as well as enhancing user trust and satisfaction.

A significant enhancement to omnichannel commerce platforms is the integration of AI in content moderation, which significantly increases a platform's ability to detect content violations quickly and mitigate them. A technology like AI moderation can only be effective if it is integrated with human oversight and AI-driven alerts. This type of system is called an integrated system. When it comes to complex cases, human moderators play an essential role in the verification of flagged content, the resolution of ambiguities, and making final judgments. By combining these two approaches, the overall moderation framework can be strengthened, ensuring a swift, accurate response to breaches and enhancing platform safety and compliance by enhancing individual and collective moderation.

The implementation of regular updates to artificial intelligence systems will ensure that they remain relevant and effective in a digital environment that is constantly evolving. The moderation algorithms must be regularly updated in order to keep up with new threats, developing societal attitudes, and advances in communication. By continuing to refine these service enhancements, we ensure that our moderation systems remain responsive, efficient, and capable of addressing new types of harmful or inappropriate content as they emerge, so they can be as responsive and efficient as possible. AI-based moderation platforms are constantly enhancing their AI-based moderation technologies in order to maintain a safe, reliable digital space, keep pace with changing challenges and improve moderation effectiveness in order to maintain a safe, trustworthy digital environment and maintain a high level of trust.

Implementation of these artificial intelligence moderation strategies has significant benefits associated with them. The omnichannel commerce platform is making sure compliance with regional norms and laws so as to mitigate legal risks in a more effective manner, by adapting moderation practices to local contexts and maintaining compliance with regional norms and laws so as to mitigate legal risks more effectively. By doing this, they have been able to enhance the reputation and credibility of their company on the global stage. It is important that AI moderation systems are continuously retrained to ensure proactive and efficient responses to emerging challenges and, as a result, to greatly reduce bias and moderation errors in the future.

It is also clear that protecting users from harmful content significantly enhances the satisfaction, trust, and retention of those users. An organization's commitment to respecting and utilizing data in a transparent manner strengthens relationships with its users, resulting in greater engagement and loyalty among them. Various audits and a diversity of training data are used to ensure fairness and equity in moderation, to protect against bias as well as discrimination. Moderation based on context-aware principles significantly reduces the number of errors, resulting in better user experiences.

There is a need for transparent moderation processes and effective appeal systems to ensure that users are confident in the fairness of moderation practices and feel assured that their interests are protected. A blend of sophisticated AI and human moderators ensures accurate, equitably-made decisions, which further solidifies the user's trust. Updates to AI moderation capabilities on a regular basis demonstrate our commitment to ensuring user safety and tracking our progress systematically.

KEY PRINCIPLES FOR SAFE AND TRUSTWORTHY OMNICHANNEL COMMERCE

Figure 2. Key principles for safe and trustworthy omnichannel commerce

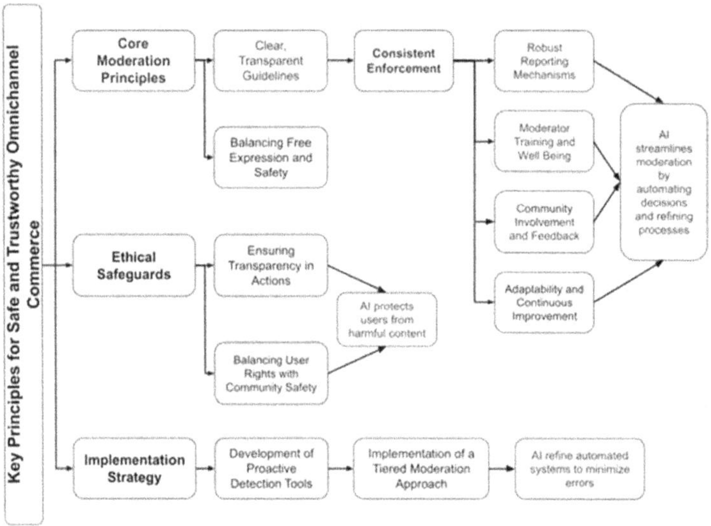

With omnichannel platforms at the heart of human retail needs, maintaining user trust and safety via content moderation has never been more crucial than it is today, as the platform has become the epicenter of human retail needs. In figure 2, the author has listed a few key principles to ensure that omnichannel commerce is safe and trustworthy. There is a comprehensive blueprint shown in figure 2 that can be used as a guide when constructing a robust system for the moderation of content in omnichannel platforms. The author has outlined three interdependent pillars of safe and respectable omnichannel commerce in figure 2 of this chapter. In order to implement fair and respectable omnichannel commerce, it is important to adhere to the principles of moderation which include ethical safeguards, implementation strategies, and policies that can help to guide the process. This framework ensures that not only consistency and fairness are guaranteed in the course of moderation, but also that it is flexible enough to expand with the changing needs of the omnichannel platforms industry. Artificial intelligence is one of the most important components of this structure, as it allows for both the automatic and enhanced moderation process to be utilized. As a foundation of this framework, core moderation principles have been formulated for platforms that are used in omnichannel environments as a way of providing a consistent and quality experience across all channels, an illustration of this can be found in figure 2. A set of these principles serves as the bedrock for creating omnichannel platforms, which serve as a base for all technical systems and human protocols that are built on top of them. A clear and transparent set of guidelines is the first of these steps that should be taken. Unless there are explicit rules for moderation, it is not consistent and predictable. It is these guidelines that provide guidance for both human moderators and machine-learning algorithms, which are used to develop algorithms for detecting violations of these guidelines. Content decisions are ensured to be based on documented standards if there is a well-defined policy set in place, rather than arbitrary decisions, which can lead to ambiguity. As a complement to clarity, platforms should also strive to find a balance between the freedom of expression and the safety of their users. The challenge here is nuanced and complex. To make sure that AI systems can distinguish between offensive content and legitimate discourse, it is imperative that they are fine tuned to take context into account, especially when contextual factors are at play. A key factor in ensuring this balance via moderation tools is the ability to apply confidence thresholds to the decision-making process and incorporate contextual cues as part of the decision-making process.

As it pertains to omnicommerce platforms, these three foundational elements are the basis for a consistent enforcement principle. There must be an impartial and systematic method of enforcing the rules across all types of users and scenarios. As a result of this, content moderation tools must be developed and deployed that are trained on a variety of datasets and are regularly audited for biases as well as tested across multiple languages and cultural contexts. Moderation efforts also need to be able to be scaled in order to maintain consistency. AI-powered automated systems are capable of scanning large volumes of text, images, as well as video at a rate that is unattainable to human teams when working with high volumes of text, images, and video. To prevent unintended consequences, such as disproportionately targeting certain groups of users or not detecting evolving forms of harmful content, these systems must be monitored and recalibrated frequently to ensure that they do not have any unintended consequences.

The omnicommerce platforms have to be able to implement several structural mechanisms in order to achieve consistent enforcement over a period of time in order to achieve the intended results. There are robust reporting tools available to users, which allow them to flag problematic content and forward it to the triage systems for review and to escalate as needed as soon as possible in order to get the problem resolved. The front end of these systems is designed with intuitive user interfaces; and on the back end, they are equipped with tools that help you manage your cases according to priority. Besides the quality of their work, the well-being and training of the moderator plays a significant role in their success. There are often sensitive and nuanced instances involving omnicommerce platform content moderators, as well as challenging situations that they are faced with frequently. Omnicommerce platforms should be able to provide their workforce with training programs, annotation environments, and wellness programs so that they can support and develop their workforce. The effectiveness of moderation policies is also strengthened as a result of the involvement of the community. Identifying inappropriate content, providing feedback, or validating decision-making may be easier to do with the assistance of trusted user groups that are able to provide assistance. An important part of this involves the development of platforms that support community governance functions such as voting, reporting hierarchies, and public accountability tools, as well as a technical component that involves the designing of the platforms.

Several factors are critical to making this process possible, but artificial intelligence is one of the most important ones. The use of artificial intelligence (AI) can enable the automatic detection of harmful content, and as a result of continuous learning, moderation strategies can be continually fine-tuned based on what is being learned. Machine learning techniques, such as supervised learning and unsupervised learning, are used by artificial intelligence systems to detect trends of abusive behavior and to adapt their responses in accordance with the trends that they detect. There are several ways in which these systems might be able to learn from correct and incorrect outcomes that are associated with moderation, including reinforcement learning. As a result of advancements in artificial intelligence, human judgment is not fully replaced, but rather extended, enabling real-time responsiveness as well as the ability to scale. The application of artificial intelligence (AI) enables the platform to recognize coordinated content moderation violations through the use of pattern recognition and predictive modeling as part of its AI capabilities. Whenever artificial intelligence and automated enforcement are employed, there must be ethical safeguards attached to ensure that fairness and transparency are not compromised by the implementation of these technologies. Keeping a transparent record of actions is one of the most important ethical obligations one can have on a person. It should be possible for those who have been flagged or had content removed to understand exactly why that content was flagged or removed. The only way to accomplish this is to log moderation decisions on backend systems, and to use explainable artificial intelligence to facilitate the interpretation of those decisions so that it can be better understood. Whenever a user appeals or questions the outcome of a moderation process, it becomes imperative that systems are auditable and capable of providing rationales for the actions taken. It is equally important to maintain a balance between user rights and the safety of the community in addition to maintaining transparency in the organization. An AI model that is well-designed must take into account the nuances of linguistics and culture in order to avoid overreaching in compliance enforcement, but at the same time protects real-world users from potential harm. In the event that the issue is ambiguous, the case is usually escalated to trained reviewers who can make appropriate decisions based on their knowledge of the context within which they are being presented. A common technique used to achieve this balance is to keep moderation systems in sync with humans at all times.

Another important ethical consideration is the role that artificial intelligence can play in preventing harmful content from appearing on websites. An examination of AI in content moderation from a decolonial perspective with a focus on its ability to address racist hate speech and discrimination is important (Siapera, 2022). The use of artificial intelligence systems must be continuously refined in order to reduce both false positives and false negatives as much as possible. The refinement process of the model consists of retraining it, labeling the data, as well as adjusting the model based on user feedback and post-incident analysis as part of the refinement process. A key element in making these systems work for omnicommerce platforms is to make sure that they can be adapted and improved. AI models must evolve as the threat landscape evolves, just as the threat landscape is evolving. Feedback loops are integrated into platforms' workflows so that they are able to continuously implement updated models and moderation policies as soon as they become available.

As part of the implementation strategy, the overall framework is grounded in the technical reality of the world. The first step is to develop proactive detection tools as a starting point. A major need of artificial intelligence (AI) is not just for enforcing but to continuously improve certain modes of moderation as well. The use of error analysis for omnicommerce platforms will provide the opportunity to enhance the solution iteratively by identifying both false removals and missed violations. The process involves ingestion pipelines for feedback, automated tools for reclassification, and periodic reviews of the performance of the system in order to achieve these goals. Using Artificial Intelligence (AI), we can refine these automated systems so that errors are minimized and the user experience is improved, which ensures that moderation efforts evolve in conjunction with the platform dynamics as it evolves.

OMNICOMMERCE PLATFORMS AND AI CONTENT MODERATION CHALLENGES

One of the crucial challenges faced by omnicommerce platforms these days is the dynamic nature of user-generated content, which is becoming more and more prevalent in a rapidly expanding e-commerce market. A vast and constantly evolving landscape of content is created as merchants upload products across omnicommerce platforms on a daily basis, creating a broad and diverse product selection. There have been many instances in the past where manual content moderation processes have been overwhelmed, inefficient, and error-prone. One of the greatest challenges that content moderators face when it comes to omnicommerce platforms is the ability to identify irrelevant, inappropriate, vulgar, illegal, political, racial, harmful, or defamatory listings accurately and promptly. Not only does this pose operational difficulties, but it also poses a risk to the integrity of the omnichannel platform and damage to user trust.

Manual content moderation, though effective, is limited by volume management, which is a result of the sheer quantity of new listings exceeding the moderators' capabilities. There is a lack of consistency and accuracy in content moderation decisions as a result of the fatigue faced by human reviewers. This leads to inconsistent content moderation decisions. There has been a dramatic increase in the amount of time consumed by content moderators at an industry level in omnicommerce platforms, which include manually reviewing every listing. This has resulted in a substantial delay in the time for legitimate listings to come live.

Managing user-generated content on omnicommerce platforms is a challenging task because of the dynamic and fast-paced nature of the content that is generated by its users. One of the key challenges in the moderation of omnicommerce platforms is the scale of the platform. With the scale of omnicommerce platforms, the amount of content that can be published skyrockets. The management of tens of thousands of product uploads on omnicommerce platforms in real-time requires systems that have the ability to verify that each piece of content complies with regulatory requirements and platform requirements. With such a massive volume of content, ensuring the relevance, appropriateness, and legality of content across such a massive volume is virtually impossible purely relying on manual moderation for the companies that offer omnicommerce platforms. The enormity of the problem brings with it a series of compounding problems that are hard to solve on their own. A high number of listings need to be reviewed each day, and content moderators are overloaded with the sheer amount of listings. There are many of these listings that include minor modifications of existing products, whereas others introduce entirely new categories and formats, making it even more difficult for the reviewer to assess them accurately. Among the many content types available on omnicommerce platforms, a number of diverse cultural, economic, and social backgrounds are represented. There is a wide range of formats and levels of quality to choose from. The diversity of products within the omnicommerce platform industry often leads to inconsistencies, noncompliance with platform norms, and confusion over how these guidelines should be implemented and interpreted in order to ensure the smooth operation of the platform. New merchants and users join the platform from time to time, resulting in new types of products and violations emerging. These range from false product claims, offensive content, and counterfeit items to illegal goods and immoral conduct.

For omnicommerce platforms to handle the influx of content, manual content moderation plays a significant role in ensuring the quality of the content. Despite the fact that this human-driven approach ensures some level of work that will be done and that contextual understanding will be taken into account, it reveals major shortcomings in terms of efficiency and scale. The volume of uploads that are made on a daily basis, regardless of the experience or training of the human moderators, makes it difficult for them to keep up. Because of this mismatch in the omnicommerce platforms industry, there are many backlogs and delays in getting products live on these platforms. Content moderation outcomes are inconsistent due to a number of factors, including fatigue, subjective interpretation, and the inherent limitations of manual review processes that affect human moderators. Depending on the content moderator, the same type of violation might be flagged by one and overlooked by the other. The tedious process of reviewing thousands of listings, many of which have similar features or repetitive violations, leads to content moderators becoming fatigued and burnt out as a result. There is a negative impact on not only the review quality but also employee morale and retention as a result. The manual moderation process significantly extends the amount of time required to review and approve listings that are submitted for publication. There is a negative impact of this delay on sellers, since longer approval times translate to an increased time to market, a reduction in sales prospects, and lower satisfaction ratings. There are times when even experienced content moderators working for companies with omni-channel platforms miss problematic listings or flag them as false flags despite their knowledge about the issues. In the end, these errors can result in content moderation violations slipping through the cracks or resulting in legitimate sellers being unfairly delisted. The ideal solution is to use both technology and human content moderators together as a means of maintaining a balance between the two.

The existing moderation processes in omnicommerce platform companies also cause bottlenecks in the processes that take place in the company. There is a direct correlation between the number of listings waiting for manual review and the amount of time it takes for legitimate listings to be approved and published. Disputes concerning takedowns or flagged content are often delayed, which makes sellers dissatisfied and leads them to lose trust in the system. Real-time visibility of content is a crucial feature in omnicommerce platforms that operate in fast-moving scenarios. Filtering and listing validation cannot be performed in real-time by manual processes. There is a possibility that the moderation bottlenecks may start to affect operations that go beyond the content team internally. A growing number of complaints related to delayed approvals or unjustified rejections of seller applications are being handled by seller support teams. There is a lot of pressure on development teams to optimize the moderation workflow or come up with workarounds to avoid inefficiencies which continue to persist. Investing in human moderation teams is neither cost-effective nor sustainable in the long run, which is why leadership must allocate more resources and budget to scale them.

It has become evident that relying solely on manual moderation is not an option that can be maintained in the long term. As a result of the risks associated with content, there is the need for a paradigm shift using artificial intelligence in order to stay ahead of the risks and to scale sustainably, in order to develop a technology driven, automated framework for content moderation in order to stay competitive.

Figure 3. AI content moderation overview vis-a-vis omnichannel commerce platforms

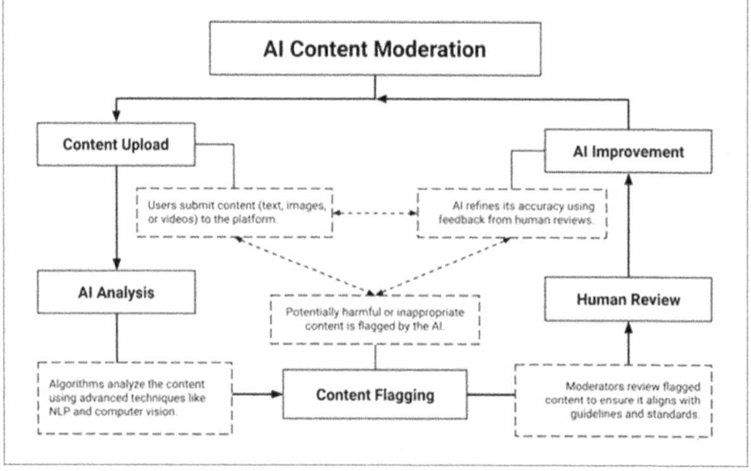

As shown in Figure 3, a comprehensive and structured approach to content moderation can be achieved by combining AI (Artificial Intelligence) analysis, content flagging, and human review of content on omnichannel commerce platforms that utilize AI (Artificial Intelligence). By keeping high standards for safety, appropriateness, and the community's standards, this systematic interaction ensures that digital platforms remain at the forefront of effectively managing user-generated content.

Merchants and users of omnichannel commerce platforms are required to submit a variety of formats for moderation, including text, images, and videos. The user and merchant generated content on omnichannel commerce platforms represents a continuous flow of information that must be evaluated systematically in order to be able to maintain an environment that is safe and productive for their users. As popular omnichannel commerce platforms encounter enormous amount of submissions in their daily operations, manual evaluation alone would be impracticable and resource-intensive due to the high volume of submissions. Figure 3 illustrates how this influx of data needs to be effectively managed by relying upon AI-driven analytics to assist in the process. By integrating context-aware AI into content moderation, content moderation can become significantly more accurate by considering the nuanced context in which content is shared in a more informed way. One of the most common limitations of traditional AI moderation tools is that they do not have the ability to recognize human emotions, such as humor, anger, love, or expressions that are culturally specific. A system that does not have context awareness risks flagging harmless content as inappropriate, leading to user frustration and eroding trust in the system. AI modes which incorporate context sensitivity can more effectively distinguish between genuinely harmful content and harmless material, thus minimizing false positives and enhancing the user experience as a result. The ability to comprehend context becomes an essential part of refining AI moderator capabilities, reducing moderation errors, and improving the overall efficiency of any moderation system as a result of contextual comprehension.

Managing large volumes of content is only part of the challenge of moderation, but it is also about maintaining operational excellence at the same time. As the digital marketplace is rapidly evolving, there is a need to build a framework to support content moderation in order to provide a safe and secure experience for omnichannel commerce while aligning with legal compliance, user safety, and brand trust in a rapidly evolving digital marketplace. The development of a solution that is both technologically driven and equally dynamic, intelligent, and scalable is necessary to address the challenges presented by this challenge. A content moderation framework has been developed by the author to provide a safe and secure omnichannel commerce experience, which is covered in the next section of this chapter. As can be seen in figure 3, the last critical component that needs to be addressed is the phase of human review. Even though AI technologies are making significant advances in the field of moderation, human intervention remains crucial. It is the nuanced judgment of the moderator as well as his or her context sensitivity that make them invaluable in the assessment of complex or ambiguous content that requires accurate interpretation. This phase of the process involves a detailed examination of flagged content in order to determine whether or not it is aligned with community guidelines and standards established by the community. There is greater reliability in a moderator's ability to distinguish legitimate expression from harmful material by meticulously analyzing the context, the intent, and the implications of their actions, than algorithms alone can.

During the flagging phase, it is especially important to define clearly the role of automated moderation in an omnichannel commerce platform since it is essential for its successful implementation. AI systems, while being highly effective at evaluating things quickly at the initial stage, shall constantly be calibrated and updated as they continue to work. Human moderators validate or correct algorithmic decisions made by AI by iterative learning processes, which are then used to refine AI accuracy by refining iterative learning processes based on its feedback loop. A continuous improvement process is enabled by the iterative interaction between AI systems and human moderators so that the sophistication and contextual responsiveness of moderation algorithms continues to be enhanced over time as a result of the iterative interaction.

OMNICHANNEL COMMERCE AND TYPES OF AI CONTENT MODERATION

As part of managing omnichannel commerce platforms, content moderation is an essential component, ensuring that the platforms remain safe and inclusive for all users as well as conducive to positive interactions with them.

Figure 4. Omnichannel commerce and types of AI content moderation

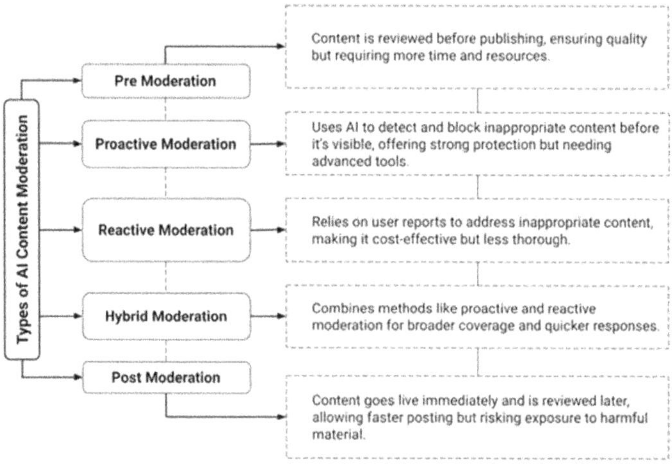

A summary of the five primary approaches to artificial intelligence-driven content moderation for omnichannel commerce platforms is shown in Figure 4: pre-moderation, proactive moderation, reactive moderation, hybrid moderation, and post-moderation. Figure 4 clearly illustrates each of these approaches. As each content moderation method is unique in terms of its characteristics, advantages, and challenges, their implementation is context-dependent and frequently complementary in terms of how they can be applied.

In the context of omnichannel commerce platforms, pre-moderation refers to a process through which content or products are reviewed before they are published in order to ensure their suitability for use as a platform for omnichannel commerce. During this stage, which is a preliminary stage, each piece of content submitted by users is evaluated by moderators whether they are AI algorithms or human moderators before it is made publically accessible by users. The effectiveness of this approach lies in the fact that it facilitates the maintenance of quality standards and prevents exposure to harmful, inappropriate, or illegal content. The pre-moderation process is intended to provide a higher level of control and protection for the audience, since harmful content does not reach them. It should be noted that the major disadvantage of pre-moderation is that it takes a substantial amount of time and resources. As this process involves significant time and labor, it may not be practical for platforms that have a high volume of user-generated content, such as social media or news forums, in which user-generated content is abundant. Premoderation is mostly used in the context of specialized platforms or communities that need rigorous content oversight due to sensitivities, legal obligations, or brand protections.

A proactive moderation system represents an advancement in AI technology that automatically detects and prevents inappropriate content from appearing on the web before it can be viewed by anyone. Using advanced AI methodologies for buyer analysis, funnel analysis and content analysis, proactive moderation tools scan and analyze content in real-time or near-real-time based on the analysis of advanced AI methodologies. By using this method, users can benefit from significant speed and scalability advantages, while being protected effectively from harmful exposure. As the world becomes more complex and dynamic, the proactive approach is especially beneficial in environments where a quick response is crucial, such as live commerce events and high-volume discussion forums, where immediacy is essential and manual moderation might not be feasible. The use of proactive moderation techniques that are innovative, continually updated, and require substantial initial and ongoing investments is imperative to ensuring their effectiveness. There can be false positives and false negatives as a result of limited technological capabilities, either leading to overly restrictive moderation or insufficient protection depending on the limitations of the technology.

There is a significant difference between reactive moderation and proactive moderation since reactive moderation is based heavily on user and trusted groups reporting inappropriate or harmful content. As a member of the moderation ecosystem, trusted users can identify potentially problematic content on the platform and bring this to the attention of the platform's moderators, which is a crucial part of the moderation process. The reason that this method is highly cost-effective is that it leverages the participation of the users to reduce the need for constant proactive monitoring, thus reducing the cost. As a consequence of its inherent limitations, reactive moderation is unable to provide thorough and timely results. Depending on user feedback, harmful content may possibly be visible to users before moderators become aware of it, and this may result in damage occurring before moderators intervene. The effectiveness of reactive moderation is also heavily dependent on the willingness of users to report issues that may be inconsistent or biased in a positive manner.

An omnichannel commerce platform with hybrid moderation combines both proactive and reactive moderation methods in order to provide both proactive and reactive moderation strategies simultaneously. It is intended that each approach will be leveraged to exploit its strengths while mitigating its weaknesses. Using hybrid moderation, advanced artificial intelligence tools are used to proactively detect and block obvious harmful content, and at the same time rely on user reports to identify content that may have bypassed the initial AI detection system. Using this unique blended approach, content moderation can offer a broader range of coverage with an increased level of accuracy and responsiveness. This is done by employing technological efficiency in sync with user insights. The concept of hybrid moderation can be considered as a custom and highly adaptable solution depending on the needs of the omnichannel commerce platform. This platform is particularly suitable for omnicommerce platforms with different types of content and more complicated requirements for moderation, especially those with diverse content types. A key benefit of this system is that it allows and even maximizes the efficient use of artificial intelligence to handle large-scale screening at the same time as taking advantage of human oversight to manage complex cases.

The last stage of post-moderation involves allowing all content to be published immediately, followed by a period of moderation afterwards. This is the stage where omnichannel commerce platforms ensure that user-generated content can be shared instantly, which will promote real-time interactions and a dynamic community engagement process with the help of user-generated content. A post moderation approach is ideal for enhancing quick communication and active participation on platforms where immediacy is key, such as social networking sites and online discussion forums. Post moderation carries a large risk. One of the major risks associated with post moderation is that harmful content can remain visible for a short period of time, potentially causing a negative user experience or causing harm to users. Developing an effective post moderation strategy requires a strong response capability, efficient AI algorithms that can detect problematic content, and a responsive moderation team that is capable of addressing and resolving any issues as they arise.

Figure 4 illustrates that each moderation method has unique considerations regarding its effectiveness, resource intensity, responsiveness, and risk exposure. Omnichannel commerce platforms can employ a variety of modes of moderation, and the platform must determine which method is most appropriate for the type of content, the type of user base, the guidelines of the community, the resources available, and the operations objectives. Moderation of users requires a number of strategic decisions. There is a direct correlation between these decisions and user safety, community standards, and overall satisfaction with the service. Developing effective, robust moderation strategies for digital platforms requires understanding and evaluating the inherent strengths and challenges associated with pre-moderation, proactive moderation, reactive moderation, hybrid moderation, and post-moderation so that effective and robust modes of moderation can be developed. Choosing a combination of these modes of moderation will ensure comprehensive, scalable, and user-responsive moderation practices, which are essential for maintaining a safe, engaging, and inclusive online community.

CONTENT MODERATION FRAMEWORK TO PROVIDE A SAFE & SECURE EXPERIENCE FOR OMNICHANNEL COMMERCE

To ensure the integrity, accuracy, and trustworthiness of content on omnichannel platforms, the author developed a content moderation strategy framework containing twelve comprehensive and interdependent factors. The author also ensured that the content moderation strategy framework complied with both community standards and regulatory requirements. As part of the framework and strategies, proactive detection, automated filtering using technology and artificial intelligence, and minimal manual intervention are all emphasized, while the user experience and platform integrity are also prioritized. Despite the fact that each of the strategies has its own distinct function, together they can be viewed as an interconnected AI system capable of moderating large scale, merchant and user generated content across a variety of omnichannel platforms.

Figure 5. Content moderation framework to provide a safe & secure experience for omnichannel commerce

Among the twelve strategies as illustrated in Figure 5 and included in this chapter as part of the framework, the first focuses on maintaining linguistic integrity. By implementing advanced language filters using artificial intelligence (AI), it becomes possible to scan for and remove content that contains racial, profanity, hate speech, violence, inappropriate words, or culturally insensitive expressions. There is a tremendous proliferation of hate speech, disinformation, and extremist content on the internet, and artificial intelligence is frequently cited as a solution for automating the identification and removal of this content. While "AI" is frequently used in policy discourse as a technical term, it is actually primarily used as a catchall for a wide array of automated detection and content analysis techniques that are becoming increasingly complex and limited (Llansó, Van Hoboken, Leerssen, & Harambam, 2020). There are a number of artificial intelligence filters that can be applied across a wide range of languages and dialects, making the moderation process inclusive and relevant to different regions. Through the use of artificial intelligence, omnichannel platforms are now equipped with a content moderation framework that analyzes the text of product titles, product descriptions, and user-generated reviews and content throughout the platform in order to ensure that it is linguistically appropriate. The framework evolves over the course of time as it discovers and is exposed to new terms, words, idioms, and slangs that are used in the day-to-day language, enabling it to adapt to the nuances of regional and local dialects.

As a second strategy, artificial intelligence rules are enforced to control the content that is posted by users and merchants on an omnichannel platform. During the process of implementing these systems, it is necessary to verify that certain types of content are limited to users based on their age, thus ensuring that minors are not exposed to offensive or otherwise sensitive material. Not only does this strategy align with the legal and regulatory requirements in many countries and regions, but it also reinforces a safe browsing environment for users as well. Based on predefined levels of sensitivity, the AI framework automatically categorizes content and flags or restricts listings according to the level of sensitivity. By implementing artificial intelligence for age gating and content labeling, this platform ensures that users of the omnichannel platform have access to tailored content based on their age and gender demographics in order to present them with the most relevant content.

The third pillar of the framework is a technology known as dynamic contextual filtering, which is a technology based on artificial intelligence (AI) that adapts real-time content filtering based on a combination of user behavior, content and product trends, and historical data sources and adapts it in real-time to meet user needs. As opposed to using only static rules to identify harmful or innocuous uses of specific keywords, the AI system depends on the concept of machine learning to dynamically evaluate context and determine, depending on the situation, whether specific keywords are being used in an innocent or harmful way. AI content moderation ensures a more accurate handling of edge cases as well as a reduction of false positives as a result of this level of content moderation. With the platform taking into consideration behavior patterns and contextual cues, it is better equipped to detect violations that may otherwise go undetected because it considers behavior patterns and contextual cues.

Using keyword blacklisting is the fourth strategy that can be used. As a traditional approach, but one that has its advantages as well, this strategy involves the creation and continuous maintenance of a database of forbidden words and terms . AI automatically flags or removes any content containing any of these blacklisted keywords as soon as it is detected by the algorithm. There is a particular benefit to this strategy when it comes to the prevention of harmful ideologies, offensive or racial language, or scam terminology spreading through social media. By using artificial intelligence, it is ensured that it works in conjunction with contextual filters, so that benign uses of certain flagged words don't get penalized. The dual approach that uses AI to enhance the accuracy of content moderation in multilingual environments greatly enhances the efficiency and accuracy of text-based content moderation.

The fifth pillar of the framework is known as commerce moderation and represents a critical part of regulating the types of products and services that can be listed on the platform as well as ensuring that they adhere to the platform's guidelines. This method involves the use of artificial intelligence (AI) to create blacklists of products that are illegal, unsafe, or ethically controversial. Keeping these blacklists up-to-date is achieved through a combination of internal compliance teams and updates from relevant regulatory authorities that is ensured by an artificial intelligence system that ensures these lists are updated on a constant basis. The purpose of this strategy is not only to protect users, but also to help omnichannel platforms comply with regulations established by local and international authorities.

The sixth pillar to the framework is a probabilistic moderation approach. As opposed to applying rigid yes or no filters to content, AI uses predictive analysis to determine the risk scores associated with each piece of content by using multiple variables as inputs. A few of the AI-driven variables that drive the results of these metrics are seller history, product category, keyword density, and user engagement metrics. A listing with a high risk score is either subjected to a human review or is subjected to a more stringent automated screening process. A scalable and nuanced moderation layer based on artificial intelligence is introduced in this approach, allowing the platform to allocate moderation resources in a more effective and proactive manner.

An analysis of user behavior represents a sophisticated predictive approach to platform oversight that is the seventh critical moderation strategy for omnichannel commerce platforms. By focusing on the overall data derived from all users' actions, within the legal framework, user behavior analysis differs from conventional methodologies that assess content exclusively on an individual merchant basis. There are numerous interactive activities, product queries, content uploads, and reporting behaviors which are meticulously logged and subject to algorithmic scrutiny in order to identify indicators of potential risk or malicious intent in these interactions with the omnichannel commerce platform. An empirical analysis of behavioral data is used to develop artificial intelligence models that are designed specifically to detect subtle yet persistent behavioral anomalies associated with abusive or manipulative behaviors. When a merchant repeatedly uploads listings that violate content guidelines without explicitly violating individual rules, then they demonstrate a behavioral pattern that may indicate a tendency to engage in exploitative behavior on a consistent basis in the future. As these subtle behavioral indicators accumulate, the predictive models can use them in a proactive manner to identify potentially problematic merchants and sellers and flag them for further investigation when necessary. As a sequel the moderation process has been enhanced in a way that has increased scrutiny to these flagged entities, increasing the frequency and intensity of manual reviews as well as possibly imposing preemptive moderation measures on them. A critical part of the user behavior analysis process is the concept of trust scoring, a dynamic metric that quantifies how reliable and compliant individual users have been over time. Based on factors such as past adherence to platform policies, interactivity within the community, and responsiveness to previous moderation actions, trust scores are calculated algorithmically based on factors such as past adherence to platform policies. It is based on these scores that essential moderation decisions are made, such as how fast content is approved, promotion visibility, and moderation strictness. The users with high trust scores benefit from leniency in the moderation process, which is a reflection of their consistent compliance history, whereas the users with lower trust scores face more strict moderation processes. As part of the technical implementation of such a system, there will be the requirement of establishing robust infrastructure for capturing behavioral events, the provision of comprehensive data warehouse solutions for aggregating historical actions and behaviors, and the application of supervised learning algorithms that can distinguish deviations from established behavioral norms. The analytical depth of user behavior analysis will enhance the effectiveness of moderation in the long run because it will allow proactive identification and mitigation of risks before they become an issue in the first place.

A similar moderation strategy to the behavioral analysis can be found for omnichannel commerce platforms and that is the enforcement of community guidelines as the eighth moderation strategy. The rationale behind this strategy highlights the commitment that omnichannel commerce platforms have to applying content policies and ethical standards in a transparent manner. The application of behavioral analysis facilitates the application of predictive moderation, while guidelines enforcement ensures that content and user conduct are governed by explicit, well-defined standards regarding acceptable content. There are several key elements to this approach, such as the application of moderation rules consistently and fairly, which is not only crucial for complying with regulatory requirements, but also for fostering user trust and reinforcing the integrity of the platform as a whole. As opposed to purely automated modes of moderation, guidelines enforcement incorporates a significant amount of human judgment along with educational and disciplinary processes to help ensure the guidelines are followed. A key component of this moderation strategy consists of a comprehensive user education process, which includes onboarding tutorials, policy reminders, as well as detailed instruction available through the help center. Whenever a violation of the guidelines occurs, the platform employs a structured and transparent escalation model, starting with warnings and educational feedback and progressing to temporary account suspensions, content removal, or permanent bans when repeated or severe violations are recorded. Technology plays an important part in enabling effective guidelines enforcement, as it requires sophisticated rule-engine systems that can manage complex policy applications and generate explanations for their application. Providing personalized feedback to users and clarifying moderation decisions through the use of artificial intelligence technologies further supports this effort. A further benefit of maintaining regular updates to social standards and legal frameworks is that they are promptly communicated to users. This ensures that the moderation system is aligned with evolving standards and legal frameworks, thereby strengthening its ethical robustness.

As a complementary strategy to the automation of omnichannel commerce platforms, as well as the explicit enforcement of policy, the ninth strategy is collaborative content filtering, which is based on the integration of community participation to enhance moderation accuracy and cultural sensitivity. As part of this strategy, users drive the process of moderation through peer reviews, user-driven reporting mechanisms, and crowd-sourced evaluations of content. A moderator designated by a community or a verified user can contribute nuanced, subjective insights that cannot always be captured by automated systems alone, especially when it comes to cultural diversity and complex contexts. Using collaboration to filter data offers distinct advantages including an increase in scalability without requiring significant operational overhead, as well as an increase in accuracy due to localized input. Participatory moderation requires sophisticated technical infrastructure to enable seamless collaboration between humans and machines, such as user-friendly interfaces for content evaluation, robust reputation scoring mechanisms, and structured moderation queues that facilitate seamless collaboration between humans and artificial intelligence. Using feedback collected from the community, iterative improvements to moderation algorithms are made over time based on the data gleaned from it. This reinforces system accuracy over time and promotes a sense of shared governance between all the users of the platform.

Considering the fact that modern omnichannel commerce platforms are eschewing a text-based approach for most of their listings, the tenth moderation strategy of visual content analysis is particularly useful as a foundational strategy for e-commerce listings. A key component of this strategy is the application of advanced artificial intelligence techniques, such as deep learning frameworks and object detection paradigms, to systematically scan graphics, images, and videos in order to find out whether or not they contain any inappropriate or misleading information. There are numerous datasets used in the training of these models that are representative of both acceptable and prohibited visual content, which enables accurate identification of racial language, violence, inappropriate images and manipulations to mislead consumers, as well as image manipulations that are meant to manipulate the image itself. In e-commerce contexts, it is very important that an effective visual moderation system is implemented in order to prevent buyer dissatisfaction, fraudulent practices, and legal disputes which may arise as a result of misleading product representations. A moderation system should be able to distinguish between legitimate, professional product images and those that are manipulated or harmful in nature. The moderation systems for video content must also be able to manage the complex analyses requiring frame-by-frame analysis and audio inspection in order to correctly assess the content. Integrating real-time visual content analysis into content delivery networks ensures that users are not exposed to inappropriate materials and improves overall user trust in platforms as well as platform reliability.

Moderation practices must be audited and policies must be adhered to in order to ensure their effectiveness and compliance in the long run. This is the eleventh strategy. A key component of this strategy is the systematic implementation of internal audits, the development of compliance verification processes, and the collaboration of the legal, compliance, and policy teams in evaluating its effectiveness. The moderation effectiveness is critically assessed, biases are identified, and recommendations are made to ensure that the enforcement process is equitable and transparent through regular audits. During audits, changes are made to automated moderation tools, trust scoring accuracy is improved, and policy refinements are incorporated as needed.

By customizing content accessibility according to user location, the twelth and the last moderation strategy addresses the legal, cultural, and regulatory frameworks that vary across different regions, which vary due to varying legal, cultural, and regulatory frameworks. It is possible to dynamically adjust the visual appearance of content on omnichannel commerce platforms based on IP geolocation data and account metadata. As a result, regionally inappropriate or legally restricted content is prevented from reaching users who are not authorized to access it. The geo-sensitive moderation approach requires state of the art geofencing technologies and localized policy applications in order to effectively manage the complexities of international regulatory requirements and cultural sensitivity inherent in global law enforcement. As a result of these sophisticated strategies, which include user behavior analysis, compliance with community guidelines, collaborative filtering, visual content analysis, auditing and policy adherence, and geographical access control, a deeply integrated, multidimensional moderation framework has been developed. A dedication to adaptability, predictive capabilities, and ethical transparency within the omnichannel commerce platforms industry ensures robust, context-aware content oversight, thus safeguarding the experience of users and supporting the growth of sustainable platforms.

CONTENT MODERATION WORKFLOW FOR OMNICHANNEL COMMERCE PLATFORM

There are multiple stages to the content moderation workflow process of an omnichannel commerce platform, including automated AI review, advanced AI analysis, human moderation, behavioral feedback systems, and ongoing monitoring, which shows how a robust and iterative approach to content moderation is used.

Figure 6. Content moderation workflow for omnichannel commerce platform

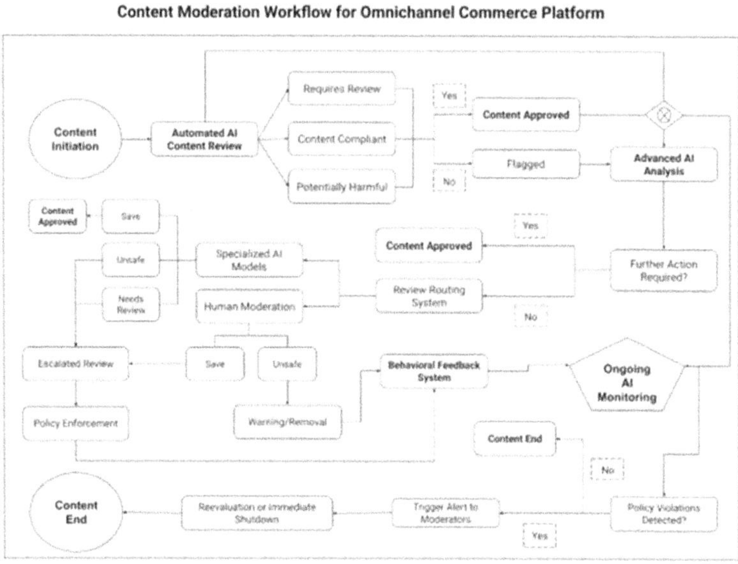

As shown in Figure 6, a comprehensive content moderation framework employing artificial intelligence (AI) and human oversight ensures safe and compliant user-generated content on omnichannel commerce platforms. Content Initiation is the first step in the moderation workflow, representing user-submitted pieces of content that enter the moderation pipeline. The content submitted is automatically reviewed by an Artificial Intelligence (AI) engine immediately after its submission. The primary objective of this evaluation is to categorize content into three distinct pathways: those requiring review, those in compliance with the law, and those that could be potentially harmful. The use of artificial intelligence algorithms allows content to be categorized based on predefined criteria and guidelines in order to manage the initial moderation burden efficiently.

Automatically identified content that is content compliant is reviewed without the need for additional human intervention, demonstrating efficient handling of material that is clearly acceptable. When content is deemed to be potentially harmful or requiring review, a more comprehensive review is conducted. Content that requires further verification advances to a decision point, where it is determined if it meets standards for approval or if it should be flagged for further review. To address subtle or ambiguous issues, flagged content is subjected to advanced artificial intelligence analysis.

Performing a sophisticated analysis of AI functions as a crucial refinement process, utilizing sophisticated techniques such as contextual evaluation. It is through this nuanced analysis that a more complex moderation scenario can be identified, reducing the amount of false positives and false negatives that are inherent in simpler automated systems. Upon completion of the analysis, the content of the article is placed in the review routing system, which is capable of either approving the article based on AI confirmation or escalating it to experts for further analysis.

There are two complementary elements that comprise the specialized moderation pathway which are specialized AI models and human moderation and they are interconnected. The use of specifically trained artificial intelligence models, which are based on the latest machine learning technology, is designed to enhance accuracy and precision in the processing of nuanced or culturally sensitive information. The idea behind human moderation is that it incorporates manual review of cases, adding context and judgment to difficult cases that may otherwise be misinterpreted by automated systems. During the review process, human moderators determine whether flagged content should be approved, saved, or classified as unsafe based on a detailed assessment.

Upon detection of unsuitable or unsafe content through human or specialized AI review, an immediate intervention will be undertaken by way of a warning/removal. The initiation of this step constitutes active moderation enforcement, directly preventing exposure to harmful or policy-infringing content as a result of active moderation. Whenever content resulting in uncertainties or controversy enters the escalated review stage, it means that another layer of moderation has been added, and policy adherence has been put under close scrutiny. This escalated review provides a link between policy enforcement and the escalating of the complaints, ensuring that actions are in strict accordance with the established guidelines, improving accountability and enhancing transparency.

A major component of the moderation framework is the behavioral feedback system which forms a significant part of the moderation process. An integrated moderation system, such as this one, aggregates the results of human and artificial moderation decisions, in essence creating a feedback loop. The feedback system enhances the accuracy, responsiveness, contextual sensitivity, and accuracy of future automated moderation processes by incorporating moderation results into AI models, and this will eventually enhance the total accuracy, responsiveness, and contextual sensitivity of the process. Continual feedback is essential for iterative learning and can significantly improve the performance of AI moderation as time goes on.

During the initial moderation phase, ongoing AI monitoring is utilized to ensure that post-approval content continues to be monitored continuously. During this monitoring stage it is essential that violations are identified if they occur after initial approval, or emerging threats and harmful behaviors are identified if they are emerging. Constant monitoring works in real time, continuously scrutinizing live content for compliance in real time. Detecting potential policy violations through ongoing AI monitoring is one of the benefits of AI. Human moderators will receive immediate alerts for rapid reassessment triggered by the tool, which reinforces the speed at which moderators respond to issues and the flexibility with which they conduct moderation actions.

Upon reassessment by the moderator, the content can either be reevaluated or an immediate shutdown can be implemented. A violation will be classified according to the severity and implications of the violation detected. There is no more effective enforcement action than an immediate shutdown, which eliminates harmful exposure in the most rapid and effective manner. The content may also re-enter the cycle of feedback so that further moderation refinement or the final implementation of the policy can be accomplished.

There are clearly defined endpoints that conclude this comprehensive moderation structure. After repeated violation or severe infractions, the content either achieves final approval and exits the moderation system or is conclusively removed from the content repository as a result of repeated violations. With this framework, robust, layered moderation is ensured, which integrates algorithm-based efficiency with human judgment while maintaining continuous quality improvement through iterative and feedback-based learning processes to ensure robust, layered moderation.

As can be seen from Figure 5 the moderation approach emphasizes automating AI efficiency complemented by targeted human oversight in addition to iterative learning via feedback based on behavioral data. The solution enables robust, context-sensitive, scalable, and robust moderation solutions critical for contemporary digital platforms. It allows equal emphasis to be placed on rapid content analysis as well as nuanced policy compliance and user safety. An implementation of this framework demonstrates the importance of integrating advanced artificial intelligence technologies, rigorous human review, and continuous feedback mechanisms to develop a comprehensive strategy that provides effective management of the complexity and scale of digital content generated by users.

CONCLUSION

Human moderators are an integral part of the algorithmic learning process. They go beyond validating and correcting AI judgments, instead they provide the foundational contextual understanding that algorithmic learning relies on. Using moderator decisions as authoritative feedback loops, AI moderation criteria, thresholds, and decision-making capabilities are refined based on moderator input. By performing evaluations, AI systems are able to comprehend subtleties and complex scenarios in a more sophisticated manner, thus enhancing their ability to perform moderation tasks. Human moderation can therefore not only improve the accuracy of immediate moderation but will also contribute to the continuous refinement and improvement of automated moderation systems as well.

As shown in the framework in the chapter with twelve strategies, this AI-human hybrid moderation strategy will be able to offer a number of important benefits. A major advantage of this approach is that it greatly improves the accuracy and efficiency of the moderation process. Human reviewers provide effective mitigation of risks associated with AI errors, thereby optimizing the overall reliability of moderation while automating large volumes of submissions, enhancing overall moderation speed. The second advantage of this collaboration lies in its active promotion of scalability. As merchant and user-generated content proliferates within omnichannel commerce platforms, they can effectively manage higher volumes of content without compromising quality or accuracy.

During the learning process, AI algorithms are continually improved together with the help of human moderators. The AI systems will become more knowledgeable with time as humans continue to input information, allowing them to develop a deeper understanding of context, which will result in fewer false positives and negatives over time. The moderation process is becoming increasingly sophisticated and effective as a result of this iterative improvement cycle, which ensures alignment with evolving user expectations and platform standards as the platform evolves.

Using a structured moderation process, users and merchants are provided with transparency and accountability, which enhances their trust and satisfaction with the program. A transparent process regarding the role of automated and human moderation processes provides the users with a more realistic perception of how fair and just moderation outcomes will be when both processes are transparent. The clear articulation of moderation procedures, the explicit criteria, and the human oversight increases the confidence of users in the fairness of the moderation process, thus reducing the frustration associated with opaque moderation decisions. The application of artificial intelligence to omnichannel commerce platforms provides a highly structured and effective approach to the moderation of content, articulating the distinct yet complementary roles that artificial intelligence analysis, content flagging, and human moderation play. The collaboration and iterative process of moderation greatly enhances its accuracy, efficiency, transparency, and adaptability. In combination with automated moderation technologies and human oversight, digital platforms efficiently manage vast quantities of user-generated content, balancing scalability with nuanced judgment. Using the depicted moderation strategy, the omnichannel commerce environment is maintained as a safe, inclusive, and compliant environment, fostering sustainable and positive online communities.

REFERENCES

Lai, V., Carton, S., Bhatnagar, R., Liao, Q. V., Zhang, Y., & Tan, C. (2022, April). Human-ai collaboration via conditional delegation: A case study of content moderation. In *Proceedings of the 2022 CHI Conference on Human Factors in Computing Systems* (pp. 1-18). DOI: 10.1145/3491102.3501999

Llansó, E., Van Hoboken, J., Leerssen, P., & Harambam, J. (2020). Artificial intelligence, content moderation, and freedom of expression.

Llansó, E. J. (2020). No amount of "AI" in content moderation will solve filtering's prior-restraint problem. *Big Data & Society*, *7*(1), 2053951720920686. DOI: 10.1177/2053951720920686

Nahmias, Y., & Perel, M. (2021). The oversight of content moderation by AI: Impact assessments and their limitations. *Harvard Journal on Legislation*, *58*, 145.

Siapera, E. (2022). AI content moderation, racism and (de) coloniality. *International Journal of Bullying Prevention : an Official Publication of the International Bullying Prevention Association*, *4*(1), 55–65. DOI: 10.1007/s42380-021-00105-7

Udupa, S., Maronikolakis, A., & Wisiorek, A. (2023). Ethical scaling for content moderation: Extreme speech and the (in) significance of artificial intelligence. *Big Data & Society*, *10*(1), 20539517231172424. DOI: 10.1177/20539517231172424

Chapter 4
Data Privacy Law in the Age of Social Media

Saikat Gochhait
https://orcid.org/0000-0003-4583-9208
Symbiosis Institute of Digital and Telecom Management, Symbiosis International University (Deemed), India

ABSTRACT

Although online social platforms are vulnerable to private information leakage, third parties can still do want with your data easily and consent. With Indeed the rapid spread of information today and changed role for social media, people more commonly worry over privacy. India's Digital Personal Data Protection Act 2023 seeks to cope with this risk by strengthening data protection. The legal framework must evolve constantly to guarantee the privacy and dignity of its recipients, permitting properly informed control over personal information in a world increasingly digital all the time.

INTRODUCTION

In the age of the Internet, many technology-based social media platforms have emerged in cyberspace to socialize and communicate with people from different places and time zones. Social media has made the communication system so easy that people can open up to each other. But if you are not careful enough, you can also expose your private information on social media, among other things. Since, nowadays one social platform is connected to another, it is easy to hack a platform and collect data. Cybercrime is constantly on the rise due to the availability of the Internet and, obviously, the lack of privacy security and openness of less protected social platforms, (Wu, 2018). Data security and the protection of user privacy are

DOI: 10.4018/979-8-3373-0335-2.ch004

the most important issues for all social media platforms today. The Internet can be a safe place, but only for those people who are progressively aware of the risk of posting private information or being on the platform and who are well aware of the 'Internet's security systems are they able to take measures to protect themselves and their information, (Martínez-de-Morentin, Lareki, & Altuna, 2021). For others, sharing information openly can be very risky. Over the past two decades, social media platforms have evolved into extensive and influential networking tools for content sharing, business activities, and information dissemination. With billions of users on major social networks such as Facebook, Instagram, TikTok, Snapchat, YouTube, Twitter, LinkedIn, Bumble, and Tinder, social media has become an integral part of our daily lives, especially during the pandemic where social commerce has become the only option for non-essential businesses to stay afloat. However, the phenomenal growth of social media has led to unprecedented access and influence over "users' personal information, activities, interests, and behaviors, raising privacy concerns among customers. The loss of privacy has become a major issue that needs to be addressed through privacy regulations, especially in the age of social media and digital technology. Global concerns have been raised about the use of consumer data by businesses for marketing purposes since social media companies often sell or manipulate user information, (Wang et al., 2021). Deloitte's report" Have it all: Protecting privacy in the age of "analytics' shows that many users are concerned about their privacy online, (Mhlanga, Maiti, & Hammer, 2021). In response to the growing concern and increasing number of cybercrimes, many countries are strengthening their systems to protect personal data. India has taken a step in this direction by introducing the Digital Personal Data Protection Act 2023 (DPDP Act 2023). The main objective of this Act is to create a transparent environment for the processing of digital data in the country. It also extends its provisions to activities conducted outside India if they involve offering goods or services in the market. With the DPDP Act 2023, India aims to address the challenges that the age of the online environment poses to individuals and promote a culture of privacy and security in the handling of personal data. This is particularly important given the amount of information that is shared and processed on social media platforms every day.

1. LITERATURE REVIEW

Social platforms are notoriously vulnerable to disclosure of user privacy. A third party can easily be tracked down by a third party, even if they have no intention of making it public. Outsiders can access the private information of a user by means of online friends, or by hacking the user's computer and publishing the information online and making it available to all without the user's consent or even without the user's knowledge, (Misra & Such, 2016). According to Warren and Brandeis, privacy refers to the right to have one's own private space away from the public gaze. This means that one can decide who has access to their personal information and keep it confidential. scholars define privacy as the degree to which others can access you through information, presence, and proximity. A person's privacy refers to their ability to protect sensitive or risky information from others during social interactions so that they do not feel restricted or uncomfortable. Social media platforms like Facebook, Twitter, Instagram, and Snapchat have made it easier for people to communicate. These platforms, however, often require users to provide personal information to the companies when using them. These platforms also record conversations and other interactions that take place on them. The main issue with privacy and social media is that users often give up their personal information in exchange for benefits such as money or access to certain features. While some users may not mind this exchange, others may be reluctant to disclose personal information if they feel the risks outweigh the benefits. Currently, there is no explicit legislation to protect personal data and privacy online, (Iwaya et al., 2022). Social media Common norms related to communication Social media is an internet-based method of communication that has become very popular in recent years. It includes various types, such as blogs, microblogs, wikis, social networks, widgets, and virtual worlds. Among these, social networks such as Facebook, Twitter, WhatsApp, Instagram, and Myspace have become extremely popular. To use these sites, users must first create a profile, which then allows them to see other 'people's' posts and communicate with them, creating a sense of community in the online world. However, this sense of community also carries potential risks, such as criminal activity. Communication privacy management theory explains how users control the boundaries of their privacy and the disclosure of personal information, both online and offline. When users voluntarily disclose personal information, it becomes co-owned, which increases the risk of misuse, (Talwar, Chaudhary, & Kumar, 2022). Therefore, people need to draw a line to distinguish between public and private information to enable deliberate disclosure of information and establish co-ownership expectations. Privacy issues arise when people are concerned about the potential misuse of personal information on social media. Technology allows for the monitoring of social media and email activity, which can lead to the theft of personal communications. Despite these risks, people continue to use social media because they believe the benefits outweigh the immediate and long-term risks. However, there is currently no explicit legislation to protect privacy and data.

2. DATA PRIVACY LAWS IN INDIA AND GLOBALLY

The right to privacy encompasses a range of freedoms that guarantee individuals the ability to keep their lives, interests and activities away from the public eye, free from interference by the government or private parties. It also protects against the unauthorized disclosure of personal information. Individuals have the right to review their information, request changes, and be notified before disclosure. The right to privacy is the right of an individual to protect themselves from direct or other forms of intrusion into their personal life, affairs or family. Social media privacy and data protection laws in India. The origins of privacy dates back to the 1935 in the Nihal Chand vs Bhagwan Dei judgment in which the High Court recognized the existence of personal privacy that transcends Indian traditions and practices. India became a member of the United Nations and signed the Universal Declaration of Human Rights (UDHR) in 1948, even before gaining independence. The Indian Constitution essentially adopted the UDHR but neglected the idea of privacy in India. While Article 19 of the Indian Constitution granted freedom of speech and expression, the UDHR prioritized privacy in Article 12. Article 19 applies to reputation, national security, and public order.

After years of debate, the Indian right to privacy is now officially recognized as a fundamental right. In the case of Justice K.S. Puttaswamy v. Union of India, the Supreme Court of India has confirmed the right to privacy as a fundamental freedom, marking a turning point in India's constitutional history. The order passed by all nine judges stated, "The right to privacy is protected as an integral part of the right to life and personal liberty under Article 21 and as part of the freedoms guaranteed under Part III of the Constitution." The advent of social media has led to a new era of online privacy concerns. There are no specific provisions for online privacy and data protection. Still, Article 21 of the Indian Constitution, which serves as a safeguard for privacy, is not enough to fully protect personal data. The Information Technology Act, 2000, is the most comprehensive legislative measure dealing with online privacy in India. Although this Act has attempted to address privacy concerns on social media, it is not sufficient to ensure complete privacy protection. However, the provisions contained in the Information Technology Act, 2000, in Sections 43, 66, 66F, and 67 serve as a measure to protect the privacy of users and provide remedies against cyber offenses. Section 43: Penalty for damaging computer systems: This section provides penalties for people who unlawfully access or obtain access to a computer system or network. It also covers offenses such as downloading, copying, or extracting data without permission and introducing computer contaminants or viruses. Penalties may also include compensation for the person concerned. Section 66 deals with offences related to computer fraud and dishonesty. Whoever commits any of the acts mentioned in Section 43 willfully or with intent to defraud is liable to imprisonment for a term that may extend to three years, a fine that may extend to five lakh rupees (currency), or both. Section 66F: Cyber Terrorism: This special section is reserved for cases of cyber terrorism where the use of a computer resource or communication device poses a threat to the sovereignty, integrity, security, friendly relations of India with other nations, maintenance of law and order, or prevention of a cognizable offense. The consequences for violations of this section are extremely harsh, as people found guilty can be punished with life imprisonment. Section 67 deals with the distribution or transmission of content in any form. This includes any lewd material, arouses the interest of lust, or has the potential to degrade people in its effect. If convicted, the punishment can include imprisonment for a maximum of three years and a fine of up to five lakh rupees. In subsequent convictions, the punishment can be imprisonment for up to five years and a fine of up to ten lakh rupees. With the publication of the Srikrishna Committee report and the draft bill on data protection titled Personal Data Protection Bill 2018, India has come a step closer to its data protection law. However, it was the Digital Personal Data Protection Act 2023 (DPDP Act 2023) that further strengthened India's commitment to data protection by introducing several important provisions.

Data and Personal Data Definitions

Data includes any form of information, facts, ideas, opinions, or instructions that can be understood, interpreted, or processed by humans or automated systems. Personal data is any information that relates to an individual (referred to as the data subject) and enables them to be identified.

Processing of Personal Data

This includes performing actions with personal data that are either fully or partially automated. These actions include collecting, storing, organizing, sharing, using, disclosing, distributing, and deleting data. Processing can only be carried out for purposes for which the consent of the data controller has been obtained or for which there are legitimate circumstances within the meaning of the law.

Applicability of the Act

The Act applies to the processing of digital personal data within India, irrespective of whether it is originally in digital format or subsequently converted into such a form. In addition, the Act extends beyond the borders when it comes to processing in connection with the offering of goods or services to individuals who are resident data holders in India. There are exceptions for domestic processing and data disclosed by the customer or due to legal obligations.

Consent for Processing

Personal data can only be processed if specific, informed, unconditional, and unambiguous consent has been obtained from the client. Consent should be obtained for specific purposes, and individuals have the right to withdraw their consent at any time. There are situations, such as responding to emergencies, ensuring government security, or providing government services, where consent is not required. It is important to note that individuals under the age of 18 or with disabilities obtain consent from their parents or legal guardians.

Rights and Responsibilities of Data Subjects

Individuals whose data is processed have the right to obtain information about how their data is processed. They may also request the rectification or erasure of their data, designate someone to exercise these rights in the event of death or incapacity, seek assistance with complaints relating to data processing, and withdraw their consent at any time. They are also obliged not to submit complaints, withhold information, or provide false information. The law stipulates sanctions for breaches of these obligations.

Data Privacy and Security Measures

Entities that handle data must implement measures to safeguard privacy and ensure protection against breaches. Organizations are obligated to conduct risk assessments, designate data protection officers, and promptly report data breaches to both authorities and affected individuals within specified timeframes.

Regulatory Framework

The DPDP Act of 2023 sets up a framework that includes the establishment of a Data Protection Authority. Its role is to oversee and enforce data protection standards, investigate complaints, and promote awareness regarding data protection among individuals and organizations handling data.

Penalties and Remedies

The law establishes sanctions for non-compliance with its provisions, which may include fines as compensation for individuals who have suffered damage as a result of breaches of data processing regulations. It also establishes a procedure for the resolution of complaints and disputes through the adjudication and appeal mechanisms provided in the Act. India has a population of more than one billion people, of which about 500 million are regular internet users. India also has the second-largest online market after China. Similar to Article 3 of the UDHR, Article 21 of the Indian Constitution also protects the freedom and life of the individual. However, it does not provide a comprehensive solution for the protection of privacy. While Article 21 provides a temporary respite, legislative measures need to be taken to include an article in the Indian Constitution that protects privacy, similar to Article 12 of the UDHR. India is on the verge of adopting significant amendments to its data and information technology regulations after a long period of inaction. These amendments are expected to enable India to fully capitalize on its status as one of the most influential data-driven economies in the world. According to reports citing government insiders, the Indian government will start drafting a new law to replace the existing Information Technology (I.T.) Act, 2000. India is currently one of the few remaining nations in the world without a clearly defined and up-to-date system of data protection laws. Given ' 'India's aspirations to establish itself as a leading digital economy with a thriving data services sector, the government needs to accelerate its efforts to create a legal framework that brings the country on par with its global competitors. Unlike other laws, data protection laws must work in conjunction with international laws and standards and cannot be limited to domestic jurisdiction only, (Awasthi, 2022).

3. FEDERAL AND STATE SOCIAL MEDIA LAWS & GDPR

US federal laws, namely the Communications Decency Act (CDA) and the Children's Online Privacy Protection Act (COPPA), aim to regulate data protection in social media. Despite various attempts to introduce comprehensive national social media privacy regulations in the United States, there is still a lack of adequate measures (unlike the GDPR in the E.U.). Several countries have introduced laws to further ensure social media privacy. These laws can be divided into three categories: Laws mandating the implementation of security measures, laws mandating accountability and criminal penalties for hackers, and laws mandating notification of data breaches.

The General Data Protection Regulation (GDPR) enshrines the "right to be forgotten" in the European Union and allows individuals and companies to request the deletion of their data from certain websites. The General Data Protection Regulation (GDPR), which came into force on May 25, 2018, is a framework that governs how the personal data of individuals within the European Union (E.U.) and the European Economic Area (EEA) is managed and protected. An important aspect of the GDPR is the introduction of the "right to be forgotten" (RTBF). This provision gives individuals and organizations the ability to request the deletion of their data from websites or online platforms in certain circumstances. For example, if their data is no longer necessary for the original purpose or if they withdraw their consent or object to processing without there being compelling reasons for doing so. The main aim behind the RTBF, as outlined in the GDPR, is to give individuals control over their data in an age where vast amounts of information are easily accessible online. The Right to Be Forgotten (RTBF) is inaccurate, with the impact of outdated, inaccurate, or irrelevant information on an individual's reputation and privacy. The General Data Protection Regulation (GDPR) seeks to strike a balance between the right to privacy and the public's access to information by allowing individuals to request the removal of data.

In contrast, there is no equivalent of the RTBF in the United States. The legal framework in the U.S. places great emphasis on the First Amendment, which protects the right to free speech. The idea of deleting or concealing information is seen as a potential violation of these rights, which complicates the adoption of an RTB-like provision. However, American tech giants like Google, which operate globally, are subject to GDPR and similar laws in their regions when doing business abroad. For example, Google has had to adapt its data processing practices to meet the requirements of the GDPR, including accommodating requests for data erasure in the E.U. and EEA. This highlights a challenge that companies face when navigating different data protection laws in different jurisdictions. The contrast between the E.U.'s focus on data protection and the U.S.'s focus on freedom of expression highlights the debate over a fair, ethical, and lawful approach to handling personal data and protecting online privacy in today's digital age. The rationale behind these regulations is that individuals should not suffer from the publication of irrelevant or outdated data. Although the United States lacks equivalent legislation on the right to be forgotten, comparable laws in other regions.

Protecting Children on Social Media

The Online Privacy Protection Act (OPPA) is a legal framework that regulates the handling of children's personal data on the Internet. Websites that target minors are prohibited from collecting personal information without first disclosing their data collection practices and obtaining written parental consent. When it comes to protecting the privacy of children on social media platforms, parents generally assume a supervisory role. Nevertheless, there may be cases where parents unintentionally or intentionally violate the privacy of their children by posting their pictures or mentioning them in a blog. However, children have no rights to social media in such situations, (Gruschka et al., 2018). Data protection laws for social media in the workplace. In the context of social media privacy, the relationship between employer and employee is a crucial aspect. As the use of social media continues to grow among employees, there are legitimate concerns about employee privacy. To address this issue, numerous regulations have been enacted to protect the privacy of job applicants and current employees as companies use social media to research potential employees. Government regulations generally prohibit employers from doing the following: requesting the username, password, or login information for an ' 'employee's or job ' 'applicant's personal social media accounts; forcing an employee to add another employee, manager, or administrator to their social media ' 'account's friend or contact list; or changing employee privacy settings, (Talwar, Chaudhary, & Kumar, 2022). European user-friendly laws. The issue of social media privacy in the context of employer-employee relations has become increasingly important due to the growing use of social media by employees. While companies use social media to research potential employees, several regulations protect the privacy of job applicants and existing employees. In general, government regulations prohibit employers from requesting or requiring employees or applicants to provide usernames, passwords, or login information for their personal social media accounts. In addition, employers are prohibited from requiring employees to add other employees, managers, or administrators to their social media ' 'account's friends or contacts list or from changing employee privacy settings. These regulations aim to protect the privacy of employees and job applicants, as disclosing information about personal social media accounts to employers poses potential risks, (Talwar, Chaudhary, & Kumar, 2022).

4. PRIVACY ISSUES RELATED TO SOCIAL MEDIA

Social media platforms have revolutionized the way people communicate and create content on the Internet. These platforms are constantly changing, with new ones emerging and old ones disappearing. As people engage in social media, privacy becomes a major concern. Privacy analysis considers both the benefits and risks associated with disclosing personal information online. It is unlikely that people will willingly sacrifice their privacy without adequate compensation. Unfortunately, social networks can jeopardize 'users' privacy by collecting and sharing personal information without their consent, leaving users vulnerable to data breaches. It is common for users not to read the intricate details of privacy policies when logging into accounts on various social media sites and platforms. The wording in these policies is intentionally designed to protect the platforms from any legal liability. Unfortunately, the security measures on many sites are inadequate, putting users at increased risk of data breaches and other cybercrimes, (Misra & Such, 2016). When signing up for a Facebook account, one must agree to the terms of service, which authorize Facebook Incorporation to collect both personal and demographic information about the user. Through the use of sophisticated algorithms, Facebook is able to track and study user behavior and patterns. It is the voluntary provision of personal data by the user that enables this type of surveillance, (Misra & Such, 2016). The improper and irresponsible use of personal data can lead to various privacy violations, as previous observations have shown. The developers believe that a single, limited method by which security can be breached is unauthorized access to social user data resulting from privacy violations or inadequately implemented safeguards. In addition, they believe that optional use, where information acquired for a specific purpose is used for different purposes without the knowledge or consent of the owner of the information, can also lead to privacy violations. However, security concerns can be addressed if appropriate information policies and practices are in place that empower individuals to decide on the disclosure and use of their personal information. The sharing of personal data on social media is subject to the consent of the platform, although the conditions for such consent are not clear. It is necessary to examine whether this consent should be interpreted generously or restrictively, and the platform's privacy policy is the only authority that can provide an answer. Both the user and the social media company have responsibilities that must be fulfilled. The user is responsible for deciding on the type and scope of personal information, including contact information, images, preferences, and other details that are published on the website. It is the responsibility of the social media platform to ensure the privacy and security of its website or mobile application and to restrict the use of the platform by marketers. However, since the social media platforms want to profit from data sharing on these sites, the security measures and access restrictions are insufficient. The most important evaluation parameters for social media platforms are related to security and confidentiality. Despite this, malicious attacks on all social networking sites continue to occur, and developing effective measures to protect potential users from such dangerous incidents remains a complicated challenge for many social analysts and technologists. The basic security attacks can be divided into three different categories. Privacy breaches: These attacks expose the connections between nodes and edges within a social network, often resulting in the disclosure of sensitive personal relationships. Passive attack: This type of attack is stealthy and unnoticed. Active attacks: This category of attacks involves the creation of new nodes and subsequent efforts to connect them to existing nodes in order to infiltrate more nodes, (Chibba & Cavoukian, 2015). The rise of big data has resulted in several cases of social media giants misguiding users about data protection. The worrying thing about this case is that whenever someone searches for something on social media and then accesses the platform again, the results are displayed based on their interests, and channels or posts are recommended that they might like. One question: if the algorithm works in this way, where is the guarantee of privacy and security on social media if users' movements can be easily monitored and investigated? This raises the question of the security of the Internet, (Sethu, 2020). Currently, Facebook is the world's largest social media platform. Thousands of people use it all over the world, and it's accessible to everyone. It should also be noted that most cases of cybercrime are linked to these platforms. Crimes such as fraud, fake identities, hacker attacks, and the disclosure of private data mostly involve Facebook users. On these platforms, users are usually the target of large companies that primarily want to obtain information about a ' 'user's age. According to the FTC, Facebook was charged in 2014 because it led consumers to believe it could keep their data private but then later shared it publicly all the time. In 2014, WhatsApp committed to its users that it would not sell their data in the future. However, in 2016, after the merger of Facebook and WhatsApp, Facebook announced that it would collect the personal data of WhatsApp users. The growing privacy furor and lawsuits have prompted social media platforms to redefine their traditional behavior towards consumers. In 2021, Facebook stated that a team of engineers was working on developing a new way to serve ads without using users' data the N.Y. Times reports Google wants to remove trackers from Chrome by 2023. Twitter is also a huge platform, although its data protection system used to be stricter. When reporting abuse, Twitter usually gives the abuser or hacker a space, which is a good sign. Although it is virtually mandatory to link Gmail and phone numbers to Twitter accounts, it is possible to connect to other social media and websites via the Twitter account. So, there is indeed a risk of exposing personal data when a social media account is linked to various other platforms. Although Twitter had strict security access, these securities are now breaking down with the new rules. Twitter has made an ambiguous statement about having to pay for account security, otherwise it is accessible and can be easily hacked. Although it is not yet confirmed, rumors of privacy invasion are circulating the Internet and people are protesting to protect their data. The term “doxxing” refers to the publication of ' 'people's information and personal data without their consent. Doxxing is a cybercrime, although it is becoming more and more difficult to stop it every day, (Basumatary & Kalita, 2022). Facebook Case study According to data from Statista (2019), there were 1.49 billion daily active Facebook users in 2018, and there were approximately 1.69 billion Facebook members worldwide in 2020. Active Facebook users frequently upload private information that may be used to follow their movements. However, the majority of users are unaware that their updates and postings are accessible to the public and in the public domain. In March 2018, Christopher Wylie, a whistleblower, revealed how Cambridge Analytica, a data company, was exploiting private user data from Facebook. After an investigation by ' 'Britain's Information ' 'Commissioner's Office, it was discovered that Cambridge Analytica violated British law in its data harvesting. Leaked documents from the firm and Facebook showed that Facebook knew about the data breach but did not do enough to notify users and secure the data of over 50 million Facebook users, (Awan et al., 2020). In response to the Cambridge Analytica scandal, Facebook and its founder Mark Zuckerberg, launched a significant public relations campaign and apology tour. ' 'Facebook's internal P.R. team immediately got to work and they also hired Definers Public Affairs to downplay and apologize for the ' 'company's involvement in the scandal. To promote this campaign, Facebook placed ads in British and American newspapers stating that if they were unable to protect users' information, they should not be allowed to do so. Zuckerberg pledged that Facebook would commit to limiting the data apps received. He also agreed to testify in a U.S. Congressional hearing and declared the company was “ready for new federal regulations”. However, these public pledges to improve appear to contradict ' 'Facebook's ongoing lobbying efforts to avoid increased data protection legislation. Documents obtained by the New York Times in December 2018 showed that Facebook allowed certain companies to access data that they claimed was restricted. Aside from breaching the right to privacy and public trust, Facebook may have also violated a 2011 agreement with the U.S. Federal Trade Commission (FTC) that requires explicit consent from users before sharing their data. The report, based on an inquiry of the British parliamentary Digital, Culture, media and Sport Committee into disinformation and fake news includes an even stronger allegation, stating that Facebook “intentionally and knowingly violated both data privacy and anti-competition laws”. Despite ' 'Facebook's public apologies and massive P.R. campaign, their actions behind the scenes suggest that the tech giant remains committed to avoiding stricter regulations when it comes to respecting the right to privacy, (Al-Asmari & Saleh, 2019).

5. CONCLUSION

The notion of digital surveillance and privacy invasion on social media platforms has led to a lack of constitutional or legislative protections for individuals in many nations. As a result, victims of such privacy violations are forced to rely on judicial decisions and interpretations to seek redress. This void in legal protection creates an undue burden on individuals who suffer from press abuses and violations of privacy. In cases of press abuse, tort law is often invoked as the sole remedy. Still, such legal mechanisms are inadequate and only cover torts such as libel, slander, defamation, morality and decency, which are often subsumed under the concept of privacy. Unfortunately, these do not fully address the need for comprehensive privacy protection that individuals demand. Although some legal codes, such as India's, offer remedies for specific offences, privacy as a general concept is not a topic that legislators have considered adequately. Courts have made rulings on some of the aforementioned offenses, but only Articles 19(2) and 19(3) remain as possible bases of legal protection for victims. The rise of social media surveillance and the widespread availability of personal information on the Internet have undercut the rights enshrined in the constitution and the principles on which democracies are built. The concept of surveillance and the invasion of privacy on media platforms have resulted in a lack of constitutional or legislative safeguards for individuals in numerous countries.

The recent implementation of the Data Privacy and Protection Act (DPPA) 2023, as mentioned earlier, is a step towards addressing these issues. Can serve as an example for other nations to follow. The DPPA 2023 establishes a framework for safeguarding data and privacy, granting individuals rights over their data while ensuring that corporations are held accountable for any misuse. In addition to legislative measures, social media networks must provide effective safety mechanisms to safeguard user data from exploitation and abuse. A comprehensive approach to privacy that extends beyond an ' 'individual's viewpoint is necessary to regulate information flows and ensure privacy in interactions with other individuals and organizations. By clarifying the risks and goods at stake, this approach can strengthen the normative power of privacy rights.

REFERENCES

Al-Asmari, H. A., & Saleh, M. S. (2019, April). A conceptual framework for measuring personal privacy risks in facebook online social network. In *2019 International Conference on Computer and Information Sciences (ICCIS)* (pp. 1-6). IEEE.

Alan, A., Al-Arnaout, Z., Topcu, A., Zaki, C., Shdefat, A., & Elbasi, E. (2022, November). How do default privacy settings on social media apps match people's actual preferences? In *2022 International Conference on Electrical and Computing Technologies and Applications (ICECTA)* (pp. 305-308). IEEE.

Ariyo, O., & Zheng, J. (2022, December). A Study On Security and Privacy Risks of Self-Disclosure On Social Networking Sites During COVID-19 Pandemic. In *2022 IEEE International Conference on Big Data (Big Data)* (pp. 2828-2832). IEEE.

Elmendili, F., Chaoui, H., & Bouzekri El Idrissi, Y. E. (2019). Social Network's Security Related to Healthcare. *Intelligent Pervasive Computing Systems for Smarter Healthcare*, 91-113.

Awan, S. M., Waheed, U., Khalid, Y., Khan, M. A., Mansoor, Y., & Rehman, S. A. (2020, February). Violation of User's Privacy Rights by Facebook. In *2020 International Conference on Information Science and Communication Technology (ICISCT)* (pp. 1-4). IEEE.

Awasthi, M. (2022, December). Verifiable and practical compliance for data privacy laws. In *2022 IEEE 29th International Conference on High Performance Computing,Data and Analytics Workshop (HiPCW)* (pp. 59-60). IEEE.

Basumatary, B., & Kalita, H. K. (2022, March). Social media forensics-a holistic review. In *2022 9th International Conference on Computing for Sustainable Global Development (INDIACom)* (pp. 590-597). IEEE.

Chibba, M., & Cavoukian, A. (2015, December). Privacy, consumer trust and big data: Privacy by design and the 3 C'S. In *2015 ITU Kaleidoscope: Trust in the Information Society (K-2015)* (pp. 1-5). IEEE.

Gruschka, N., Mavroeidis, V., Vishi, K., & Jensen, M. (2018, December). Privacy issues and data protection in big data: a case study analysis under GDPR. In *2018 IEEE International Conference on Big Data (Big Data)* (pp. 5027-5033). IEEE.

Iwaya, L. H., Iwaya, G. H., Fischer-Hübner, S., & Steil, A. V. (2022). Organisational privacy culture and climate: A scoping review. *IEEE Access : Practical Innovations, Open Solutions*, *10*, 73907–73930.

Martínez-de-Morentin, I., Lareki, A., & Altuna, J. (2021). Risks Associated With Posting Content on the Social Media. *IEEE Revista Iberoamericana de Technologias del Aprendizaje, 16*(1), 77–83. DOI: 10.1109/RITA.2021.3052655

Mhlanga, M. X., Maiti, R. R., & Hammer, B. (2021, March). Privacy and Security Matters Related To Use Of Mobile Devices and Social Media. In *SoutheastCon 2021* (pp. 1–6). IEEE.

Misra, G., & Such, J. M. (2016). How socially aware are social media privacy controls? *Computer, 49*(3), 96–99.

Sethu, S. G. (2020, July). Legal protection for data security: a comparative analysis of the laws and regulations of European Union, US, India and UAE. In *2020 11th International Conference on Computing, Communication and Networking Technologies (ICCCNT)* (pp. 1-5). IEEE.

Tabassam, S., Shah, H., Alghamdi, K., & Badshah, A. (2019, July). Social Netwoks and Digital Security. In *2019 International Conference on Electrical, Communication, and Computer Engineering (ICECCE)* (pp. 1-7). IEEE.

Talwar, A., Chaudhary, A., & Kumar, A. (2022, October). Encryption Policies of Social Media Apps and Its Effect on User's Privacy. In *2022 10th International Conference on Reliability, Infocom Technologies and Optimization (Trends and Future Directions)(ICRITO)* (pp. 1-4). IEEE.

Wang, X., Luo, W., Bai, X., & Wang, Y. (2021, November). Research on big data security and privacy risk governance. In *2021 International Conference on Big Data, Artificial Intelligence and Risk Management (ICBAR)* (pp. 15-18). IEEE.

Hu, M., & Wu, X. (2018, June). Research on children's network privacy protection in mobile social media. In *2018 IEEE 20th International Conference on High Performance Computing and Communications; IEEE 16th International Conference on Smart City; IEEE 4th International Conference on Data Science and Systems (HPCC/SmartCity/DSS)* (pp. 1135-1138). IEEE.

Chapter 5
Full Stack Powered Documentary Review App to Foster Documentary Enthusiasts

Angelin Gladston
https://orcid.org/0000-0003-3899-2474
Anna University, Chennai, India

Jessica Constance Paul
Anna University, Chennai, India

P. Elavarasi
Anna University, Chennai, India

ABSTRACT

Documentary Review Application designed to provide users with a platform to explore, review, and discuss documentaries. React, offers a user-friendly interface that allows users to easily navigate through a diverse collection of documentaries, read detailed reviews, and contribute their own insights. Features such as user authentication and personalized profiles enable tailored experiences for users, fostering a sense of community. Spring Boot serves as the back-end framework, providing a robust environment for developing RESTful APIs that facilitate seamless interaction between the front-end and back-end. This ensures efficient handling of user requests, data processing, and real-time updates. MongoDB, a NoSQL database, is utilized to store a wide array of documentary data and user-generated content. Its flexible schema design supports the dynamic nature of the application, allowing for easy scaling and efficient data retrieval. Users can view documentaries by various

DOI: 10.4018/979-8-3373-0335-2.ch005

criteria, such as genre, director, or release year and reviews.

1. INTRODUCTION

The rise of digital media has transformed how we consume information, making documentaries more accessible than ever before. With the proliferation of streaming platforms, audiences can explore a vast array of documentaries covering diverse topics, from social issues and history to science and nature. However, despite this abundance of content, finding quality documentaries and engaging with them meaningfully can still be a challenge. This gap presents an opportunity for a specialized platform that not only helps users discover documentaries but also fosters a community where they can share insights, reviews, and discussions.

The Documentary Review Application aims to bridge this gap by providing a comprehensive platform for documentary enthusiasts. Unlike traditional movie review applications, which primarily focus on entertainment films, this application emphasizes educational and socially impactful content. This focus on documentaries is particularly relevant in today's context, where media literacy and informed consumption of information are crucial (Kondel S et.al., 2019). By creating a dedicated space for users to explore and discuss documentaries, the application promotes awareness of significant social issues and encourages users to engage critically with the content they consume.

The development of the Documentary Review Application involves a full-stack approach, incorporating both front-end and back-end technologies. The front end is built using React.js, a popular JavaScript library known for its ability to create dynamic and responsive user interfaces. React allows for the creation of single-page applications that provide a seamless user experience, making navigation intuitive and efficient (Liu C et.al., 2012). Users can easily browse through a collection of documentaries, view trailers, read reviews, and contribute their own insights without the disruptions typically associated with traditional web applications.

On the back end, Spring Boot is employed as the framework for developing RESTful APIs. Spring Boot simplifies the process of building production-ready applications with minimal configuration. It offers features like dependency injection, which enhances modularity and testability, making it easier to manage the application's logic and data interactions. The use of RESTful APIs ensures that the front end can communicate effectively with the back end, facilitating the retrieval and submission of data in real-time.

Data management is handled using MongoDB, a NoSQL database that allows for the storage of unstructured and semi-structured data. Unlike traditional relational databases, MongoDB's flexible schema enables the application to adapt to the dynamic nature of documentary content and user-generated reviews. This is particularly advantageous for our application, as it allows for easy scaling and efficient data retrieval, accommodating an expanding library of documentaries and a growing user base.

Documentaries play a crucial role in educating the public and raising awareness about various social issues. They often provide in-depth insights and diverse perspectives that are essential for informed citizenship. In an era where misinformation is rampant, documentaries can serve as a reliable source of knowledge, helping audiences understand complex topics and fostering critical thinking. The Documentary Review Application not only aims to facilitate access to these valuable resources but also encourages users to engage with the material actively.

By focusing on documentaries that offer educational and socially relevant content, the application aims to support the dissemination of meaningful information. It recognizes that viewers often seek recommendations from peers when choosing documentaries to watch. Therefore, providing a platform where users can review, discuss, and recommend documentaries enhances the discovery process and enriches the viewing experience.

User engagement is at the heart of the Documentary Review Application. The platform is designed to foster a sense of community among documentary enthusiasts, allowing them to share their thoughts and experiences. Features such as user authentication and personalized profiles enable users to create tailored experiences. Users can curate their watchlists, follow others with similar interests, and receive personalized recommendations based on their viewing history and preferences.

The ability to contribute reviews and ratings is a vital aspect of the application. It empowers users to express their opinions on documentaries, providing valuable feedback to both filmmakers and fellow viewers. User-generated content enriches the platform, offering diverse perspectives that can influence viewing choices. The application aims to create an interactive environment where discussions can flourish, further enhancing the understanding and appreciation of documentaries.

Moreover, the application incorporates features that allow users to view trailers for documentaries, enabling them to gauge interest before committing to a full viewing. This feature enhances the decision-making process, making it easier for users to discover content that resonates with them. By offering a platform that combines discovery, review, and community engagement, the Documentary Review Application seeks to elevate the documentary-watching experience.

In an age where digital literacy is increasingly important, the Documentary Review Application also plays a role in enhancing media literacy. By encouraging users to critically analyze and discuss documentaries, the application fosters an environment of informed consumption. Users are prompted to consider the source of the content, the perspectives presented, and the social issues addressed (Mahalakshmi T et.al.

2023). This critical engagement with media is essential for developing a discerning audience that can navigate the complexities of modern information landscapes.

The platform will include educational resources, such as articles and guides on media literacy, to support users in developing their analytical skills. These resources can help users understand the context of the documentaries they watch, the techniques employed by filmmakers, and the impact of the subjects presented. By integrating educational components into the application, users are not only passive consumers of content but active participants in the discourse surrounding documentaries.

The Documentary Review Application is designed to be a living platform, adaptable to the evolving needs and preferences of its users. Future enhancements may include advanced search features that utilize machine learning algorithms to personalize recommendations further, based on user behavior and preferences. Integrating social media sharing capabilities will allow users to share their favorite documentaries and reviews across platforms, expanding the reach and impact of the application.

Additionally, collaborations with filmmakers and documentary distributors can provide users with exclusive content, behind-the-scenes access, and special events such as virtual screenings or Q&A sessions. Such partnerships would enrich the user experience and strengthen the community around the application.

The Documentary Review Application represents a significant step forward in the way audiences interact with documentary content. By focusing on socially relevant themes, promoting community engagement, and enhancing media literacy, the application aims to empower users to discover and appreciate documentaries in a meaningful way. As digital media continues to evolve, this platform seeks to adapt and grow, fostering a culture of informed viewing and critical engagement with the world around us. Through this initiative, we aspire to create a vibrant community of documentary enthusiasts who value education, awareness, and the power of storytelling.

2. LITERATURE SURVEY

Overview of Existing Systems

In the realm of digital media, user-generated content has become a critical component of the consumer experience, particularly in applications focused on movie and documentary reviews. As the demand for informative and engaging platforms continues to grow, existing literature provides valuable insights that inform the design and functionality of the Documentary Review Application. This review examines several key works, highlighting their contributions and relevance to our work.

Kondel and Sing (2019) delve into the development of a mobile-based movie review application utilizing Android technology. Their work emphasizes user interface (UI) design and essential functionality for reviewing films. By prioritizing user feedback and ratings, the application serves as a foundational model for mobile movie review platforms. They stress the significance of user experience (UX) as a driving force for engagement, suggesting that a well-designed interface not only attracts users but also encourages them to participate actively in the review process.

The principles laid out by Kondel et al. are particularly relevant for the Documentary Review Application, where creating an intuitive and visually appealing UI is paramount. Just as their application focused on feedback mechanisms, our platform will incorporate features that allow users to rate and comment on documentaries. By fostering an engaging environment where users feel their opinions are valued, we can enhance community interaction and promote a culture of shared learning and exploration.

Liu et al. (2012) introduce a movie rating and review summarization system that employs latent semantic analysis (LSA) for feature extraction and sentiment classification. Their study centers on summarizing and classifying reviews to assist users in making informed decisions based on sentiment and content characteristics. This approach is not only innovative but also highly relevant for our application, as it underscores the importance of quality in user-generated content.

The techniques explored by Liu et al. can be adapted to improve the presentation of reviews within the Documentary Review Application. For instance, integrating LSA could enhance our ability to analyze user feedback and extract sentiment trends from reviews. This capability would enable us to present users with a more comprehensive overview of documentary reception, facilitating more informed viewing choices. Moreover, by categorizing reviews based on sentiment, we can tailor the user experience, highlighting positive feedback for potential viewers and guiding them towards documentaries that resonate with their interests.

Khan et al. (2020) investigate a feature extraction method called the bag of words (BoW) to create a vector space model for movie reviews. Their research illustrates how the Naïve Bayes algorithm classifies reviews into positive and negative categories, demonstrating effective techniques for processing user-generated data. This work is complemented by the application of a graph-based ranking algorithm to summarize reviews, showcasing advanced data processing methodologies that could enhance the summarization features of our application.

The insights from Khan et al. provide a framework for implementing robust data analysis tools within the Documentary Review Application. By utilizing BoW and Naïve Bayes, we can classify reviews and present summaries that reflect the overall sentiment of user feedback. This approach not only improves the efficiency of review processing but also enriches the user experience by providing clear, categorized insights. Such functionalities would be crucial in enabling users to navigate a growing database of documentaries with ease, thereby enhancing their overall engagement with the platform.

Mahalakshmi et al. (2023) discuss the development of a movie review application, focusing on UI and functionality for searching and reviewing films. Their findings highlight the necessity of employing various technologies to create an interactive and responsive application, similar to traditional movie review platforms. They underscore the importance of a seamless user experience, which is a central objective of the Documentary Review Application.

The emphasis on responsiveness and interactivity in M G and Mahalakshmi's work aligns with our goals for the Documentary Review Application. By ensuring that users can easily navigate the platform and access content without friction, we aim to replicate the success of traditional review applications while adapting their features to a documentary-focused context. This involves not only aesthetic considerations but also functional ones, such as implementing search filters and personalized recommendations that cater to users' specific interests in documentaries.

In a further exploration, Khan et al. (2020) present a machine learning approach for summarizing large volumes of online movie reviews. Their system employs techniques like word2vec and semantic clustering to generate concise summaries of reviews, illustrating the potential for advanced data processing in user feedback analysis. This innovative approach is essential for the Documentary Review Application, where the ability to distill user feedback into easily digestible formats will significantly enhance user experience.

Implementing machine learning techniques from Khan et al. can transform how we manage and display user reviews within our application. By employing word2vec and clustering algorithms, we can create dynamic summaries that adapt to user interactions and emerging trends. This adaptability not only keeps content fresh but also allows users to quickly grasp the essence of user feedback without sifting through extensive reviews. Such features would be particularly beneficial for users who seek quick recommendations or insights before committing to a documentary viewing.

A literature survey by Pentheny, J. R. (2015) on the impact of online word-of-mouth (eWOM) on consumer decisions, particularly regarding movie ticket purchases, highlights that both professional critics' reviews and consumer-generated reviews influence decisions, but their effects differ. Professional reviews, though often seen as more authoritative, may not be as impactful as consumer reviews, which are perceived as more relatable and trustworthy. Studies suggest that positive reviews, whether from critics or consumers, tend to have a stronger effect on consumer choices, with negative reviews generally deterring purchases. Psychological factors, such as the Need for Cognitive Closure (NFC), indicate that individuals with high NFC are more influenced by clear, decisive positive reviews. Additionally, the Self-Monitoring (SM) trait affects review preferences, with low self-monitors more likely to value reviews over personal preferences, though this relationship remains underexplored and warrants further investigation.

Wallentin, E. (2016) examines the impact of professional critics' reviews on cinema demand, highlighting differences between critics' preferences and audience choices. Using Swedish data from 1966 movies (2001–2009), it finds that critics favor documentaries and Asian films, while audiences prefer Swedish and U.S. productions. Despite these differences, review scores positively correlate with ticket sales.

A two-step analysis uses ordered logit models to study critics' review scores and OLS models to assess box office demand. While limited by the lack of dynamic review data, the findings provide insights into factors driving cinematic success. This research offers valuable implications for producers and distributors aiming to balance critical acclaim with audience appeal.

Kim, E et al. (2023) examines the role of "topic consistency," or the overlap between critic and user review content, in influencing movie demand. Using topic models and U.S. box office data, the research finds that higher topic consistency enhances information recall, making movie attributes more memorable and positively impacting revenue. This effect is especially pronounced for movies with average review ratings and when critic and user ratings are closely aligned. Lab experiments confirm a causal relationship between topic consistency and consumer willingness to watch a movie, mediated by information recall.

The findings suggest that movie producers and advertisers can boost demand by promoting central themes that encourage overlapping discussions among critics and users. By aligning review content, they can improve audience engagement and financial outcomes.

According to Pang, J. et al. (2022) the relationship between critics' and consumers' opinions in the movie industry is complex and evolving. Traditionally, critics were considered independent opinion leaders, whose assessments were expected to influence consumer decisions. However, with the rise of user-generated content (UGC) on platforms like IMDb and Rotten Tomatoes, consumers now have a direct voice in shaping public opinion before or alongside critics' reviews. Recent research challenges the assumption of critic independence, suggesting that critics may actually conform to popular consumer opinions when forming their own ratings, particularly when a movie has a high volume of consumer reviews. This shift is driven by the need for critics to align with popular tastes to maintain credibility and attract public attention in a media environment dominated by consumer feedback. This dynamic is particularly evident when critics publish in general media outlets, where there is more pressure to reflect popular sentiment, compared to niche entertainment industry media. The implications for the film industry are significant, as studios may need to reconsider how they leverage both critic and consumer opinions in their marketing strategies. Understanding the mutual influence between critics and consumers can provide deeper insights into how movie reviews impact box office revenue and the role of word-of-mouth marketing.

Haw, W. Y. et al. (2013) explores factors influencing movie consumption, focusing on trailers, critics' reviews, star power, and word of mouth (WOM) using Kotler's Black Box Model. Through a survey of 200 undergraduates in Klang Valley, the analysis reveals WOM as the most influential factor in movie decisions, while gender shows no significant impact. The findings highlight WOM's critical role in shaping consumer preferences, surpassing trailers and star power. Marketers can leverage this by fostering audience discussions and promoting social proof to enhance engagement and boost movie attendance and sales.

Research by Boatwright, P et al. (2007) on the relationship between critics' opinions and consumer reviews highlights a complex interaction, where critics are influenced by consumer ratings, but their own preferences and professional characteristics also play a significant role. Studies show that critics' ratings tend to align with consumer ratings, particularly when there is a higher volume of consumer reviews, reflecting the influence of popular taste on critic opinions. Critics are more likely to rate a movie higher when it is widely discussed by consumers or when their peers also give favorable reviews. However, critics are less influenced by consumer ratings when they evaluate movies in specialized media outlets, suggesting that elite critics may still rely more on their personal taste when addressing a movie's quality. Additionally, movie characteristics such as fame of the director or producer can influence critic ratings, with famous names often leading to higher ratings. The results emphasize that critics' conformity to consumer opinions is stronger in environments where consumer feedback is more abundant, while other factors like release strategy and production budget do not significantly moderate this effect. This suggests that critics' ratings are not only based on personal aesthetic judgments but are also shaped by the dynamics of consumer reviews and the broader media context.

Reinstein, D et al. measured the influence of expert reviews on the demand for experience goods, such as movies, is complicated by the potential for spurious correlations between positive reviews and high demand, often due to underlying unobservable quality signals. To address this, a difference-in-differences approach was used, focusing on the timing of reviews by two prominent movie critics, Siskel and Ebert, in relation to opening weekend box office revenue. This methodology helps to eliminate spurious correlation, providing a clearer understanding of the impact of expert reviews. After accounting for these confounding factors, the influence of expert reviews on demand was found to be smaller but still significant. Positive reviews were especially impactful for dramas and narrowly-released movies, where audience demand is more sensitive to expert opinion.

Improvements in Our System

The Documentary Review Application enhances existing platforms by focusing specifically on documentaries, emphasizing their educational and social value rather than just entertainment. Unlike general movie review systems, it prioritizes content with meaningful societal impact, supporting the spread of informative and thought-provoking material. Additionally, the app offers trailer viewing, allowing users to preview documentaries before watching, which helps them make more informed decisions about the content they choose to engage with.

3. ARCHITECTURE DESIGN

Figure 1. Documentary review application architecture diagram

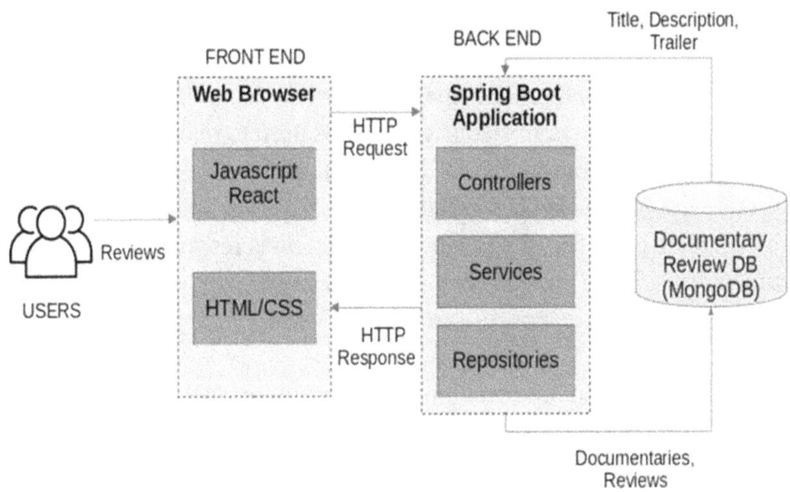

The architecture of the "Documentary Review" web application illustrated in Fig.1 is designed with a clear separation between the front end and back end. On the front end, the user interface is built using React, a popular JavaScript library, complemented by HTML and CSS for styling. This interface allows users to interact with the application by submitting reviews and viewing documentary details, providing a smooth and responsive experience.

On the back end, the application is powered by a Spring Boot framework, which is responsible for handling HTTP requests and responses. The back-end logic is organized into several components: Controllers, which manage incoming requests from the front end; Services, which implement the business logic to process those requests; and Repositories, which handle the interaction with the database to store and retrieve data.

The database used for storing documentary information, including titles, descriptions, trailers, and user reviews, is MongoDB, a NoSQL database. MongoDB is well-suited for this application due to its flexibility in storing diverse, unstructured data. Communication between the front end and back end occurs through HTTP requests, with the back end querying and updating the MongoDB database as needed to provide users with the most up-to-date documentary information and reviews.

Frontend Tasks (React.js)

Setup API Calls

To set up API calls in the "Documentary Review" application, Axios is imported from a configuration file (axiosConfig.js) and is used to make HTTP requests to the backend. In the configuration file, the base URL of the API is set, which streamlines interactions with the backend by ensuring all requests are directed to the correct endpoint. In the App.js file, the getdocus() function is responsible for fetching a list of documentaries. This function sends a GET request to the /api/v1/docus endpoint, and upon receiving the response—an array of documentary objects—it stores this data in the docus state.

For fetching detailed information about a single documentary, the getdocuData(docuId) function sends a GET request that includes the documentary's ID (docuId). The response provides the documentary's full details, as well as its associated reviews, which are stored in the docu and reviews state variables, respectively. This approach allows for both a general list of documentaries and specific, detailed information about individual documentaries to be accessed and displayed in the user interface.

Error handling is implemented in App.js using try-catch blocks. This ensures that if an API request fails—whether due to network issues or server errors—the error is caught and logged via console.log or console.error. To improve the user experience, developers can enhance this by displaying user-friendly error messages in the UI, such as "Failed to load data" or "Server is unavailable," informing users of issues in a clear and accessible way.

Documentary List Display (Home Component)

In the “Documentary Review” application, the `getdocus()` function is responsible for retrieving an array of documentary objects from the backend. Once the data is fetched, it is passed as a prop called `docus` to the `Home` component. This prop contains key information about each documentary, such as titles, posters, and ratings, which is essential for presenting the documentaries to the user in a visually appealing way.

Within the `Home.js` component, the `docus` prop is further passed to a child component called `Hero.js`, where the actual rendering takes place. Although the specific implementation of `Hero.js` isn't provided in the code, it can be assumed that this component maps over the `docus` array and displays the relevant information for each documentary. For example, posters would be displayed as images using the `src` attribute pointing to the poster URL, titles would be shown as text, and ratings—if available—could be rendered either as stars or numerical values. This layout provides a quick, visual overview of the documentaries, allowing users to browse through them effectively.

To ensure a clean and organized presentation, a grid or list layout can be used within `Hero.js` to arrange the documentary items. CSS or a styling library like Bootstrap, which is already being used in the application, can be applied to refine the design and provide a polished, responsive look. This setup allows for an intuitive, user-friendly experience when navigating through the available documentaries.

Documentary Details and Trailer Page

In the “Documentary Review” application, routing to documentary details is handled using react-router-dom, which enables navigation between different pages without reloading the browser. When a user clicks on a specific documentary, they are directed to a details page that displays more information about the selected film. This routing is managed in App.js, where a route is defined as /Reviews/:docuId. Here, docuId is a dynamic URL parameter that represents the unique ID of the documentary being viewed.

Once the user is routed to the Reviews component, the component accesses the docuId from the URL using the useParams() hook. This ID is then passed to the getdocuData(docuId) function, which sends an API request to retrieve the specific documentary's data, including its full details and associated reviews. The retrieved data is stored in state variables and displayed on the page for the user to read and explore.

Additionally, to enhance the user experience, a separate route /Trailer/:ytTrailerId is used to show the YouTube trailer of the selected documentary. The Trailer component extracts the ytTrailerId from the URL parameters and uses it to embed the corresponding YouTube video within the page. This allows users to watch the trailer directly within the application, providing a seamless way to preview the documentary before deciding to watch it in full.

Review List

Once the documentary details are fetched, including its reviews, they are stored in the reviews state in App.js. The Reviews.js component then renders this list of reviews by mapping over the reviews array and displaying each review's content within a Bootstrap-styled grid. Each review could be displayed as a separate row or card, and additional details such as the user's name (if available) or a timestamp could be shown alongside each review.

To allow users to add their own reviews, the ReviewForm component includes a form with a textarea where users can enter their review text. When the form is submitted, it triggers the addReview() function in Reviews.js. This function prevents the default form submission, retrieves the review text from the ref (using revText.current.value), and sends a POST request to the /api/v1/reviews endpoint, passing the review body and the documentary's ID (docuId). Upon successful submission, the new review is added to the reviews state, which updates the list of reviews on the page without requiring a page refresh.

Error Handling

The wildcard route (path="*") ensures that any unmatched route directs the user to the NotFound component, which displays a simple message like "This page could not be found." This can be further improved by adding a button that redirects users back to the homepage or including a fun illustration to make the user experience more engaging. Additionally, handling errors in API requests, such as failed data fetching, can be incorporated by showing error messages on the relevant pages. These messages could prompt users to retry or inform them of any server issues, improving overall communication and user experience when something goes wrong.

Backend Tasks (Spring Boot + MongoDB)

Documentary Data Management

To manage documentary data in the backend of the Documentary Review Application, the first task is to define the Documentary schema and model. This involves creating a Documentary class in Java that will map to a MongoDB collection. The class will contain fields such as id, title, description, genre, releaseYear, director, and trailerUrl. The @Document annotation will be used to designate the class as a MongoDB document, and the @Id annotation will mark the unique identifier for each documentary. This structure will be used to store documentary details in the database.

Implement Endpoints to Fetch Documentaries

Once the Documentary model is defined, the next task is to create RESTful endpoints to retrieve documentary data. This will involve defining a DocumentaryController class, which will handle HTTP requests related to documentaries. A core endpoint in this controller will allow the application to fetch all documentaries from the database. This endpoint will return a list of documentaries, providing users with a comprehensive view of available content.

Review Data Management

In addition to managing documentary data, the application will need to handle user reviews. This begins by defining a Review schema and model in a Review class. This class will include fields such as id, documentaryId, userId, reviewText, and rating. The documentaryId field will link each review to the corresponding documentary, ensuring that reviews are correctly associated with the films they pertain to.

Endpoints to Create and Associate Reviews

To manage review operations, a ReviewController class will be implemented. This controller will expose endpoints to allow users to interact with the review system. The "Create Review" endpoint will allow users to submit new reviews for documentaries, while the "Fetch Reviews by Documentary ID" endpoint will enable the retrieval of all reviews associated with a particular documentary. These endpoints ensure that users can contribute to the review system and see others' feedback on documentaries.

Database Operations

Before any data can be stored or retrieved, the MongoDB database must be set up with appropriate collections. The collections named documentaries and reviews will be created to store documentary and review data, respectively. This can be done manually in MongoDB or automatically configured within Spring Boot using MongoDB repositories. Proper setup of these collections is essential for smooth data operations.

MongoTemplate to Manage Documentary-Review Relationships

To effectively manage the relationship between documentaries and reviews, MongoTemplate will be used. MongoTemplate is a powerful class in Spring Data MongoDB that simplifies database access and manipulation. By using MongoTemplate, custom queries can be created to fetch documentaries along with their associated reviews. This ensures that users can view documentaries along with all related reviews in a seamless and efficient manner.

4. IMPLEMENTATION AND RESULTS

Steps Followed

1. Technology Stack Setup: The development environment was established, including Node.js for React, Java for Spring Boot, and MongoDB for data storage.
2. Frontend Development: The front-end was developed using React, implementing components for documentary listings, details, and review submissions.
3. Backend Development: The backend was constructed using Spring Boot, creating RESTful APIs for data management and user interactions.
4. Database Integration: MongoDB was integrated for persistent storage, with schemas defined for both documentaries and reviews.
5. Testing and Debugging: Comprehensive testing was conducted to ensure functionality, usability, and error handling were robust.

Figure 2. Documentary home page

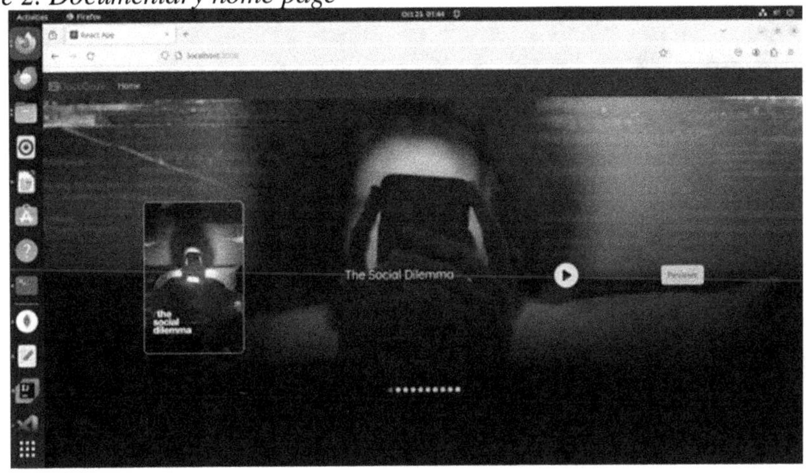

Figure 2 presents the Documentary home page, which facilitates documentary review as in Figure 3, trailer review, analyzing review collections as shown in Figure 4

Figure 3. Documentary review page

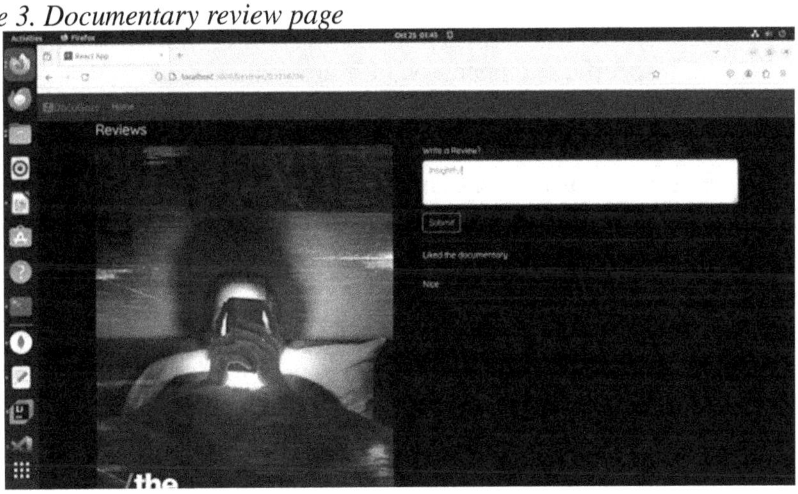

Figure 4. MongoDB review collection

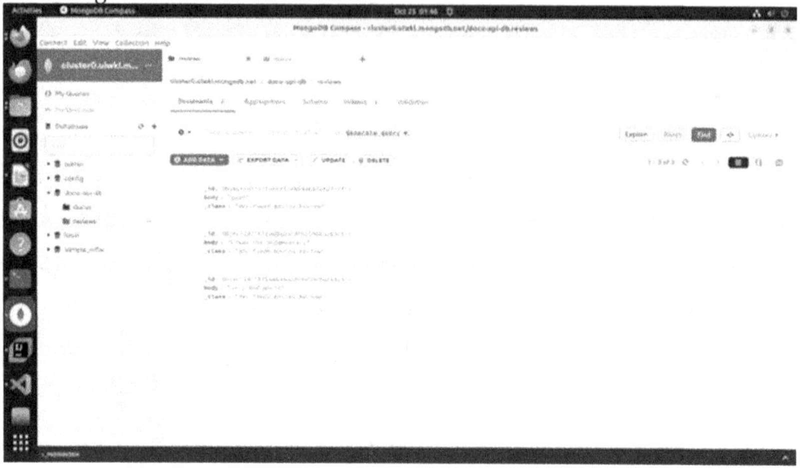

Documentary Details and Trailers Page

Routing to Documentary Details:

`react-router-dom` is used to handle routing between different pages. When a user clicks on a specific documentary, they are routed to a details page. This is managed in `App.js` by the route `/Reviews/:docuId`, where `:docuId` is a dynamic URL parameter.

The `Reviews` component fetches the specific documentary's data based on the `docuId` from the URL using `useParams()` and calls `getdocuData(docuId)` to get the details.

Embedding YouTube Trailers:

A separate route `/Trailer/:ytTrailerId` is defined for showing the YouTube trailer of a selected documentary. The `Trailer` component likely uses the `ytTrailerId` from the URL parameters to embed the YouTube video.

This can be done using an `<iframe>` to display the trailer:

```
jsx
<iframe
width="560"
height="315"
src={`https://www.youtube.com/embed/$ytTrailerId`}
frameborder="0"
allow="accelerometer; autoplay; encrypted-media; gyroscope; picture-in-picture"
```

allowFullScreen
></iframe>

Documentary Data Management

a. **Define the Documentary Schema and Model (Documentary.java)**

In Spring Boot, the first step in managing documentary data is to define the schema and model for the documentary entity. This typically involves creating a `Documentary` class that maps to a MongoDB collection. The class includes fields such as `id`, `title`, `description`, `genre`, `releaseYear`, `director`, and `trailerUrl`.

java
import org.springframework.data.annotation.Id;
import org.springframework.data.mongodb.core.mapping.Document;

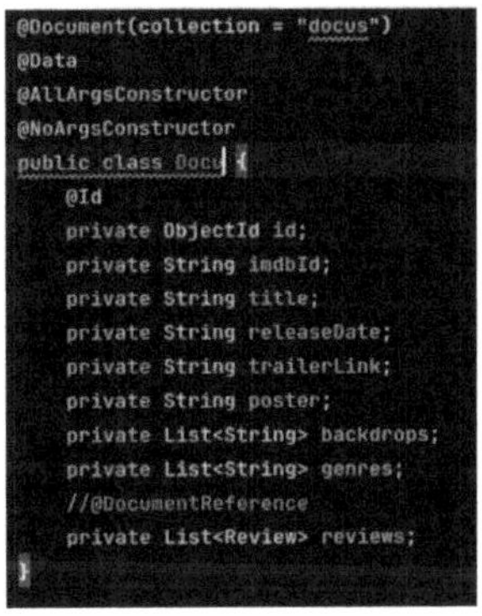

Figure 5. Spring boot

b. Implement Endpoints to Fetch Documentaries

Next, we need to create RESTful endpoints to fetch documentary data. This involves defining a `DocumentaryController` class that handles HTTP requests.

Fetch All Documentaries: This endpoint retrieves all documentaries from the database.

```java
@RestController
@RequestMapping("/api/v1/movies")
@CrossOrigin(origins = "*")
public class DocuController {
    @Autowired
    private DocuService docuService;
    @GetMapping
    public ResponseEntity<List<Movie>> getAllDocu() {
        return new ResponseEntity<List<Docu>>(DocuService.allDocu(), HttpStatus.OK);
    }
```

```java
@Service
public class DocuService {
    @Autowired
    private DocuRepository docuRepository;
    public List<Docu> allDocu() { return docuRepository.findAll(); }

    public Optional<Docu> singleMovie(String imbdId) { return DocuRepository.findDocuByImdbId(imbdId);
}
```

Review Data Management

a. Define the Review Schema and Model (Review.java)

Similar to documentaries, we need to create a `Review` class that represents user reviews for documentaries. This class includes fields such as `id`, `documentaryId`, `userId`, `reviewText`, and `rating`.

b. Implement Endpoints to Create and Associate Reviews

We then define a `ReviewController` class to manage review operations.

- Create Review: This endpoint allows users to submit a review for a documentary.
- Fetch Reviews by Documentary ID: This endpoint retrieves all reviews associated with a specific documentary.

Database Operations

a. Setup MongoDB Collections for Documentaries and Reviews

Before executing operations, we ensure the MongoDB database is properly set up to store our documentary and review documents. This involves creating collections named `documentaries` and `reviews`, which can be done directly in MongoDB or configured in Spring Boot using MongoDB repositories.

```
import ...

@Repository  no usages
public interface DocuRepository extends MongoRepository<Docu, ObjectId> {
    Optional<Docu> findMovieByImdbId(String imdbId);  no usages  1 related problem
}
```

b. Use MongoTemplate to Manage Documentary-Review Relationships

To manage relationships between documentaries and reviews effectively, we use `MongoTemplate`, a powerful class in Spring Data MongoDB that simplifies data access and manipulation. Fetching Documentaries with Reviews: We can create a custom query to fetch documentaries along with their associated reviews.

The backend implementation of the Documentary Review Application involves a well-structured approach using Spring Boot and MongoDB. By defining appropriate schemas, implementing RESTful endpoints, managing database operations effectively, and ensuring robust error handling, we create a scalable and user-friendly platform that facilitates the exploration and review of documentaries. This foundation will enable us to build a dynamic application that engages users and fosters a community of documentary enthusiasts.

6. CONCLUSION

The Documentary Review Application represents a significant advancement in the way users discover and interact with documentaries. By focusing on socially impactful content the application aims to enhance the visibility and accessibility of educational and socially relevant documentaries. This approach not only supports informed decision-making but also contributes to the broader dissemination of valuable content.

REFERENCES

Boatwright, P., Basuroy, S., & Kamakura, W. (2007). Reviewing the reviewers: The impact of individual film critics on box office performance. *Quantitative Marketing and Economics*, *5*(4), 401–425. DOI: 10.1007/s11129-007-9029-1

Haw, W. Y., Ho, E., Lim, Y. L., & Wong, J. W. (2013). *The effect of trailer, critics review, star power, and word of mouth toward decision making on movie consumption*. UTAR Institutional Repository.

Khan, A., Gul, M. A., Uddin, M. I., Shah, S. A. A., Ahmad, S., Al Firdausi, M. D., & Zaindin, M. (2020). "Movie review summarization using supervised learning and graph-based ranking algorithm", Computational Intelligence and Neuroscience, 2020. *Article ID*, *7526580*, 1–10.

Khan, A., Gul, M. A., Uddin, M. I., Shah, S. A. A., Ahmad, S., Al Firdausi, M. D., & Zaindin, M. (2020). "Summarizing Online Movie Reviews: A Machine Learning Approach to Big Data Analytics", Scientific Programming, 2020. *Article ID*, *5812715*, 1–12.

Kim, E., Ding, M., Wang, X. S., & Lu, S. (2023). Does Topic Consistency Matter? A Study of Critic and User Reviews in the Movie Industry. *Journal of Marketing*, *87*(3), 428–450. DOI: 10.1177/00222429221127927

Kondel, S., & Sing, N. (2019). A Paper on Movie Review by Implementing Movie Review App Using Android Technology. *JETIR*, *6*(5), 1–5.

Liu, C.-L., Hsaio, W.-H., Lee, C.-H., Lu, G.-C., & Jou, E. (2012). Movie Rating and Review Summarization in Mobile Environment. *IEEE Transactions on Systems, Man, and Cybernetics. Part C, Applications and Reviews*, *42*(3), 345–358. DOI: 10.1109/TSMCC.2011.2136334

MG, A. & Mahalakshmi, T. (2023). Movie Review Application [IJARSCT]. International Journal of Advanced Research in Science. *Tongxin Jishu*, *3*(1), 50–55.

Pang, J., Liu, A. X., & Golder, P. N. (2022). Critics' conformity to consumers in movie evaluation. *Journal of the Academy of Marketing Science*, *50*(4), 864–887. DOI: 10.1007/s11747-021-00816-9

Pentheny, J. R. (2015). *The Influence of Movie Reviews on Consumers*. Honors Theses and Capstones.

Reinstein, D. A., & Snyder, C. M. (2005). The influence of expert reviews on consumer demand for experience goods: A case study of movie critics. *The Journal of Industrial Economics, 53*(1), 27–51. DOI: 10.1111/j.0022-1821.2005.00244.x

Wallentin, E. (2016). Demand for cinema and diverging tastes of critics and audiences. *Journal of Retailing and Consumer Services, 33*, 72–81. DOI: 10.1016/j.jretconser.2016.08.002

Chapter 6
Human-AI Collaboration in Moderating AI-Generated Harmful Content

Sameer Saharan
https://orcid.org/0000-0002-7487-6297
Mody University of Science and Technology, India

Mridu Sharma
Mody University of Science and Technology, India

Meha Khiria
Mody University of Science and Technology, India

Abhaya Gupta
https://orcid.org/0009-0006-2575-0096
Mody University of Science and Technology, India

ABSTRACT

Increasing AI-generated hazardous objects like deep fake and side create big difficulties for content moderation. Effective solutions demand human-AI cooperation to make a balance between efficiency of artificial intelligence and human decisions on relevant and moral problems. Major approaches have hybrid models, openness and continuous learning systems. While platforms should apply active moderation and empower users by digital literacy, regulatory framework should encourage responsibility. To reduce new dangers requires the development of forensic artificial intelligence technologies and cross-platform cooperation. This structure guarantees

DOI: 10.4018/979-8-3373-0335-2.ch006

the ethical digital environment as well as the planet's quick AI-powered environment.

INTRODUCTION

In recent years, there has been an increase in artificial intelligence (AI) capabilities and use in the digital sector. The impact of AI has spread over various industries, thereby changing areas such as healthcare, banking, entertainment and materials building. Nevertheless, there exists a more unclear and anxious reality within these achievements - the increasing prevalence of harmful AI-generated materials. From malicious AI-generated content, fake news and deep fakes to AI-fuel hate speech and wrong information campaigns, not only growing, but also getting challenging to refined and regulate rapidly (Marzuki et al., 2023).

AI-generated material refers to any material produced or converted by artificial intelligence systems. Progress in generative models like machine learning, natural language processing (NLP), and generative adversities network (GAN) and large language models (LLMs) have enabled highly realistic text, pictures, audio and video generation (Jamal, 2024; Pirone, 2024; Walczak & Cellary, 2023; Y. Zhang et al., 2024). It has facilitated new and efficient applications, including automatic writing tools, vibrant virtual character and AI-advanced video editing (Pirone, 2024). Nevertheless, these technologies can be used to generate harmful materials, which can cause a huge problem for material control.

Harmful AI-generated content includes (Henderson et al., 2023; Kendon et al., 2023; Lyu, 2024; Romero Moreno, 2024):

i. Deep Fakes: Such AI-generated videos or images substitute real content in order to produce misleading media, which is mainly used for spreading misinformation or differentiating people.
ii. AI-Generated Fake News: The wide language models produce praise-worthy yet false concepts that lead to the propagation of false news, political exploitation, or social unrest.
iii. AI-Generated Hate Speech: Systems can generate autonomously vitriolic or vicious speech against individuals or teams, which also heightens social tensions.
iv. Artificial Identities: AI constructs profiles, pictures or voices for use in campaigns of identity theft, fraud, or spying.

How the informational damage produced by AI can be shocking in terms of magnitude and velocity, given the point at which AI will create enormous data within minutes, at which point the traditional filtering approaches are seriously limited. It is a technological challenge, but also the social, political, and ethical issue since the information which AI generates may influence elections, destroy communities, and ruin private reputations.

Complexity of Moderating AI-Generated Harmful Content

Keeping dangerous AI-generated content under control is harder than regular content moderation because it's made the way it is. The increased use of AI is a big problem. AI can make thousands or millions of rapidly harmful materials, which is so much for human moderators and even automatic systems that aren't made to handle so many. The level of difficulty is another problem because the AI-generated content looks very real, so it often takes up a past detecting system (Mansour, 2024). For example, DeepFake meets very much with real sounds and faces, which makes it difficult for computers or people to tell the difference between real and fake (Lyu, 2024). In the same way, the AI-generated text can be written so well that it looks like a piece of real news or opinion, making it difficult for review systems to recognize as fake news. At the same time, harmful content always keeps changing because AI ways are changing so quickly. AI models are always getting better, and as systems are getting better at finding some sort of harmful material, new ways of creating materials are very fast. For example, as algorithms get better to find deep fakes, AI writers bring even better ways to avoid these systems. It becomes a never-ending game of cat and rat, where the equipment for control always keep trying to catch up. These problems show that we need a new way to moderate content that's not limited to only systems run by automatic or people (Kučinskas; Romero Moreno, 2024; Zhou et al., 2023).

Role of AI in Content Moderation

Rather, AI itself plays a crucial role in solving the very problems it provides. Social media and other digital communities are increasingly reliant on AI-powered automated moderation systems to scan through copious volumes of user-generated content in real time and flag as inappropriate in hope of taking them out of circulation or for assessment. On the one hand, AI works pretty well with a lot of data. The really tricky judgments, though, are not its strong points-about context, cultural difference, or complex ethical issues. For example, an AI may flag correctly on content that's using offending language, but it doesn't actually know the context of the language that's in use. A statement that is legally acceptable in one jurisdiction will be hate speech in another. Without effective contextual understanding, moderation often goes astray into deleting harmless content and letting offending content slip through (Ferraz et al., 2024; Molina & Sundar, 2024; Stockinger et al., 2023).

In addition, AI is biased. Where there exists a biased dataset, the algorithm trained upon it may reflect such biases in moderation choices to potentially continue reinforcing stereotypes or unfairly target specific groups. This may then lead to the over-policing of marginalized communities while failing to address more complex and harmful content generated by bad actors who know how to exploit the weaknesses in AI detection systems. Such weaknesses require human moderation because then content, passed to the screen by humans, can give crucial context, judgment, and ethics reasoning that is currently missing in AI systems (De Gregorio & Stremlau, 2023; S. Wang, 2023).

Need for Human-AI Collaboration

Given the complexity, scale, and evolving nature of harmful AI-generated content, human-AI collaboration is emerging as the most effective approach for content moderation. In such a collaborative model, AI systems handle the initial heavy lifting—scanning vast amounts of content, detecting patterns, and flagging potential threats—while human moderators review and make the final judgment on borderline cases or complex ethical issues. This collaboration allows for a more nuanced and flexible response to the challenges posed by AI-generated harmful content. AI systems can filter out obvious cases of harmful content at scale, enabling human moderators to focus their attention on the more ambiguous or context-specific cases that require human judgment (Alowais et al., 2023; Fui-Hoon Nah et al., 2023; Sezgin, 2023). Over time, AI systems can also learn from human decisions, improving their accuracy and reducing the burden on human moderators.

Human-AI collaboration in content moderation can take several forms (Lykouris & Weng, 2024):

i. **AI-Assisted Moderation**: AI systems flag potentially harmful content for human review, providing tools and insights to help moderators make informed decisions.
ii. **Continuous Learning Systems**: AI models are regularly updated based on feedback from human moderators, adapting to new trends in harmful content generation.
iii. **Task Prioritization**: AI systems prioritize cases based on severity or urgency, allowing human moderators to focus on the most pressing issues.

This combination of human judgment and AI efficiency can lead to a more effective and scalable content moderation process, capable of keeping up with the evolving nature of AI-generated content.

This chapter shall attempt to explore why such harmful AI-created content is becoming difficult to regulate, outline what complexities such content moderation poses, and propose a collaborative human-AI framework for content regulation. The two main objectives of this chapter are:

- To analyze the types of harmful AI-generated content and the technologies behind them, such as GANs and NLP models.
- To evaluate the advantages and disadvantages of existing moderation techniques, encompassing both human and artificial intelligence-driven approaches.
- Propose solutions to improve human-AI collaboration in detecting, analyzing, and moderating hate speech.

This chapter will describe how human-AI collaboration can effectively deal with the unique challenges created by negative AI-generated content using different case studies and illustrative examples that will make the digital environment safer and more responsible. It addresses the ethical dimensions also, which involve reconciling free speech with moderation needs, confronting biases hidden in the systems, and promoting transparency in the AI-aided decision-making processes.

These complexities indicate the need to apply collaborating solutions to content moderation systems so they can become more adaptive and responsive in the fight against the rapidly emerging threat of harmful AI-generated content.

UNDERSTANDING AI-GENERATED HARMFUL CONTENT

Artificial intelligence technologies have evolved so much that so has their ability to produce content to reflect the change, often hiding the difference between a real and artificial product. While advancements in AI-generated content creation have introduced many benefits, they have also created new forms of damaging content. The following classes of harmful AI-generated content, the technical processes involved in creating them, the effects they bear on society, and case studies that show their real-life impact are explored in the following sections.

Detrimental content generated by artificial intelligence can take many different forms, each posing uniquely different threats to individuals, organizations, and to societies. This paper outlines the main categorizations of harmful content produced by AI:

1. Deep Fakes: Highly realistic manipulated content, particularly in the area of videos or images, where faces or voices are replaced by artificial intelligence generating a kind of fabricated reality. The machine learning algorithms, such as Generative Adversarial Networks (GANs), can produce deep fakes when they are very sophisticated, portraying individuals as doing things or saying things they actually did not do. While deep fakes sometimes serve entertaining or artistic purposes, they are more often used to commit fraud, defamation, or coercion. A relevant example is found in political campaign usage, through which deep fakes manipulate public perception of those targeted by making them appear to say something false or inflammatory. Additionally, these technologies have been used to generate non-consensual pornography, where the faces of individuals are superimposed on pornography (Habgood-Coote, 2023; Lal & Saini, 2023; Rafique et al., 2023).
2. AI-Generated Hate Speech: Technologies and tools can be designed with the capacity to create offensive or harmful language. A malicious actor can use AI tools to mass-produce hate speech in relation to race, religion, gender, and other characteristics protected by law. AI-generated hate speech can have varied psychological and social effects, spreading incitement to violence and exacerbating social divisions. For example, autonomous hate-speech-generating bots have been deployed on social media platforms to target political opponents or marginalized groups, amplifying extremist ideologies and leading to online harassment campaigns (Song et al., 2024; Vetagiri et al.).
3. Disinformation Campaigns: Artificial intelligence-produced disinformation refers to the development of fake news, articles, or online materials created by AI language tools, including OpenAI's GPT-3. These can design highly convincing narratives that are intended to deceive the greater population, create confusion, and influence political, economic, or societal outcomes. Disinformation campaigns often rely on AI to influence public opinion, diminish institutional confidence, or spark social chaos. For example, in electoral campaign articles, AI products have been used to influence public opinion, spread conspiracy theories, or undermine trust in democratic systems (Abuhamad; Kivimaki).
4. Artificial Intelligence Synthetic Identifications: AI also produces synthetic identities, which include fake social media profiles, pictures, and even synthesized voices. Some AI can mimic realistic personas that do not really exist and can create fraud, espionage, or even influence public policy by creating a grassroots movement. For example, AI-created avatars and personas are used in disinformation campaigns to promote false narratives on social media platforms by setting up fictitious accounts that support baseless claims, hence giving them more credibility (Bird & Lotfi, 2024; D'amico et al., 2023; Veturi et al., 2023).

TECHNICAL PROCESSES BEHIND CONTENT GENERATION

The harmful production through artificial intelligence is now eased by a number of highly advanced technical methodologies. Among all such methodologies, the most sophisticated systems include Generative Adversarial Networks (GANs), NLP models, and other machine learning approaches, among others.

1. Generative Adversarial Networks: GANs are among the most popular models applied in producing synthesized media, especially deepfakes. A Generative Adversarial Network consists of two related components: a generator and a discriminator. The generator makes synthetic data such as image or video. Meanwhile, the discriminator evaluates the authenticity of that synthetic data as the real or as a fake. In the long term, this could permit an enhancement apparently real media generation utilizing discriminator feedback that potentially results in highly surprisingly realistic outputs (De Souza et al., 2023; Pan et al., 2023).
    - Application: GANs have already been utilized to generate Deepfake videos that sometimes appear incredibly realistic. Celebrity, politicians, or ordinary people faces are inserted easily into scenes where they were not originally.
2. Models in Natural Language Processing: The main elements that empower an AI in text generation capabilities are NLP models from the transformers to GPT-3. Such models create meaningful text by employing patterns obtained from large-scale datasets. They can even manufacture news articles, social media posts, and even user interaction through harmful language and spread misinformation (Pokhrel & Banjade, 2023; Reddy & Reddy, 2024).
    - Application: GPT-3 can write about completely imaginary news stories, so real-looking that a reader will believe the material is true journalism.
3. Deep Learning and Voice Synthesis: Deep learning techniques may be used with artificial intelligence for the generation of synthetic voice. This has immense value for voice deepfakes as it will enable the synthesis of someone's voice and hence creates their speech they never said. It can very convincingly make audio, to be used for fraud, impersonation, or defamation (Nishimura et al., 2016).
    - Application: Deepfake speech technology has been misappropriated in fraudulent activities whereby the offenders imitate high-ranking executives in order to fool employees into transferring significant money.

IMPACT AND PROLIFERATION OF AI-GENERATED HARMFUL CONTENT

The proliferation of AI-generated harmful content poses significant risks to society, individuals, and organizations. Its impact is wide-ranging and can include the following (Basta, 2024; Divya & Mirza; Romero Moreno, 2024; Y. Wang, 2023):

1. Erosion of Trust: The increasing sophistication of AI-made content seriously threatens the value of trust in online media. Individuals may begin to question any information discovered online and increasingly find it difficult to differentiate between fact and fiction. This impacts journalism, democratic systems, and societal debate. For instance, even after the video deepfakes have been proved false, the damage caused by spreading such content can be long-term due to creating a state of distrust. At times, the mere presence of deepfakes may challenge the credibility of authentic evidence.
2. Hate Speech and Violence Spread: AI-generate hate speech can easily spread through all the platforms, leading to real-world violence as social tensions increase. AI with its ability to automate content generation allows bad individuals to flood social media portals and fill up the moderators with hateful statements that influence public opinion. Where there have been increases in ethnic violence, AI-generated hate speech has been linked to incendiary information that fuels conflict between groups.
3. Political and Social Manipulation: Operations involving AI-generated misinformation have the potential to disrupt political frameworks by shaping public perceptions, spreading conspiracy theories, and diminishing confidence in democratic institutions. Through the automation of deceptive content production, malicious actors could influence electoral outcomes, weaken governmental authority, and fracture societal cohesion. Disinformation campaigns that deploy AI-generated false news articles have been linked to electoral interference, affecting public sentiment through the propagation of misleading narratives.
4. Psychological and Emotional Harm: Persons with exposure to deepfakes or AI-created misinformation often suffer psychological trauma, reputational damages, and emotional distress. Victims of non-consensual deepfake pornography experience tremendous emotional and social implications of such realistic adulterated content. Most individuals who fall victim to deepfake porn have reported long-lasting psychological trauma among them anxiety, depression, and embarrassment in the public.

Case Studies of Significant Incidents

1. Deep Fake Political Manipulation: In 2020, a deep fake video hit the circulation of social media, where a prominent European politician went saying things which were never said, and which were inflammatory in nature. The video hit millions of viewers before it later got climaxed with actions to disprove it. The politicians' reputation was damned. It generated public opinion leading to protests due to sowing distrust in the political system (Paterson & Hanley, 2020).
2. Artificially Created Election Misinformation: NLP models generated artificially created election misinformation dominantly for the 2016 U.S. Presidential election and spread them on social media. Fake news articles were created by the use of NLP models to alter voters' perceptions about the candidates. Election misinformation brought about polarization and fueled fear about the possible use of AI in elections (Hashemi, 2023; Mundra et al., 2023).
3. Non-consensual AI-generated pornography: Several cases of non-consensual deep fake pornography have been brought to public attention over the past few years and many have involved celebrities as well as private individuals. Their faces were superimposed on videos, which were then shared anonymously all over the internet and caused public outrage as well as challenges in court. Victims of deep fakes suffered reputational damage and emotive distress as well as psychological damage, which argued for greater regulation and better content moderation (Brigham et al., 2024).

This proliferation of harmful AI-generated content made it necessary to develop different content moderation strategies supposed to alleviate its impacts. The variations include traditional human-based moderation and more advanced AI-driven detection tools. However, despite all these methods offering such crucial solutions, they also come with tremendous limitations. It will talk about the current state of existing moderation strategies, the shortcomings of traditional techniques, and raises the issue of AI-driven detection tools and ongoing challenges with trying to adapt to rapidly evolving generation methods in harmful AI-generated content.

There are two broad categories of modern content moderation strategies used today: human-based moderation and automated systems (Chandrasekharan et al., 2019). These content moderation approaches have been applied by social media sites, news establishments, and other digital service providers to identify and control undesirable content, including AI-generated material.

1. **Human Moderation**: In this case, for over two decades, most internet platforms' content control has primarily relied on human moderation. Under this strategy, teams of human reviewers look at, for example, flagged material where it is

most likely breaching community standards including hate speech, false information, and other explicit materials. Using human moderation has benefits in that context is kept and moderators make overall choices depending on cultural and situational settings.

- Strength: Human moderators will be great at knowing what they know about contextual data that has to do with material-that's to say, know when to separate humor from deception or when a certain phrase constitutes hate speech through intent and contextual use.
- **Weaknesses**: Human moderators are unable to moderate the sheer volume of content produced online. It is further expensive, time-consuming, and can be psychologically taxing for reviewers who have to receive distressing material (Chandrasekharan et al., 2019; Sander, 2019).

2. **Automated Moderation Systems**: In the growth of content production on digital platforms, systems that automatically scan large volumes of data in search of matching defined criteria and flag them are becoming increasingly critical. These systems, including ones using machine learning models whose precision increases over time through "learned" patterns of identified harmful content, will help automatically flag hate speech, disinformation, or explicit material.
   - Advantages: The chief benefit of automated systems lies in their ability to process massive volumes of data in real time while offering scalable solutions for content moderation. For instance, such automated systems could prove very helpful when cases are clearly defined and demand simple decision-making procedures, such as explicit content or well-documented hate symbols.
   - Weakness: Automatic systems become weak at minute details of languages, contexts, and cultural issues. For instance, an algorithm may warn someone that 'Sensitive words' are included in the context; yet fails to consider irony or context and over-censors or under-censors (Gorwa et al., 2020; Sander, 2019).
3. **Hybrid Approaches**: To mitigate such inadequacies both in purely human as well as automated moderation frameworks, hybrids of moderation are commonly found on platforms these days. Hybrids combine the scalable nature of AI with nuances and context-aware decision making by humans themselves. AI would then scan most of the content it analyzes and only flag problematic ones for human review when deemed appropriate. This way, the workload burden on humans can be avoided, but more complex judgments will still be allowed to be made.
   - Strength: Hybrid models balance efficiency with an element of accuracy. The AI gets used mainly on content, but the human reviewers gear to manage those edge cases that require an understanding.

- Weaknesses: Hybrid systems continue to retain some of the inherent limitations of AI and human moderators, particularly regarding how fast harmful content generation techniques can be understood (Nguyen et al., 2024; Wu, 2019).

However, although traditional methods of moderation, such as human moderation, still hold good to a greater or lesser extent, they stand at their greatest challenge against AI-generated deleterious content. To name a few of the key shortcomings (Lehtimäki, 2024; Lloyd et al., 2023; Reichwein, 2024; Wach et al., 2023):

1. Scalability: Human moderators cannot keep pace with the sheer volume of content being generated, especially as AI makes it easier to create harmful material at scale. In contrast, AI systems may be scalable but are unable to interpret context, leading to many missing harmful contents and falsely flagging benign content.
2. Contextual Understanding: Perhaps the biggest weakness of AI technology is its failure to understand the context in which an utterance was made-be it cultural, linguistic, or situational. For example, in making distinctions between satire or parody and actionable disinformation, AI over-moderate. And human moderators understand nuances of the context but lack consistency in applying standards across large datasets.
3. Bias and Fairness: Bias in content moderation can be inflicted both by human and AI-based moderation systems. As the datasets used by AI systems reflect the bias of their creators, these systems often flag some content coming from certain demographics or favoring a particular kind of speech over another. Inconsistent decision-making is also due to implicit bias brought into content moderation by humans.
4. Lag Time: Traditional human moderation techniques take longer to catch up on very viral content. A disinformation campaign may spread like wildfire within hours, while human moderation can only respond once it's been processed days, or even weeks later. Faster automation still does not enable real-time moderation, at least in cases of new threats like deep fakes and AI-generated disinformation.

AI-DRIVEN DETECTION AND MODERATION TOOLS

Platforms are increasingly relying on AI-based detection tools as the more complex the harmful stuff generated out from AI. Detection tools, using machine learning and NLP, flag, detect, and remove harmful content at speeds and scales human moderators cannot beat (Marsoof et al., 2023; Zhu, 2022).

1. Machine learning models: Patterns of offensive behavior in text, images, or video-based content can be highlighted by machine learning models. These models depend on huge datasets containing harmful and benign data for training purposes, and with enough time and correct feedback from human moderators or additional data inputs, they can progress to accuracy improvement. For example, Facebook and YouTube utilize machine learning models to automatically identify hate speech and violent content and automatically mark it for review or delete it as appropriate based on the degree of violence (Simon et al., 2022).
2. Natural Language Processing (NLP): NLP algorithms also constitute the identification of hostile AI-generated text, such as hate speech or disinformation. These algorithms process text in terms of both form and meaning to detect abusive language patterns or strategies of disinformation. The latest transformer models, such as GPT-3, have further enhanced the dexterity of NLP tools in detecting more subtle content. Twitter has leveraged these NLP models for their harmful language flagging of tweets and subsequent human review or automated action (Hutchens, 2023).
3. Deep Fake Detection Algorithms: Deep fakes have become prevalent, and as such have influenced platforms to create AI systems designed to detect manipulated images, audio, and video. Such tools scan for media that may have been manipulated through inconsistency in the lighting, texture, or lip-syncing, as a means of enabling identification of deep fakes, which otherwise are very reliable when viewed by a human being. News agencies use deep fake detection tools as a check to verify the authenticity of videos before publishing them (Masood et al., 2023).
4. Content Verification Systems: AI-based technologies can also be useful in validating information credibility. The verification systems of user-generated content will cross-check the content against known sources to determine any cases of false and misleading information. Such applications are very helpful in incidences of fake news. AI systems cross-reference claims with verified databases. For instance, Google uses its content verification tools to verify news stories using its AI functionality to cross-check news articles against their original source and mark suspicious content (Kolluri & Murthy, 2021; Rubin, 2022).

CHALLENGES IN ADAPTING TO RAPIDLY EVOLVING GENERATION METHODS

While the benefits of AI-driven detection tools seem groundbreaking, they raise quite a number of significant challenges in how quickly, and quite often perilously, methods for generating and propagating damaging content are changing.

1. Improving AI Capabilities: More and more content moderation tools evolve, and with that method, so do ways to create harmful content. AI-generated disinformation, deep fakes, and hate speech are emerging in increasingly scalable matters and cannot be tracked as effectively by detection systems. New generation techniques can bypass existing moderation algorithms within a cycle of continuous improvement (Gilbert & Gilbert; Shoaib et al., 2023).
2. Adversarial Attack: The adversarial attack these bad actors seek to conduct is to manipulate AI detection systems by modifying content minimally. For example, a few pixels in an image or changed text can easily make AI classify harmful content as harmless and therefore undermine the capability of detection systems (Gongane et al., 2022).
3. False Positives and False Negatives: AI systems are usually lousy at the balance between precision and recall; they may flag benign content so that there are too many false positives, but most harmfully fail to flag inappropriate content so that it leads to false negatives. This is a tough spot for platforms, because sites that are too lenient with moderation allow abusive or inappropriate content to spread, while sites that are too strict severely stifle free expression (Plevris, 2024; Sharma et al., 2024).
4. Ethical Considerations: Deep ethical issues are involved in the application of AI in content moderation. Particularly, stated as concerns by users and advocacy groups about over-censorship and invasion of privacy were the lack of full transparency on how decisions were made. Moreover, biases in an AI system may end up in a more unfair targeting on certain communities or views (Udupa et al., 2023).
5. Resource intensity: AI-based moderation requires quite a lot of resources because you are having big datasets and lots of power to compute on besides developing machine learning expertise. In the smaller platforms, you might find that these tools will not work all that well and thus leave them open to all kinds of harmful content (Shao et al., 2024).

A bottom line in that regard would be that although AI-driven detection tools may offer promising solutions for the moderation of content generated from harmful AI, much is still left to be done. As the nature of content generation strategies continues to evolve, the strategies used by platforms must constantly be adjusted in order to maintain the ethical implications of using AI-driven moderation. Innovation and collaboration in the same direction between humans and AI will become highly important in meeting such challenges and making digital spaces safe and trustworthy.

HUMAN-AI COLLABORATION IN DETECTING AND MODERATING AI-GENERATED CONTENT

As AI-generated harmful content increases in complexity and quantity, human and AI-driven moderation systems alone cannot suffice anymore. In fact, the future of content moderation only in human-AI collaboration is there. Here, initial screening and high-volume tasks are done by artificial intelligence and human expertise is applied for nuanced judgment and context-sensitive judgment. This way of collaboration must surely enhance efficiency while also improving accuracy in detection and moderation of harmful content. Here, we'll see how AI can be used within the screening process, the input human moderators can provide to give a contextual understanding, AI-assisted tools that augment human moderation, and the need to have continuous learning systems to adapt to the shifting nature of AI-generated content (Haupt et al., 2024; M. Zhang et al., 2024).

Using AI for Initial Content Screening and Prioritization

AI systems are particularly well suited to scanning initial content from the message itself, especially concerning massive amounts. The technology will scan, classify, and flag material accordingly to set rules or learned patterns so that possibly harmful material is quickly identified. AI does exceptionally well on volume applications, such as real-time pattern identification in a mass content so that suspect material can be flagged for closer scrutiny:

- Speed: Automated systems can quickly detect and prioritize harmful content so that the time taken for harmful material to be online is minimized.
- Consistency: AI systems apply moderation rules uniformly for all the content. Therefore, if the content is flagged, it exceeds the predefined thresholds.

For example, Facebook's AI monitors the content for deep fakes, hate speech, and disinformation by finding the appearance of specific keywords or even image patterns and audio anomalies. These systems flag the content that matches their criteria for potential harmful behavior and pass them on to humans when discretion is needed (Ahti, 2024; Hamel et al., 2020; Radwan et al.).

AI also aid in the prioritization of content for human review on the basis of urgency or potential harm. Thus, slightly more serious cases of hate speech, fake news, or manipulated media can be sent directly to human review, while a less serious case may be treated by the automatic systems.

Human Expertise in Providing Context and Making Nuanced Decisions

Although AI systems excel at pattern discovery and processing vast amounts of data, they are rather weak at making decisions of contextual understanding, which still require human expertise at the present moment. Human moderators contribute very important elements to moderation processes that AI currently lacks in moderation.

i. Cultural Context: Meaning and working within the cultural, linguistic, and social context of content gives one an idea of what is essentially, indeed harming, versus what might be simply misunderstood. What is offensive in one place would not remotely carry any similar connotation in another.
ii. Gradations of Judgment Some content may be ambiguous, complex, or in a gray area, and some decisions are best left to human judgment either to remove it or allow it. For instance, satire, parody, or commentary might appear so damaging but really carry a different message that only human sensibility can discern.
iii. Ethical Issues: Human monitors would be able to grapple with sticky issues of morality, such as balancing free speech with content restriction, or estimating the potential harm of removing or not deleting specific content from the web.

Human monitors could review flagged content with regard to community standards, bringing an aspect of nuance involving context, intent, and reasonable ethical considerations. For example, although AI might flag a content item with objectionable terms, humans can decide that a piece is used in an educational or even satirical manner rather than out of hatred. This minimizes false positives-that is, content that was flagged but has no relation to harm-and false negatives-the content was not flagged and in fact does entail harm (Jarrahi, 2018; Lai et al., 2021; Mcdonald, 2000; Sulastri, 2023).

AI-Supported Tools for Human Moderators

In this collaborative environment, AI does not confine itself to flagging content. Rather, AI tools would help human moderators in even more sophisticated jobs of vetting, analyzing, and contextualizing flagged material. A few examples of these AI-supported tools are listed below (Bankins et al., 2022; Lai et al., 2021):

1. Forensic analysis tools: Artificial intelligence can aid human moderators by offering forensic tools that will help in the analysis of the origin and authenticity of the content. For instance, AI can detect whether a video was created with deep fake technology by picking up inconsistencies in visual data, such as irregularities in lighting, texture, and facial movements. It is an analytical process of which moderators make decisions on removing credibility from content.
   - Application: A forensic AI tool could, through pixel-level inconsistencies or unnatural voice syncing, determine that an amateur viral video involving a political figure stating controversial statements is indeed a deep fake, and human moderators could issue the final ruling.
2. Content Verification Systems: AI-driven content verification systems enable human moderators to cross-check flagged material against verified databases or trusted sources. These verification systems thus help generate disinformation by cross-checking claims against known facts, allowing the human moderator to easily verify the authenticity of articles, posts, or images.
   - Application: It flags a news story which may potentially be false when an election campaign goes on. After it has been flagged, it can then be verified against credible news sources and government databases with the help of human moderators that are supported with AI-powered content verification systems.
3. Algorithmic Classification: AI can help classify unsafe content; it can, for example, classify the same types of similar content to masquerade as human moderation. This enables moderators to monitor certain trends, patterns, or behaviors, which then may make it easier to identify a coordinated campaign of disinformation, mass hate speech attacks, or the spread of deep fakes.
   - Application: AI machines can group thousands of posts that follow the same fabricated story across social media, thereby saving human moderators for the task of breaking down campaigns and not the isolated incidents.
4. Translation and Interpretation of Languages: AI-based tools for real-time translation and interpretation of languages enable the human moderators to read all this content in multiple languages. It's helpful, therefore, for network platforms with a global user base where harmful content can appear in a wide variety of languages.
   - Application: An AI-supported translation tool may be employed by a human moderator based in the U.S., who analyses hate speech that is indeed being posted in some non-English languages, thus adhering to moderation standards worldwide.

These AI-supported tools do lighten the load of human moderators as they can be deployed solely for high-impact tasks and in doing so ensure decisions are driven by right and verified information.

Continuous Learning Systems to Keep Up With Evolving Harmful Content

One of the biggest challenges in controlling AI-generated content is the continuous change of how bad actors adapt their approach toward creating malicious content. And if new methods are adapted to circumvent the current detection systems, AI systems and human moderator expertise must continually improve alongside it. Continuous learning systems counter this challenge by allowing AI systems the opportunity to learn from new data to adapt emerging threats and improve with time (Mhlanga, 2023).

1. Feedback Loops: Continuous learning systems depend on the principle of feedback loops between AI systems and human moderators. Human moderators review the content flagged by AI and return feedback regarding the accuracy of AI's decision, which is then used to retrain AI models, thus making AI models more capable of detecting similar types of content in the future. For example, if an AI model tends to classify satire as disinformation frequently, feedback from human moderators will contribute to the refinement of AI understanding of satire and will make similar errors less likely to occur.
2. Retraining on New Datasets: As new forms of harmful contents emerge, the AI models must be retasked with updated datasets that reflect the change. Continuous learning systems enable AI to include new examples of harmful content within their training, always remaining one step ahead of emerging, evolving threats like more complex deep fakes or AI-generated disinformation campaigns. For example, once emerging techniques for deep fakes are discovered, AI systems can be updated through the retraining via the updated datasets- and so with examples of the new deep fakes being detected.
3. Instant updates: Continuous learning real-time update systems can update AI systems to respond to emerging threats instantaneously when they appear. This way, an AI system will continue to be effective with the invention of fresh types of harmful content and their spread across the web. If it's a campaign of disinformation that spreads instantly, then real-time updates allow an AI system to detect new narratives and flag related content before it goes viral.
4. Cross-Platform Collaborative Learning: Learning is inter-exchanged across each platform and shared in different industries. AI systems on one platform could be updated based on harmful content detected on another, so moderation

systems benefit from a better understanding of new threats across them. For example, when someone detects a new deep fake technology on a social media forum, that information can be relayed to other platforms to inform updates to the AI mechanisms for detection of updates; this makes a more comprehensive defense against the threat.

5. Human-AI Collaboration: Balancing and Adaptive Approach in Modulating Harmful Content Generation with AI. The use of an AI initial filtration with regards to human capabilities for contextual understanding and nuanced decision-making steps up the content moderation efforts of the platform with accuracy and improved efficiency. AI-supported tools continue to enhance human moderators' capabilities, and continuous learning systems ensure that both AI and human moderators remain ahead of the curve of harmful content generated over time.

ETHICAL CONSIDERATIONS IN COMBATING AI-GENERATED CONTENT

AI use in content moderation is an issue that raises many critical debates with heavy moral implications. In the case of harmful AI-generated content, the fight against it through the establishment of such platforms prompts a multitude of ethical questions on free speech, bias, transparency, accountability, and privacy. Fair, just operation, and respect for users' rights within systems powered by AI balance out the need to successfully moderate all these factors. In the subsequent section, we discuss in detail these key ethical issues (Y. Wang, 2023).

Balancing Content Moderation With Free Speech Rights

The urgent ethical question relates to balancing the removal of harmful content on one hand and free speech on the other. Although AI-generated harmful content for instance hate speech, deep fakes, or disinformation may cause quite a deal of damage to individuals and their societies, excessive moderation hampers legitimate speech, artistic creativity, and political discourse (Dias Oliva, 2020).

1. Over-Moderation: AI-based content moderation systems can become over-moderating at times by flagging or deleting material that is not hate speech and should remain under the protection of free speech. Satiric, ironic, or provocative content would be flagged as hate speech or disinformation since AI systems cannot fully understand the tone and the contextual meaning of words. In this way, free speech may include legitimate discussion, creative writing, or even social comment; the outcome might be that debate, artistic expression, and

even sharp social commentary remain silenced. Using satire, satirical articles and political cartoons criticizing leaders or ideologies are flagged by an AI as disinformation or hate speech, curtailing the public from having open political dialogue.

2. Finding a Balance: The effort towards moderation needs to be well-balanced so that harming the users through content is not easily possible, and yet at the same time, should not cross the freedom of expression lines set by the platforms. Human-AI collaboration is one such necessity because human moderators can assess the context and intent with which the content has been created. Thus, all appropriate moderations can be done while not leaving a mark of unnecessary censorship.
    - Ethical Dilemma: Whether to err on the side of caution by removing borderline harmful content and possibly over-censor or favor free speech by allowing more content to stay online by risking the spread of harmful content.

Tackling Potential Biases in AI Moderation Tools

As AI moderation systems are trained on massive volumes of data, biases inherent in the data that is used to train them come out inadvertently within it. Biases inherent in the data can thus sway the decisions made by AI systems and result in unbalanced content moderation practices that settle unevenly on some sets of people or communities (Ferraz et al., 2024; Nahmias & Perel, 2021).

1. Bias in Training Data: AI systems learn based on the datasets they are trained upon, and if those datasets are biased, then so will be the systems' replications of and reinforcement of those biases. The moderation system may over-police content written by the groups determined to be the active perpetrators in a skewed dataset of the very same racial or ethnic group. Such a system will perfect a biased outcome. For example, a language model mainly trained on the basis of data available from the West countries in English would fail miserably to identify hate speech in other languages or cultures, effectively causing content moderation policies to vary widely between populations of users.
2. Minimizing Bias: Developers of AI moderation have to make the data used to train the AI as varied as possible and representative of all sets of people. This would range from multiple languages to cultures and opinions so that the system becomes balanced and fairer. Additionally, the technology has to self-audit regularly to determine existing biases and correct the biases with improvement of the models over real-world performance.

- Ethical Dilemma: In implementing such systems, AI developers are first faced with the task of ensuring that the systems they implement are fair but not intentionally biased, especially while managing global platforms with users of different disciplines.

3. Correction by Human Reviewers: This would be highly effective in correcting biases if human reviewers are really involved in scrutinizing flagged content and giving relevant feedback that AI systems can learn from and apply. Human reviewers have a better contextual understanding, empathy, and capacity for complex cases, such as when AI systems are biased.

Ensuring Transparency and Accountability in Decision-Making

Ethical principles actually enshrined in the management of these contents are certainly transparency and accountability, particularly in terms of using AI. Users ought to know how moderation decisions are being made, and the platforms have to be made accountable for the outcome of their AI moderated systems (Diakopoulos, 2020; Pillai, 2024).

1. Opaque decision-making: One of the criticisms against AI-driven moderation, however, pertains to the opacity in how the decision is being made. Algorithms work like "black boxes" most of the time, where the reasoning behind a certain content being removed or retained cannot even be adequately comprehended by the deployment platforms. This raises questions of equity and fair process because users whose content is taken down do not understand why the decision was made or how to appeal it. For example, a user may find his content flagged out or removed without an apparent explanation as to whether such removal was justified or based on AI misinterpretation.
2. Developing Transparent Systems: Such platforms should ensure that transparency serves as a basis or foundation from which moderation policies are built upon. This can be where the detailed but understandable explanations of moderation decisions to the users explaining why the content was flagged, how it was decided, and what to do about an appeal. Transparency also comes in disclosing development on moderation systems, including disclosure of training and auditing procedures of AI models to promote fairness.
    - Ethical Dilemma: The transparency required needs to be balanced off against the danger that ill actors may employ such information for taking advantage of the system if much more than prudent regarding AI moderation tools gets out into the open.

3. Accountability and Redress: Accountability refers to the fact that the platforms need to come up with processes wherein challenges made by users can be raised on moderation decisions, seeking redress. For instance, when AI errors occur, such as failing to classify harmful material or misclassifying content. Such users should therefore, have clear avenues of appeal and recourse offered to them, and also through AI audited periodically for better accuracy as well as fairness in many instances.

Addressing Privacy Concerns With Advanced Content Analysis Techniques

As increasingly sophisticated AI-driven moderation tools emerge, they increasingly rely on forensic analysis and behavioural profiling, cross-referencing user-generated content against external data sources. Their accuracy does increase content moderation. However, huge privacy concerns are involved (Kleinheksel et al., 2020):

1. Data Collection and Surveillance: For an AI moderation system to function efficiently, it requires large amounts of data concerning the user-whether personal information, private messages, or behavioral patterns. In fact, such levels of surveillance are problematic, particularly as such techniques used by platforms are invasive in monitoring and analyzing activity on different services. For example, AI scans private messages for harmful content. This is questionable regarding the degree to which consent is obtained from the users themselves and the degree at which private conversations can be monitored by platforms.
2. Balancing Privacy and Security: In this aspect, the question is how this can be done without making it hard to strike a balance between protecting the users from harmful content and respect for privacy among the users. Advanced AI techniques in deep fake detection or content verification call for extensive analysis on the content of the users, which may be an infringement upon their right to privacy. The capability of data collection and analysis should not infringe upon personal space but still be an effective product for moderation.
    - Ethical Dilemma: How much information should AI systems possess about users? How do platforms make sure that access to personal information to make accurate moderations is used responsibly and in a transparent manner?
3. Consent and User Control: User privacy has to be addressed by ensuring that users fully understand what the platform is going to collect, namely data on content moderation, so that one has respect for privacy. Giving users control of their data can be done by providing users with a choice, for instance, opting out.

- Ethical Dilemma: How Can Platforms Provide Meaningful Control over Data to Users without Compromising AI-driven Content Moderation?

CONCLUSION: THE ETHICAL IMPERATIVE IN HUMAN-AI COLLABORATION

Thus, the ethical considerations beneath content moderation with harmful AI-generated content are very intricate and complex. In so far as platforms seek to balance the need for effective moderation of such content with the protection of free speech and the prevention of biases in AI systems, these decision-making processes should be transparent and accountable. Finally, privacy concerns will be met as well, given that more data analysis techniques are required to operate sophisticated content moderation using AI.

It is thus crucial to human-AI collaboration in addressing these ethical issues. Platforms can create more fair, transparent, and respectful content moderation systems by complementing AI's scalability and efficiency with the human moderators' ethical judgment and understanding of the context. Still, as the technology progresses, it is continually demanding a watchful mind from the companies making it to bring the system in tune and serve the interests of individual users and the larger society.

Technical Challenges and Opportunities

Therefore, part of the development of AI-generated content should include better tools and techniques in moderating and managing such content. The technical challenges are huge, but so is the innovative locked up in detecting those noxious forms of AI-generated content. In this section, we discuss the advancement in deep fake detection and content authenticity verification, the challenge of benign and malicious AI-generated content, the future of blockchain and distributed ledger technologies, and the future of forensic AI with an emphasis on content traceability.

Progress in Detecting Deep Fakes and Verifying Content Authenticity

1. Deep fakes: AI-generated videos, images, and audio that convincingly mimic real people are probably among the most challenging content moderation tasks today. AI-powered videos/images/audio that are nearly realistic but entirely fabricated have led to anxiety about using them for mis- and disinformation campaigns, political manipulation, and personal defamation. At the same time,

tremendous progress has been made in the last two years in the development of tools and techniques to identify deep fakes and authenticate original content.

2. Advances in Deep Fake Detection. AI-based detection models have been further advanced to pick up on some very faint tampering hints from media. Some rely on artifact-based detection - proper defects in fabricated output - such as inconsistent lighting, unnatural facial movements, or irregular audio syncing, for instance. Others utilize biometric markers, such as the detection of the beating heart in videos, to indicate whether content is real or AI generated. For example, for scientists, researchers have developed a system of detection of deep fakes that can analyze how the eyes or facial muscles move, which AI models are designed not to do convincingly.
3. Content Authentication Tools In addition to deep fake detection, there is good research and development into content authentication tools that authenticate the source and integrity of the media. These tools depend on the analysis of metadata, watermarking, and cryptography to determine whether a piece of content has been tampered with or otherwise altered from its original state. Other technologies under testing include blockchain and distributed ledger technologies, which are further described below, to authenticate content across digital ecosystems. For example, Many media companies have started introducing media authentication tools whereby platforms verify the origin of an image or video and supply users with information about whether the content has been altered or manipulated.

Differentiating Between Benign and Harmful AI-Generated Content

Perhaps the most difficult burden of moderation is to separate safe from harmful material. It's certainly not all bad: most AI-generated content does not belong in that category, but serves instead a legitimate purpose-in the creative arts, entertainment, or as an educational tool. The challenge, therefore, lies in creating mechanisms that can do just that: separate the harmless from dangerous content.

1. Contextual Intelligence: AI moderator does not have contextual understanding while it generates or shares a content. The deep fake used for a comical video may be harmless, but the very same technology applied by some miscreants to create fake news can be highly damaging. Lack of contextual awareness in such AI systems lays it up for false positives: benign content marked as harmful, and false negatives: harmful content failing to go noticed. Example: a parody video using deep fake technology might get flagged as disinformation by an AI moderation tool, even though the intent was to appear humorous rather than malicious (Jiang et al., 2023).

2. Ethical and Legal Considerations: What is bad versus benign will eventually depend on perspectives, legal frameworks, and the platforms on which it operates. Moderation models have to deal with these subtle nuances of ethics and legalities to not over-moderate, which stifles free expression, nor under-moderate and allow bad content. Building this distinction in AI models is a big technological challenge.

The Potential of Blockchain and Distributed Ledger Technologies

Improvement in traceability, authenticity, and security of digital content This applies to the blockchain and DLT technologies; they can create a decentralized, tamper-proof record of content by ensuring transparency and verification on information regarding the origin, modifications, and ownership (Farahani et al., 2021; Sunyaev & Sunyaev, 2020).

1. Content Authenticity and Provenance: Blockchain technology generates a "fingerprint" of the content at inception, and that fingerprint, or hash, would be then recorded on the decentralized ledger so that the authenticity can resurface at any point afterward by users. When the contents are altered, the hash would no longer match, and the change would be indicated to the user. For example, a news agency could use blockchain to timestamp each of the published articles so that all subsequent changes made to that text can be tracked and proved readable to viewers.
2. Combating Misinformation and Deep Fakes: Blockchain can be used to prove the origin of media files and their integrity, thus reducing the chances of spreading misinformation or deep fake videos. The content can be traced back to its creator since it makes it easier for people who spread altered or fake content to be traced and removed from the platforms. For example, a social media platform can utilize blockchain so that video authenticity is guaranteed for that video of a user posted on it so that that is a deep fake or digitally altered cannot be a real event.
3. Adoption Challenges. It is not that blockchain does not hold great promises, but the development, as a whole, faces some challenges. The implementation of a blockchain system on a large scale requires many resources and processing of vast data that makes it impossible to scale for most content platforms, which post hundreds of contents daily. Also, applying blockchain with the current system of content moderation would take much investment in infrastructure and technology.

Future Advancements in Forensic AI and Content Traceability

Forensic AI will represent the future of AI in content moderation, those systems not only detecting the presence of harmful content but also tracing the origin, tracking its spread, and analyzing its impact. This way, those systems will be able to provide much deeper insights into how such bad stuff is created and propagated, enabling platforms to respond in a more targeted fashion to emerging threats.

1. Deep Fake Forensic AI: As deep fake technologies advance, forensic AI tools have to keep abreast of the ways manipulations will become increasingly impossible to miss. Techniques bound to include a variety of biometric analysis, audio-visual synchronization, and behavioral pattern recognition to identify fake media. Forensic AI will help trace back the origin of deep fakes and track perpetrators so that platforms may ban such actors along with their associated content. For example, it could be tracked using forensic AI that the viral deep fake video was actually coming from a particular account so that platforms can shut down the source before such content goes viral (Pappachan et al., 2024).
2. Content Traceability and Attribution: Forensic AI will be able to trace and attribute content to much finer specifics than ever before, enabling the platforms to know exactly where this noxious content is flowing, who amplifies this disinformation, and to what extent are users suffering its implications. Such data will enable platforms to undertake more targeted interventions, such as clearing out the harmful content before it even starts to spread or issuing corrections to users who have already been reached with false information. To take one example, a forensic AI system may trace the journey of disinformation across several social media platforms, identify critical influencers in spreading the misinformation, and alert moderators to act accordingly (Singh).
3. Automated collection of evidence of harmful content: There is extreme potential in the use of forensic AI to automate evidence collection that is connected with harmful content, especially for law enforcement or regulatory bodies while conducting investigations into crimes of disinformation, harassment, or violation of privacy. To be more efficient and dependable, digital evidence's automated collection and preservation for legal purposes are offered through forensic AI systems. For example, a forensic compilation-based AI system will automatically generate a report of a deep fake video, complete with metadata, timestamps, and traces of manipulation, all ready to be presented in a courtroom (Ganesh et al., 2022).

CONCLUSION: NAVIGATING TECHNICAL CHALLENGES AND EMBRACING OPPORTUNITIES

Technical challenges regarding the control of noxious content generated by AI, in turn, are really quite diverse, but at the same time do represent some big opportunity for innovation. Among other bright spots of deep-fake detection, content authentication, blockchain, and forensic AI, is solution to the issue of increasing digital harms of every kind. The more that such technologies become more accepted, applied, and further developed, the more will such platforms develop safer and more trustworthy digital environments.

These innovations must be put side by side with serious consideration of the ethical, legal, and social implications of the issues to ensure that technological solutions respect rights and freedoms while effectively mitigating the risks of AI-generated harmful content.

Policy and Industry Recommendations

The complex challenges posed by AI-generated harmful content should not be addressed alone with technological solutions but with proper regulatory frameworks and industry best practices that ensure responsible use of AI in content creation and moderation. Besides protecting user rights, this will establish a clear dimension for enhancing digital literacy. This section outlines key policy recommendations, best practices for platforms, empowerment of users through digital literacy, and the strategies to promote responsible AI development.

Regulatory Frameworks for Managing AI-Generated Content

As AI technologies grow and advance, governments and regulatory agencies must create effective guidelines that will address the dangers of AI-generated malign content. Proper regulation allows for the placement of clear lines that cannot be crossed by demonstrating the capability to stay secure against such harmful content while still promoting innovation responsibly (Xuan, 2023).

1. Definition of Key Terms and Standards: Defining deep fakes, AI-generated disinformation, and synthetic media are two of the foundational steps to regulate AI-generated content. Definitions help lay down clear standards that policy analysts can use in establishing clear-cut criteria of harmful AI-generated content and guide the development of laws regarding its creation and dispersal. For instance, laws may draw a distinction between a use of AI-generated content for bona fide purposes such as entertainment and education and others harmful,

like disinformation or defamation, in order that legitimate creators are not left with undue burdens.

2. Transparency and Accountability Legislation: The law should guarantee that all the regulatory frameworks demand that platform businesses be transparent concerning the practices that their content moderation follows, especially where AI is engaged. This includes informing the users of the extent to which the AI tools apply to moderation, reasons for the removal of their contents, and clear dispute resolution channels. There should also be accountability over the misuse of AI technologies to inflict harms, as might be the case in the rampant spread of disinformation or deep fakes. An instance is requiring laws to label AI-generated content explicitly where such deep fakes have been identified by users, enabling them to make informed choices about the consumption habits of what they ingest.
3. Traceability of Content and Digital Provenance: The use of authentication systems of content should be encouraged or ensured by regulatory bodies. This includes blockchain and other digital media authentication. This will prevent the online spreading of manipulated content and restrain creators from producing such harmful media. For instance, the requirement that all political ads, news, or other elections-related material in the media have to be digitally watermarked and traceable back to the source can be used by authorities to prevent deep fake use during elections.
4. Inter-jurisdictional Coordination: As globalization has digitalized the world of the internet, harmful AI-generated content usually involves multiple jurisdictions. Regulations need to interlock across jurisdictions to set international standards for AI-generated content. That will mean aligning the regulations amongst themselves so that there is no discrepancy in regulations which otherwise can be exploited by malefactors. For example, International agreements may be found setting worldwide standards to label AI-generated content so the bad news of disinformation does not spread itself across borders where regulations vary.

Best Practices for Platforms in Mitigating Harmful AI-Generated Content

While governments contribute to the regulation of AI-generated content, the task doesn't end there. The online platforms themselves must do their part through the adoption of best practices to mitigate the risks accompanying hate-fueled AI-generated material. Best practices point to step-by-step implementations that allow for proactive protection of the users on the platforms while creating an environment where responsible content creation becomes a part of the culture (Lyu, 2024; Menczer et al., 2023; Wang & Zheng, 2024).

1. Proactive content monitoring and detection: Platforms should invest in proactively developed monitoring systems that use AI in real-time detection of harmful content- deepfakes, AI-generated hate speech, disinformation-not allowing them to spread widely once they have been discovered. In this manner, by slowly upgrading the effectiveness of detection tools, platforms are better at preventing viralizing harmful content. To give an example, AI specifically trained to identify the newest forms of AI-generated disinformation may be used by social media for high-stakes events, be it elections or a public health crisis.
2. Hybrid Approach to Moderation: Platforms should take on the hybrid approach where AI automatically scans voluminous contents for its detection tools and passes on hard or context-dependent cases to human moderators to make their verification and ensure accuracy. An example would be where a platform made AI scans of millions of posts to detect disinformation, marking suspicious content for further assessment by human moderators who decide whether the content in question was done with malicious intent and applied according to its context before taking a decision on action taken.
3. AI Moderation Transparency Report: The online platforms would submit to the public transparency reports of how often AI moderation tools are utilized, the total number of contents AI flagged, and the AI-success rate in identifying such harmful content. The online platforms would also ensure the capability of users to appeal decisions taken by the AI-based systems, with details about the reasons why the content was removed or flagged by these AI systems. For example, Twitter or Facebook can publicly release quarterly reports citing the number of content identified and marked as problematic by AI, and the portion flagged that was later found to be indeed harmful by human moderators.
4. User Empowerment and Controls: Sites should empower users to control their exposure to content; thus, they should allow users to filter AI-generated content, opt out of the view of deep fakes, or control their feed in order to maximize fact-checked news. The above accounts give users confidence and diminish the negative effects of such content. For example, a video-sharing site could offer users a toggle that would automatically filter out AI-generated deep fakes, so the users only have a view of verified, authentic media.

The Importance of Digital Literacy and Empowering Users

Digital literacy can be one of the most potent tools to counter negative AI-generated material. Awareness of the possible harms of AI-generated material and educating the public on how to identify it will empower individuals to secure themselves better against misinformation, scams, and deep fakes (Diseiye et al., 2024; Setiadi et al., 2023).

1. Digital Literacy Initiatives: The governments, educational institutions, and platforms will have to put forth their efforts in the digital literacy initiatives as well that educate users about AI-generating material, techniques for detecting manipulated media, and the risks associated with misinformation. Such campaigns might also give instructions about checking material before it spreads and how to use fact-checking sources more efficiently. Digital literacy classes can be enforced by the schools to clarify the AI technology within the terminologies of deep fakes, such that students can identify manipulated content and assess its credibility.
2. act-checking and media verification tools: for example, websites can include fact-checking capabilities on the front ends, such that customers will easily verify the news stories, images, or videos through the sites. Improving on these technologies will also help minimize misinformation and responsible provision and sharing of information. Social media can have a "fact-check" button to the right of posts, where users will quick-check something against truth sources before engaging or sharing.
3. Reporting Mechanisms for Users: Facilitating content moderation through reporting mechanisms by users helps detect the dangerous content that AI cannot. Platforms must make it easy to report misinformation, deep fakes, or AI-generated hate speech with fair judgment within time limits. A video sharing platform may make an effective reporting mechanism in which viewers might identify deepfake content by just a few clicks that can notify the moderators instantly about the problem.

Encouraging Responsible AI Development in Content Creation

To minimize the risk of adverse material production through AI, responsible AI production in content creation is very much essential. There should be more impetus to AI developers and content platform creators towards considering ethical and openness insights while developing their AI models.

1. Ethical AI Protocols: The use of AI systems should be guided by rules that emphasize securing transparency, justice, and liability within the design of their respective systems. They should be cautioned against inflaming already damaging prejudices, and against behaving in a way that might infringe upon user privacy and, more broadly, to obscure information about the origins of content. AI model creators can refer appropriately to widely accepted ethical guidelines such as those from the Partnership on AI for instance, transparency in ensuring the construction of AIgenerated content and minimization of unintended harmful effects.

2. Safety measures: AI development platforms offering content production mechanisms utilizing artificial intelligence technologies must have in place safety measures so that the same tools might not be misused. For instance, the utilization of labels or watermarks on AI-generated content could alert the viewer that the contents provided are not originally created by a human actor. For instance, on an AI content production platform, the "This content is AI-generated" disclaimer would automatically appear with all media created by AI, making it clear to the explicit information of what one views-the material.
3. Interaction with Experts and Policymakers: Developers of AI and users of AI technologies should continually interact with relevant experts, policymakers, and civil society to further ensure responsible development and application of the technology. It will guide legislation, show where the potential perils are and provide safeguards against certain dangerous application of AI-generated content. This could occur when a group of developers of AI meet with policy academics to generate best practices for limiting spread of dangerous techniques for detection of deep fakes across platforms.

Regulatory frameworks must allow the building of substantial resilience into them by incorporating industry practices and gradually ease the empowerment of the users through a more complex approach. While the platforms will therefore proactively take the risks with regard to AI-generated content, the legislators will work on the appropriate technology rules that will protect consumers but do not impede innovation. Digital literacy and ethical AI development will empower consumers and experts to cross much more complex digital landscapes (Buhmann & Fieseler, 2021).

Policymakers and platforms can deliver a safer and more trustworthy digital environment that foster innovation but respect rights through the promotion of openness, accountability, and ethical AI development.

CONCLUSION

i. A Framework for Effective Human-AI Collaboration

The unprecedented challenge to digital platforms, governments, and users alike is the creation of harmful content through AI. Effective content moderation frameworks that co-opt best-of-breed human expertise and AI capabilities have become imperative, but need to address this in a way that balances efficiency with scalability and contextual understanding: preventing harm without infringing on basic rights like free speech. In this final section, we outline core principles for handling AI-generated dangerous content; we offer advice to platforms, policymakers, and researchers on how best to handle the issue at hand; and we reflect on the future of content moderation in an AI-driven environment.

Core Principles for Addressing AI-Generated Harmful Content

Such a powerful framework for human-AI cooperation in content moderation shall form a set of foundational principles from which both AI and human moderators can operate synergistically to address the dynamic and constantly evolving nature of AI-generating content that harms people.

1. Balancing Algorithmic Analysis with Human Judgment: AI systems excel at processing enormous volumes of content extremely quickly while also detecting patterns that indicate harmful content. However, the AI system lacks understanding of nuances, context, and intent behind specific types of content. It is the human moderators who bring cultural, ethical, and contextual understanding to this exercise of moderation when AI goes wrong. This indicates that a balance must be achieved between complete automation, which may eliminate the possibility of human oversight, and human oversight, which negatively affects efficiency.
2. Transparency and Accountability: AI-based Content Moderation with Transparency Users should know how AI is working, content is flagged or actually removed, and how to make decisions to dispute. The platforms are responsible for their moderation outcomes, making sure that the decision-making system is fair, not biased. Transparency builds user trust, and accountability ensures that mistakes or unintended consequences lie upon the shoulders of the platforms.
3. Continuous Learning and Adaptation: Harmful content, produced by AI, will evolve; so too must the tools and systems placed within to detect and moderate it. AI systems must be updated continuously by engaging in feedback loops with human moderators who learn from reality cases and improve over time. Humans should also be trained continually in such a system regarding the novel threats, new content generation techniques, and the ethical implications of AI-driven moderation.
4. Ethical Concerns and Rights of Users: Prevention of Violation of Rights of the User-the rights to free speech and privacy are entitled to the users. AI-developed moderation needs to be delicately calibrated so as not to enable over-censorship and to protect users' rights over freedom of speech. Simultaneously, the platforms must explore the ethical considerations of the harmful content such that measures adopted towards the creation of disinformation, hate speech, and

deep fakes should be done in such a manner that does not enable biasness while safeguarding vulnerable communities from the harms caused by the latter.

Recommendations for Platforms, Policymakers, and Researchers

Effective human-AI collaboration for content moderation will depend on the synergy that can be generated between the involved stakeholders: platforms, regulators, and academics. To properly guide each category, here are a few key guidelines:

1. For Platforms:
    - Hybrid Models in Moderation: frameworks designed by platforms should strike a balance between the scalabilities of advantage AI can bring about with the level of discernment human moderators would have. While using AI for preliminary screening and flagging, the decision on intricate cases to be taken up should be done by humans, based on contextual understanding.
    - Improve Transparency and Control of the Choices Users Want to See: Platforms should explain in clear terms processes that govern content moderation and allow choices for individuals on what they see-that is, empower the users to control blocking AI-generated content or opting out of personalized recommendations of content that they will be exposed to.
    - Establish Near Real-Time Threat Detection Systems: Companies should identify near real-time threat-detection systems for deepfakes and coordinated disinformation campaigns, among others. Further, rapid response teams could be established across different departments for prompt response to high-impact incidents that occur.
2. For Policymakers:
    - Regulate AI-Generated Content: Policymaking bodies should create robust legislations that constrain the ills brought about by harmful AI-generated content without obstructing free speech and innovation. Such regulatory frameworks should feature legal requirements regarding labeling of AI-generated content, transparency in moderation policies and traceability of contents.
    - Encourage Interoperability Collaboration: The governments would encourage interoperability collaboration between cross-platforms, academia, and regulatory agencies to set out common practices and standards for filtering and best practices around content filtering which will

incorporate support for international cooperation to deny hazardous information reaching the world.
    - Investment on Digital Literacy and Public Education: It should invest in activities on digital literacy educating the general public on how to check whether material is generated by AI, how to evaluate the credibility of media, and how to be safe while surfing online ecosystems.
3. To Researchers
    - Ethical AI Development must be accorded highest importance: The developers of AI for content moderation, researchers should stress the ethical issues when the AI system is to be developed with transparency, fairness, and accountability. Less bias in AI models and the ability to understand the subtleties of cultures and contexts should take place with activities.
    - Researchers should engage with platforms in developing and enhancing AI detection technologies that could detect deep fakes, misinformation, and other poisonous material. More powerful open-source tools and datasets will help smaller platforms build more cohesive defenses against malicious content.

Therefore, researchers should also continue their analysis into the social and psychological effects of such harmful AI-generated content for users so that they can assist in the design of the procedure for content moderation measures and public policy decisions.

The Future of Content Moderation in an AI-Driven Environment

Content control will grow less because of its massive impact on the digital world. The improvement in content control will largely depend on the ability of the platforms, governments, and society at large to adapt to new technologies within the limits of democracy and moral principles. Here are a few possible trends in content moderation for the next few years:

1. AI-based scalable solutions: Since the digital platforms are getting larger and larger, their handling of large volumes of material will largely depend on AI systems. AI would have become increasingly smart so that it could be able to identify subtle manipulation or deep fakes or texts generated by an AI system. They would also be in a position to distinguish better safe and unsafe content.
2. Improved Human Judgment in AI Processes: More and more, human reviewers will play a big role for content moderation, even while AI technologies improve. In the future, processes will bring together more closely both AI systems and

human reviews. AI will handle routine tasks with human moderators focused upon tough cases with much at stake. Besides tracking tools for content, forensic AI will make it easier for human users to tell whether the content is real or fake and where they came from.

3. Agreed, proactive content moderation and crisis management: As time goes by, content filtering is likely to shift from reactive to proactive. Platforms will use real-time tracking and prediction analytics to discover threats early and often, before they spiral out of control. It will be the best to have crisis reaction teams with the latest AI tools ready for a pandemic or information warfare during election time.
4. Better working, more open ecosystem: The problematic material that AI is unleashing has started to become a major concern around the world. Thus, as such, platforms have to work together with each other and be more open. Open-source AI detection tools use the best practices from partners will be typical. This means that a better chance of minimizing such risks of problematic material of this kind is achieved as the platforms work together. It would also become easier for users to help in moderating material. The tools available include those for fact-checking and reporting problems.

   ii. Building a Safer and More Ethical Digital Future

Human-AI collaboration in content moderation holds the most promising future toward the eradication of AI-generated harmful content. It will allow the platforms to create safer and more responsible digital environments by efficient contributions of AI along with ethical and contextual insights of human moderators. Transparency, accountability, and respect for user rights must form a basis for this collaboration.

Policymakers, platforms, and researchers must collaborate on creating ethical standards and rule-based frameworks as well as innovation technologies that will keep pace with this changing digital landscape. In parallel, the empirical ability for users to be empowered through digital literacy and transparency helps everyone have the tools to operate in an AI-driven environment safely. Therefore, promoting cooperation and responsible AI development will allow society to "reap the rewards of AI responsibly-to focus on the most secure as well as innovative exploitation of AI within a digital future".

REFERENCES

Abuhamad, A. (2024). *Algorithmography: Intersections of Truth*. Authenticity and Representation of AI Generated Visual Content in Journalism.

Ahti, J. O. A. (2024). Systematic prioritization of AI initiatives: implementation factors and achievable value.

Alowais, S. A., Alghamdi, S. S., Alsuhebany, N., Alqahtani, T., Alshaya, A. I., Almohareb, S. N., Aldairem, A., Alrashed, M., Bin Saleh, K., Badreldin, H. A., Al Yami, M. S., Al Harbi, S., & Albekairy, A. M. (2023). Revolutionizing healthcare: The role of artificial intelligence in clinical practice. *BMC Medical Education*, *23*(1), 689. DOI: 10.1186/s12909-023-04698-z PMID: 37740191

Bankins, S., Formosa, P., Griep, Y., & Richards, D. (2022). AI decision making with dignity? Contrasting workers' justice perceptions of human and AI decision making in a human resource management context. *Information Systems Frontiers*, *24*(3), 857–875. DOI: 10.1007/s10796-021-10223-8

Basta, Z. (2024). The Intersection of AI-Generated Content and Digital Capital: An Exploration of Factors Impacting AI-Detection and its Consequences. In.

Bird, J. J., & Lotfi, A. (2024). Cifake: Image classification and explainable identification of ai-generated synthetic images. *IEEE Access : Practical Innovations, Open Solutions*, *12*, 15642–15650. DOI: 10.1109/ACCESS.2024.3356122

Brigham, N. G., Wei, M., Kohno, T., & Redmiles, E. M. (2024). " Violation of my body:" Perceptions of AI-generated non-consensual (intimate) imagery. *arXiv preprint arXiv:2406.05520*.

Buhmann, A., & Fieseler, C. (2021). Towards a deliberative framework for responsible innovation in artificial intelligence. *Technology in Society*, *64*, 101475. DOI: 10.1016/j.techsoc.2020.101475

Chandrasekharan, E., Gandhi, C., Mustelier, M. W., & Gilbert, E. (2019). Crossmod: A cross-community learning-based system to assist reddit moderators. *Proceedings of the ACM on human-computer interaction, 3*(CSCW), 1-30. DOI: 10.1145/3359276

D'amico, S., Dall'Olio, D., Sala, C., Dall'Olio, L., Sauta, E., Zampini, M., Asti, G., Lanino, L., Maggioni, G., Campagna, A., Ubezio, M., Russo, A., Bicchieri, M. E., Riva, E., Tentori, C. A., Travaglino, E., Morandini, P., Savevski, V., Santoro, A., & Della Porta, M. G. (2023). Synthetic data generation by artificial intelligence to accelerate research and precision medicine in hematology. *JCO Clinical Cancer Informatics*, *7*(7), e2300021. DOI: 10.1200/CCI.23.00021 PMID: 37390377

De Gregorio, G., & Stremlau, N. (2023). Inequalities and content moderation. *Global Policy, 14*(5), 870–879. DOI: 10.1111/1758-5899.13243

De Souza, V. L. T., Marques, B. A. D., Batagelo, H. C., & Gois, J. P. (2023). A review on generative adversarial networks for image generation. *Computers & Graphics, 114*, 13–25. DOI: 10.1016/j.cag.2023.05.010

Diakopoulos, N. (2020). Accountability, transparency, and algorithms. *The Oxford handbook of ethics of AI, 17*(4), 197.

Dias Oliva, T. (2020). Content moderation technologies: Applying human rights standards to protect freedom of expression. *Human Rights Law Review, 20*(4), 607–640. DOI: 10.1093/hrlr/ngaa032

Diseiye, O., Ukubeyinje, S. E., Oladokun, B. D., & Kakwagh, V. V. (2024). Emerging technologies: Leveraging digital literacy for self-sufficiency among library professionals. *Metaverse Basic and Applied Research, 3*, 59–59. DOI: 10.56294/mr202459

Divya, V., & Mirza, A. U. (2024). Transforming content creation: The influence of generative AI on a new frontier. *Exploring the frontiers of artificial intelligence and machine learning technologies, 143.*

Farahani, B., Firouzi, F., & Luecking, M. (2021). The convergence of IoT and distributed ledger technologies (DLT): Opportunities, challenges, and solutions. *Journal of Network and Computer Applications, 177*, 102936. DOI: 10.1016/j.jnca.2020.102936

Ferraz, T. P., Duarte, C. H. D., Ribeiro, M. F., Takayanagi, G. G. B., Alcoforado, A., Lopes, R. D., & Susi, M. (2024). Explainable AI to Mitigate the Lack of Transparency and Legitimacy in Internet Moderation. *Estudos Avançados, 38*, 381–405. DOI: 10.1590/s0103-4014.202438111.020

Fui-Hoon Nah, F., Zheng, R., Cai, J., Siau, K., & Chen, L. (2023). *Generative AI and ChatGPT: Applications, challenges, and AI-human collaboration* (Vol. 25). Taylor & Francis.

Ganesh, N. G., Venkatesh, N. M., & Prasad, D. V. V. (2022). A systematic literature review on forensics in cloud, IoT, AI & blockchain. *Illumination of Artificial Intelligence in Cybersecurity and Forensics*, 197-229.

Gilbert, C., & Gilbert, M. A. (2024). The Role of Artificial Intelligence (AI) in Combatting Deepfakes and Digital Misinformation. *International Research Journal of Advanced Engineering and Science (ISSN: 2455-9024), 9*(4), 170-181.

Gongane, V. U., Munot, M. V., & Anuse, A. D. (2022). Detection and moderation of detrimental content on social media platforms: Current status and future directions. *Social Network Analysis and Mining, 12*(1), 129. DOI: 10.1007/s13278-022-00951-3 PMID: 36090695

Gorwa, R., Binns, R., & Katzenbach, C. (2020). Algorithmic content moderation: Technical and political challenges in the automation of platform governance. *Big Data & Society, 7*(1), 2053951719897945. DOI: 10.1177/2053951719897945

Habgood-Coote, J. (2023). Deepfakes and the epistemic apocalypse. *Synthese, 201*(3), 103. DOI: 10.1007/s11229-023-04097-3

Hamel, C., Kelly, S., Thavorn, K., Rice, D., Wells, G., & Hutton, B. (2020). An evaluation of DistillerSR's machine learning-based prioritization tool for title/abstract screening–impact on reviewer-relevant outcomes. *BMC Medical Research Methodology, 20*(1), 1–14. DOI: 10.1186/s12874-020-01129-1 PMID: 33059590

Hashemi, M. (2023). Geographical visualization of tweets, misinformation, and extremism during the USA 2020 presidential election using LSTM, NLP, and GIS. *Journal of Big Data, 10*(1), 125. DOI: 10.1186/s40537-023-00797-2

Haupt, M., Freidank, J., & Haas, A. (2024). Consumer responses to human-AI collaboration at organizational frontlines: Strategies to escape algorithm aversion in content creation. *Review of Managerial Science*, •••, 1–37.

Henderson, P., Hashimoto, T., & Lemley, M. (2023). Where's the Liability in harmful AI Speech? *J. Free Speech L., 3*, 589.

Hutchens, J. (2023). *The Language of Deception: Weaponizing Next Generation AI*. John Wiley & Sons.

Jamal, S. (2024). *Applications of Predictive and Generative AI Algorithms: Regression Modeling*. Customized Large Language Models, and Text-to-Image Generative Diffusion Models.

Jarrahi, M. H. (2018). Artificial intelligence and the future of work: Human-AI symbiosis in organizational decision making. *Business Horizons, 61*(4), 577–586. DOI: 10.1016/j.bushor.2018.03.007

Jiang, N., Liu, X., Liu, H., Lim, E. T. K., Tan, C.-W., & Gu, J. (2023). Beyond AI-powered context-aware services: The role of human–AI collaboration. *Industrial Management & Data Systems, 123*(11), 2771–2802. DOI: 10.1108/IMDS-03-2022-0152

Kendon, T., Wu, L., & Aycock, J. (2023). AI-Generated Code Not Considered Harmful. Proceedings of the 25th Western Canadian Conference on Computing Education, Kivimaki, V. P. Open-Source Information for Intelligence Purposes: The Challenge of Disinformation. In *Routledge Handbook of Disinformation and National Security* (pp. 283-294). Routledge.

Kleinheksel, A., Rockich-Winston, N., Tawfik, H., & Wyatt, T. R. (2020). Demystifying content analysis. *American Journal of Pharmaceutical Education*, *84*(1), 7113. DOI: 10.5688/ajpe7113 PMID: 32292185

Kolluri, N. L., & Murthy, D. (2021). CoVerifi: A COVID-19 news verification system. *Online Social Networks and Media*, *22*, 100123. DOI: 10.1016/j.osnem.2021.100123 PMID: 33521412

Kučinskas, G. (2024). *Negative Effects of Revealing Ai Involvement in Products: Mediation by Authenticity and Risk, Moderation by Trust in Ai and Familiarity with Ai*. Moderation by Trust in Ai and Familiarity with Ai.

Lai, V., Chen, C., Liao, Q. V., Smith-Renner, A., & Tan, C. (2021). Towards a science of human-ai decision making: a survey of empirical studies. *arXiv preprint arXiv:2112.11471*.

Lal, K., & Saini, M. L. (2023). A study on deep fake identification techniques using deep learning. AIP Conference Proceedings, Lehtimäki, M.-L. (2024). Navigating Ethical and Practical Challenges in AI-Driven Visual Content Creation. DOI: 10.1063/5.0154828

Lloyd, T., Reagle, J., & Naaman, M. (2023). " There Has To Be a Lot That We're Missing": Moderating AI-Generated Content on Reddit. *arXiv preprint arXiv:2311.12702*.

Lykouris, T., & Weng, W. (2024). Learning to defer in content moderation: The human-ai interplay. *arXiv preprint arXiv:2402.12237*.

Lyu, S. (2024). *DeepFake the menace: mitigating the negative impacts of AI-generated content. Organizational Cybersecurity Journal: Practice*. Process and People.

Mansour, M. (2024). The Moderation effect of AI Image Generator on the Relationship Between Evidences and Accurate Judgment. [IJTOP]. *International Journal of Theory of Organization and Practice*, *4*(1), 44–58.

Marsoof, A., Luco, A., Tan, H., & Joty, S. (2023). Content-filtering AI systems–limitations, challenges and regulatory approaches. *Information & Communications Technology Law*, *32*(1), 64–101. DOI: 10.1080/13600834.2022.2078395

Marzuki, W., Widiati, U., Rusdin, D., Darwin, , & Indrawati, I. (2023). The impact of AI writing tools on the content and organization of students' writing: EFL teachers' perspective. *Cogent Education, 10*(2), 2236469. DOI: 10.1080/2331186X.2023.2236469

Masood, M., Nawaz, M., Malik, K. M., Javed, A., Irtaza, A., & Malik, H. (2023). Deepfakes generation and detection: State-of-the-art, open challenges, countermeasures, and way forward. *Applied Intelligence, 53*(4), 3974–4026. DOI: 10.1007/s10489-022-03766-z

Mcdonald, D. W. (2000). *Supporting nuance in groupware design: Moving from naturalistic expertise location to expertise recommendation.* University of California.

Menczer, F., Crandall, D., Ahn, Y.-Y., & Kapadia, A. (2023). Addressing the harms of AI-generated inauthentic content. *Nature Machine Intelligence, 5*(7), 679–680. DOI: 10.1038/s42256-023-00690-w

Mhlanga, D. (2023). Open AI in education, the responsible and ethical use of ChatGPT towards lifelong learning. In *FinTech and artificial intelligence for sustainable development: The role of smart technologies in achieving development goals* (pp. 387–409). Springer. DOI: 10.1007/978-3-031-37776-1_17

Molina, M. D., & Sundar, S. S. (2024). Does distrust in humans predict greater trust in AI? Role of individual differences in user responses to content moderation. *new media & society, 26*(6), 3638-3656.

Mundra, S., Reddy, J., Mundra, A., Mittal, N., Vidyarthi, A., & Gupta, D. (2023). *An Automated Data-driven Machine Intelligence Framework for Mining Knowledge To Classify Fake News Using NLP.* ACM Transactions on Asian and Low-Resource Language Information Processing. DOI: 10.1145/3607253

Nahmias, Y., & Perel, M. (2021). The oversight of content moderation by AI: Impact assessments and their limitations. *Harvard Journal on Legislation, 58*, 145.

Nguyen, A., Rai, A., & Maruping, L. (2024). Understanding the Unintended Effects of Human-Machine Moderation in Addressing Harassment within Online Communities. *Journal of Management Information Systems, 41*(2), 341–366. DOI: 10.1080/07421222.2024.2340831

Nishimura, M., Hashimoto, K., Oura, K., Nankaku, Y., & Tokuda, K. (2016). Singing Voice Synthesis Based on Deep Neural Networks. Interspeech, Pan, Z., Lau, S. L., Yang, X., Guo, N., & Wang, X. (2023). Automatic pavement crack segmentation using a generative adversarial network (GAN)-based convolutional neural network. *Results in Engineering, 19*, 101267.

Pappachan, P., Adi, N. S., & Firmansyah, G. (2024). Deep Learning-Based Forensics. *Digital Forensics and Cyber Crime Investigation: Recent Advances and Future Directions*, 211.

Paterson, T., & Hanley, L. (2020). Political warfare in the digital age: Cyber subversion, information operations and 'deep fakes'. *Australian Journal of International Affairs*, *74*(4), 439–454. DOI: 10.1080/10357718.2020.1734772

Pillai, V. (2024). Enhancing Transparency and Understanding in AI Decision-Making Processes. *Iconic Research and Engineering Journals*, *8*(1), 168–172.

Pirone, N. A. (2024). Determinants of Generative Artificial Intelligence Large Language Model Exploration Intent for Software Development.

Plevris, V. (2024). Addressing the Pitfalls of Image-Based Structural Health Monitoring: A Focus on False Positives, False Negatives, and Base Rate Bias. *arXiv preprint arXiv:2410.20384*.

Pokhrel, S., & Banjade, S. R.Shiv Raj Banjade. (2023). AI Content Generation Technology based on Open AI Language Model. *Journal of Artificial Intelligence and Capsule Networks*, *5*(4), 534–548. DOI: 10.36548/jaicn.2023.4.006

Radwan, A. M., Abdel-Fattah, M. A., & Mohamed, W. AI-Driven Prioritization Techniques of Requirements in Agile Methodologies: A Systematic Literature.

Rafique, R., Gantassi, R., Amin, R., Frnda, J., Mustapha, A., & Alshehri, A. H. (2023). Deep fake detection and classification using error-level analysis and deep learning. *Scientific Reports*, *13*(1), 7422. DOI: 10.1038/s41598-023-34629-3 PMID: 37156887

Reddy, V. S. S., & Reddy, N. (2024). AI-Powered Language Models Enhancing Natural Language Understanding And Generation. [IJAIML]. *International Journal of Artificial Intelligence and Machine Learning*, *3*(02), 101–115.

Reichwcin, F. L. (2024). *Ethical and societal implications of generative AI-Models*. Technische Hochschule Ingolstadt.

Romero Moreno, F. (2024). Generative AI and deepfakes: A human rights approach to tackling harmful content. *International Review of Law Computers & Technology*, *38*(3), 1–30. DOI: 10.1080/13600869.2024.2324540

Rubin, V. L. (2022). Investigation in Law Enforcement, Journalism, and Sciences. In *Misinformation and Disinformation: Detecting Fakes with the Eye and AI* (pp. 123-156). Springer.

Sander, B. (2019). Freedom of expression in the age of online platforms: The promise and pitfalls of a human rights-based approach to content moderation. *Fordham Int'l LJ*, *43*, 939.

Setiadi, D., Nurhayati, S., Ansori, A., Zubaidi, M., & Amir, R. (2023). Youth's digital literacy in the context of community empowerment in an emerging society 5.0. *Society*, *11*(1), 1–12. DOI: 10.33019/society.v11i1.491

Sezgin, E. (2023). Artificial intelligence in healthcare: Complementing, not replacing, doctors and healthcare providers. *Digital Health*, *9*, 20552076231186520. DOI: 10.1177/20552076231186520 PMID: 37426593

Shao, Y., Huang, C., Song, Y., Wang, M., Song, Y. H., & Shao, R. (2024). Using Augmentation-Based AI Tool at Work: A Daily Investigation of Learning-Based Benefit and Challenge. *Journal of Management*, •••, 01492063241266503. DOI: 10.1177/01492063241266503

Sharma, A., Kumar, V., & Poojari, A. (2024). *Prioritize Threat Alerts Based on False Positives Qualifiers Provided by Multiple AI Models Using Evolutionary Computation and Reinforcement Learning. Journal of The Institution of Engineers.* Series B. DOI: 10.1007/s40031-024-01175-z

Shoaib, M. R., Wang, Z., Ahvanooey, M. T., & Zhao, J. (2023). Deepfakes, misinformation, and disinformation in the era of frontier AI, generative AI, and large AI models. *2023 International Conference on Computer and Applications (ICCA).*

Simon, H., Baha, B. Y., & Garba, E. J. (2022). Trends in machine learning on automatic detection of hate speech on social media platforms: A systematic review. *FUW Trends in Science & Technology Journal, 7*(1), 001-016.

Singh, A. P. Safeguarding Authenticity in the Digital Realm: A Holistic Approach Integrating Content Provenance, Secure Watermarking, and Transparent Labeling to Combat Deepfakes.

Song, X., Mamidisetty, S., Blanco, E., & Hong, L. (2024). Assessing the Human Likeness of AI-Generated Counterspeech. *arXiv preprint arXiv:2410.11007.*

Stockinger, A., Schäfer, S., & Lecheler, S. (2023). Navigating the gray areas of content moderation: Professional moderators' perspectives on uncivil user comments and the role of (AI-based) technological tools. *new media & society*, 14614448231190901.

Sulastri, R. (2023). Unveiling the Nuances of Human Interaction within Organizational Settings. *Advances in Human Resource Management Research*, *1*(3), 150–163. DOI: 10.60079/ahrmr.v1i3.197

Sunyaev, A., & Sunyaev, A. (2020). Distributed ledger technology. *Internet computing: Principles of distributed systems and emerging internet-based technologies*, 265-299.

Udupa, S., Maronikolakis, A., & Wisiorek, A. (2023). Ethical scaling for content moderation: Extreme speech and the (in) significance of artificial intelligence. *Big Data & Society, 10*(1), 20539517231172424. DOI: 10.1177/20539517231172424

Vetagiri, A., Mogha, P., & Pakray, P. Multilate Classifier: A Novel Emsemble of Cnn-Bilstm with Resnet-Based Multimodal Classifier for Ai-Generated Hate Speech Detection. *Available atSSRN* 4951337. DOI: 10.2139/ssrn.4951337

Veturi, Y. A., Woof, W., Lazebnik, T., Moghul, I., Woodward-Court, P., Wagner, S. K., de Guimarães, T. A. C., Varela, M. D., Liefers, B., & Patel, P. J. (2023). SynthEye: Investigating the impact of synthetic data on artificial intelligence-assisted gene diagnosis of inherited retinal disease. *Ophthalmology Science, 3*(2), 100258. DOI: 10.1016/j.xops.2022.100258 PMID: 36685715

Wach, K., Duong, C. D., Ejdys, J., Kazlauskaitė, R., Korzynski, P., Mazurek, G., Paliszkiewicz, J., & Ziemba, E. (2023). The dark side of generative artificial intelligence: A critical analysis of controversies and risks of ChatGPT. *Entrepreneurial Business and Economics Review, 11*(2), 7–30. DOI: 10.15678/EBER.2023.110201

Walczak, K., & Cellary, W. (2023). Challenges for higher education in the era of widespread access to Generative AI. *Economics and Business Review, 9*(2), 71–100. DOI: 10.18559/ebr.2023.2.743

Wang, S. (2023). Factors related to user perceptions of artificial intelligence (AI)-based content moderation on social media. *Computers in Human Behavior, 149*, 107971. DOI: 10.1016/j.chb.2023.107971

Wang, X. S., & Zheng, J. (2024). Can Banning AI-generated Content Save User-Generated Q&A Platforms? *Jinyang, Can Banning AI-generated Content Save User-Generated Q&A Platforms.*

Wang, Y. (2023). Synthetic realities in the digital age: Navigating the opportunities and challenges of ai-generated content. *Authorea Preprints.*

Wu, T. (2019). Will artificial intelligence eat the law? The rise of hybrid social-ordering systems. *Columbia Law Review, 119*(7), 2001–2028.

Xuan, G. (2023). Risks And Regulatory Framework of AI-Generated Content (AIGC) in the Judicial Field. *Journal of Education. Humanities and Social Sciences, 19*, 278–282.

Zhang, M., Xu, Y., & Wei, X. (2024). AI-centered vs. Human-centered: Exploring Users' Attitude toward AIGC in Varying Forms of Human-AI Collaboration.

Zhang, Y., Yang, X., Xu, X., Gao, Z., Huang, Y., Mu, S., Feng, S., Wang, D., Zhang, Y., & Song, K. (2024). Affective Computing in the Era of Large Language Models: A Survey from the NLP Perspective. *arXiv preprint arXiv:2408.04638*.

Zhou, J., Zhang, Y., Luo, Q., Parker, A. G., & De Choudhury, M. (2023). Synthetic lies: Understanding ai-generated misinformation and evaluating algorithmic and human solutions. *Proceedings of the 2023 CHI Conference on Human Factors in Computing Systems*.

Zhu, W. (2022). *NLP measures for cyber environment safety: Detection, mitigation and intervention*. University of Illinois at Urbana-Champaign.

Chapter 7
Leveraging AI Applications to Combat Misinformation:
A Comparative Analysis of University Students in Malaysia and Egypt

Sharon Wilson
https://orcid.org/0000-0002-9030-386X
Universiti Tunku Abdul Rahman, Malaysia

George Latif Zaki Sedhom
https://orcid.org/0000-0001-7560-3891
Galala University, Egypt

ABSTRACT

Misinformation poses a significant challenge in the digital age, affecting public opinion and societal trust. The advent of artificial intelligence (AI) provides promising solutions for identifying, countering, and preventing the spread of false information. This study investigates the effectiveness and perceptions of AI applications in combating misinformation among students from two universities with distinct socio-cultural backgrounds. Our research objectives are threefold: to assess the awareness and understanding of AI tools among university students, to evaluate the effectiveness of specific AI applications in identifying and reducing misinformation, and to compare the perceptions and attitudes towards these AI tools among students from both countries. This exploratory study employed a survey method of (n=80) student. This study contributes to the understanding of how AI can be effectively

DOI: 10.4018/979-8-3373-0335-2.ch007

deployed to combat misinformation and provides insights for educators, policymakers, and technology developers on enhancing the adoption and trust in AI solutions across diverse educational settings.

INTRODUCTION

Artificial Intelligence (AI) is becoming increasingly integral to modern society, with significant implications for education, employment, and daily life. AI literacy, which includes understanding AI concepts, applications, and impacts, is essential for students to navigate and thrive in this evolving landscape. This study aims to compare AI literacy among students in Malaysia and Egypt, focusing on their knowledge, perceptions, and attitudes towards AI. Artificial Intelligence (AI) plays a dual role in the realm of misinformation, acting as both a tool for its creation and dissemination, as well as a means to combat it. AI technologies, such as deepfakes and content generation, can be exploited to spread false information (Luchko, 2023; Xu et al., 2023). However, AI also offers powerful solutions for detecting and countering misinformation through pattern recognition and fact-checking algorithms (Luchko, 2023; Tomassi et al., 2024). The rise of Artificial Intelligence Generated Content (AIGC) presents new challenges in identifying and mitigating misinformation, requiring innovative approaches to detection (Xu et al., 2023). Implementing AI-supported methods for combating disinformation faces epistemic and ethical challenges, including defining disinformation and navigating the ethical risks of countermeasures (Lange & Lechterman, 2021). To address these issues, strategies such as improving digital literacy and promoting critical thinking among social media users are proposed (Tomassi et al., 2024).

AI IN MALAYSIA AND EGYPT

The use of artificial intelligence (AI) in Malaysian media is a rapidly evolving phenomenon, impacting various aspects of news production, distribution, and audience engagement. This essay explores the current landscape of AI utilization in Malaysian media, drawing insights from newspaper articles, government documents, and academic journals.

AI is increasingly being integrated into Malaysian media workflows, with newsrooms leveraging AI-powered tools for tasks such as content generation, data analysis, and audience targeting. According to a report by the Malaysian Communications and Multimedia Commission (MCMC), AI is seen as a transformative technology that can enhance the competitiveness of the media industry in Malaysia. Newspapers like *The Star* and *New Straits Times* have started using AI to automate certain news writing processes, such as generating sports reports or financial news updates. This allows journalists to focus on more in-depth and investigative reporting, while AI handles routine tasks efficiently. However, concerns have been raised about the potential bias in AI algorithms, which could lead to the perpetuation of stereotypes or discrimination in news reporting. There are also concerns about the impact of AI on jobs in the media industry, with fears that automation could lead to job losses among journalists and other media professionals.

The use of artificial intelligence in Malaysian media is a trend that is likely to continue growing in the coming years. While AI offers numerous benefits in terms of efficiency, audience engagement, and fact-checking, it also presents challenges in terms of bias, job displacement, and ethical considerations. It is crucial for Malaysian media organizations to carefully navigate these challenges and ensure that AI is used responsibly and ethically to enhance the quality and credibility of news content.

A range of studies have explored the use of AI in journalism, with a focus on its benefits and concerns. Yasin (2021) and Aissani (2023) both highlight the potential of AI to enhance the quality of work and transform traditional journalism, but also raise concerns about deepfake news, bias, job displacement, transparency, and ethics. Kothari (2021) and Noain Sánchez, A. (2022) call for further research into the use of AI in newsrooms, particularly in African and Spanish contexts, and identify a need for more comprehensive theoretical frameworks and methodological approaches. They emphasized the need for transparency and the balancing of algorithms with editorial and ethical parameters. While AI has the potential to improve journalism, its use must be carefully managed to ensure the integrity and trustworthiness of the content. These studies collectively underscore the need for a balanced approach to the use of AI in journalism, one that maximizes its potential while addressing its potential pitfalls.

In recent years, there have been significant changes in the media industry including journalism related to advances of information and communication technology (Jamil 2021). In developed countries, newsrooms are bracing for the impending surge in AI-supported data journalism (Goni & Tabassum, 2020), More and more we are hearing of AI in newsrooms when it used to be just stories about the innovation sides. Using AI helps in robot and machine handling of tasks, diminishing the role of humans necessarily (Huang & Rust 2021). AI is revolutionizing the world of journalism where it changes how news is collected, edited and delivered. That means robots can produce real news stories — and AI algorithms transform complex information into simpler news pieces for the general public. It can convert data as well as long form to turn them into sentences written like human journalists and is programmed on a software known as WordSmith (Guanah et al., 2020). The rise of AI technologies has signaled a revolution in the types of journalistic labor performed (Tejedor & Vila, 2021). While journalists are clearly better off with this automation, incorporating such tools into newsrooms remains difficult. There is a panic sweeping the globe where people came to realization that AI can theoretically write articles from scratch and replace human journalists in the process of completing simple tasks, as revealed by several studies. Scholarly discussions about the influence of AI on human journalistic creativity raise also ethical and professional dilemmas (see, for example Hossain 2021; Abdulmajeed & Fahmy 2023).

Traditionally, the conventional journalist's work was to produce news from a specific place where something important had taken place. Indeed, the user generated content and social media platforms are gaining popularity, which has led to the evolution of the conventional practice of seeking information and news gathering from the official sources only. For one, the digital revolution pushed media organizations to experiment with new ways of news presentation. In the context of shifting media landscape, the journalists as news producers still remain under an eternal "construction" challenges though predicaments witnessed by journalist on the shift from traditional ways of making news into digital conforms impressionable standards of best practices. Most importantly, the emerging shift in the working culture within the news industry has surely transformed the business model making use of the functions of the journalists who are content creators. In order to hold the audience interest and make search engines and other social media use their content, investments and returns on investments are affecting the news ecology.

In the same manner, the incorporation of Twitter within the Newsroom has altered the gatekeeping function and it can be anticipated that, the new technology is changing the professional communication practices of journalists and other assessments in order to perform better in the journalism.

Where a journalist can create an integrated blend of the written word, images, audio, and video with other forms of digital information, curation and distribution of news on Twitter become increasingly engaging to today's audience, enabled by the latest leaps in technology. Innovative seekers "actively seek knowledge of new technologies which, in turn increases their knowledge of how the technology works, leading them to perceive its use as less burdensome." The concept of MOJO allows the journalists to do several jobs all at once: reporting, writing, photographing and editing of news stories as a single person a task that was traditionally done by a news team (Blankenship 2016). Apart from the skills, Lee, Lindsey and Kim, 2017 have argued that routine newsroom activities needed one to get accustomed to social media use especially by the journalists of all stages. Similarly, it was found by Wu, 2019, that in their 20's and 30's journalists want to get themselves trained to adapt to social media and interest in social networking is higher as compared to the senior journalists who ignored the usage of social media in daily work.

Wu claims that senior journalists are content with their jobs as professional journalists, but the acquisition and mastering of new skills are not an easy task since they rarely use new media in their daily activities. The decentralization of media has resulted in an increasingly discriminating audience in terms of their news selection; an audience which has nowadays become a key factor in newsgathering and news processing processes of the news industry, both nationally and internationally. Normah et al. (2017) suggested that modern media consumers have entered an era in which they are no longer passive watchers due to the myriad of choices offered by continuous advancement within technology. This also meets the changing needs of audiences that tend to look for creativity in news that comes through social media, apart from being the fastest source of breaking news and offering the broadest range of options in several dimensions. Thus, the challenge is in finding the best, most influential, innovative, and creative ways of storytelling to secure continued interaction with media users. Traditional media, such as newspaper publishing divisions and television networks, face a number of challenges today as they seek to adapt to the changing nature of their activities and investments in the digital sphere for the purpose of viability and importantly in response to changing community needs. Consequently, in response to the evolving behavior of media consumers, news organizations utilize Twitter as a platform for news distribution, story promotion, and client acquisition. Conversely, journalists employ it as a means to identify and connect with sources (Hanusch & Bruns, 2017).

Wu expressed the view that veteran journalists will find satisfaction when roles played and assigned align them with conventional modes of doing journalism; however, learning new competencies and being flexible is challenging and minimal engagement in new media in everyday tasks. Decentralization of media has created a segment of audiences that are very selective in choosing any news, which has become critical in the routines of newsgathering and news processing in news industries both locally and internationally. Normah et al. (2017) assert that contemporary media consumers have entered an era in which they are no longer mere 'passive watchers' of media, owing to the plethora of options afforded by evolving technologies. This would satisfy the growing needs of viewers who tend to look for new things in news presented through social media, as well as be the fastest way to show what is happening, and a range of choices from different views. Therefore, a challenge remains: how to put up narratives in the most efficient, impactful, inventive, and imaginative ways to stay engaged with media consumers. The print newspaper industry and television broadcasting companies face many challenges in trying to re align business models and investments into the digital world in order to sustain themselves and more importantly remain relevant for the changing needs of the consumers. News producers, therefore, make use of Twitter by releasing news, stories, as well as securing new customers to keep up with the up and coming trends with media audiences. This system allows journalists to locate sources and reach out to them.

A number of studies have pointed out the flexibility in using other digital and social media tools to disseminate news, such as Hanusch and Bruns (2017), McGregor (2019), and Brandtzaeg, Følstad, & Chaparro (2018). The use of social media reveals lots of aspects: it shows the view of the journalists towards technology, readiness regarding the new role assigned to them, and the role of news organizations in facilitating the adoption of social media within routine reporting by journalists. These have been highlighted as the key routes through which the journalists can keep themselves updated regarding various news and ongoing social phenomena. Also, it was put that more news agencies are now embracing social media as a new means for information collection, reporting, as well as for disseminating newsflash. As campus journalism in the ASEAN region increasingly becomes a witness to changes brought about by AI-powered content creation, so also does the need for ethical guidelines and regulations on responsible AI adoption in journalism grow. For example, Santos (2017) showed that AI tools could enable student journalists in the Philippines to build data-driven stories pertinent to local audiences, find meaning in telling their stories, and give meaning to the larger media ecology.

Specifically in Malaysia, Tan et al. (2022) conducted a study on how audiences perceive AI-generated news content and its impact on reader engagement. This research underscores the importance of understanding reader preferences and receptivity toward AI-created content, while also raising concerns about credibility and trust in AI-generated news. Similarly, studies in other ASEAN countries such as Cambodia (Cheng et al., 2019) and Myanmar (Aung et al., 2021) have examined issues like bias in AI-generated content and the potential for misinformation.

In Egypt, Artificial Intelligence (AI) is increasingly integrated into journalism, offering benefits like improved efficiency and data reporting, but also raising ethical concerns and challenges (Amponsah & Atianashie, 2024). Egyptian journalists recognize AI's importance in journalistic work but perceive negative effects on news quality and media coverage (Habib, M. R., 2023). AI tools like ChatGPT and Bard can assist with tasks such as language translation and data scraping, but concerns exist about accuracy and data hallucination (Dhiman, 2023). Media coverage of AI in journalism reveals a tension between industry hopes and professional pitfalls, highlighting the need to assess AI's role in news-making within the economic and contextual complexity of journalism (Moran & Shaikh, 2022). While AI offers potential benefits, challenges include understanding human emotions, addressing biases, and maintaining ethical standards. Recommendations include training journalists, developing ethical guidelines, and adopting a balanced approach to AI integration in newsrooms (Habib, M. R., 2023; Amponsah & Atianashie, 2024).

The role of artificial intelligence in tackling misinformation comes with a set of intricate challenges, particularly in the realms of ethics, human psychology, and regional digital inequalities. Ethical dilemmas stem from the potential biases in AI systems, the risk of suppressing free speech, and the need for greater transparency in algorithmic decision-making, particularly in politically charged settings like Malaysia and Egypt. Human psychology also plays a crucial role, as individuals tend to believe information that aligns with their existing views, making misinformation difficult to counteract. This has been evident in Malaysia, where misleading narratives have influenced political discourse, and in Egypt, where misinformation has been used to manipulate nationalistic sentiments. Additionally, disparities in digital accessibility create barriers to effective AI-driven misinformation control, as rural communities and economically disadvantaged groups often lack the technological resources to verify information.

Effectively addressing these concerns requires a deeper cultural insight into the unique misinformation patterns prevalent in Malaysia and Egypt, where factors like religion, ethnicity, and politics heavily influence the spread of false narratives. AI tools that are predominantly trained on Western data struggle to navigate these complex regional contexts, leading to unintended biases in content moderation. Several initiatives demonstrate practical applications of AI in misinformation detection, such as Malaysia's SEBENARNYA.MY platform and Egypt's AI-powered tools like SAHEEH.NEWS, AKHBARMETER.ORG, DABEGAD.COM for detecting propaganda and fake news that are also created using AI . However, AI alone is insufficient, as it faces challenges in distinguishing between satire, genuine content, and maliciously altered media, such as deepfakes. This underscores the importance of combining AI moderation with human oversight. Collaboration between governments, tech companies, and civil society has shown promise, as seen in Malaysia's partnership with social media platforms to curb misinformation during the COVID-19 pandemic and Egypt's academic efforts in building Arabic-language AI models for better accuracy, and the efforts of the Egyptian higher council of Journalism to design models and web based apps to detect fake news and AI biased narratives.

For AI-based misinformation detection to be truly effective, there must be clear standards to assess its success, including measures such as accuracy rates, false detection percentages, and public trust evaluations. Advances in artificial intelligence, particularly in natural language processing and adaptive learning, are enhancing real-time misinformation detection. Furthermore, global policy discussions, such as those led by UNESCO and the World Economic Forum, emphasize the importance of establishing regulations that ensure ethical AI usage. Malaysia's Anti-Fake News Act 2018 and Egypt's Anti-Cyber and Information Technology Crimes, (2018) showcase differing approaches to regulating misinformation, highlighting the need for policies that balance the fight against false information with the preservation of free speech. By implementing these considerations, AI-driven misinformation control can become more precise, culturally aware, and ethically responsible.

PERCEPTION OF AI USAGE AMONG STUDENTS

Recent studies have explored university students' awareness and understanding of artificial intelligence (AI). Research indicates that while most students show a fundamental understanding of AI, there is significant variance in AI literacy levels (Hornberger et al., 2023). Students with technical backgrounds or prior AI experience tend to have higher AI literacy (Hornberger et al., 2023; Lee et al., 2024). Many students express interest in learning about AI, but educational barriers may hinder their ability to effectively engage with the technology (Lee et al., 2024). Prior software education, particularly during K-12 schooling, appears to enhance students' AI knowledge and skills (Lee et al., 2024). While students generally demonstrate good AI awareness levels, their understanding of concepts like mind and intelligence may be insufficient (Dergunova et al., 2022). Students recognize the importance of technology in education and believe AI tools can facilitate teaching. However, concerns exist about AI's potential impact on employment (Dergunova et al., 2022). These findings highlight the need for effective AI courses tailored to diverse student populations. Recent studies in Egypt have explored the acceptance and attitudes of Egyptian students towards artificial intelligence (AI) in education. Research on higher education students found significant impacts of performance expectancy, effort expectancy, and social influence on intentions to accept chatbot technology, though demographic factors did not moderate these relationships (Mohamed A. Ragheb et al., 2022). Another study revealed positive attitudes among media students towards using AI applications in education, with a high percentage of students familiar with AI terminology (Al-Halfawy et.al, 2023). Similarly, medical students at Ain Shams University demonstrated moderate to good knowledge and attitudes regarding AI in medical education and practice. Over 80% of these students emphasized the need to integrate AI education into medical curricula, and more than 85% showed enthusiasm for learning about AI applications in medicine (A. Khater et al., 2023). These findings highlight the growing acceptance and interest in AI among Egyptian students across various disciplines.

It was found that students show positive attitudes towards AI tools, appreciating their accessibility, adaptability, and benefits for tasks like grammar checking and essay outlining (Phan, 2023; Malik et al., 2023). AI tools are seen to enhance productivity, personalize learning, and improve linguistic capabilities (Zhou et al., 2024). However, concerns exist regarding academic integrity, over-reliance on AI, and potential impacts on creativity and critical thinking (Malik et al., 2023; Zhou et al., 2024). Factors influencing perceptions include gender, degree level, and prior AI knowledge, with male students and those with higher AI knowledge generally showing more positive attitudes (Daher & Hussein, 2024). While students express high intention to use AI tools, their perceptions of efficiency, interaction, and affect are moderate (Daher & Hussein, 2024). These findings highlight the need for balanced integration of AI in higher education

AI AND MISINFORMATION

Recent research has explored various AI applications for identifying and reducing misinformation. Personalized AI systems can learn from individual user assessments to predict content accuracy, potentially influencing user judgment over time (Jahanbakhsh et al., 2023). Studies have also examined AI-generated misinformation, revealing linguistic differences from human-created content and challenges for existing detection models (Zhou et al., 2023). Comparative analyses of AI-based fact-checking solutions have shown varying levels of comprehensiveness and accuracy, with some highly-discussed systems performing poorly (Školkay & Filin, 2019). Convolutional Neural Network approaches, such as CAMI, have demonstrated effectiveness in misinformation identification and early detection by extracting key features and shaping high-level interactions among them (Yu et al., 2017). These studies highlight the potential of AI in combating misinformation while also revealing limitations and areas for improvement in current systems. Recent research highlights the potential of AI in combating misinformation while acknowledging its dual nature as both a tool and a challenge. Large Language Models (LLMs) offer opportunities for fighting misinformation due to their knowledge and reasoning abilities, but they can also generate deceptive content at scale (Chen & Shu, 2023). The rise of Artificial Intelligence Generated Content (AIGC) presents new challenges in detecting misinformation, necessitating examination of manipulation traces at various levels (Xu et al., 2023). Combining AI with media literacy education is proposed as a potential solution to mitigate the influence of false information (Washington, 2023). Additionally, blockchain technology, when integrated with AI, could provide tamper-proof evidence of content authenticity and transparent utility of fake news detection models (Seneviratne, 2022). These studies emphasize the need for interdisciplinary efforts and innovative approaches to address the evolving landscape of misinformation in the digital age.

AI technologies are increasingly recognized as powerful tools in the fight against misinformation and disinformation. While AI has been used to create misleading content, it also offers several critical advantages for detecting and mitigating false information. AI algorithms can be trained to identify specific linguistic cues and emotional language often associated with disinformation. Techniques like sentiment analysis help flag content that may be manipulative or misleading (*AstroAwani*, 2024). AI can automate the fact-checking process by cross-referencing claims with credible sources and established knowledge bases. This capability allows for rapid identification of potentially false statements and can track how information disseminates across social media platforms, identifying suspicious patterns that may indicate disinformation campaigns. This enables early detection and intervention strategies (*AstroAwani*, 2024; Li and Callegari, 2024).

Combating misinformation effectively requires a multi-faceted approach. Collaboration between technology and human oversight is essential. Users, journalists, and content moderators play a vital role in reporting and verifying information, which can help refine AI detection tools (Meyers and Feerrar, 2024; Flemming, 2024). Industry initiatives, such as watermarking and content authenticity projects, are also being developed to address concerns about disinformation while maintaining ethical standards (*The Chronicle of Higher Education*, 2024).

AI holds significant promise in the battle against misinformation, providing sophisticated tools for detection and analysis. However, its effectiveness hinges on ethical implementation, continuous adaptation to new disinformation tactics, and collaboration with human expertise. By leveraging AI responsibly, stakeholders can enhance the integrity of information in the digital landscape. Therefore this research questions the awareness and understanding of AI tools among university students, to evaluate the effectiveness of specific AI applications in identifying and reducing misinformation and to compare the perceptions and attitudes towards these AI tools between students.

THEORETICAL FRAMEWORK

The theoretical framework for this study is based on the AI Trust and Effectiveness Model (AITEM) (Mylrea & Robinson, 2023) which proposes that the perceived effectiveness of AI in combating misinformation is influenced by several interconnected factor the level of an individual's awareness and experience with misinformation affects their perception of AI's potential in combating it and greater familiarity with AI applications leads to more nuanced perceptions of AI's capabilities and limitations in misinformation detection. This model suggests that these factors interact to form an individual's overall perception of AI's effectiveness in combating misinformation. The balance of these elements determines the level of trust and perceived utility of AI applications in this domain. The AITEM can be used to predict and explain variations in public perception and acceptance of AI tools for misinformation detection and prevention. It also provides a framework for identifying areas of improvement in AI applications and public education efforts to enhance the effectiveness of AI in combating misinformation. A few of the items that the model focuses on include belief in AI's ability to provide accurate information, worries about potential biases in AI algorithms, the perceived need for human involvement alongside AI, perceived effectiveness, identification efficacy such as how well AI is thought to identify misinformation, how effective AI is perceived in preventing misinformation spread and user satisfaction with specific AI-based tools influences overall perceptions of AI effectiveness. The model also weighs the perceived advantages (e.g., rapid analysis, pattern detection) against disadvantages (e.g., context struggles, potential for misuse) shapes overall attitudes.

METHODOLOGY

This study employed a quantitative cross sectional survey design to assess the effectiveness of AI tools in identifying and preventing the spread of misinformation. The survey approach was chosen to collect data efficiently from students across two different cultural contexts, providing insights into their awareness, perceptions, and usage of AI tools. The sample consisted of 80 media students, with 40 students from Malaysia and 40 students from Egypt. These participants were selected through convenience sampling, targeting media students who were accessible and willing to participate. This approach ensured that students with relevant exposure to both media literacy and AI tools were included. To maintain balance, the sample size was equally divided between the two countries. Participants were undergraduate and postgraduate students, reflecting a typical university demographic as seen in Table 1.

Table 1. Sample demographics

Country Demographic Information		Egypt		Malaysia		Total	
		N	%	N	%	N	%
Gender	Male	23	28.8%	11	13.8%	34	42.5%
	Female	17	21.2%	29	36.2%	46	57.5%
Age	18-24	40	50.0%	40	50.0%	80	100.0%
Education level	Undergraduate	36	45.0%	38	47.5%	74	92.5%
	Postgraduate	4	5.0%	2	2.5%	6	7.5%
Total		40	50.0%	40	50.0%	80	100.0%

Data Collection Instrument

A structured survey questionnaire was used as the primary data collection instrument. The questionnaire included multiple choice and Likert scale questions focusing on:

1. Awareness and usage of AI tools
2. Effectiveness of AI in identifying and preventing misinformation
3. Trust and satisfaction with AI based tools
4. Challenges and limitations of AI systems

The questionnaire was administered online to ensure ease of access for participants in both countries. The survey was distributed to participants via email and messaging platforms, with each student completing the questionnaire independently. The data collection took place over a two-week period, ensuring enough time for participation from both Malaysian and Egyptian students. Participants were briefed on the study's objectives, and informed consent was obtained before they proceeded with the survey. The collected data were analyzed using descriptive statistics to summarize respondents' awareness, perceptions, and experiences with AI tools. Chi square tests were employed to identify statistically significant differences between the two student groups. Additionally, correlation analysis was conducted to explore relationships between trust, usage, and satisfaction with AI systems. This research adhered to ethical guidelines by ensuring participants' voluntary participation, anonymity, and confidentiality. All responses were anonymized, and participants had the right to withdraw from the study at any time. Institutional approval was obtained from both Malaysian and Egyptian universities to conduct the survey.

Analysis of Findings

Awareness and Understanding of AI Tools Among University Students

This section explores the research objective of assessing the awareness and understanding of AI tools among university students, based on the survey conducted in Egypt and Malaysia.

The findings indicate that a combined 40% of respondents are either very or somewhat familiar with AI tools used to combat misinformation. However, familiarity varies significantly between the two countries. The Egyptian respondents demonstrate higher familiarity, with 16.2% stating they are "very familiar," compared to only 2.5% of Malaysians. Malaysian respondents show more neutrality, with 26.2% expressing neither familiarity nor unfamiliarity.

This suggests that the exposure to or education about AI applications differs between the two countries. Egypt's higher familiarity could reflect better integration of AI related discussions or workshops, whereas Malaysia may benefit from targeted awareness campaigns. A significant 68.8% of respondents reported having used AI based tools to verify information. Mobile applications were the most utilized tool (61.8%), followed by browser extensions (54.5%). Social media platforms, however, exhibited notable disparity: only 12.7% of Egyptian respondents reported using them for AI based verification compared to 27.3% of Malaysians. This suggests students rely heavily on mobile and web integrated tools, but cross platform use is still limited. The gap in social media platform utilization may reflect differing cultural or technological environments between the two countries.

50% of the respondents expressed either strong or moderate trust in AI applications to provide accurate information. However, trust patterns differ between the two groups where the Egyptian respondents are more likely to report strong trust, while Malaysians lean toward neutral or somewhat distrustful attitudes. No respondents expressed strong distrust, indicating an overall willingness to engage with AI tools, albeit with some reservations. This variance highlights the need to foster greater trust in Malaysia through educational initiatives that emphasize AI's potential and limitations. A positive perception exists, with 90.1% of respondents agreeing that AI tools can identify misinformation effectively to some extent. Egyptians are more optimistic about AI's effectiveness, with more respondents rating it as "extremely effective" or "very effective." Malaysians, in contrast, predominantly see AI as "moderately effective," indicating cautious optimism but also a need for better demonstrations of AI's capabilities. The different levels of confidence highlight varying expectations, suggesting that promotional efforts should be tailored to match these perceptions. While many respondents are aware of AI applications, understanding remains limited. Only 22.5% reported actively educating themselves about misinformation detection using AI tools.

Students proposed enhancements such as AI's ability to understand context and nuance (43.8% of respondents), developing realtime misinformation tracking systems (42.5%) and cross referencing information across platforms to enhance trust (35%). These findings underline the importance of further refining AI tools to meet user expectations and improving educational programs to increase awareness and usage.

AI Effectiveness in Identifying Misinformation

This section evaluates the effectiveness of artificial intelligence (AI) in identifying misinformation based on the responses from university students in Egypt and Malaysia. The survey reveals that 90.1% of respondents believe AI can identify misinformation effectively to varying degrees. This positive perception highlights an optimistic view of AI's potential in mitigating false information where 12.5% rated AI as "extremely effective." 28.8% found AI "very effective." 48.8% judged AI to be "moderately effective." Egyptian respondents displayed more confidence in AI's efficacy, with higher proportions selecting "extremely" and "very effective." In contrast, Malaysian students were more likely to assess AI as "moderately effective." This divergence suggests a difference in technological engagement, awareness, or expectations. A notable 45% of respondents expressed concern that AI tools lack the ability to understand the context of misinformation, which is critical for distinguishing between deliberate misinformation and satire or misinterpretations. 37.5% of respondents indicated that overreliance on AI might reduce human critical thinking, emphasizing the importance of human oversight in the process. While 22.5% worried that AI systems could perpetuate biases from their training data, with Malaysian students reporting higher levels of concern than their Egyptian peers. In terms of trust levels, it was found that 12.5% of respondents stated that they "strongly trust" AI driven tools for accuracy while 37.5% "somewhat trust" these applications, indicating a cautious optimism. However, 36.2% remained neutral, reflecting the need for further evidence of AI reliability to build stronger trust. The findings suggest that while students are generally open to using AI for misinformation detection, many remain skeptical of its performance, pointing to the need for improvement and transparency in AI systems.

Respondents (58.8%) also identified fact checking algorithms as the most effective AI tool for combating misinformation. This aligns with the preference for tools that offer direct validation against trusted sources. Social media monitoring tools were more popular among Malaysian respondents (25%) compared to Egyptian respondents (6.2%), likely reflecting differing patterns of misinformation exposure. Meanwhile Natural Language Processing (NLP) models were considered effective by 45% of respondents, showing recognition of AI's role in understanding language. 43.8% valued image and video verification tools, demonstrating awareness of the need for multimodal verification capabilities. Nearly half (48.7%) of the participants reported being satisfied or very satisfied with the AI tools they used. Notably, Egyptian respondents reported higher satisfaction levels compared to Malaysian respondents, who were more likely to express neutrality (35%). No respondents expressed dissatisfaction with AI tools, suggesting a generally positive or neutral experience.

AI Effectiveness in Preventing the Spread of Misinformation

This section evaluates the effectiveness of AI in preventing the spread of misinformation based on survey data from university students in Egypt and Malaysia. 55% of respondents rated AI as "moderately effective," indicating a belief that AI can partially contain the spread of misinformation but with limitations. 20% of the sample considered AI to be "very effective," while 5% rated it as "extremely effective." The remaining 18.8% found AI "slightly effective," with only 1.2% saying it was "not effective at all." This distribution suggests that students recognize AI's potential but believe it is not yet optimized to prevent misinformation fully. The high percentage of "moderately effective" responses reflects cautious optimism toward AI's capabilities. Egyptian students were more likely to rate AI as "very" or "extremely effective." This aligns with their generally higher confidence in AI observed throughout the study. Malaysian respondents leaned toward "moderately effective," indicating a more reserved perspective on AI's performance. The differing views may reflect variations in exposure to misinformation or the maturity of AI initiatives in each country. 45% of respondents expressed concern that AI tools struggle with contextual interpretation, a key challenge for misinformation prevention. AI's difficulty in distinguishing satire from harmful misinformation is a significant hurdle in content moderation. 32.5% of respondents were concerned that AI could inadvertently censor legitimate content. This suggests skepticism about AI's ability to strike a balance between curbing false information and protecting freedom of speech. Interestingly, 46.2% of respondents expressed concern that AI could be misused to create more sophisticated misinformation, reflecting awareness that AI itself could contribute to the problem it aims to solve. 71.2% of respondents agreed that AI tools should be used alongside human judgment to enhance effectiveness. This suggests that while AI plays a crucial role, it is not seen as sufficient on its own. Malaysian respondents expressed higher confidence in tools such as social media monitoring and factchecking algorithms, which are key components in preventing the viral spread of false information. Egyptian respondents, while also supportive, were more balanced in their trust toward different types of AI tools. 68.8% of respondents reported using AI based tools such as mobile applications and browser extensions for information verification. This indicates that students actively engage with AI systems to identify and stop misinformation from spreading. 61.8% of participants reported using mobile apps to verify information, reflecting the importance of accessible, onthego solutions in combating misinformation. Nearly half (48.7%) of respondents were either satisfied or very satisfied with the performance of AI tools in preventing misinformation spread. However, 51.2% expressed neutrality, suggesting that while AI tools are generally functional, improvements are still needed to enhance user experience. Egyptian respondents were more likely to express satisfaction with the AI tools they used, whereas Malaysian respondents maintained a more neutral stance. This discrepancy points to differing expectations or experiences with AI in both countries.

CONCLUSION

The findings suggest that university students possess a foundational awareness of AI tools, though gaps in understanding and trust remain. Egyptian students demonstrate higher familiarity and trust in AI applications, while Malaysian students express more neutral attitudes, signalling the need for more education and engagement in the latter. Both groups recognize AI's potential to combat misinformation but emphasize the importance of integrating human oversight to mitigate risks like bias and misuse. Targeted initiatives focusing on enhancing AI literacy, promoting cross platform verification, and building trust in AI tools could significantly improve students' understanding and usage of these applications. The findings show that students in both Egypt and Malaysia believe AI can be effective in identifying misinformation, though the level of confidence and trust varies between the two countries. Egyptian respondents generally exhibit higher confidence in AI, while Malaysian respondents adopt a more measured perspective. Despite these differences, there is widespread agreement that AI tools are valuable, especially when combined with human oversight.

There is a strong demand to enhance AI's ability to interpret nuanced language and detect subtle forms of misinformation at the same time addressing concerns about bias in AI systems will be critical to building trust as AI tools continue to evolve to function effectively across different platforms, including social media. These insights suggest that AI has the potential to become a cornerstone in combating misinformation, but ongoing development and better user education are essential to maximize its effectiveness.

DISCUSSION

The findings indicate that students acknowledge AI's role in preventing the spread of misinformation but see room for improvement. While most respondents view AI as moderately effective, they also highlight key challenges, including AI's struggle with nuance, the potential for misuse, and concerns about over censorship. Both countries agree on the importance of combining AI tools with human oversight to enhance effectiveness. Moving forward, efforts should focus on improving AI's ability to understand context and prevent unintended censorship. Additionally, fostering greater trust through transparency and better performance of AI tools will be critical in enhancing their role in misinformation prevention. This study evaluated the awareness, usage, and perceived effectiveness of AI tools in identifying and preventing the spread of misinformation among university students in Egypt and Malaysia. The findings reveal nuanced insights into students' interactions with AI-based tools, highlighting both the strengths and limitations of these technologies. The data demonstrates that a large majority (90.1%) of respondents believe AI is capable of identifying misinformation to some degree, though many (48.8%) perceive this capability as only moderately effective. This aligns with existing literature that emphasizes the potential of AI for rapid detection but acknowledges its limited ability to capture context and nuanced content (Akhtar et al., 2023). The findings also reveal variations between countries: Egyptian students generally express higher confidence in AI, with more respondents rating it as "extremely" or "very effective," compared to Malaysians who lean towards moderate evaluations. These differences likely reflect variations in exposure to technological tools, media literacy, and misinformation patterns in each context. Despite the optimism, respondents highlighted several limitations, such as AI's inability to interpret context accurately (45%) and the potential for over censorship (32.5%). This aligns with concerns from scholars that AI driven systems may struggle with complex content, such as satire or emotionally charged misinformation (OECD, 2024). Additionally, the fear that AI could inadvertently generate more convincing misinformation (46.2%) underscores the double-edged nature of these technologies. These concerns reflect the importance of improving AI models while integrating them with human oversight to mitigate risks associated with bias and false positives. While 55% of respondents viewed AI as moderately effective in preventing the spread of misinformation, the reliance on AI tools alone was not seen as sufficient. A significant 71.2% of participants stressed the importance of combining AI with human oversight. This preference supports existing frameworks advocating for hybrid approaches to misinformation management, where AI tools assist but do not replace human judgment (OECD, 2024). The greater trust in factchecking algorithms and social media monitoring tools—especially among Malaysians—indicates that students are aware of the tools available, though further improvement in these systems' reliability is needed. The findings reveal a cautious optimism toward AI tools, with 50% of respondents indicating some level of trust in AI for providing accurate information. However, trust varied by country, with Egyptians expressing stronger trust and satisfaction compared to Malaysians, who showed more neutral attitudes. This disparity suggests that cultural and technological factors influence perceptions of AI's credibility. Despite these differences, no respondents expressed strong distrust in AI tools, indicating that students are generally open to using them, provided they meet expectations. Furthermore, while nearly half of the respondents (48.7%) were satisfied with AI tools, the high percentage of neutral responses (51.2%) signals an opportunity to enhance user experiences. The study found that mobile applications (61.8%) and browser extensions (54.5%) were the most commonly used AI tools for misinformation management, underscoring the importance of easily accessible, integrated solutions. The relatively low use of social media platforms for AI based verification among

Egyptians (12.7%) compared to Malaysians (27.3%) points to differing patterns in digital behavior and engagement. The findings also highlight that while students are actively engaging with these tools, many still perceive gaps in AI's ability to prevent misinformation from spreading effectively.

CONCLUSION

This study contributes to the understanding of AI's role in combating misinformation by offering empirical insights into students' awareness, trust, and satisfaction with AI tools in Egypt and Malaysia. The findings suggest that while AI is recognized as a valuable tool for identifying and managing misinformation, its effectiveness remains limited by challenges such as context interpretation, potential biases, and the risk of misuse. Additionally, differences in perceptions between Egyptian and Malaysian students highlight the need for tailored strategies that address the specific cultural and technological environments of each country. The research underscores the importance of hybrid models that combine AI with human oversight to enhance the effectiveness and reliability of misinformation management efforts. There is also a need for further education and awareness campaigns to build students' trust in AI tools and encourage their use. Improvements in AI algorithms, especially in areas like contextual analysis and bias mitigation, will be critical to increasing the tools' impact.

Future research should explore the long term effectiveness of AI tools in real-world misinformation scenarios and assess how improvements in AI design influence trust and adoption among students. As AI technologies continue to evolve, their role in combating misinformation will become even more crucial, provided that ethical considerations, transparency, and user education remain central to their development and deployment.

This study provides a foundation for policymakers, educators, and developers to design more effective AI based solutions that align with the needs and expectations of users in diverse cultural settings. With careful implementation, AI has the potential to become an essential tool in the fight against misinformation, ensuring that it supports rather than replaces human decision making processes.

This study evaluated the effectiveness of AI tools in identifying and preventing the spread of misinformation among university students in Egypt and Malaysia. The findings highlight that while most students believe AI can identify misinformation, many see it as only moderately effective. Egyptian students expressed more confidence in AI than their Malaysian counterparts, suggesting cultural or technological differences in engagement.

Key challenges include AI's struggle with understanding context and the risk of over censorship. Additionally, concerns that AI could generate more convincing misinformation reflect the dual risks posed by these tools. These insights emphasize the need to refine AI's capabilities and incorporate human oversight, a solution supported by the respondents. Respondents emphasized that AI alone is insufficient. Greater trust should be placed in fact checking algorithms and social media monitoring tools. Although 50% of participants expressed some trust in AI, the prevalence of neutral responses signals room for improvement in AI performance and user experience. The study also revealed that mobile applications and browser extensions are the most commonly used tools, reflecting a preference for accessible platforms. While engagement with AI tools is high.

In conclusion, AI shows potential in combating misinformation, but challenges remain, particularly in interpreting nuanced content and avoiding misuse. A hybrid approach combining AI with human oversight is essential for maximizing effectiveness. To improve trust and adoption, further education and improvements in AI algorithms are needed. Policymakers and developers should tailor solutions to fit the needs of diverse cultural contexts, ensuring AI serves as a complement to, not a replacement for, human judgment.

LIMITATIONS

The study employed convenience sampling, which may limit the generalizability of the findings. Additionally, the reliance on self-reported data introduces the possibility of response bias. Future research could explore larger and more diverse samples to validate the findings further.

REFERENCES

Abdul, K. L., & Tan, M. N. (2018). Overcoming barriers to AI adoption in Mindanao campus journalism. *Journal of Communication Technology*, *5*(1), 34–48.

Abdulmajeed, M., & Fahmy, N. (2022, May). Meta-analysis of AI research in journalism: Challenges, opportunities and future research agenda for Arab journalism. In *European, Asian, Middle Eastern,North African Conference on Management & Information Systems* (pp. 213-225). Cham: Springer International Publishing.

Aissani, R., Abdallah, R. A. Q., Taha, S., & Al Adwan, M. N. (2023, June). Artificial Intelligence Tools in media and journalism: Roles and concerns. In *2023 International Conference on Multimedia Computing, Networking and Applications (MCNA)* (pp. 19-26). IEEE. DOI: 10.1109/MCNA59361.2023.10185738

Aung, Z. M., Kyaw, T. Z., & Htay, T. (2021). Unpacking the ethics of AI-generated content in Myanmar campus journalism. *Media Ethics in Southeast Asia*, *10*(4), 234–250.

Awani, A. (2024) How AI can help us spot its own fakes. https://www.astroawani.com/berita-dunia/how-ai-can-help-us-spot-its-own-fakes-473818

Al-Halfawy, Aya, Ibrahim, Al-Ashry, & Walid, Mahmoud Hatab, Abdel-Hakam, ... & Amal. (2023). Trends of media students in Egyptian universities towards the use of artificial intelligence applications in the educational process. *Scientific Journal of Specific Educational Sciences*, *18*(18), 1013–1038.

Blankenship, J. C. (2016). *Solo journalism and news routines: Using the hierarchical influences model to study the organizational and individual influences of solo journalism in local television news* (Doctoral dissertation, The University of North Carolina at Chapel Hill).

Brandtzaeg, P. B., Følstad, A., & Chaparro Domínguez, M. Á. (2018). How journalists and social media users perceive online fact-checking and verification services. *Journalism Practice*, *12*(9), 1109–1129. DOI: 10.1080/17512786.2017.1363657

Cheng, S., Kim, S., & Pheng, L. S. (2019). Ethical considerations of AI in Cambodian journalism. *Ethics in Media Communication*, *26*(3), 201–215.

Flemming, M. (2024) How Can We Tackle AI-Fueled Misinformation and Disinformation in Public Health? https://www.bu.edu/ceid/2024/04/25/how-can-we-tackle-ai-fueled-misinformation-and-disinformation-in-public-health/

Gomez, H. I., & Rodriguez, J. M. (2020). Enhancing engagement through AI-driven chatbots: A study in Visayas campus journalism. *Journal of Interactive Media, 15*(3), 112–129.

Goni, A., & Tabassum, M. (2020). Artificial Intelligence (AI) in journalism: Is Bangladesh ready for it? A study on journalism students in Bangladesh. *Athens Journal of Mass Media and Communications, 6*(4), 209–228. DOI: 10.30958/ajmmc.6-4-1

Guanah, J. S., Agbanu, V. N., & Obi, I. (2020). Artificial intelligence and journalism practice in Nigeria: Perception of journalists in Benin City, Edo State. *International review of humanities. Studies, 5*(2), 16.

Habib, M. R. (2023). The role of social media in shaping the social capital of the new republic in light of the global challenges. *The Egyptian Journal of Media Research, 2023*(82), 383–432.

Hanusch, F., & Bruns, A. (2017). Journalistic branding on Twitter: A representative study of Australian journalists' profile descriptions. *Digital Journalism (Abingdon, England), 5*(1), 26–43. DOI: 10.1080/21670811.2016.1152161

Hossain, L. (2021). *The extent to which Jordanian journalists are aware of the concept of robot journalism and its professional and ethical challenges.* Jordan Publishing Media Institute.

Huang, M. H., & Rust, R. T. (2021). A strategic framework for artificial intelligence in marketing. *Journal of the Academy of Marketing Science, 49*(1), 30–50. DOI: 10.1007/s11747-020-00749-9

Jamil, S. (2021). Artificial intelligence and journalistic practice: The crossroads of obstacles and opportunities for the Pakistani journalists. *Journalism Practice, 15*(10), 1400–1422. DOI: 10.1080/17512786.2020.1788412

John Den Saul, L. D., & Enciso, R. E. Exploring the Impact of Artificial Intelligence on Campus Journalism: A.

Kothari, A., & Cruikshank, S. A. (2022). Artificial intelligence and journalism: An Agenda for journalism research in Africa. *African Journalism Studies, 43*(1), 17–33. DOI: 10.1080/23743670.2021.1999840

Lee, S. K., Lindsey, N. J., & Kim, K. S. (2017). The effects of news consumption via social media and news information overload on perceptions of journalistic norms and practices. *Computers in Human Behavior, 75*, 254–263.

Li, C., & Callegari, A. (2024) Stop AI disinformation: Protecting truth in the digital world. https://www.weforum.org/agenda/2024/06/ai-combat-online-misinformation-disinformation/

Luchko, Y. I., & Dobrovichka, O. O. (2023). Application of cloud technologies in the educational process of higher education institutions.

McGregor, S. C. (2019). Social media as public opinion: How journalists use social media to represent public opinion. *Journalism*, *20*(8), 1070–1086. DOI: 10.1177/1464884919845458

Mustaffa, N., Sannusi, S. N., Hasan, A. S. A., & Saad, M. Z. M. (2017). Journalism and news industry in Malaysia: new media, new challenges. *e-BANGI Journal, 12*.

Myers, C., & Feerrar, F. (2024) *AI and the spread of fake news sites: Experts explain how to counteract them*https://news.vt.edu/articles/2024/02/AI-generated-fake-news-experts.html

Noain Sánchez, A. (2022). Addressing the Impact of Artificial Intelligence on Journalism: The perception of experts, journalists and academics.

Reyes, L. P., & Cruz, R. S. (2021). AI-assisted data analysis for investigative reporting: Exploring the potential in Northern Luzon. *Journal of Investigative Journalism*, *12*(4), 156–172.

Santos, A. B., Lim, C. D., & Tan, E. F. (2019). AI powered news generation for increased efficiency: A case study in Metro Manila. *Journal of Medical Technology*, *8*(2), 45–58.

Santos, M. A. (2017). Data-driven storytelling by AI-assisted student journalists in the Philippines. *Journal of Emerging Media Studies*, *5*(2), 78–92.

Taibi, M. A. L. I. A., & Na, T. Y. (2020). The changes of media landscape in Malaysia: How citizen journalism poses threats to traditional media. *Jurnal Komunikasi: Malaysian Journal of Communication*, *36*(1), 396–380.

Tan, R. M., Wong, L. S., & Ahmad, N. (2022). Audience reception of AI-generated news content in Malaysia. *Digital Journalism (Abingdon, England)*, *19*(5), 678–693.

Tejedor, S., & Vila, P. (2021). Exo journalism: a conceptual approach to a hybrid formula between journalism and artificial intelligence. *Journalism and media, 2*(4), 830-840.

The Chronicle of Higher Education, 2024. https://sponsored.chronicle.com/how-ai-is-being-used-to-fight-fake-news/index.html

Wu, Y. (2019). How age affects journalists' adoption of social media as an innovation: A multi-group SEM analysis. *Journalism Practice*, *13*(5), 537–557. DOI: 10.1080/17512786.2018.1511821

Chapter 8
Psychological Impact of AI Moderation

Satya Subrahmanyam
https://orcid.org/0000-0003-0441-2742
Holy Spirit University of Kaslik, Lebanon

ABSTRACT

This chapter explores the psychological effects of AI-driven content moderation on users, content creators, and human moderators. While AI enables efficient, large-scale moderation of digital content, its opaque, automated processes often introduce emotional and behavioral challenges. Users may experience frustration and distrust due to AI's lack of transparency, potentially leading to self-censorship or disengagement. Content creators, especially those monetizing their work, face stress and anxiety from unpredictable AI decisions, impacting their creativity and autonomy. Human moderators also encounter psychological strain, caught between AI efficiency and empathy. Addressing algorithmic bias and promoting transparency, fairness, and human oversight are crucial for mitigating these impacts and fostering a healthier digital environment.

1. INTRODUCTION

1.1 The Rise of AI in Content Moderation

In today's digital ecosystem, the scale and speed of online content generation have rendered traditional human moderation increasingly insufficient. To address the overwhelming volume of user-generated material across platforms such as Facebook, YouTube, Twitter, and TikTok, technology companies have turned to artificial intelligence (AI) as a scalable and efficient solution. AI-powered content

DOI: 10.4018/979-8-3373-0335-2.ch008

moderation tools utilize machine learning (ML), natural language processing (NLP), and computer vision to detect and remove harmful, inappropriate, or policy-violating content in real time.

This shift toward automation marks a significant transformation in the landscape of online governance. Unlike human moderators, AI systems can operate 24/7, analyze vast data streams instantly, and execute decisions consistently, making them attractive to platforms under pressure to ensure user safety and compliance with regulatory standards (Gillespie, 2018). While the functional benefits of AI moderation are well-documented, its psychological consequences—particularly for stakeholders such as users, human moderators, developers, and the wider digital society—are less thoroughly explored.

1.2 From Human Judgment to Algorithmic Decisions

The integration of AI into content moderation represents more than a technological upgrade; it signals a shift in how decisions are made and who makes them. Traditionally, content moderation involved nuanced human judgment, allowing for cultural sensitivity, emotional intelligence, and contextual understanding. In contrast, AI systems often rely on patterns derived from data and historical decisions, which can lack the subtlety required to distinguish between harmful content and benign expression, such as satire, political critique, or regional dialects (Jhaver et al., 2019).

This mechanization of judgment has profound psychological implications. As users become increasingly subject to automated decision-making, questions arise about fairness, transparency, and accountability. When users are not informed about the reasons behind content takedowns or bans—or worse, when those reasons appear inconsistent—they may experience confusion, anxiety, or distrust toward the platform. Such experiences can lead to emotional disengagement and a chilling effect on speech, where individuals preemptively censor themselves to avoid penalties (Gorwa, 2019).

Emotional Consequences for Users - For everyday users, the psychological toll of AI moderation is tied to perceived injustice and a lack of control. Content that is erroneously flagged or removed may trigger feelings of helplessness, especially when appeal mechanisms are unclear or ineffective. Users may feel that their voices are silent or misinterpreted by machines, undermining their sense of agency and participation in digital communities. These experiences are especially pronounced among marginalized or minority groups whose cultural expressions are often misunderstood or misclassified by algorithmic systems (Noble, 2018).

Repeated exposure to punitive actions—such as warnings, suspensions, or shadow bans—can create an environment of fear and hyper-vigilance. Rather than fostering open dialogue, AI moderation may inadvertently contribute to anxiety, social isolation, or disengagement from online platforms.

Psychological Toll on Human Moderators - While AI is often seen as a means to reduce human exposure to disturbing content, human moderators still play a critical role in evaluating edge cases and reviewing flagged material. Ironically, AI may intensify the emotional strain on these workers by reserving the most ambiguous or controversial content for human evaluation. This "residual burden" leaves moderators confronting highly distressing material—violence, abuse, and hate speech—without the support systems necessary to protect their mental well-being (Roberts, 2019).

The increasing reliance on AI can lead to job insecurity, de-skilling, and feelings of devaluation among human moderators. Their work may be seen as subordinate to algorithmic judgment, reducing their autonomy and psychological resilience.

Designers and Developers: Ethical Strain and Emotional Labor - The psychological impact of AI moderation also extends to those who design and maintain the systems. Developers face unique ethical dilemmas as they encode complex social values into algorithmic logic. Determining what constitutes hate speech, misinformation, or harmful content is not merely a technical task—it involves cultural awareness, legal compliance, and moral responsibility.

The emotional labor involved in making such determinations can result in cognitive dissonance and moral injury, especially when designers witness the real-world consequences of flawed or biased systems. Concerns about reproducing systemic inequalities or enabling censorship can generate long-term psychological stress, burnout, or disillusionment with the field (Binns, 2018).

Societal Implications and Psychological Spillovers - Beyond individual stakeholders, AI moderation has broader psychological consequences for society. When algorithms regulate digital discourse, they shape not only what is said but also how people feel about participating in online spaces. Over-moderation can suppress diversity of thought, while under-moderation can create toxic environments, discouraging constructive engagement. In both cases, the psychological safety of users is compromised, which can erode trust in platforms and democratic dialogue (Gillespie, 2018).

Marginalized communities, in particular, bear the brunt of algorithmic blind spots. Their experiences of misrecognition or exclusion reflect deeper psychological harm—the denial of visibility and representation in digital public life (Noble, 2018). These patterns of exclusion contribute to digital inequalities and compound existing social disparities.

1.3 Scope and Purpose of the Chapter

Given the complex interplay between AI technology and human psychology, this chapter aims to unpack the multifaceted psychological impacts of AI-driven content moderation. By examining the experiences of users, human moderators, developers, and broader digital communities, the chapter seeks to foreground the emotional and mental health dimensions often overlooked in discussions of AI governance. In doing so, it advocates for a more human-centered and psychologically informed approach to the design and implementation of content moderation technologies.

2. UNDERSTANDING AI MODERATION

Artificial intelligence (AI) moderation is the process of autonomously checking material on various digital platforms for compliance with rules and regulations. It entails finding dangerous, improper, or infringing materials including hate speech, sexual content, or disinformation. To improve efficiency and decrease human supervision, AI moderation systems use machine learning and natural language processing (NLP) to evaluate and filter material in real-time.

2.1 Defining AI Moderation

When algorithmic algorithms are used to identify, assess, and respond to user-generated material on various online platforms, this practice is known as artificial intelligence (AI) moderation. In order to evaluate text, pictures, audio, and video, these systems are trained using large datasets and use methods from computer vision, natural language processing (NLP), and machine learning (ML). The primary objective is to detect and remove objectionable content, including but not limited to hate speech, violent images, false information, and sexually explicit content (Gorwa et al., 2020). As guardians of community norms and legal and regulatory compliance, AI moderation systems protect the peace.

The functioning of AI moderation is grounded in classification algorithms. These models learn patterns from labeled data and use them to categorize new content. NLP models may be trained to recognize hate speech by learning linguistic features from previously flagged instances. Once deployed, the system can scan incoming content in real-time and determine whether it violates platform policies. Depending on the platform's governance structure, the AI may autonomously remove the content, issue a warning, or escalate it to a human reviewer for final judgment (Gillespie, 2018).

2.2 Types of AI Moderation

AI moderation systems can be broadly categorized into three main types: automated detection, flagging systems, and decision-making algorithms. Each type serves a specific function within the content governance framework and often operates in combination with the others.

Automated Detection Systems: Automated detection is the frontline mechanism in AI moderation. These systems are trained to scan and identify content that potentially violates platform policies without human intervention. Image recognition tools can detect nudity or graphic violence using pattern recognition and pixel analysis, while NLP models evaluate text for abusive or threatening language (Schmidt & Wiegand, 2017). Automated detection systems are designed for scale and speed, allowing platforms to preemptively address problematic content.

Flagging Systems: Flagging systems operate as hybrid mechanisms where AI algorithms highlight or "flag" questionable content for human moderators. These systems rely on predictive scoring models that assess the likelihood of content being harmful. Flagging is particularly useful in ambiguous contexts where definitive classification is difficult. Content containing political satire, dark humor, or regional slang may require human discernment due to the contextual and cultural sensitivity involved (Jhaver et al., 2019).

Flagging systems are instrumental in optimizing moderator efficiency by reducing the volume of benign content they must review. The effectiveness of these systems depends heavily on the quality and diversity of training data, which influences the algorithm's ability to generalize across different cultural, linguistic, and social contexts.

Decision-Making Algorithms: At a more advanced level, decision-making algorithms are empowered to enforce moderation actions such as content removal, user bans, and suspension of accounts. These algorithms operate under a rule-based framework augmented by probabilistic assessments. If an AI system detects a high probability of hate speech in a user comment and this exceeds a predetermined threshold, it may automatically delete the comment and notify the user.

Decision-making algorithms are increasingly employed in real-time scenarios where rapid response is crucial—such as during live video streams or trending conversations. This form of AI moderation has raised concerns over transparency, accountability, and user rights, especially when moderation outcomes are not clearly communicated (Barrett, 2020).

2.3 Platforms Utilizing AI Moderation

AI moderation is now a central component of digital governance across various online ecosystems. Social media platforms such as Facebook, Instagram, YouTube, Twitter (now X), and TikTok have integrated AI systems to manage billions of user posts daily. Facebook, for instance, uses machine learning models to detect hate speech, graphic violence, and misinformation in over 40 languages, claiming that over 90% of content removals are now initiated by AI systems (Facebook Transparency Report, 2023).

Beyond social media, online gaming platforms such as Xbox Live, Discord, and Twitch employ AI moderation to monitor in-game chats, livestreams, and user interactions. These platforms face unique challenges due to the spontaneous and informal nature of communication, requiring real-time detection and action (Kowert, 2020).

Online forums like Reddit and Quora use AI to assist with spam detection, policy violations, and user reporting systems. Even professional platforms like LinkedIn have adopted AI tools to address issues of harassment, misinformation, and discriminatory language.

The deployment of AI moderation is also expanding into e-commerce platforms (e.g., Amazon, eBay), dating apps (e.g., Tinder, Bumble), and customer review sites (e.g., Yelp), where it helps to maintain the credibility and trustworthiness of user interactions.

2.4 Strengths of AI Moderation

One of the most significant strengths of AI moderation is its ability to process massive volumes of content at unparalleled speed. In contrast to human moderation, which is labor-intensive and slow, AI offers scalability and round-the-clock performance. This is particularly advantageous in crisis situations, such as during political unrest or public health emergencies, when harmful misinformation can spread rapidly (Hosseini et al., 2021).

AI systems also offer consistency in applying platform rules, reducing the variability and subjectivity often associated with human moderators. This can lead to more uniform enforcement of community guidelines and potentially reduce bias when designed and trained appropriately. AI moderation helps protect human moderators from psychological harm by filtering out the most extreme or traumatic content before it reaches them (Roberts, 2019).

Limitations and Challenges - Despite their advantages, AI moderation systems face significant limitations—particularly in their handling of nuanced, contextual, and culturally sensitive content. One major issue is the risk of false positives (content incorrectly flagged as harmful) and false negatives (harmful content that goes undetected). Satirical content, political dissent, and minority dialects often fall prey to misclassification due to a lack of contextual understanding within the algorithm (Noble, 2018).

AI systems also suffer from data biases inherited from their training datasets. These biases can perpetuate systemic inequalities, leading to disproportionate targeting of marginalized communities. Research has shown that some hate speech classifiers are more likely to flag content written in African American Vernacular English (AAVE) than Standard English, revealing discriminatory outcomes embedded in algorithmic processes (Sap et al., 2019).

Another limitation is the lack of transparency in how AI moderation decisions are made. Users are frequently not informed about why their content was flagged or removed, nor are they given clear mechanisms for appeal. This opacity undermines user trust and raises ethical concerns about accountability and due process (Gorwa, 2019).

Finally, while AI can reduce exposure to harmful content, it cannot entirely replace the need for human judgment. Human moderators remain essential for edge cases and policy interpretation, and the continued reliance on AI moderation must be balanced with strong human oversight.

Understanding AI moderation is key to analyzing its psychological influence on digital ecosystems. AI brings efficiency, scalability, and some respite to human moderators, but it also increases misclassification, bias, and user disenfranchisement threats. As digital platforms increasingly use AI to manage content, it's important to critically assess their methods, strengths, and weaknesses. AI moderation must combine technological, ethical, and psychological insights to maintain online safety and fairness.

3. PSYCHOLOGICAL IMPACT ON USERS

As AI moderation becomes an increasingly prominent feature of digital content governance, it is critical to explore its psychological implications on users. While AI-driven systems promise speed, scalability, and consistency, they often introduce concerns related to trust, fairness, transparency, and emotional well-being. This section explores how AI moderation shapes user perceptions, influences behavior, and impacts mental health in both direct and subtle ways.

3.1 Trust and Transparency Issues

A central psychological impact of AI moderation lies in users' perceptions of trust and fairness in content governance systems. Many users expect platforms to offer clear, consistent, and equitable moderation. AI moderation frequently operates within what has been termed the "**black box**" — a metaphor for the opaque nature of algorithmic decision-making where users are unable to understand or question how and why moderation decisions are made (Pasquale, 2015).

AI moderation systems often fail to offer meaningful explanations when content is flagged or removed. Users receive generic or automated messages stating that community guidelines have been violated, but without context or clarity. This lack of transparency fosters confusion and erodes trust in the platform (Gillespie, 2018). Research shows that when users perceive moderation to be unfair or arbitrary, they experience negative psychological reactions such as irritation, alienation, and a reduction in platform engagement (Jhaver et al., 2019).

Algorithmic bias poses a significant challenge to user trust. AI systems trained on imbalanced or culturally limited datasets may over-police marginalized communities or misinterpret context-specific language. African American Vernacular English (AAVE) has been disproportionately flagged as toxic by certain hate speech detection algorithms (Sap et al., 2019). Such biases not only undermine the legitimacy of moderation but also intensify feelings of exclusion and discrimination among affected users.

3.2 Censorship and Self-Censorship

AI moderation also alters user behavior through the mechanisms of censorship and self-censorship. In many cases, users fear that their content may be automatically flagged or removed without justification. This fear, whether based on past experiences or anticipated risks, often leads users to restrict their own expression preemptively—a phenomenon known as the **chilling effect** (PEN America, 2020).

Self-censorship is particularly pronounced in politically sensitive discussions or emotionally charged topics such as race, religion, gender, or mental health. Users who once felt comfortable expressing dissenting opinions or sharing personal experiences may begin to withdraw due to perceived surveillance or algorithmic scrutiny (Roberts, 2019). The automated nature of AI moderation, devoid of human empathy or cultural sensitivity, intensifies this issue.

AI moderation also struggles with cultural and contextual nuances, which can lead to misinterpretation of benign content. Sarcasm, satire, or regional dialects may be wrongly classified as offensive or threatening by AI systems. When users feel misunderstood or wrongly penalized, they may begin to feel alienated from the platform and community (Gorwa et al., 2020).

The broader implications of this include the erosion of digital public spheres where users engage in critical dialogue. When moderation disproportionately impacts certain groups or opinions, it can lead to the suppression of diverse viewpoints, fostering ideological homogeneity and digital echo chambers.

3.3 Mental Health and Emotional Responses

Beyond issues of expression and trust, AI moderation can also directly affect users' mental health and emotional well-being. The experience of having one's content removed, account suspended, or reputation questioned due to AI decisions can provoke intense emotional responses. Users often report feelings of frustration, confusion, and anger when faced with unjust or unclear moderation actions (Jhaver et al., 2019).

These emotional responses are exacerbated when users are denied the opportunity to contest decisions or communicate with a human moderator. In such cases, they may feel powerless, marginalized, and dehumanized by a faceless system (Gillespie, 2018). The lack of recourse contributes to a broader sense of digital alienation, where users perceive themselves not as active participants in an online community but as subjects to automated surveillance and control.

For content creators, influencers, and professionals whose livelihoods depend on digital platforms, AI moderation presents an additional layer of psychological strain. Account suspensions, demonetization, or content takedowns can threaten financial stability and professional credibility. The anticipatory anxiety over whether content will be flagged can lead to compulsive self-monitoring and stress (Cunningham & Craig, 2019). These mental burdens, although less visible, are part of the broader psychosocial landscape shaped by algorithmic governance.

Younger users, particularly teenagers, are more vulnerable to the emotional consequences of AI moderation. Adolescents place significant value on online validation, peer approval, and social identity formation. When their content is removed or labeled inappropriate without explanation, it can contribute to feelings of shame, embarrassment, or low self-worth (Nesi, 2020). In severe cases, repeated moderation experiences may correlate with increased levels of anxiety or depressive symptoms, especially when coupled with cyberbullying or online exclusion.

3.4 Coping Strategies and User Adaptations

Despite these challenges, users are not passive recipients of AI moderation. Many engage in coping strategies and adapt their behavior in creative ways to navigate algorithmic systems. Some users deliberately alter their language—using euphemisms, symbols, or alternative spellings—to evade automated detection. Others turn to private groups or alternative platforms where moderation is perceived to be more transparent or less invasive (Matias, 2019).

Collective responses such as public criticism, activism, and platform accountability campaigns have emerged, demanding more transparent, explainable, and participatory moderation systems. These actions reflect a growing recognition of the need to balance platform safety with user rights and psychological dignity.

Users experience various psychological effects from AI-powered content regulation. Trust, transparency, censorship, and emotional effect affect how people utilize digital platforms and see online communities. AI moderation may be efficient, but it lacks emotional intelligence and cultural sensitivity to maintain a psychologically healthy digital environment. Future AI moderation must stress human-centric design, inclusive training data, and accessible appeal procedures to reduce these harms and build platform-user trust.

4. PSYCHOLOGICAL IMPACT ON CONTENT MODERATORS

As artificial intelligence (AI) systems become increasingly integral to online content moderation, the roles and experiences of human content moderators are evolving. Although AI moderation aims to enhance efficiency and reduce human exposure to harmful content, its implementation raises profound psychological and professional concerns for the very people it is designed to assist or replace. This section explores the psychological impact of AI moderation on content moderators, focusing on their emotional wellbeing, professional identity, and the ethical dilemmas they face in working alongside or under algorithmic systems.

4.1 AI as a Support Tool vs. AI as a Job Replacement

AI was initially introduced into content moderation with the promise of support. Its capacity to automatically scan, flag, and categorize vast volumes of user-generated content—ranging from hate speech to graphic violence—offers significant advantages in scale and speed (Gorwa et al., 2020). In theory, this should relieve human moderators from the most repetitive and harmful tasks. However, this narrative has not always held true in practice.

For many content moderators, AI feels less like a supportive partner and more like a threat to job security. The increasing reliance on automated tools has raised fears of redundancy among human workers, especially as corporates seek to optimize costs by outsourcing or automating moderation (Roberts, 2019). This shift can create anxiety and insecurity about long-term career prospects. When AI systems are presented as infallible or superior to human judgment, moderators may experience a diminished sense of professional worth, leading to feelings of being devalued or marginalized within their roles.

On the other hand, human moderators often remain critical to AI moderation systems because algorithms still struggle with context, nuance, and cultural sensitivity. In such hybrid systems, humans are called upon to resolve ambiguities and make final decisions—an increasingly stressful responsibility when placed against opaque and sometimes faulty AI recommendations (Gillespie, 2018).

4.2 Increased Emotional Burden from Reviewing Flagged Content

One of the paradoxes of AI moderation is that while it aims to reduce the emotional burden on human moderators, it can inadvertently concentrate on that burden. Algorithms frequently flag the most egregious, ambiguous, or controversial content for human review. Consequently, human moderators are routinely exposed to the most traumatic materials that AI cannot confidently categorize—images of violence, child abuse, hate crimes, and suicide attempts (Newton, 2019).

This exposure can have lasting psychological effects, including depression, desensitization, anxiety, and even symptoms akin to post-traumatic stress disorder (PTSD) (Chen, 2014). Compounding the issue is the high-speed, repetitive nature of moderation work, where moderators must make rapid decisions with limited context, leading to emotional exhaustion and compassion fatigue. Many moderators operate under strict quotas and time limits, which leave little room for decompression or reflection.

These psychological effects are often exacerbated by insufficient mental health support. While some tech companies have introduced counseling and wellness programs, these are frequently inadequate, especially for moderators working in outsourced environments with limited protections or resources (West, 2021). In many cases, moderators are discouraged from speaking openly about their work due to confidentiality clauses, adding a layer of isolation to their already difficult roles.

4.3 Psychological Toll of Relying on AI Decisions

Another psychological dimension of AI integration is the tension created when moderators must trust or override machine-made decisions. AI moderation systems often function as black boxes, providing little or no explanation for their classifications. Moderators may be asked to affirm or challenge decisions made by algorithms without fully understanding the logic behind them, leading to confusion, ethical conflict, and reduced confidence in their own judgment (Pasquale, 2015).

This can produce a form of **moral injury**, a term originally used to describe the psychological distress resulting from actions that contradict a person's ethical or moral beliefs (Feinstein et al., 2018). If an AI flags a post as hate speech, but the human moderator interprets it as satire or political commentary, being required to remove the content can create internal dissonance. Repeated experiences of moral injury can lead to burnout, cynicism, and disengagement from work.

This reliance on AI shifts the locus of accountability. Moderators may be held responsible for decisions influenced or determined by AI, creating a disempowering environment where blame can be difficult to assign and agency is diluted (Gillespie, 2018). This erosion of human authority undermines the ethical core of moderation work, reducing it to a mechanical task rather than a nuanced, judgment-driven role.

4.4 De-skilling and Identity Loss among Professional Moderators

AI moderation also poses a threat to the professional development and identity of content moderators. As AI systems take over more cognitive and decision-making tasks, human moderators may find themselves confined to lower-order tasks such as confirming AI decisions or processing algorithmically sorted content. This creates a risk of **de-skilling**, where moderators have fewer opportunities to apply and refine critical thinking, ethical reasoning, and contextual judgment skills (Crawford & Paglen, 2021).

Over time, this de-skilling can lead to **professional stagnation** and identity loss. Moderators who once saw themselves as ethical custodians of online discourse may begin to feel like replaceable cogs in an automated system. The lack of recognition for their labor—combined with the invisibility of their role in public discourse—compounds this identity erosion. Despite their essential contributions, moderators rarely receive credit or visibility, reinforcing feelings of undervaluation and alienation (Roberts, 2019).

This invisibility is particularly acute in outsourced or offshore moderation contexts. Many global platforms outsource moderation to countries in the Global South, where workers are paid less and given fewer protections. These moderators often face the same or worse psychological risks, with even less recognition, voice, or support (West, 2021).

AI-powered content filtering systems bring potential and difficulties. AI can help manage massive online material, but it shouldn't hurt human moderators' mental health or careers. These demands and opinions must guide a more ethical and sustainable moderate ecology. This involves creating visible, explainable, and responsible AI systems, providing moderators with mental health support, and including their voices in AI tool design and deployment. Platforms must adopt a human-centered ethic that acknowledges moderation as a very human and psychological role rather than a techno-solutionist one.

5. PSYCHOLOGICAL IMPACT ON DEVELOPERS AND DESIGNERS

Designing AI systems for content moderation requires ethical awareness, emotional resilience, and deep cognitive involvement, not just technical expertise. Developers and designers, the unseen builders of AI moderation, shape online content management, flagging, and removal. They have great responsibility. This section discusses moral harm, empathy fatigue, and cognitive-emotional strain caused by ethical issues, poisonous material, and prediction technology limits.

5.1 Cognitive and Emotional Burden in Designing Ethical Moderation Systems

AI developers and designers working on moderation tools often grapple with complex ethical challenges. Content moderation is not a neutral or purely technical task—it involves value judgments about what is harmful, offensive, or inappropriate. In the absence of universally agreed-upon standards, developers must encode subjective and often culturally specific norms into algorithms that operate across diverse digital communities (Gillespie, 2018).

This process creates significant cognitive and emotional stress. Developers must anticipate how algorithms behave in varied real-world contexts, account for edge cases, and address potential misuse or overreach of the system. The knowledge that their decisions could silence marginalized voices or overlook harmful content weighs heavily on many practitioners (Raji et al., 2020). Unlike typical software engineering tasks, moderation systems require constant reflection on societal impact, fairness, and unintended consequences—demands that can lead to chronic mental strain and burnout.

The pressure to "get it right" is compounded by public scrutiny and the risk of reputational damage for companies and developers alike. Ethical AI design involves long hours of deliberation over training data, classifier thresholds, and review protocols, all while navigating tight production timelines. This balance between technical performance and moral responsibility can be mentally exhausting, especially when trade-offs must be made between user safety, freedom of expression, and platform profitability (Madaio et al., 2020).

5.2 Moral Injury from Designing Systems with Unjust Consequences

Developers may also experience **moral injury**—a psychological response that arises when individuals perpetrate, fail to prevent, or witness actions that contradict their moral beliefs (Feinstein et al., 2018). In the context of AI moderation, moral injury can manifest when developers realize that their algorithms are being used in ways that cause real-world harm, such as the silencing of activists, misclassification of culturally specific expressions, or amplification of extremist content due to algorithmic bias.

Such outcomes are not always immediately visible during development but become apparent after deployment. Biased training data may lead to the over-policing of certain dialects, like African American Vernacular English (AAVE), while failing to detect hate speech cloaked in coded language (Sap et al., 2019). Developers who become aware of these impacts may feel complicit in systemic injustice, particularly if organizational pressures limit their ability to address the problems.

These experiences can lead to a loss of professional purpose and ethical disillusionment. Developers often enter the field with a desire to build beneficial technologies, yet they may find themselves entangled in corporate agendas or bureaucratic constraints that prioritize efficiency over justice. The internal conflict between personal ethics and organizational directives can generate deep emotional unrest and moral fatigue (Benkler, 2019).

5.3 Empathy Fatigue and Moral Disengagement During System Training

Another significant psychological challenge for developers involves the training of AI systems, which often requires direct interaction with harmful or distressing content. To build effective moderation tools, developers must curate datasets that include examples of hate speech, pornography, graphic violence, suicide content, and more. This exposure, while less continuous than that experienced by human moderators, still poses risks for empathy fatigue and emotional desensitization (Crawford & Paglen, 2021).

Repeated exposure to toxic content, even in controlled environments, can erode a developer's emotional capacity and lead to **empathy fatigue**—a condition marked by emotional numbing, reduced compassion, and psychological withdrawal. Over time, this can progress into moral disengagement, a psychological process where individuals distance themselves from the ethical implications of their actions to cope with distress or avoid burnout (Subrahmanyam, 2021).

Moral disengagement may manifest as detachment from the social consequences of algorithmic decisions or rationalization of harmful outcomes as necessary trade-offs. While this mechanism can offer short-term psychological relief, it risks creating a culture of ethical apathy within development teams. When empathy is sacrificed for efficiency or emotional self-preservation, the quality and fairness of moderation systems can deteriorate, perpetuating the very harm they are designed to mitigate (Whittaker et al., 2018).

The organizational culture of many tech firms does not adequately address these risks. Developers are rarely provided with trauma-informed support structures or ethical reflection spaces. Conversations about emotional labor are often confined to content moderation teams, excluding those who architect the systems from the discourse. This omission overlooks the full spectrum of psychological impacts associated with AI development and leaves many developers to cope in isolation (West, 2021).

5.4 Toward Ethical and Emotionally Sustainable Development Practices

To mitigate these psychological burdens, there is a growing call for ethical and emotionally sustainable development practices in AI. These include incorporating **ethics-by-design** frameworks, promoting interdisciplinary collaboration with ethicists and social scientists, and embedding ongoing impact assessments throughout the development lifecycle (Morley et al., 2020). Such practices can help developers feel more empowered and less morally isolated in their work.

Mental health support should not be limited to content moderators. Developers and designers should have access to counseling services, peer support groups, and decompression protocols when dealing with distressing training data. Organizations must also create a culture where ethical concerns are welcomed, not sidelined, and where employees can raise red flags without fear of retaliation.

Transparency and accountability mechanisms are equally crucial. When developers are given a voice in how systems are implemented and monitored post-deployment, they are more likely to feel aligned with their work and less vulnerable to moral injury. The inclusion of diverse perspectives within development teams can also enhance cultural sensitivity and reduce the risk of harmful bias, contributing to a more just and psychologically safe ecosystem (Raji & Buolamwini, 2019).

Without notice, developers and designers change the digital information environment using AI moderation systems. Their task is vital but dangerous, causing moral injury, empathic fatigue, cognitive overload, and ethical disillusionment. Organizations that prioritize productivity over mental wellness worsen these concerns. Human-centered, ethical development is essential to preserve AI system architects' mental health and provide democratic and human rights-compliant moderating tools. Recognition and treatment of psychological consequences are needed to improve technology and create more humane and equitable digital communities.

6. ETHICAL AND PSYCHOLOGICAL FRAMEWORKS FOR RESPONSIBLE AI MODERATION

AI-mediated digital content management requires comprehensive frameworks that incorporate ethical and psychological well-being. Algorithmic fairness and prejudice have received significant attention, but AI systems' mental health effects on moderators, developers, users, and society have not. Thus, responsible AI moderation must include all parties' psychological resilience, emotional intelligence, and mental health as well as ethical principles like transparency, accountability, and justice. Four essential elements of an ethical and psychological content moderation ecosystem are listed below.

6.1 Incorporating Psychological Well-Being in AI Design

Integrating psychological well-being into AI design is a foundational step toward responsible moderation systems. Most AI content moderation tools are optimized for accuracy, speed, and scalability, often overlooking the psychological consequences of their decisions. Whether it is the emotional burden on moderators who must review flagged content or the mental toll on users whose posts are unfairly removed, AI systems can have wide-ranging emotional impacts (Crawford & Paglen, 2021). As such, it is critical to design AI with an awareness of mental health outcomes.

This involves several practical strategies. First, moderation systems should be designed with sensitivity to trauma exposure, especially when human review is required. Content previews, blur filters, and tiered exposure protocols can help reduce the **risk of secondary traumatic stress** among human moderators (Roberts, 2019). For developers and engineers, organizations should introduce "well-being checkpoints" throughout the AI development lifecycle—periods when teams assess potential emotional harms, receive psychological support, and participate in ethical reflection exercises (Madaio et al., 2020).

Second, AI tools can incorporate features to support the user's mental health. Rather than simply removing content, AI moderators might offer empathetic explanations or refer users to support services in cases involving self-harm, bullying, or grief-related content. By embedding psychological well-being as a design goal—alongside traditional performance metrics—developers can create systems that are more humane, responsive, and aligned with users' emotional needs.

6.2 Explainability, Fairness, and Accountability as Psychological Safeguards

Ethical frameworks for AI moderation frequently highlight the principles of explainability, fairness, and accountability. While these are usually considered legal or operational imperatives, they also serve as psychological safeguards for all stakeholders. Explainability, in particular, is essential in reducing cognitive distress and emotional frustration when users are subjected to moderation decisions.

When users receive opaque or inconsistent explanations for why their content has been removed or their account suspended, it can lead to anxiety, helplessness, and feelings of being unfairly targeted (Binns et al., 2018). Transparent and comprehensible justifications not only uphold democratic values but also promote psychological clarity and trust in the system. Similarly, fairness ensures that moderation does not disproportionately affect vulnerable or marginalized groups, which can prevent the emotional alienation and disenfranchisement of these communities (Noble, 2018).

Accountability mechanisms, such as appeal processes and independent audits, offer users a sense of procedural justice, mitigating the stress and powerlessness associated with unilateral AI decisions. Developers and moderators also benefit psychologically from working in environments where accountability is shared and ethically grounded. These mechanisms help buffer against moral injury and ethical fatigue, creating a more sustainable ecosystem for content governance (Whittaker et al., 2018).

6.3 The Role of Human-in-the-Loop (HITL) in Mitigating Psychological Harms

A critical component in ethical and psychologically responsive AI moderation is the **Human-in-the-Loop (HITL)** model. HITL refers to the inclusion of human judgment at various stages of the AI decision-making process—especially in ambiguous, high-risk, or emotionally charged scenarios. This approach counters the risks of **automation bias** and helps maintain empathy, context sensitivity, and cultural awareness in moderation systems (Amershi et al., 2014).

From a psychological standpoint, HITL mitigates several forms of harm. For human moderators, it creates shared responsibility, reducing the burden of making unilateral decisions in isolation. For developers, it provides ongoing feedback loops that refine algorithmic behavior while preserving ethical alignment. For users, knowing that a human has reviewed or is available to review a contested decision helps restore dignity and reduce emotional alienation.

HITL systems must be designed with care. Human reviewers should be supported with proper mental health resources, trauma-informed training, and manageable caseloads to prevent burnout and secondary trauma (Newton, 2019). HITL should not be seen as a patch to flawed automation, but rather as a structural commitment to **ethical humility**—acknowledging that machines alone cannot arbitrate the moral and emotional complexities of digital life.

6.4 Emotional Intelligence in AI: Emerging Research and Its Potential

One of the most exciting and underexplored frontiers in responsible AI moderation is the integration of **emotional intelligence (EI)** into AI systems. Emotional intelligence refers to the capacity to perceive, interpret, and respond to emotions effectively. While traditional AI systems are logic-driven and emotionally neutral, emerging research in **affective computing** seeks to imbue AI with the ability to detect sentiment, tone, and emotional context (Picard, 2000).

In the domain of content moderation, emotionally intelligent AI could enhance sensitivity to user distress signals—distinguishing between satire and hate speech, or between venting and actual threats. This emotional granularity can improve both accuracy and fairness, while also reducing the psychological harm caused by inappropriate censorship or inaction. Emotionally intelligent systems can be programmed to deliver empathetic responses, enhancing user experience during difficult interactions, such as content takedowns involving personal trauma or bereavement.

Nevertheless, emotional AI must be approached with caution. There are risks of emotional manipulation, overreach, and privacy invasion if such technologies are deployed without clear ethical guidelines. Transparency about the emotional capabilities of AI systems is essential to maintain user trust and agency. The potential for psychological benefit is significant—but only if developed with user dignity, consent, and well-being as primary goals (Cowie & Cornelius, 2003).

Content filtering affects psychology, morality, and technology. The emotional dynamics of AI decision-making affect developers, moderators, and customers. Effective moderation systems need robust algorithms and ethical and psychological design. Create more humane, safer, and fair content moderation ecosystems by integrating psychological well-being into AI research, improving transparency via explainability and accountability, applying human-in-the-loop models, and studying emotional intelligence in AI. They are preparing for a digital future where technology reduces harm, boosts psychological resilience, and maintains ethics.

7. CASE STUDIES AND EMPIRICAL EVIDENCE

Users, moderators, and developers have seen complicated psychological effects from content moderation using AI. Facebook, YouTube, and TikTok use AI to identify hate speech, disinformation, graphic violence, and other dangerous material. Automation promotes efficiency and scalability, but empirical research shows conflicting effects, notably on mental health. Real-world examples, mental health and user engagement research, and human-machine supervision achievements and failures are examined in this area.

7.1 Real-World Examples: Facebook, YouTube, and TikTok

One of the most cited case studies on the psychological toll of AI-assisted moderation comes from Facebook's content moderation centers. In 2019, *The Verge* published a groundbreaking exposé on the working conditions of content moderators contracted by Facebook through Cognizant (Newton, 2019). While AI filtered out a vast quantity of content, human reviewers were tasked with assessing edge cases—often the most disturbing ones that AI could not effectively judge. The psychological impact was severe: employees reported post-traumatic stress disorder (PTSD) symptoms, anxiety, and depression. Even with AI handling the majority of low-level filtering, human moderators remained overwhelmed due to the concentration of traumatic content in their workflow.

YouTube also faced scrutiny for its content moderation practices. Following major criticism in 2017-2018 regarding extremist and harmful content slipping through the cracks, YouTube accelerated its deployment of machine learning to identify and remove content violating its policies. According to its **2019 Transparency Report**, more than 90% of videos flagged for removal were first detected by AI (YouTube, 2019). Whistleblower reports and independent investigations revealed that this automation sometimes led to the unjust removal of educational, historical, or artistic content, triggering frustration, emotional distress, and reduced trust among content creators (Green, 2019).

Similarly, **TikTok** has employed advanced AI to monitor content across its vast user base. The platform has been both praised and criticized for its rapid response to potentially harmful content. A 2022 study found that TikTok's moderation algorithms frequently misidentified mental health-related videos, such as those discussing eating disorders or self-harm recovery, flagging them as harmful and removing them without context (Chancellor & De Choudhury, 2022). This not only silenced important conversations but also inflicted emotional harm on users, especially adolescents, who felt alienated and misunderstood.

7.2 Studies on User Stress, Mental Health Reports, and Platform Engagement

Empirical research has increasingly drawn attention to the psychological ramifications of AI-based moderation. A 2021 study by Gillespie and Karizat found that users exposed to AI-based moderation, particularly automated takedowns without explanations, experienced increased perceived injustice, helplessness, and stress, especially among marginalized communities. This was closely tied to a lack of transparency and the absence of meaningful appeal processes.

In a survey conducted by Mozilla Foundation (2020), nearly 60% of online creators reported experiencing moderation-induced anxiety due to the unpredictability and opaqueness of AI decisions. Respondents noted that they often self-censored content to avoid penalties, even when their posts were within guidelines. This phenomenon, known as "algorithmic anxiety", reflects the cognitive and emotional toll of navigating AI-driven ecosystems.

Research also points to a correlation between AI implementation and user engagement. A 2022 study by the Pew Research Center indicated a drop in active engagement on platforms like Facebook and Instagram following the aggressive rollout of AI-based moderation, with users citing "unfair content removals" and "lack of appeal options" as reasons for their disengagement (Pew Research Center, 2022). Conversely, platforms that combined AI moderation with clear communication and human review saw better retention and more positive user sentiment.

7.3 Successes in Balancing Automation with Human Oversight

Despite the challenges, several platforms have made notable progress in balancing AI and human moderation. **Reddit** employs a community-based moderation model supplemented by AI. Here, automated systems filter content based on predefined criteria, but subreddit moderators—actual users—make nuanced decisions. This hybrid model has been credited with preserving user trust and emotional investment in the platform (Matias, 2019).

Twitter has also iterated its approach. In 2021, it launched a system where tweets flagged by AI for possible rule violations are first reviewed by a human moderator before being removed. Initial results showed a decrease in false positives and an increase in user satisfaction (Twitter Transparency Report, 2022). Twitter began notifying users with detailed explanations when their content was moderated, which helped reduce user stress and perceived bias.

Another promising initiative is **YouTube's Creator Support program**, which provides content creators with moderation reports, personalized feedback, and access to human reviewers. While not perfect, this model has helped mitigate psychological harm by offering clarity and recourse, particularly for creators whose livelihoods depend on platform algorithms.

7.4 Failures and Challenges

Nonetheless, failures continue to surface. **Meta's Oversight Board**, established to provide ethical guidance and appeals for moderation decisions, has faced criticism for being underutilized and lacking enforcement power. A 2022 review of its cases revealed that fewer than 1% of contested decisions were actually reviewed, and the recommendations made were often not implemented on scale (Kaye, 2022). This limited effectiveness contributes to a persistent trust deficit, which has psychological consequences for users who feel voiceless and powerless.

TikTok, too, has struggled to correct its biases in AI moderation. Reports from LGBTQ+ and BIPOC users indicate that content from these communities is disproportionately flagged or demoted, often due to poorly trained algorithms or implicit bias in training data (Noble, 2018). These missteps result in identity-related stress, emotional distress, and in some cases, withdrawal from the platform.

The over-reliance on AI continues to desensitize human reviewers. Interviews with moderators suggest that they become emotionally numb over time, particularly when required to review content only after it passes through AI filters—typically the most violent or distressing material (Roberts, 2019). Without adequate psychological support and systemic change, this trend may lead to widespread burnout and disengagement.

Real-world case studies and empirical research demonstrate AI-based content moderation's psychological difficulties. Automation has improved content governance efficiency and scalability, but it has also added emotional costs, unexpected consequences, and psychological pressures for users, moderators, and developers. Successful platforms embrace mixed approaches, stress openness and user communication, and invest in mental health services. Overreliance on automation, lack of redress, and inadequate human monitoring cause failures. As AI evolves, platforms must emphasize psychological safety, fairness, and ethical alignment in content management to preserve community standards and safeguard mental health.

8. FUTURE DIRECTIONS AND RECOMMENDATIONS

As AI is used for content moderation across platforms, it's important to consider both its operational efficiency and the mental health of users, moderators, and developers. AI moderation has changed how platforms control material, but it has also raised mental health, justice, and trust concerns. AI systems must emphasize psychological resilience, ethical responsibility, and transparency going ahead. This section discusses how to improve the psychological impact of AI moderation by designing AI with resilience, fostering cross-disciplinary collaboration, implementing regulatory frameworks, and creating mental health and digital literacy resources.

8.1 Designing AI Moderation with Psychological Resilience in Mind

One of the most pressing needs in AI moderation is the incorporation of **psychological resilience** into the design and operation of these systems. Psychological resilience refers to the capacity to cope with the stresses and challenges associated with content moderation and mitigate the potential psychological harms. Designing AI systems with psychological resilience in mind involves creating algorithms that not only identify harmful content but also minimize the emotional toll on users and content moderators.

A key consideration is reducing algorithmic bias, which can lead to unfair treatment and stress for marginalized communities. AI systems should be designed to account for cultural, linguistic, and contextual nuances in content to ensure fairness and inclusiveness. Transparency is crucial in this regard. Platforms must implement feedback mechanisms where users and moderators can understand how decisions are made and, if necessary, challenge automated decisions. This could involve integrating AI systems with clear notification processes and user-friendly appeal options to reduce feelings of helplessness and frustration (Gillespie, 2021).

For content moderators, resilience can be enhanced by providing psychological support and mental health resources. Creating systems where human moderators are actively supported—both in terms of emotional support and professional development—could help alleviate the emotional burden of reviewing potentially distressing content. The use of empathetic AI that takes emotional nuances into account when making decisions could further reduce the emotional toll on users and moderators alike (Scherer, 2022).

8.2 Need for Cross-Disciplinary Collaboration

Designing ethical AI moderation systems requires collaboration across various disciplines, including artificial intelligence, psychology, ethics, and law. A successful AI moderation system must not only use advanced machine learning algorithms but also integrate psychological insights on human behavior, emotions, and cognitive biases. This requires collaboration between computer scientists, ethicists, psychologists, sociologists, and legal professionals to create a holistic framework that addresses both technical and psychological aspects of AI moderation.

Psychologists and sociologists can contribute by helping developers understand the emotional impact of content and designing systems that consider user welfare. Psychology experts can help identify patterns of emotional distress caused by certain types of content and advise on mitigation strategies. Ethicists and legal experts are essential in ensuring that AI systems adhere to ethical guidelines and legal standards, ensuring that content moderation is not only effective but also fair and just (Jobin et al., 2019).

This interdisciplinary collaboration can also help establish common standards for AI systems that govern content moderation across different platforms, ensuring consistency and transparency in the way content is handled. Establishing guidelines for emotional impact assessments in content moderation systems will be key to fostering both public trust and user satisfaction (Gillespie, 2021).

8.3 Calls for Regulatory Frameworks and Transparency Mandates

Given the increasing reliance on AI in content moderation, there is a growing call for regulatory frameworks that set clear standards for how AI systems should operate in this context. Governments and international organizations have begun to recognize the importance of ensuring ethical AI practices in content moderation. The European Union's Digital Services Act (DSA) mandates that platforms disclose how their moderation systems work, how content is flagged, and how users can challenge automated decisions (European Commission, 2022). These frameworks promote transparency and accountability, which are critical to mitigating the psychological harm associated with content moderation.

Beyond transparency, regulatory frameworks can also enforce psychological safeguards by setting mandatory standards for the mental health of both users and moderators. This might include requiring platforms to provide mental health resources for moderators and offering users more robust tools to manage their emotional well-being when engaging with AI moderation systems. Regulations could mandate the inclusion of human oversight in automated decisions, especially in sensitive cases, to prevent unjust content removals that may trigger emotional distress in users (European Commission, 2022).

Transparency mandates could also ensure that platforms disclose how AI systems are trained—ensuring that diverse datasets are used to prevent discrimination against vulnerable groups. This would be a key step in reducing user stress and frustration stemming from unfair algorithmic decisions.

8.4 Building Digital Literacy and Mental Health Resources

As AI-powered content moderation systems become more prevalent, there is a need for digital literacy initiatives that help users and moderators navigate the complexities of AI moderation. Users should be informed about how AI works, its limitations, and the processes through which decisions are made. By improving digital literacy, users can better understand why their content may have been flagged, which could reduce feelings of anger or anxiety associated with unjust moderation decisions (Scherer, 2022).

For content moderators, digital literacy also extends to mental health awareness. Providing training on coping mechanisms for dealing with traumatic or disturbing content is essential to ensure that moderators can take the psychological toll of their work. Regular psychological check-ins and access to support networks can help mitigate burnout and emotional fatigue. It is crucial to educate moderators on the ethical implications of their work and the psychological effects of making difficult decisions regarding content removal.

Platforms should develop and implement mental health resources for both users and moderators. This can include providing on-demand counseling, support groups, and stress management techniques for moderators who may encounter distressing content. For users, platforms can offer resources such as mental health hotlines or self-care tips to help individuals cope with the emotional effects of content moderation and censorship (Jobin et al., 2019).

Looking toward the future of AI-powered content moderation, the psychological impact on users, moderators, and developers requires urgent attention. By incorporating psychological resilience into the design of AI systems, promoting cross-disciplinary collaboration, establishing regulatory frameworks, and building digital literacy and mental health resources, we can create a more approach to content moderation. These steps will help to mitigate the psychological harm caused by AI moderation while ensuring that content platforms continue to uphold their responsibility to their users and communities.

9. CONCLUSION

AI-powered content moderation has significantly reshaped the digital landscape, offering remarkable efficiency in managing vast amounts of user-generated content across platforms. The psychological dimensions of AI moderation are profound and multifaceted. On one hand, AI enhances efficiency by automating content review processes, identifying harmful content faster than human moderators ever could. On the other hand, this efficiency comes with psychological challenges, including issues of trust, emotional distress, and the potential for dehumanization in content moderation. The dual-edged nature of AI lies in its balance between operational effectiveness and emotional sensitivity. While AI can execute tasks rapidly and at scale, it lacks the empathy and contextual understanding that human moderators provide, which can result in unintended harm to users and moderators alike.

The psychological implications for users include issues like bias, censorship, and mental health distress resulting from content flagging and removal. For moderators, the emotional toll of reviewing flagged content, especially in cases where AI systems fall short, raises concerns about burnout and identity loss. Developers also face ethical dilemmas when designing AI systems, further contributing to emotional and moral strain.

To ensure AI moderation systems are humane and effective, the future must focus on psychologically sound practices that prioritize fairness, transparency, and empathy. Cross-disciplinary collaboration, ethical design, and regulatory oversight are necessary to create systems that not only perform well but also support the emotional well-being of all stakeholders involved. Ultimately, the challenge lies in integrating humanity into AI-driven processes, ensuring that content moderation in the age of AI remains not only efficient but also ethically responsible and psychologically supportive.

REFERENCES

America, P. E. N. (2020). *No excuse for abuse: What social media companies can do now to combat online harassment*. https://pen.org/report/no-excuse-for-abuse/

Amershi, S., Cakmak, M., Knox, W. B., & Kulesza, T. (2014). Power to the people: The role of humans in interactive machine learning. *AI Magazine*, *35*(4), 105–120. DOI: 10.1609/aimag.v35i4.2513

Barrett, P. M. (2020). *Who moderates the social media giants?* New York University Stern Center for Business and Human Rights.

Benkler, Y. (2019). Don't let industry write the rules for AI. *Nature*, *569*(7754), 161. DOI: 10.1038/d41586-019-01413-1 PMID: 31043715

Binns, R. (2018). Algorithmic accountability and public reason. *Philosophy & Technology*, *31*(4), 543–556. DOI: 10.1007/s13347-017-0263-5 PMID: 30873342

Binns, R., Veale, M., Van Kleek, M., & Shadbolt, N. (2018). 'It's reducing a human being to a percentage': Perceptions of justice in algorithmic decisions. *Proceedings of the 2018 CHI Conference on Human Factors in Computing Systems*, 1–14. DOI: 10.1145/3173574.3173951

Chancellor, S., & De Choudhury, M. (2022). "When AI Gets It Wrong": Examining the Psychological Toll of AI Misclassification on Mental Health Discourse. *CHI Conference on Human Factors in Computing Systems*.

Chen, A. (2014, October 23). The laborers who keep dick pics and beheadings out of your Facebook feed. *Wired*. https://www.wired.com/2014/10/content-moderation/

Cowie, R., & Cornelius, R. R. (2003). Describing the emotional states that are expressed in speech. *Speech Communication*, *40*(1-2), 5–32. DOI: 10.1016/S0167-6393(02)00071-7

Crawford, K., & Paglen, T. (2021). *Atlas of AI: Power, politics, and the planetary costs of artificial intelligence*. Yale University Press.

Cunningham, S., & Craig, D. (2019). *Social media entertainment: The new intersection of Hollywood and Silicon Valley*. NYU Press.

European Commission. (2022). *Digital Services Act: Ensuring a safe and accountable online environment*. https://ec.europa.eu/info/business-economy-euro/banking-and-finance/digital-finance_en

Feinstein, A., Pavisian, B., & Storm, H. (2018). Moral injury in the context of humanitarian aid work: A review of current research. *European Journal of Psychotraumatology*, *9*(1), 1462834.

Gillespie, T. (2018). *Custodians of the Internet: Platforms, content moderation, and the hidden decisions that shape social media.* Yale University Press.

Gillespie, T., & Karizat, N. (2021). Algorithmically Unjust: How Automated Moderation Contributes to the Silencing of Marginalized Voices. *Social Media + Society*, *7*(3).

Gorwa, R. (2019). The platform governance triangle: Conceptualising the informal regulation of online content. *Internet Policy Review*, *8*(2), 1–22. DOI: 10.14763/2019.2.1407

Gorwa, R., Binns, R., & Katzenbach, C. (2020). Algorithmic content moderation: Technical and political challenges in the automation of platform governance. *Big Data & Society*, *7*(1), 1–15. DOI: 10.1177/2053951719897945

Green, D. (2019). YouTube's moderation problems: Creators speak out. *The Guardian*. https://www.theguardian.com

Hosseini, H., Kannan, S., & Mani, M. (2021). The limits of AI content moderation: A cautionary case study. *Proceedings of the AAAI/ACM Conference on AI, Ethics, and Society*, 173–179.

Jhaver, S., Bruckman, A., & Gilbert, E. (2019). Does transparency in moderation really matter? User behavior after content removal explanations on Reddit. *Proceedings of the ACM on Human-Computer Interaction, 3*(CSCW), 1–27.

Jobin, A., Ienca, M., & Vayena, E. (2019). The health implications of AI and big data in medical research. *Lancet, 394*(10210), 2134–2145.

Kaye, D. (2022). Oversight Board Accountability Review. *Center for Human Rights & Policy*. https://www.ohchr.org

Kowert, R. (2020). Toxic gaming: The impact of content moderation and the need for community-based approaches. *Cyberpsychology (Brno)*, *14*(4), 7.

Madaio, M., Stark, L., Wortman Vaughan, J., & Wallach, H. (2020). Co-designing checklists to understand organizational challenges and opportunities around fairness in AI. *Proceedings of the 2020 CHI Conference on Human Factors in Computing Systems*, 1–14. DOI: 10.1145/3313831.3376445

Matias, J. N. (2019). Preventing harassment and increasing group participation through social norms in 2,190 online science discussions. *Proceedings of the National Academy of Sciences of the United States of America, 116*(20), 9785–9789. DOI: 10.1073/pnas.1813486116 PMID: 31036646

Morley, J., Floridi, L., Kinsey, L., & Elhalal, A. (2020). From what to how: An initial review of publicly available AI ethics tools, methods and research to translate principles into practices. *Science and Engineering Ethics, 26*(4), 2141–2168. DOI: 10.1007/s11948-019-00165-5 PMID: 31828533

Mozilla Foundation. (2020). Creators and Moderation: A Stressful Relationship. https://foundation.mozilla.org

Nesi, J. (2020). The impact of social media on youth mental health: Challenges and opportunities. *North Carolina Medical Journal, 81*(2), 116–121. DOI: 10.18043/ncm.81.2.116 PMID: 32132255

Newton, C. (2019). *The trauma floor: The secret lives of Facebook moderators in America.* The Verge.

Noble, S. U. (2018). *Algorithms of oppression: How search engines reinforce racism.* NYU Press. DOI: 10.18574/nyu/9781479833641.001.0001

Pasquale, F. (2015). *The black box society: The secret algorithms that control money and information.* Harvard University Press. DOI: 10.4159/harvard.9780674736061

Pew Research Center. (2022). Social Media Engagement and User Trust. https://www.pewresearch.org

Picard, R. W. (2000). *Affective computing.* MIT Press. DOI: 10.7551/mitpress/1140.003.0008

Raji, I. D., & Buolamwini, J. (2019). Actionable auditing: Investigating the impact of publicly naming biased performance results of commercial AI products. *Proceedings of the 2019 AAAI/ACM Conference on AI, Ethics, and Society*, 429–435. DOI: 10.1145/3306618.3314244

Raji, I. D., Smart, A., White, R., Mitchell, M., Gebru, T., Hutchinson, B., & Barnes, P. (2020). Closing the AI accountability gap: Defining an end-to-end framework for internal algorithmic auditing. *Proceedings of the 2020 Conference on Fairness, Accountability, and Transparency*, 33–44. DOI: 10.1145/3351095.3372873

Report, F. T. (2023). *Community Standards Enforcement Report.* Meta. https://transparency.fb.com

Report, T. T. (2022). https://transparency.twitter.com

Roberts, S. T. (2019). *Behind the screen: Content moderation in the shadows of social media.* Yale University Press.

Sap, M., Card, D., Gabriel, S., Choi, Y., & Smith, N. A. (2019). The risk of racial bias in hate speech detection. *Proceedings of the 57th Annual Meeting of the Association for Computational Linguistics*, 1668–1678. DOI: 10.18653/v1/P19-1163

Scherer, L. (2022). Building emotionally intelligent AI: A new frontier in human-centered design. *Journal of AI and Society*, *37*(3), 85–102.

Schmidt, A., & Wiegand, M. (2017). A survey on hate speech detection using natural language processing. *Proceedings of the Fifth International Workshop on Natural Language Processing for Social Media*, 1–10. DOI: 10.18653/v1/W17-1101

Subrahmanyam, S. (2021). The Psychodynamics of Apprehension in the Corporate World – A Hermeneutic Review of Literature. *Psychology and Education*, ISSN: 0033-3077, Volume-58 | Issue-3, 1684-1698.

West, S. M. (2021). Content moderation and the labor question. *Social Media + Society*, *7*(3), 1–12.

Whittaker, M., Crawford, K., Dobbe, R., Fried, G., Kaziunas, E., Mathur, V., & Schwartz, O. (2018). *AI Now Report 2018.* AI Now Institute.

YouTube. (2019). Transparency Report. https://transparencyreport.google.com/youtube-policy

Chapter 9
Psychological Well-Being of Human Content Moderators and Wellness Strategies in AI-Driven Content Moderation Organizations

Adi Fahrudin
https://orcid.org/0009-0005-1990-7440
Universitas Bhayangkara Jakarta Raya, Indonesia

Siddhartha Paul Tiwari
https://orcid.org/0000-0003-1596-1501
Google Asia Pacific, Singapore

Kus Hanna Rahmi
https://orcid.org/0009-0005-1990-7440
Universitas Bhayangkara Jakarta Raya, Indonesia

ABSTRACT

As the digital landscape becomes an increasingly central part of daily life, the psychological well-being of individuals is shaped not only by personal and social factors but also by the technological systems that govern online spaces. Among these, AI-driven content moderation organizations play a pivotal role in curating digital interactions and regulating harmful content. This chapter explores the intersection of psychological well-being and AI-powered moderation, examining how algorithms

DOI: 10.4018/979-8-3373-0335-2.ch009

affect emotional experiences, identity formation, and online safety. By integrating psychological theory with emerging concerns around artificial intelligence in content governance, the paper offers a nuanced understanding of how digital systems can both support and challenge mental health.

INTRODUCTION

Considering the fact that content moderation organizations are relatively new to the scene, it can be very challenging to prioritize mental health. Even with technological advances and the use of artificial intelligence, there is still a high number of people working in content moderation organizations who face working conditions and norms that can take a cumulative toll on their health. Scales for the measurement of some work attitudes as well as aspects of psychological well being appear to be correlated in a very strong way (Warr et al., 1979). The promotion of the psychosocial well-being of human content moderators in AI-driven content moderation organizations requires that improvements be made in the work organization, culture, and practices in order to provide a supportive working environment. Mental health programs and continuous training have numerous benefits for companies, including increased employee productivity, safety, and retention. The concept of psychological well-being is of great interest to social psychologists and is closely related to the general literature on adjustment, competence, mood indicators, and so on (Cherlin & Reeder, 1975). Failure to implement effective strategies to support the psychosocial well-being of human content moderators can result in employee burnout and withdrawal from the work environment, higher absenteeism, higher employee attrition and conflict at work due to poor mental health. The implementation of positive changes could have a significant impact on improving mental health for content moderators and creating a psychologically healthy work environment. The issue of content moderation in the modern world is at a crucial juncture and it needs to be prioritized, as both AI and human content moderators are now working together to solve the issues surrounding this critical function in a sensitive and important manner. The concept of psychological well-being has been neglected for a long time in scientific literature. (Ruini et al., 2003). The creation of a psychologically healthy work environment leads to more engaged, productive employees, as it promotes an environment in which employees feel valued, empowered, and motivated, which all contribute to the development of more engaged and productive employees. Human content moderators work in a fast-paced industry, and where repetitive tasks, irregular work schedules, and safety concerns are part of their day-to-day duties, nurturing their mental well-being often takes a backseat in their daily routine. With the right approach and correct wellness strategies in AI driven content moderation organizations, this does not have to be the case.

In content moderation organizations, the primary problem with dealing with workplace mental health is that human content moderators are not aware that the content they are viewing can be harmful to their mental health, which is one of the main problems when it comes to addressing this issue. Due to the nature of shift work and the limited HR channels available to employees in this field, many human content moderators do not fully understand the extent of their benefits, and they may have little time to ask questions. Passion, and especially harmonious passion, play an important role in ensuring sustainable psychological well-being (Vallerand, 2012). There is a relationship between perceived stress in family, school, and peer-group situations, namely anxiety, depression, social dysfunction, and a sense of anergia, in a relationship with four measures of psychological well-being (Siddique & D'Arcy, 1984). Language barriers can also pose a problem and some employees may not have the access to the technology that they need to be able to take advantage of a HR digital helpline platform if they are unable to communicate in their native language.

There is another significant obstacle to improving mental human content moderators aside from awareness, and that is stigma. The stigma is a way for employees to describe how their work involves watching harmful and sensitive content they need to eliminate in order to work in sync with artificial intelligence. AI-driven content moderation organizations remain a male dominated industry in India and South East Asia that prioritizes hiring employees who are ready to work in the US and Europe time zones so that they can eliminate content on the go, while mental health and well-being concerns are usually dismissed. Psychological well-being is strongly correlated with the quality of one's health (Vázquez et al., 2009). The environment is often high-pressure, with the goal to keep the content moderation production line moving at all costs to make sure that the process remains effective. There may be aspects of the workplace culture that discourage employees from slowing down and seeking help or seeking out the support they need for their mental health when they need it.

FOUNDATIONS OF PSYCHOLOGICAL WELL-BEING IN DIGITAL CONTEXTS

The literature surrounding content moderation in online mental health forums reveals a complex interplay between user safety, moderator practices, and the evolving challenges digital environments pose. The foundational work by Cohan et al. (2017) highlights the critical need for timely responses to posts indicating acute distress, suggesting that an automated triaging framework can significantly enhance moderators' ability to prioritize severe content. This framework is essential given the overwhelming volume of daily posts that moderators face, emphasizing the importance of effective content categorization in preventing self-harm. The literature on content moderation and its implications for mental health challenges offers a nuanced exploration of how online environments can both support and endanger vulnerable users. The scoping review by Perry et al., (2021) emphasizes the essential role of moderators in fostering safe online spaces, particularly in health communities where users may exhibit suicidal behaviors. Their findings reveal a gap in understanding the professional practices of moderators, highlighting that most research has focused on volunteer moderators rather than qualified mental health professionals. This lack of insight into how moderators respond to crises raises concerns about the effectiveness of online forums in mitigating risks associated with suicidal behaviors.

Building on this foundation, Klaus Scheuerman et al. (2021) introduce a framework for assessing the severity of harmful content online. They argue that while moderation is crucial for compliance with legal standards and corporate responsibility, current human moderation practices may not sufficiently reduce perceptions of toxicity in online communities. The authors point out the limitations of automated moderation, which, despite its efficiency, often lacks the cultural sensitivity required to address nuanced issues such as hate speech. This highlights a critical tension in moderation practices: the need for human oversight in contexts where emotional and contextual understanding is vital.

Nichele et al. (2022) further this discussion by identifying the challenges and needs in digital mental health moderation, particularly for young users. They advocate for a balanced approach that promotes the positive aspects of social media while addressing its potential harms, such as anxiety and cyberbullying. Their research underscores the importance of moderators as facilitators of information flow and community support, suggesting that effective moderation can significantly influence user participation and commitment to online communities.

The study by Singhal et al., (2022) expands on the governance mechanisms of online communities by detailing the interconnected components of moderation policies and practices. They emphasize the role of both human moderators and automated systems in enforcing community guidelines, while also acknowledging the complexities surrounding the definitions of harmful content. This research underscores the need for clearer guidelines and definitions to navigate the often ambiguous landscape of online moderation.

Trujillo and Cresci (2022) provide empirical evidence on the effects of moderation interventions, revealing a mixed bag of outcomes. While some interventions reduced user activity, they often failed to decrease toxicity, and in some instances, led to increased radicalization among users. This inconsistency suggests that moderation strategies require careful consideration and adaptation to specific community dynamics to be effective. Deng et al., (2023) highlight the critical role of moderators in online mental health communities, emphasizing their potential to enhance the safety and effectiveness of peer support. Their qualitative study suggests that continuous and effective moderation is essential for maximizing the positive impacts of these platforms, indicating a need for further research into the moderators' roles and their interactions with community members. Cai et al. (2024) explore user perceptions of content moderation, emphasizing the importance of transparency and fairness in moderation practices. Their findings suggest that users are more likely to engage positively with platforms that provide clear explanations for content removal, thus enhancing perceived justice and fairness. This insight is crucial for platforms seeking to improve user trust and satisfaction in their moderation practices.

Finally, Vahed et al., (2024) address the moral implications of content moderation, particularly concerning harmful behaviors promoted on social media. They highlight the significant role users play in identifying harmful content through reporting mechanisms, underscoring the need for platforms to understand the factors influencing users' reporting decisions. This research aligns with the broader discourse on the necessity of effective moderation in safeguarding mental health and addressing the complexities of online harm. Together, these articles present a comprehensive view of the challenges and solutions associated with content moderation in relation to mental health. They underscore the necessity for ongoing research and adaptation of practices to better support vulnerable populations in online spaces.

Perry et al. (2021) expand on this theme by examining the broader responsibilities of moderators in maintaining safe online spaces, particularly for individuals exhibiting suicidal behaviors. Their scoping review underscores the necessity for qualified health professionals in moderation roles, revealing a significant gap in research concerning the professional practices of these moderators. The authors argue for a deeper understanding of how moderators navigate the complexities of online interactions, especially when dealing with vulnerable populations. In response to these challenges, Scheuerman et al. propose a Framework of Severity that could serve as a vital tool for content moderation across various platforms. This framework not only assists moderators in prioritizing content based on user experiences but also alleviates the burden of managing the most harmful content. By establishing clear categories of severity, the framework aims to enhance the efficacy of moderation practices and improve user outcomes.

Nichele et al. (2022) further contextualize the discussion by addressing the duality of moderation approaches—manual versus automated. Their case study of Kooth highlights the complexities of moderating digital mental health spaces, particularly the need for responsible AI tools that can effectively navigate the nuances of social interactions. The authors emphasize that while algorithmic solutions aim to remove harmful content, they often fall short in addressing the contextual subtleties required for effective moderation. Singhal et al. (2022) contribute to the understanding of moderation practices by analyzing community guidelines across various social media platforms. Their study identifies significant gaps in current research and highlights the diverse moderation techniques employed, which can lead to varying user experiences and perceptions of safety. This analysis is crucial in understanding how different platforms manage harmful content and the implications for user mental health.

Trujillo and Cresci (2022) examine the effects of moderation interventions more closely, revealing a complex landscape where such interventions can lead to both desired and unintended consequences. Their findings indicate that while moderation can reduce user activity, it may also exacerbate toxicity in certain communities, underscoring the need for nuanced strategies that consider users' diverse reactions to moderation efforts. Deng et al. (2023) emphasize the pivotal role of moderators in fostering peer-to-peer support within online mental health communities. Their qualitative study highlights the potential benefits of effective moderation in enhancing user safety and engagement, suggesting that moderators can significantly influence the overall health of these online spaces. The authors call for further research to explore how moderators can be better supported and trained to maximize their impact.

Cai et al. (2024) and Vahed et al. (2024) delve into the perceptions of justice and fairness in content moderation. Their studies reveal that transparency in moderation decisions can enhance user engagement and satisfaction, indicating the importance of clear communication in moderating practices. These insights are crucial for platforms aiming to maintain user trust while effectively managing harmful content. Overall, the literature illustrates the multifaceted challenges of content moderation in online mental health contexts, highlighting the critical role of moderators and the need for frameworks that support their efforts in safeguarding vulnerable users.

Cohan et al. (2017) present a significant contribution to the discussion surrounding content moderation in mental health online communities. The authors address a pressing challenge faced by moderators: the overwhelming volume of content generated daily in these forums, which complicates their ability to identify and respond to posts indicating severe self-harm ideation. The framework proposed by the authors categorizes user content into four severity levels, allowing for a more systematic approach to triaging posts based on the risk of self-harm. This classification not only aids moderators in prioritizing their responses but also enhances the overall safety and support provided within these online environments. The authors' methodology demonstrates a marked improvement over existing techniques, indicating a substantial advancement in the field of content moderation for mental health forums.

A critical evaluation of the material reveals that the authors effectively leverage quantitative analysis to support their claims. Their findings suggest that long-term engagement in these forums correlates with a decrease in users' reported severity of risk, which underscores the potential therapeutic benefits of online community support. However, the study could benefit from a more detailed exploration of the implications of these findings for moderators' training and the ethical considerations surrounding automated content moderation. Furthermore, while the proposed model shows promise in identifying critical content, the article does not extensively address the potential limitations of relying on automated systems in sensitive contexts. The nuances of mental health discussions may not always be captured accurately by algorithms, raising questions about the balance between automation and the human element in moderation practices.

Perry et al. (2021) offers a critical examination of the role of moderators in online health communities, particularly in the context of supporting individuals experiencing suicidal behaviors. The authors highlight a significant gap in the literature regarding the professional practices of moderators, noting that most existing studies have focused on volunteer moderators rather than those with formal qualifications in mental health. This distinction is crucial, as the effectiveness of moderation in providing safe online spaces is closely tied to the moderators' training and expertise. The article underscores the importance of moderators in maintaining the safety of online environments, which can have a positive impact on mental health outcomes for users seeking support. However, the authors point out that there is a lack of research detailing how moderators respond to suicidal crises, the specific skills and knowledge they employ, and their emotional experiences while working in these high-stress situations. This lack of insight raises concerns about the adequacy of support provided to vulnerable populations, as moderators may not always be equipped to handle the complexities of mental health crises effectively.

Moreover, the review reveals that the transition from face-to-face interactions to online moderation presents unique challenges, such as the absence of visual cues and the potential for anonymity. These factors can complicate the moderators' ability to assess situations accurately and provide appropriate interventions. The findings indicate that there is considerable variability in the training and preparedness of online moderators, which further complicates the evaluation of their effectiveness in crises. The article was presenting a critical examination of the current state of content moderation and its intersection with mental health, particularly in terms of the perceived severity of harmful content. The authors argue that existing platform policies, often shaped by legal standards, do not necessarily align with users' perceptions of harm. This disconnect highlights a significant challenge in content moderation practices, as legal definitions of harmful content may not adequately capture the nuanced ways in which such content affects individuals and communities.

One of the central insights provided by the authors is the notion that legality does not equate to perceived harm. Their findings suggest that experts within companies view legal frameworks as overly contextual and not universally applicable when assessing the potential impact of harmful content. For instance, while child grooming and child pornography are recognized as illegal, the authors emphasize that the harm associated with these forms of content transcends their legal status. Instead, the authors propose that the dimensions leading to severely negative outcomes should guide the evaluation of harmful content, thereby informing moderation strategies that prioritize user safety and well-being. The proposed Framework of Severity is a significant contribution to the discourse on content moderation. It offers a structured approach for researchers, practitioners, and policymakers to assess and categorize harmful content based on its severity rather than solely its legality. This framework could enhance platforms' ability to prioritize moderation efforts, ensuring that the most severely harmful content receives the necessary attention. Additionally, the framework has implications for labor management within moderation teams, as it can help distribute workloads more effectively among moderators by focusing on content that poses the greatest risk to users.

Moreover, the article underscores the importance of integrating user perspectives into content moderation practices. By acknowledging the subjective nature of harm, the authors advocate for a more empathetic approach to moderation that considers the psychological impacts of harmful content on users. This perspective is particularly relevant in the context of mental health, as the emotional and psychological toll of exposure to harmful content can be significant.

Nichele et al. (2022) presents a comprehensive examination of the intersection between digital mental health support and moderation practices. The authors emphasize the critical role of moderation in fostering safe online environments for vulnerable users, particularly those grappling with self-harming behaviors and eating disorders. Their insights are particularly relevant in an era where digital platforms serve as both sources of support and potential triggers for mental health issues. One of the central arguments of the article is the need for effective moderation strategies that balance the promotion of positive interactions while mitigating risks associated with negative behaviors, such as anxiety and cyberbullying. The authors reference the Royal Society for Public Health's call to action, highlighting the necessity of leveraging social media's benefits while addressing its drawbacks. This dual approach underscores the complexity of digital environments where users, often labeled as 'vulnerable publics,' seek both connection and support.

Nichele et al (2022) also delineates various forms of moderation—automatic and manual—and discusses the implications of each. Automated moderation, powered by AI tools, is presented as a double-edged sword; while it allows for rapid removal of harmful content, it is often criticized for its opacity and ineffectiveness in nuanced situations. This critique raises critical questions about the reliability of algorithmic systems in understanding context and the potential for misinterpretation of user intent. On the other hand, manual moderation, while more contextually aware, faces its own set of challenges, including scalability and the emotional toll on moderators who must engage with distressing content regularly. Moreover, the authors highlight the role of moderators as brokers of information within online communities. This perspective is crucial as it positions moderators not merely as gatekeepers but as facilitators of community engagement and support. The influence of moderation on user participation and commitment is a vital consideration, as effective moderation can enhance the sense of safety and belonging, thereby encouraging individuals to seek help and share experiences.

The article Trujillo & Cresci (2022) provides a comprehensive examination of content moderation practices across various social media platforms, emphasizing the importance of effective guidelines and enforcement mechanisms. The authors systematically analyze existing community guidelines and moderation policies, aiming to highlight both the successes and shortcomings of current approaches to combating hate speech and misinformation. One of the key contributions of this article is its identification of research gaps in the field of content moderation. The authors meticulously review over two hundred interdisciplinary research papers, which allows them to uncover inconsistencies and variations in moderation techniques between mainstream and fringe platforms. This distinction is crucial, as it underscores the varying degrees of effectiveness and accountability that different platforms exhibit in their moderation efforts. The article suggests that understanding these differences can inform better practices and policies tailored to the unique challenges faced by each type of platform.

The introduction of three taxonomies based on their analysis serves as a valuable framework for categorizing content moderation strategies. This classification not only aids in understanding the landscape of moderation practices but also facilitates the identification of specific areas that require further research and development. The authors argue that a more nuanced understanding of these taxonomies can lead to improved enforcement mechanisms that are sensitive to the context and nature of the content being moderated. In their discussions of practical challenges, Trujillo & Cresci (2022) highlight the psychological toll that content moderation can impose on moderators, particularly when they are exposed to harmful or distressing content. This aspect is particularly relevant to the intersection of content moderation and mental health, as the emotional and psychological impacts on moderators can have significant implications for the overall effectiveness of moderation strategies. The authors advocate for the implementation of support systems and training programs that prioritize the mental well-being of moderators, thereby enhancing their ability to perform their roles effectively while mitigating the adverse effects of their work.

Furthermore, the article addresses the broader implications of content moderation policies on user behavior and community dynamics. By analyzing the enforcement of guidelines, the authors suggest that inconsistent application of moderation policies can lead to user distrust and a decline in community engagement. This observation highlights the necessity for platforms to not only establish clear guidelines but also to ensure their consistent enforcement to foster a healthier online environment. Trujillo & Cresci, 2022) also presents a comprehensive examination of the effects of moderation interventions on user behavior within online communities, particularly focusing on the subreddit. The authors synthesize findings from various studies to assess how different moderation strategies, such as quarantine and restriction, impact user activity and community dynamics.

A key insight from the article is the recognition that while moderation interventions can reduce the activity of moderated users, they may inadvertently increase toxicity within the community. (Trujillo & Cresci, 2022) found that quarantine and restriction measures led to a decrease in user engagement but did not necessarily mitigate harmful behaviors. Notably, the authors concluded that restriction had a more pronounced effect than quarantine, indicating that the type of intervention employed can significantly influence user responses and community health. The article also highlights the challenges associated with user migration from banned communities to new platforms, where increased toxicity and radicalization were observed. This finding raises concerns about the efficacy of moderation strategies in addressing harmful content, as users may simply relocate rather than alter their behavior. Furthermore, the authors point out that moderation interventions on platforms like Instagram and Twitter have yielded mixed results, with some interventions failing to curtail problematic content effectively.

Trujillo and Cresci (2022) emphasize the need for a deeper understanding of user-level effects, as most existing research has focused on platform or community-level outcomes. The article suggests that user reactions to moderation interventions can vary significantly, which complicates the development of effective moderation strategies. This heterogeneity in user responses underscores the importance of tailoring interventions to the specific context of the community and its users. Deng et al. (2023) presents a nuanced examination of the critical role that moderators play in shaping online mental health communities. The authors argue that effective moderation is essential for maximizing user safety and enhancing the positive impact of peer support interactions. This assertion is particularly relevant in the context of increasing reliance on digital platforms for mental health support, especially during the pandemic, which has highlighted both the potential benefits and risks associated with unmoderated environments.

The study employs qualitative methods to explore the mechanisms through which moderators influence community dynamics. The findings suggest that moderators are not merely gatekeepers but also active facilitators of supportive interactions. They help to cultivate a safe space that encourages open dialogue while simultaneously mitigating harmful behaviors that could arise in peer-to-peer settings. This dual role is critical, as it underscores the importance of having trained individuals who can navigate the complexities of mental health discussions online. Moreover, the article raises important considerations regarding the scalability of moderator roles. The authors call for further research to investigate how these roles can be effectively expanded across various platforms and cultural contexts. This is particularly pertinent for low- and middle-income countries, where access to mental health resources is often limited. By emphasizing the need for a diverse range of studies that include perspectives from community members and users, the authors advocate for a more comprehensive understanding of how online peer support can be optimized.

The implications of this research extend beyond academic inquiry; they suggest practical applications for mental health initiatives that leverage digital platforms. The authors propose that online peer support could serve as a valuable adjunct to traditional mental health care, potentially enhancing public health efforts. However, they caution that unmoderated communities may pose significant risks, indicating a pressing need for ongoing research into the specific attributes and challenges of these digital environments.

Cai et al. (2024) provide a comprehensive examination of the complexities surrounding content moderation in social media environments. The authors articulate that content moderation, which involves the screening of user-generated content to assess its appropriateness, is essential for maintaining safe online spaces. They highlight the dual approach of employing algorithms and human moderators to manage harmful content, a practice that has become increasingly sophisticated as platforms strive to create a balance between user safety and freedom of expression.

One of the critical insights from the article is the variability in users' perceptions of fairness and justice in moderation decisions. The authors note that many users express dissatisfaction when their content is removed without adequate explanation, leading to frustration and even disengagement from the platform. This point underscores the importance of transparency in content moderation practices. The article presents evidence that providing explanations for content removal can enhance users' perceptions of fairness, suggesting that platforms should prioritize clear communication about moderation decisions to foster trust and maintain user engagement.

Furthermore, the authors conducted an online experiment to investigate how contextual explanations surrounding harmful content influence users' perceptions of moderation fairness. This empirical approach adds significant value to the discussion, as it grounds theoretical insights in practical findings. The results of the experiment indicate that the context in which content moderation occurs can significantly affect user perceptions, highlighting the need for platforms to tailor their moderation strategies to the specific circumstances surrounding each case of harmful content. In terms of implications for practice, the article advocates for a more nuanced understanding of user perceptions in content moderation. By recognizing that users may react differently based on the context and the clarity of the moderation process, social media platforms can refine their policies to better align with user expectations. This could lead to more effective moderation strategies that not only protect users from harmful content but also promote a sense of justice and fairness in the digital space.

Vahed et al., (2024) provides a comprehensive examination of the complexities surrounding content moderation on social networking sites (SNSs) and its implications for mental health. The authors articulate the pressing need for effective content moderation strategies in light of the increasing prevalence of harmful online content, which has been linked to adverse mental health outcomes, including self-harm and suicidal ideation, particularly among vulnerable populations. One of the article's key insights is the role of individual users in the content moderation process. The authors highlight that users can submit complaints through reporting mechanisms, thereby actively participating in the regulation of online content. This participatory approach is further underscored by recent legislative developments, such as the European Union's Digital Services Act (DSA), which emphasizes the importance of user engagement in moderating objectionable content. However, the article also points out that while users have the potential to influence content moderation, there is limited empirical research on the factors that motivate users to report harmful content. This gap in understanding is critical, as it affects the overall efficacy of content moderation efforts and raises questions about the moral and ethical responsibilities of users in the digital landscape. The authors effectively situate their discussion within the broader context of societal concerns about online harm and its consequences for mental health. They reference research that correlates exposure to negative online content with increased psychological distress, thereby reinforcing the urgency of addressing online harm through robust moderation practices. However, the article could benefit from a more in-depth exploration of the psychological mechanisms that drive user behavior in reporting content. Understanding these mechanisms could enhance the effectiveness of content moderation strategies and potentially mitigate the negative mental health impacts associated with online harm.

HUMAN CONTENT MODERATORS: PROMOTING THE PSYCHOSOCIAL WELL-BEING OF THE MODERATORS

The psychosocial wellbeing of human content moderators is an issue that requires a holistic and comprehensive understanding due to the unique nature of their jobs and the unique challenges that they face every day. Moderators play a critical role in maintaining the trust and safety of online communities by continuously reviewing potentially harmful, distressing, or inappropriate content in order to keep their communities safe and trustworthy. A person's mental, emotional, and physical well-being can be considerably affected when they are exposed to such material that is not typically seen by normal people on a day-to-day basis. It is especially important for the well-being of moderators, the well-being of the broader society, as well as the efficiency of the organization, to keep their psychosocial health top of mind.

Media conglomerates and technology companies using human moderators should establish institutional support systems as the foundations of their moderator welfare programs. A variety of essential resources, including access to HR, counseling services, employee assistance programs, and easy access to mental health support, all play an essential role in providing moderators with immediate and continuous support. Having a robust peer-to-peer support network can help eliminate feelings of isolation among moderators and promote a sense of community among them by removing feelings of isolation that may be present. There are a number of ways in which we can further enhance the well-being of moderators if we offer them clear, transparent and consistent channels of communication. This will reduce uncertainty and reinforce the commitment of the organization to ensure the well-being of moderators.

Figure 1. Human content moderators: Promoting the psychosocial welfare of the moderators

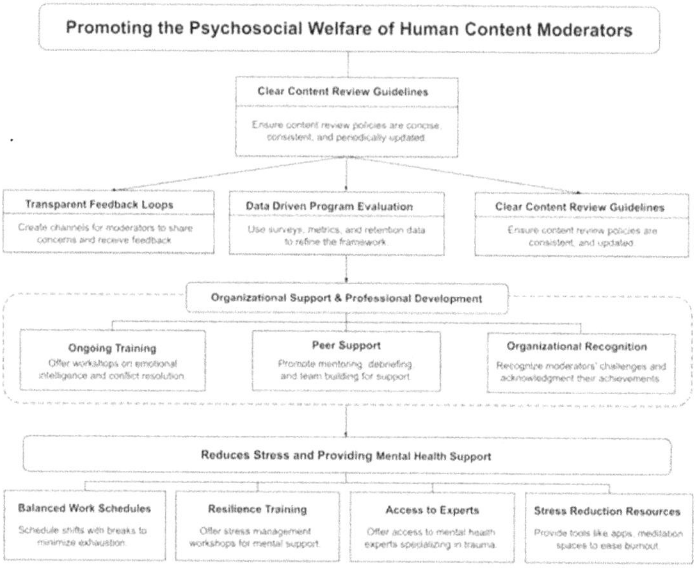

Educating, learning, and developing for moderators according to their needs can have a significant impact on their psychosocial resilience. The media and technology industry should regularly implement training programs that focus on stress management, coping skills, resilience-building, and psychological safety in order to help employees cope with stress. Providing moderators with DIY tools to manage emotional responses effectively, technology companies enable moderators to maintain their mental health more effectively by providing them with self-help tools. Providing moderators with ongoing education will ensure that they remain informed of moderating policies and practices that are continually evolving, decreasing confusion and stress caused by constantly changing guidelines and policies.

Moderators' psychosocial welfare can also be promoted through flexible working arrangements, which needs to be discussed per shift so that it is feasible to work out flexible working arrangements. The technology and media industries must recognize the detrimental impact that work scheduling has on the health and well-being of moderators as well as their fitness. Flexibility in shifts and schedules tailored to the needs of the individual promotes a healthier work-life balance through policies that enable such flexibility. Taking frequent breaks from work and providing rest periods throughout work shifts may minimize fatigue, reduce burnout risk, and enhance the overall productivity of employees. Providing moderators with access to flexibility ensures they are allowed adequate time to recover from psychological strain, reinforcing their resilience against the stresses of their jobs.

Figure 1 illustrates how health and wellness programs that are integrated within the workplace can dramatically improve the overall well-being of moderators. Physical wellness initiatives are a great way to promote a healthy lifestyle. There are several ways to address the connection between physical and psychological health, such as providing healthy meal options, encouraging hydration, and offering exercise programs. Stress and emotional responses can be managed better with wellness activities, like mindfulness sessions, meditation exercises, and relaxation techniques, which provide moderators with valuable tools for coping with stress and managing emotions. Employee engagement, especially engagement with HR, and morale are boosted as a result of participation in wellness initiatives on a regular basis, fostering an atmosphere in which holistic health is prioritized, resulting in a healthier work environment.

As shown in figure 1, recognition and appreciation significantly contribute to the psychosocial welfare of moderators. The authors would like to highlight the importance of developing formal recognition programs and incentives that acknowledge moderator contributions as well as facilitate peer workers' feeling more valued and belonging within the company by recognizing their contributions. Taking time to recognize achievements, milestones, and consistent performance can elevate morale, reduce feelings of unappreciation, and positively influence the culture of the workplace by elevating morale. It is important to recognize moderators for the critical role they play, as well as to motivate them to perform at their best and engage in high levels of participation. Figure 1 elaborates on how dedicated human resource interventions can further enhance moderators' psychosocial support in more detail. There needs to be established crisis intervention teams within organizations that are trained to provide immediate psychological assistance during critical incidents or emotional breakdowns caused by distressing content reviews. Debriefing sessions should be scheduled on a regular basis so moderators are able to process their experiences, address emotional distress proactively, and strengthen their capacity to cope with future challenges. The implementation of proactive HR interventions signals an organizational awareness and receptiveness, which reinforces trust and fosters an environment where all employees feel valued. A number of policies have been adopted in an attempt to improve the working conditions of moderators. These reforms have a considerable influence on their psychosocial well-being. There is a need for organizations to implement policies restricting overtime work, ensuring reasonable workloads, and providing adequate equipment and resources to ensure that moderators are protected from work-related hazards. Psychological safety at work encourages open communication within a work environment, allowing moderators to voice concerns and seek support without fear of being stigmatized or retaliated against as a result. Having a supportive work environment improves employee satisfaction and performance, reduces the likelihood of burnout, and promotes mental health among moderators by reducing the incidence of burnout.

Figure 2. Wellness initiatives in content moderation organizations

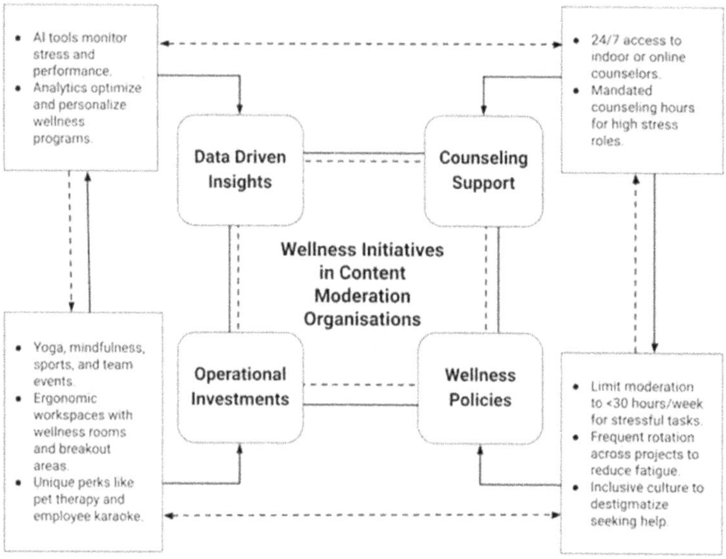

Engaging in a meaningful way with the wider community even if its via social media its fine and this is also an essential part of improving the welfare of moderators. As shown in figure 2 inclusive culture to seek help is important and a public awareness campaign can be a valuable way to address misconceptions about the nature of content moderation work, thus reducing the stigmatization and harassment that moderators face from the outside world. The goal of fostering community engagement and understanding is to foster mutual respect, create a supportive external environment in which moderators are recognized for their important role in maintaining online safety, and create an environment of mutual respect among them. By utilizing technological advancements and artificial intelligence, human moderators will be better able to support their psychosocial needs. Moderators have easy access to psychosocial support resources through technology-enabled platforms such as remote counseling, virtual peer support groups, and online wellness resources, thanks to technology-enabled platforms. By combining technology-driven solutions with human moderation strategies, organizations are able to create more resilient and sustainable moderation practices while balancing workload demands and moderator health in a more effective manner. With these 360 degree strategies, it highlights the necessity of putting psychosocial welfare at the center of content moderation roles, ultimately contributing to healthier work environments, increased productivity, and continued employee engagement in the workplace.

LEVERAGING AI AND MAINTAINING BALANCE BETWEEN HUMAN AND AI

Due to the volume of information being generated from technology and media companies and the complexity of online content, it is necessary to have effective and robust modes of moderation. The use of Artificial Intelligence (AI) has of late emerged as a powerful tool to complement human efforts in content moderation, offering speed, efficiency, and scalability, allowing the management of vast amounts of data to be carried out with little manual effort. Moderation is not solely reliant on technology; it requires a balanced collaboration between human moderators and artificial intelligence systems in order to ensure accuracy, sensitivity towards everything, social and ethical considerations are adequately taken into consideration when moderation is carried out.

Figure 3. Benefits of AI content moderation in partnership with human moderators

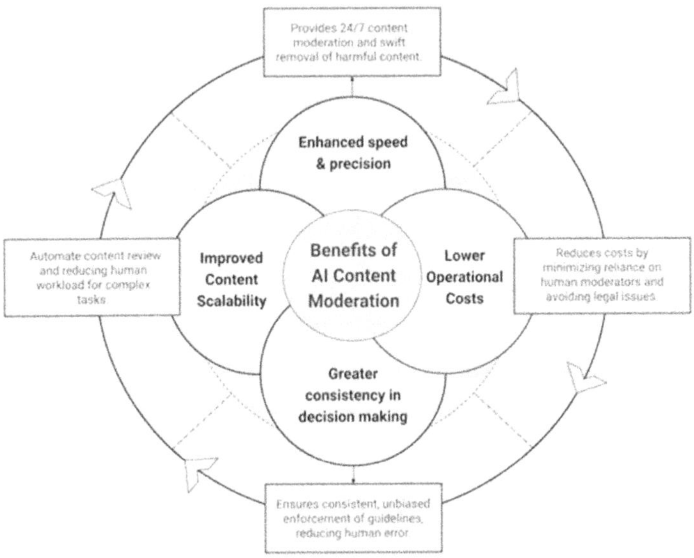

In Figure 3, many advantages can be seen of AI-driven content moderation, including the ability to detect, analyze, and classify content rapidly by utilizing machine learning algorithms, natural language processing, and image recognition technologies in a hybrid environment. There are several automated systems that can reduce the workload of a human moderator by filtering out a large portion of obviously harmful content, such as explicit imagery, violent material, hate speech, and spam, thus significantly reducing the workload of humans. The ability of artificial intelligence to quickly sort through massive datasets and identify content violations provides key support for human moderators, allowing them to focus on more complex and context-sensitive cases that AI might find challenging to interpret accurately without the help of AI.

There are many limitations associated with AI algorithms, such as the fact that they tend to operate based on patterns learned from historical data, which can lead to bias and inaccuracies, especially when dealing with context-sensitive data. There are many cases where content concerning the latest satire, political commentary, elections, cultural nuances, or individual or sensitive mental health discussions often requires human judgment in order to interpret correctly. Though AI systems are becoming more advanced, they do not currently possess the nuanced understanding and emotional intelligence required to fully comprehend context, intent, and subtleties involved in human communication due to their lack of nuance and emotional intelligence. Due to this limitation, the need for integrating human oversight into the moderation process is highlighted.

A human moderator is essential in the process of verifying AI's decisions and addressing ambiguous content which might be mistakenly classified by the AI. They are capable of applying ethical reasoning, cultural awareness, as well as emotional intelligence, which enables them to complement AI's computational efficiency. Technology companies should create clear protocols explaining how moderation tasks are to be divided and escalated in order to ensure effective collaboration between humans and artificial intelligence. As soon as content is flagged by AI systems, it should be reviewed by human moderators to make sure they are fair, accurate, and respecting the rights and intentions of the users, whenever an uncertainty arises.

There is no substitute for continuous training and iterative learning processes in the refinement of AI moderation systems. The role of human moderators is crucial to providing valuable feedback to the AI developers, highlighting incorrect classifications, biased outcomes, or misunderstandings about the context of the results. By continually receiving human feedback, AI systems improve their accuracy over time, which, in turn, reduces the number of false positives and negatives as time goes. AI moderation systems should be regularly updated based on insights gained from human moderators in order to ensure their adaptability to emerging trends, evolving linguistic patterns, and new types of online content that appear on a regular basis.

As important as transparency in AI-driven moderation processes is, it is equally important that they be transparent. Whenever automated systems are used to influence moderation decisions affecting a user's content, the user must be informed of that fact. A clear explanation of why specific content was flagged or removed helps maintain trust and engagement between users and the company. Users' perception of fairness is enhanced by transparency, not only because it enhances their perception of fairness, but also because it creates accountability in moderation practices, allowing users to appeal decisions if necessary. There is also the chance for organizations to further reinforce trust by explaining openly the roles of the AI and human moderators, clarifying that they are collaborative.

There is a need for comprehensive moderator training programs and technological literacy programs to help maximize the effectiveness of human-AI collaboration. Whenever a moderator receives inputs from an automated system or interprets them, they should be trained on how to manage the system effectively. A good training program should include guidelines for maintaining AI systems, recognizing biases in the system, and employing critical thinking when making decisions about moderation. Having an education program such as this ensures that manual moderators remain effective collaborators rather than passive overseers of the decisions made by robots.

In spite of the effectiveness of AI moderation tools, they are not without their limitations. Considering ethical considerations for technology companies is a foundational part of the planning and development of AI moderation systems. A number of recommendations should be made by technology companies in order to mitigate biases, avoid over-reliance on automation, uphold privacy standards, and uphold human rights in the workplace. Regulatory compliance guidelines and ethical and moral frameworks for AI should lead the development process, to ensure that moderation practices respect freedom of expression and cultural diversity as well as ensuring user safety and community integrity are protected.

Using artificial intelligence as a tool for content moderation has tremendous potential for managing online environments efficiently if it is done in the right way. The use of artificial intelligence alone will not be sufficient to address the complex human interactions online with a nuanced moderation that is necessary. As a moderation system, the ideal system incorporates the efficiency and scalability of artificial intelligence with the nuanced judgment and ethical reasoning of humans. Assuring a successful human-artificial collaboration requires clear operational protocols as well as continuous training and feedback, transparent operations, and robust ethical oversight. Online communities that collaborate in this way are more likely to be safer, more inclusive, and more responsive.

CONTENT MODERATION AND MENTAL HEALTH

The literature on content moderation in online mental health forums reveals significant challenges and potential solutions for ensuring user safety and well-being. (Cohan et al., 2017) emphasize the urgent need for timely responses to posts indicating acute distress, advocating for an automated triaging framework that can aid moderators in prioritizing severe content. This framework is crucial in light of the overwhelming volume of posts that moderators encounter daily, which can hinder their ability to identify and address critical situations effectively.

(Perry et al., 2021) further explore the responsibilities of moderators, particularly in the context of supporting individuals exhibiting suicidal behaviors. Their scoping review highlights a gap in research regarding the professional practices of moderators, emphasizing the need for qualified health professionals in these roles. The complexities of online interactions with vulnerable populations necessitate a deeper understanding of how moderators navigate their responsibilities.

propose a Framework of Severity for content moderation, which categorizes harmful content based on user experiences. This framework aims to enhance moderation efficacy and improve user outcomes by providing clear categories for prioritization. (Nichele et al., 2022) contribute to this discussion by examining the dichotomy between manual and automated moderation approaches, illustrating the necessity for responsible AI tools that can effectively handle the nuances of social interactions in digital mental health spaces.

(Singhal et al., 2022) analyze community guidelines across various platforms, identifying significant gaps in research and highlighting the diversity of moderation techniques. This analysis is essential for understanding how different platforms manage harmful content and its implications for user mental health. (Trujillo & Cresci, 2022) delve into the effects of moderation interventions, revealing that while such measures can reduce user activity, they may also inadvertently exacerbate toxicity in certain communities.

(Deng et al., 2023) emphasize the pivotal role of moderators in fostering peer-to-peer support within online mental health communities. Their qualitative study underscores the potential benefits of effective moderation in enhancing user safety and engagement, calling for further research to explore how moderators can be better supported and trained. (Cai et al., 2024) and (Vahed et al., 2024) investigate perceptions of justice and fairness in content moderation, revealing that transparency in moderation decisions can significantly enhance user satisfaction and engagement.

PROMOTING THE PSYCHOSOCIAL WELFARE OF HUMAN CONTENT MODERATORS

The implementation of AI-driven content moderation can play an important role in managing the amount of news and daily content that is being published on social media. When faced with such challenging content and times, the ability of the organization to provide adequate content moderators is largely dependent on the psychosocial well-being of its workforce. The mental and emotional strain experienced by human content moderators can have lasting effects in the long run if they are not addressed adequately in a timely manner. While reviewing harmful or sensitive material, there will definitely be a range of emotions that are experienced, including anxiety, apprehension, and stress as well as fear, and it is important not to misinterpret these emotions as signs of weakness or incompetence as they are the natural reactions to crisis situations. To effectively manage and mitigate the psychological toll of crises on their human content moderators as part of a comprehensive crisis management strategy, AI-powered content moderation organizations need to implement a comprehensive support system that cultivates both institutional and individual resilience in order to effectively manage and mitigate the psychological toll of crises.

The psychological challenges faced by organizations that use AI and human content moderation can be categorized as follows:

Organizations that employ artificial intelligence to moderate content and the workers who work for them are exposed to a variety of stressors during their normal day-to-day activities, which can adversely affect their mental, emotional, and physical well-being. Here are a few of the main challenges:

1. During their shifts (specially during night shifts), content moderators are isolated from their friends and family, as well as physically isolated from colleagues at times when reviewing sensitive content. Human content moderators may suffer from feelings of loneliness and emotional distress as a result of prolonged separations from their families and peers. A correlation exists between the efficacy of selected personality, behavior, and social/organizational variables as predictors of how well a person adapts to night work in terms of personality and organizational variables (Bohle & Tilley, 1989). Having limited social interactions and watching harmful and inappropriate content on a constant basis can exacerbate feelings of alienation and the absence of emotional support.
2. Reactions that are emotionally charged. When reviewing sensitive content for an extended period of time, situations can trigger intense emotions such as anger, anxiety, and fear, which can interfere with the ability to make decisions and perform the overall job duties in a competent manner. Chronic stress and

feelings of exhaustion are caused by a prolonged exposure to stress-inducing environments.

3. During certain world events, there can be burnout and overwhelming workloads. Workloads are increasing, shifts are being extended, and events such as world events are contributing to burnout, which leads to physical and mental exhaustion. As a result of a feeling of helplessness and loss of normalcy, motivation and job satisfaction can be lowered.
4. Reviewing inappropriate content can result in moral distress. A human content moderator may face ethical dilemmas that challenge their professional as well as moral standards, if they are working day to day on inappropriate content, or if they are seeing and moderating content that they do not understand. Having to make difficult decisions at a time when resources are scarce or difficult choices need to be made about sensitive political content, for example, can result in psychological distress over the course of a lifetime.
5. There is an insufficient amount of resources available. A lack of proper HR support during shift times on the floor while working, a lack of good quality software and hardware, as well as staffing shortages may be factors that contribute to increased stress levels. Insufficient resources can often lead to mental challenges as a result of the extremely hard work, coupled with insufficient resources, and a feeling of frustration when it comes to reviewing sensitive content that contains highly sensitive information.
6. Physical stress and fatigue occur as a result of an increase in mental workload and activity, resulting in physical strain and fatigue. Human content moderators often work long hours and perform irregular sleep patterns, which can lead to fatigue and physical exhaustion as a result of chronic fatigue. There is an association between health status and cultural participation and psychological well-being, with particular attention to the interaction between patterns of cultural access and other factors known to affect psychological well-being (Grossi et al., 2012). The psychological well-being of a person is inextricably linked to the quality of their sleep (Hamilton et al., 2007). Rest and nutrition are essential to ensure the immune system is functioning properly and for maintaining overall health.
7. Human editors who are in charge of reviewing the content sometimes have to work under a great deal of pressure to keep informed as they may have to review the content as soon as possible, and the review process requires discretion from them. There is a great deal of cognitive burden on content moderators due to the fact that they must keep up with ever changing policies, political situations, and regulatory procedures. There is an increasing number of guidelines and policies constantly changing, which can cause confusion and increase the level of stress in our lives.

8. Stress related to secondary traumatic events. As a result of reviewing threatening content and experiencing traumatic experiences, human content moderators can develop secondary traumatic stress as a result of their reviews. Repeated exposure to trauma and viloence is likely to lead to compassion fatigue and numbness on an emotional level.
9. Reductions in the number of employees and financial pressures. A reduction in staff due to sickness, layoffs, or furloughs can lead to increased workloads and pressure on the human content moderators as a result. There can be uncertainty and anxiety within content moderation organizations that are powered by artificial intelligence (AI).
10. Harassment and stigmatization within the community. Human content moderators may face stigmas, blame, or harassment from the public due to the perceived nature of their job, which involves watching harmful, pornographic, and sensitive content on a daily basis. Having negative perceptions of your organization can have a negative impact on your morale and increase your emotional burdens.
11. The amount of content being moderated by human content moderators is high. A continuous exposure to distressing and harmful news and social media content can make content moderators feel more anxious and stressed as a result of increased anxiety. There is no doubt that information overload and the flood of content can contribute to feelings of helplessness and despair among employees.

Promoting Psychosocial Wellbeing in AI Driven Content Moderation Organizations

Those organizations that employ AI driven content moderation should implement holistic strategies that address the mental, emotional, and physical needs of the human content moderators in order to support them and enhance their resilience. Here are some of the key strategies (from the authors research, which is selective and not exhaustive):

1. The institutional support system is an important part of this process. The provision of mental health resources, such as counseling services and employee assistance programs (EAPs), to employees is essential. Social support, as conceived and assessed from a socio-psychological perspective, has been found to be related to psychological well-being in a way that has been validated through research (Turner, 1981). Peer support networks are an effective way to foster a sense of community and a sense of belonging through shared experiences. To keep staff informed and eliminate uncertainty, it is important to establish clear channels of communication.

2. Human content moderators need to receive training and education in order to be effective. Provide training in stress management, resilience-building, and coping skills to employees. Maintaining regular updates and providing educational resources for staff so that they are informed of new procedures as they evolve.
3. The ability to work in a flexible manner. AI-driven content moderation companies need to implement a flexible scheduling policy that enables them to meet the individual's needs and to encourage a work-life balance among their employees, so that the employees can maintain a balance between their work and their personal lives. To prevent exhaustion, regular breaks and rest periods should be encouraged as much as possible.
4. Providing health and wellness programs to the community. Promote physical wellness through initiatives such as healthy meal options, water stations, and exercise programs in order to promote physical wellness. Meditation and relaxation exercises are good ways to encourage mindfulness practices, such as meditation and relaxation.
5. Appreciation and recognition should be given. Providing recognition programs and incentives for healthcare workers in order to acknowledge their contributions. The purpose of celebrating milestones and achievements is to boost morale among employees.
6. For human content moderators, HR intervention may be required as and when necessary. Creating dedicated crisis intervention teams for human content moderators will provide them with immediate psychological support in the event of a breakdown or stress from an inappropriate content review process. It is important to offer staff debriefing sessions in order to help them cope with traumatic situations.
7. Policy adjustments within the organization. Creating policies that prioritize employee well-being, such as limiting overtime and making sure that proper protective equipment is available to everyone. Creating a culture of psychological safety and open communication in the workplace is a key component to improving organizational performance. A correlation exists between psychological well-being and the ability to perform well at work as predictors of future performance in the workplace (Wright & Cropanzano, 2000).
8. Engaging the community in the process of development. Creating a sense of mutual support and understanding within the community by engaging with them. Public awareness campaigns can be used to address misconceptions and promote positive interactions between people.
9. Utilization of technology and AI in the workplace. Utilising technology and artificial intelligence as a means of providing remote counseling and mental health support. Providing well-being resources and virtual peer support through digital platforms as a means of disseminating well-being resources. The relationship

between psychological well-being and reduced cardiovascular mortality has been demonstrated in healthy population studies as well as in studies involving patients with renal failure and HIV infection (Chida & Steptoe, 2008).

CONCLUSION

AI driven content moderation faces unique challenges when fostering a mental health culture. Employers can strengthen their content moderators' health by encouraging conversations about mental health among them and making small but meaningful changes to the work environment. Creating compassionate and supportive environments for content moderators can enhance productivity, job satisfaction, and employee morale. Long-term damage can occur when a person is consistently exposed to high levels of harmful and inappropriate content over a prolonged period of time. It is possible for content moderators to develop trauma when they are consistently exposed to harmful and inappropriate content. A person who experiences trauma may experience insomnia, behavioral difficulties, anxiety, irritation, depression, and a tendency to disagree with others frequently as well as post traumatic stress disorder (PTSD). In AI driven content moderation organizations, it is imperative that we take a proactive approach to the well-being of the content moderators by implementing strategies and by taking a proactive approach to managing behavioral issues that might be causing them to experience other symptoms, such as substance abuse or behavioral disorders.

The reviewed literature underscores the critical need for ongoing research and adaptation of content moderation practices to effectively support vulnerable populations in online environments. It highlights the importance of professional training for moderators, the necessity of clear guidelines for harmful content, and the significance of user perceptions of fairness in moderation strategies. Collectively, these insights point to a multifaceted approach that balances the complexities of online interaction with the imperative of mental health protection. Overall, the literature underscores the multifaceted challenges of content moderation in online mental health contexts. It highlights the critical role of moderators, the need for frameworks that support their efforts, and the importance of integrating user perspectives into moderation practices. As digital environments continue to evolve, ongoing research is essential to address the complexities of moderation and its implications for mental health.

The role of human moderators is irreplaceable and organizations that operate artificial intelligence-driven content moderation must collaborate with human moderators, but without adequate support, many of them may suffer from trauma as a result. There is a need for employers to continue to provide and leverage technology in order to help mitigate this growing issue, and it is imperative that they utilize more and more AI for the content moderation process. As it stands today, it is evidently necessary to strike a fine balance between advancements in technology and artificial intelligence, as well as human support, in order to address the challenges faced by content moderators in a way that truly addresses their needs.

REFERENCES

Bohle, P., & Tilley, A. J. (1989). The impact of night work on psychological well-being. *Ergonomics, 32*(9), 1089–1099. DOI: 10.1080/00140138908966876 PMID: 2806232

Cai, J., Patel, A., Naderi, A., & Wohn, D. Y. (2024). Content moderation justice and fairness on social media: Comparisons across different contexts and platforms.

Cherlin, A., & Reeder, L. G. (1975). The dimensions of psychological well-being: A critical review. *Sociological Methods & Research, 4*(2), 189–214. DOI: 10.1177/004912417500400203

Chida, Y., & Steptoe, A. (2008). Positive psychological well-being and mortality: A quantitative review of prospective observational studies. *Psychosomatic Medicine, 70*(7), 741–756. DOI: 10.1097/PSY.0b013e31818105ba PMID: 18725425

Cohan, A., Young, S., Yates, A., & Goharian, N. (2017). Triaging content severity in online mental health forums.

Deng, D., Rogers, T., & Naslund, J. A. (2023). The role of moderators in facilitating and encouraging peer-to-peer support in an online mental health community: A qualitative exploratory study. *JMIR Formative Research, 7*, e43541. DOI: 10.2196/43541 PMID: 36810998

Grossi, E., Tavano Blessi, G., Sacco, P. L., & Buscema, M. (2012). The interaction between culture, health and psychological well-being: Data mining from the Italian culture and well-being project. *Journal of Happiness Studies, 13*(1), 129–148. DOI: 10.1007/s10902-011-9254-x

Hamilton, N. A., Nelson, C. A., Stevens, N., & Kitzman, H. (2007). Sleep and psychological well-being. *Social Indicators Research, 82*(1), 147–163. DOI: 10.1007/s11205-006-9030-1

Nichele, E., Lavorgna, A., & Middleton, S. E. (2022). Identifying key challenges and needs in digital mental health moderation practices supporting users exhibiting risk behaviours to develop responsible AI tools: The case study of Kooth. *Frontiers in Digital Health, 4*, 901169. DOI: 10.3389/fdgth.2022.901169 PMID: 36196212

Perry, A., Pyle, D., Lamont-Mills, A., du Plessis, C., & du Preez, J. (2021). Suicidal behaviours and moderator support in online health communities: A scoping review. *BMJ Open, 11*(1), e047905. DOI: 10.1136/bmjopen-2020-047905 PMID: 34193497

Ruini, C., Ottolini, F., Rafanelli, C., Tossani, E., Ryff, C. D., & Fava, G. A. (2003). The relationship of psychological well-being to distress and personality. *Psychotherapy and Psychosomatics*, *72*(5), 268–275. DOI: 10.1159/000071898 PMID: 12920331

Scheuerman, M. K., Jiang, J. A., Fiesler, C., & Brubaker, J. R. (2021). A framework of severity for harmful content online

Siddique, C. M., & D'Arcy, C. (1984). Adolescence, stress, and psychological well-being. *Journal of Youth and Adolescence*, *13*(6), 459–473. DOI: 10.1007/BF02088593 PMID: 24306949

Singhal, M., Ling, C., Paudel, P., Thota, P., Kumarswamy, N., Stringhini, G., & Nilizadeh, S. (2022). SoK: Content moderation in social media, from guidelines to enforcement, and research to practice.

Trujillo, A., & Cresci, S. (2022). One of many: Assessing user-level effects of moderation interventions on r/The_Donald.

Turner, R. J. (1981). Social support as a contingency in psychological well-being. *Journal of Health and Social Behavior*, *22*(4), 357–367. DOI: 10.2307/2136677

Vahed, S., Goanta, C., Ortolani, P., & Sanfey, A. G. (2024). Moral judgment of objectionable online content: Reporting decisions and punishment preferences on social media. *New Media & Society*. Advance online publication. DOI: 10.1177/14614448241244995 PMID: 38527036

Vallerand, R. J. (2012). The role of passion in sustainable psychological well-being. *Psychology of Well-Being: Theory. Psychology of Well-Being*, *2*(1), 1–21. DOI: 10.1186/2211-1522-2-1

Vázquez, C., Hervás, G., Rahona, J. J., & Gómez, D. (2009). Psychological well-being and health: Contributions of positive psychology. *Anuario de Psicología Clínica y de la Salud*, *5*, 15–27.

Warr, P., Cook, J., & Wall, T. (1979). Scales for the measurement of some work attitudes and aspects of psychological well-being. *Journal of Occupational Psychology*, *52*(2), 129–148. DOI: 10.1111/j.2044-8325.1979.tb00448.x

Wright, T. A., & Cropanzano, R. (2000). Psychological well-being and job satisfaction as predictors of job performance. *Journal of Occupational Health Psychology*, *5*(1), 84–94. DOI: 10.1037/1076-8998.5.1.84 PMID: 10658888

KEY TERMS AND DEFINITIONS

Algorithmic Bias: The term algorithmic bias refers to systematic and repeatable errors in a computer system that result in "unfair" results, such as prioritizing one category over another contrary to the algorithm's intended purpose.

Artificial Intelligence in Content Moderation: As part of the content moderation process, artificial intelligence (AI) involves the use of machine learning algorithms and other AI technologies to analyze and manage digital content. The use of user-generated content across a variety of online platforms is essential to enhancing the safety and trustworthiness of that content on an ongoing basis.

Algorithmic Moderation: The use of algorithms and artificial intelligence to automate the review, filter, and management of user-generated content on platforms to identify and deal with content that violates community guidelines or service terms. The algorithmic moderation of content consists of scanning and filtering user-generated content, such as images, videos, and audio, for compliance with predefined standards using artificial intelligence and machine learning algorithms.

Digital Harm vis-à-vis Content Moderation: In content moderation, the term "digital harm" refers to content that has the potential to negatively impact individuals or communities online. Content containing harmful, offensive, or illegal materials, such as hate speech, misinformation, cyberbullying, and explicit material, may negatively impact anyone accessing this information whether its a user or a moderator.

Desensitization in Content Moderation: The concept of desensitization, in content moderation, refers to the process through which prolonged exposure to certain types of content can lead to diminished emotional reactions as well as diminished capacity to empathize or be concerned when it comes to certain types of content (such as racial abuse, violence, or violated imagery).

Stress Inoculation Training (SIT): Stress Inoculation Training (SIT) is a type of cognitive behavioral therapy which provides moderators with coping skills to help them cope with the stress and trauma associated with regularly encountering disturbing or harmful content, enhancing their resilience and well-being as a result.

Social Support Networks: A social support network is a process or structure that provides assistance and resources to people working as content moderators, especially in terms of addressing the emotional and psychological toll of reviewing potentially harmful or disturbing content. It can be part of a wider social network, including one that is geographically diverse.

Trigger Management: The trigger management process, particularly in content moderation, refers to the process of identifying and handling situations where content or user actions violate the platform's guidelines, resulting in automated or manual actions like content removal, warnings for users, or suspensions of accounts.

Chapter 10
Reducing the Workload: AI as a Support Tool for Human Content Moderators

J. K. Lalchhanhima
https://orcid.org/0009-0008-0567-7252
Christ University, India

Vijayalaxmi Rajendran
https://orcid.org/0000-0002-8378-9750
Christ University, India

Aradhana Madhusudanan
Christ University, India

ABSTRACT

Content moderation on digital platforms has evolved into a critical challenge due to the volume and complexity of user-generated content. This chapter explores the transformative role of Artificial Intelligence (AI) in addressing this issue, highlighting its capacity for scalability, efficiency, and consistent enforcement of policies. However, AI's limitations—such as interpreting context, navigating cultural nuances, and avoiding bias—underscore the necessity of human involvement. The hybrid AI-human approach emerges as the most effective model, leveraging AI's data-processing capabilities to alleviate workload while relying on moderators for nuanced judgments and ethical oversight. Through case studies of major platforms like Meta, Reddit, and YouTube, this chapter demonstrates the potential and challenges of integrating AI into moderation. It advocates for transparency, ethical AI practices, and research to refine hybrid models, aiming to balance efficiency, fairness, and trust. This chapter contributes to the discourse on sustainable, ethical frameworks in the digital age.

DOI: 10.4018/979-8-3373-0335-2.ch010

1 INTRODUCTION

The explosive surge in digital platforms and user-generated content has created an unprecedented challenge for content moderation. With billions of posts, comments, images, and videos uploaded daily, maintaining safe and inclusive online spaces has become a formidable task (Huertas-García et al., 2023). In this fast-evolving digital landscape, **Artificial Intelligence (AI)** has emerged as a powerful tool, offering unmatched scalability, speed, and consistency in identifying and flagging potentially harmful content (Kniazieva, 2023). By leveraging advanced algorithms trained on vast datasets, AI systems can process and analyze large volumes of content at speeds far beyond human capabilities, enabling platforms to proactively manage harmful material.

However, despite these technological advancements, the question remains: **Can AI truly replace human judgment in content moderation?** While AI excels at rule-based decision-making, it struggles with interpreting contextual nuances, humor, and evolving cultural references, areas where humans outperform machines (Mantri, 2021; Singh, 2019). The limitations of AI, such as its inability to understand intent or manage ambiguous content, underscore the critical role of human moderators. This has led to the rise of a **hybrid AI-human model**, which combines the strengths of AI with the ethical oversight and contextual understanding of human judgment.

To understand this dynamic, it is essential to analyze the distinct strengths and weaknesses of AI and human moderators. The following subsections examine the capabilities and limitations of both, emphasizing why a balanced, collaborative approach to content moderation remains indispensable.

1.1 AI Without Human Intervention

AI has revolutionized content moderation by automating large-scale tasks that are otherwise insurmountable for human moderators. It offers unmatched advantages such as **scalability**, **efficiency**, and **objectivity**, but also faces challenges like limited contextual understanding, adaptability, and bias. The following explores these strengths and limitations in detail:

Scalability and Efficiency: AI's most significant advantage is its ability to manage vast amounts of content efficiently. Platforms like Facebook and YouTube generate millions of posts daily, making manual moderation unfeasible (Mantri, 2021). AI systems, built on Natural Language Processing (NLP), computer vision, and deep learning, can analyze textual, visual, and audio content in real time, flagging harmful material such as hate speech, graphic imagery, and misinformation. This unparalleled speed allows AI to perform proactive screening, ensuring that inappropriate content is detected before it spreads (Kniazieva, 2023). For instance, AI models can scan millions of images or videos for known harmful patterns and compare them against extensive databases to identify and flag violations quickly (L, 2024).

Objectivity and Consistency: AI also brings objectivity to content moderation. Unlike humans, who may vary in their judgments due to emotions, fatigue, or biases, AI applies predefined criteria and rules uniformly across all content. This consistency reduces the risk of subjective or inconsistent decisions, promoting a fairer enforcement of moderation policies (Hartmann, 2020).

Despite these advantages, AI's ability to operate without human intervention is fundamentally limited.

Challenges of Context and Nuance: While AI excels at identifying patterns, it struggles with understanding the complexities of human communication. Context-dependent content, such as sarcasm, humor, and cultural idioms, often confounds AI systems, leading to false positives—harmless content mistakenly flagged as harmful—and false negatives, where harmful material is overlooked (Ozanne et al., 2022; Singh, 2019). For example, a satirical meme may be flagged as hate speech because the AI lacks the ability to discern the creator's intent.

Evolving Nature of Online Communication: Online communication is dynamic, with new slang, memes, and coded language emerging continuously. AI models, trained on static datasets, may fail to adapt to these changes, rendering them less effective over time (Singh, 2019). This inability to keep up with evolving user behavior highlights the limitations of AI in addressing the full scope of harmful content.

Ethical Concerns and Bias: AI systems are not inherently neutral; they reflect the biases present in their training data. This can result in unfair or discriminatory moderation decisions, disproportionately impacting marginalized communities (Noble, 2018; Gorwa et al., 2020). Additionally, AI's opaque decision-making processes—often referred to as "black-box" algorithms—pose challenges to transparency and accountability (Gorwa et al., 2020; Hartmann, 2020). Users may find it difficult to understand or challenge moderation decisions, eroding trust in these systems.

Thus, while AI provides scalability and objectivity, its limitations necessitate human oversight to ensure moderation decisions are accurate, contextually informed, and ethically sound.

1.2 Human Moderation Without AI

Human moderators have long been central to content moderation, providing critical judgment, empathy, and ethical oversight. Unlike AI, they excel at understanding **context**, **nuance**, and **emotional impact**, making them indispensable for complex cases. However, human moderation also comes with significant challenges, such as scalability, bias, and mental health risks. The following examines both the strengths and limitations of human moderators:

Understanding Nuance and Context: Unlike AI, human moderators excel at interpreting the context and intent behind user-generated content. They can distinguish between a joke and a genuine threat, recognize satire, and account for cultural differences that influence communication styles (Kniazieva, 2023; Ozanne et al., 2022). This ability to grasp subtle nuances ensures that moderation decisions are more accurate and culturally sensitive.
Adaptability to Evolving Trends: Human moderators are inherently flexible and can adapt quickly to emerging trends in online communication, such as new slang, memes, or coded language. Unlike AI systems, which require retraining to address new patterns, human moderators can intuitively learn and adjust their decisions in real time (Singh, 2019).
Empathy and Ethical Judgment: Human moderators bring empathy and ethical considerations to their decisions. This is particularly crucial when handling sensitive content related to mental health, harassment, or hate speech, where a thoughtful, compassionate approach is necessary (Ozanne et al., 2022). By considering the emotional and social impact of their actions, human moderators contribute to a moderation process that is both fair and humane.

However, human moderation also faces significant challenges, such as:

Scalability and Fatigue: The sheer volume of content on platforms like Facebook and Twitter far exceeds the capacity of human moderators to manage effectively (Gillespie, 2020). Reviewing millions of posts manually is not only unsustainable but also inefficient compared to AI's processing capabilities.
Cognitive Biases and Inconsistencies: Human judgment is inherently subjective, influenced by personal biases, fatigue, and emotional responses. This can result in inconsistent moderation decisions, where the same content might be judged differently by different moderators (Kniazieva, 2023).

Mental Health Toll: Continuously reviewing harmful and graphic content takes a significant psychological toll on human moderators. Exposure to such material can lead to burnout, emotional distress, and long-term mental health issues (Lai et al., 2022).

While human moderators are indispensable for handling complex and sensitive cases, these limitations emphasize the need for support systems that alleviate their workload and safeguard their well-being.

1.3 The Need for a Collaborative Approach

Given the strengths and limitations of both AI and human moderators, the most effective solution lies in a **collaborative hybrid model**. In this approach, AI serves as a first line of defense, automating repetitive and large-scale tasks such as filtering spam, identifying clear policy violations, and flagging suspicious content for further review. Human moderators, in turn, handle complex cases requiring contextual understanding, nuanced judgment, and empathy (Gray & Suri, 2019; Vössing et al., 2022).

This collaboration not only enhances the efficiency and accuracy of content moderation but also mitigates the risks associated with relying solely on either AI or human judgment. By leveraging AI's processing capabilities alongside human expertise, platforms can achieve a more balanced, ethical, and effective moderation process.

This chapter explores the transformative role of AI in supporting human moderators, advocating for a balanced AI-human hybrid model. It examines AI's strengths in scalability and efficiency, human moderators' unique ability to navigate context and empathy, and the challenges inherent in both approaches. Through a review of case studies, ethical concerns, and practical recommendations, this chapter aims to provide insights into building sustainable and responsible content moderation systems.

To provide a clearer overview of the chapter's structure and flow, the following figure outlines the key themes and subtopics discussed thus far, including the role of AI, human moderators, and their collaboration in content moderation.

Figure 1. Chapter overview: AI as a support tool for human content moderators

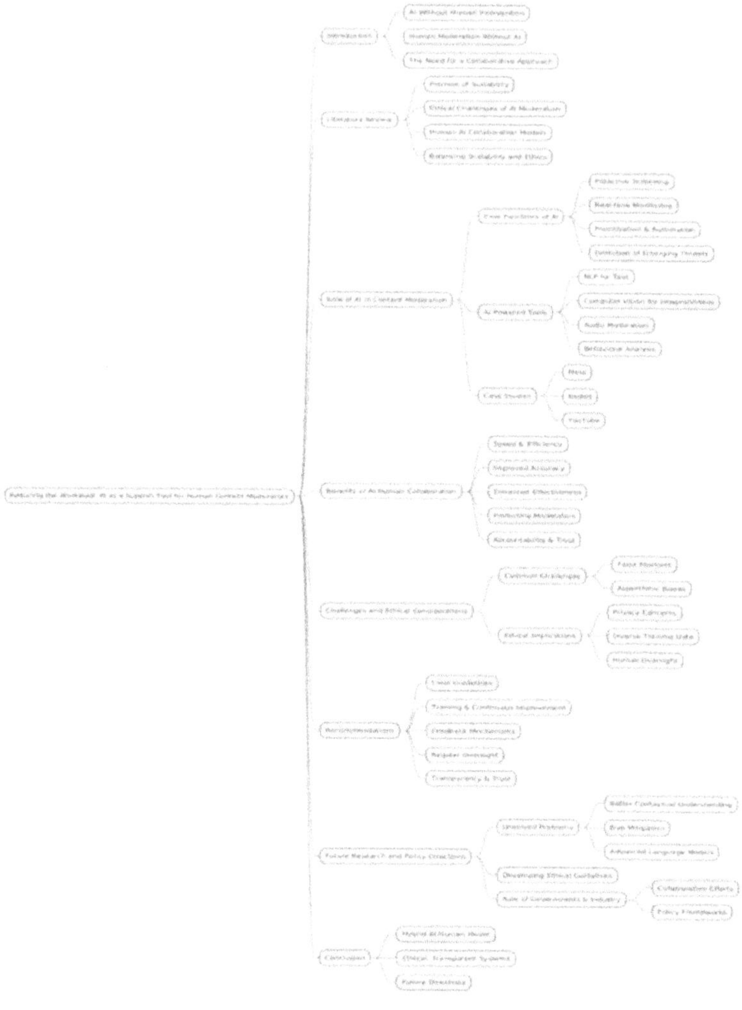

2 LITERATURE REVIEW

The integration of Artificial Intelligence (AI) into content moderation has been the subject of extensive academic inquiry, with researchers examining its capabilities, limitations, and ethical implications. This review explores key themes in AI-enabled content moderation, focusing on scalability, technical challenges, ethical concerns, and the evolving dynamics of human-AI collaboration.

2.1 The Promise of Scalability in Content Moderation

AI's ability to manage vast amounts of user-generated content has been widely recognized as a cornerstone of modern content moderation systems. Platforms such as Facebook, YouTube, and Reddit generate massive volumes of posts, images, and videos daily, posing a challenge that exceeds human capacity. Gillespie (2020) highlights AI's unparalleled scalability and speed, emphasizing its role in identifying and filtering inappropriate content efficiently, particularly at the scale required for global platforms. AI-powered tools utilizing Natural Language Processing (NLP), computer vision, and deep learning have emerged as vital components in managing this deluge of information. Mantri (2021) further underscores the significance of these technologies, arguing that automated systems can swiftly flag harmful content—such as hate speech, graphic imagery, and misinformation—that would otherwise overwhelm human moderators.

However, the promise of scalability is tempered by concerns about **accuracy**. Scholars note that AI systems are prone to algorithmic errors, resulting in false positives, where benign content is flagged erroneously, and false negatives, where harmful material goes undetected (Gorwa, Binns, & Katzenbach, 2020). Such limitations raise concerns about the over-reliance on automation and highlight the need for human oversight. Without human intervention to verify and refine AI decisions, moderation outcomes risk undermining fairness and user trust.

2.2 Limitations and Ethical Challenges of AI Moderation

Despite its strengths, AI-driven content moderation faces significant limitations, particularly in understanding **context** and **cultural nuances**. Content often relies on subtle cues such as sarcasm, satire, or regional dialects, which AI struggles to interpret accurately. For instance, Singh (2019) points out that AI systems trained on static datasets fail to adapt to the evolving nature of online language, such as slang or coded expressions, reducing their effectiveness in dynamic digital spaces.

In addition to technical limitations, ethical challenges have drawn considerable attention. Noble (2018), in *Algorithms of Oppression*, highlights how biases embedded in AI algorithms can perpetuate systemic discrimination, disproportionately impacting marginalized communities. Crawford (2022), in *Atlas of AI*, expands on this critique, emphasizing how biased datasets and opaque decision-making processes exacerbate existing inequalities. These findings underscore the risks of deploying AI systems that lack transparency and fairness.

Accountability remains another key ethical concern. Ryan (2020) argues that AI systems, by their very nature, lack the capacity for interpersonal trust and ethical reasoning. The responsibility for ensuring fairness, transparency, and accountability therefore shifts to developers and operators, who must adhere to ethical design principles. Regulatory frameworks such as the European Union's General Data Protection Regulation (GDPR) reflect this perspective, mandating transparency in automated decision-making and safeguarding user privacy.

2.3 Human-AI Collaboration in Content Moderation

Recognizing the limitations of AI, researchers advocate for **human-AI collaboration** models that leverage the strengths of both systems. Hybrid frameworks, often referred to as "human-in-the-loop" systems, combine AI's scalability with human moderators' contextual understanding and ethical judgment. Lai et al. (2022) propose a **"conditional delegation"** model, wherein AI manages routine moderation tasks while escalating ambiguous or complex cases to human reviewers. This approach optimizes efficiency by allowing AI to operate within predefined parameters, while humans intervene in nuanced situations requiring cultural sensitivity or ethical reasoning.

Transparency within human-AI collaboration is another critical factor for success. Vössing et al. (2022) emphasize that **agent transparency**, where AI systems provide clear explanations for their decisions, fosters trust and improves collaboration outcomes. By making AI decisions interpretable, platforms enable human moderators to verify and refine automated outputs, thereby mitigating errors and ensuring fairness.

The practical implementation of hybrid systems further illustrates their effectiveness. Meta (formerly Facebook) employs AI for the initial screening of content, flagging material that requires human review (Singh, 2019). Similarly, Reddit's decentralized moderation model incorporates **AutoModerator**, an AI-powered tool that automates rule enforcement while allowing subreddit moderators to manage context-specific decisions (Chandrasekharan et al., 2019). These examples highlight the potential of AI-human collaboration to address the scale and complexity of content moderation effectively.

2.4 Balancing Scalability with Ethical Responsibility

The interplay between scalability and ethical responsibility remains a recurring theme in the literature. While AI offers significant advantages in speed and efficiency, its inability to fully grasp context and its susceptibility to bias pose critical challenges. Scholars agree that hybrid moderation models, combining AI-driven automation with human oversight, present the most balanced approach. This collaboration ensures that the scale of content moderation is managed effectively while safeguarding fairness, transparency, and accountability.

Future research must continue to address unresolved questions surrounding AI's contextual understanding, bias mitigation, and ethical design. By refining hybrid frameworks and ensuring ethical implementation, platforms can navigate the complexities of content moderation in ways that align technological advancements with societal values.

3 ROLE OF AI IN CONTENT MODERATION

Artificial Intelligence (AI) plays a transformative role in modern content moderation, offering scalable and efficient solutions to manage the vast and ever-growing volume of user-generated content. As digital platforms continue to expand, the challenges of moderating harmful material—ranging from hate speech to misinformation—have intensified. AI has emerged as a critical tool, providing the ability to process large datasets, detect subtle patterns, and enhance moderation efficiency through automation (Frank L, 2024; Kniazieva, 2023; Mantri, 2021). This section explores AI's pivotal functions in content moderation, its core applications, and the sophisticated tools that enable platforms to address the complexities of online content governance.

3.1 Core Functions of AI in Content Moderation

AI's contributions to content moderation can be categorized into several fundamental functions that address the challenges of managing large-scale, dynamic, and potentially harmful content. These functions collectively enhance platforms' ability to proactively screen material, monitor live content streams, prioritize resources, and detect emerging threats. The following explores these core capabilities in detail:

Proactive Content Screening: One of AI's primary functions is its ability to screen content before it is made public, minimizing the risk of harmful material reaching users. Platforms deploy AI algorithms to analyze textual, visual, and audio content in real time, flagging content that violates predefined rules or patterns. By identifying inappropriate material early, AI creates safer online environments and reduces user exposure to offensive or harmful content (L, 2024; Kniazieva, 2023).

Real-Time Content Monitoring: The speed and precision of AI enable continuous monitoring of live content streams, a function particularly crucial for platforms that support live streaming or real-time communication, such as gaming or broadcasting applications. AI systems can quickly identify and flag harmful material as it appears, facilitating swift removal and mitigating potential damage. This ensures that violations, such as abusive speech or violent imagery, do not proliferate unchecked, preserving the platform's integrity (Mantri, 2021).

Prioritization and Automation: AI enhances the efficiency of content moderation by prioritizing high-risk material for human review. While AI systems handle the bulk of routine and repetitive tasks, they can also flag ambiguous or complex content requiring human judgment. This process optimizes the allocation of resources, allowing moderators to focus on nuanced cases while AI processes most of the less ambiguous content. The result is a streamlined moderation workflow that improves outcomes and reduces manual effort (L, 2024).

Detection of Emerging Threats: AI's ability to analyze patterns and trends enables platforms to identify new and evolving threats, such as emerging hate speech, misinformation tactics, or coordinated harmful behavior. By detecting shifts in user behavior or new forms of malicious activity, AI allows platforms to adapt their moderation strategies preemptively. This proactive capability helps maintain a secure and evolving content moderation ecosystem in response to dynamic online challenges (Gillespie, 2020).

3.2 AI-Powered Tools and Techniques

To fulfill its core functions, AI relies on a diverse range of tools and techniques that enhance its precision, adaptability, and scope. These technologies empower AI to analyze and moderate content across multiple formats—including text, images, videos, and audio—allowing platforms to address moderation challenges comprehensively. The following discussion explores the key tools and techniques that enable AI to detect, analyze, and respond to harmful content effectively:

Text Moderation with Natural Language Processing (NLP): Natural Language Processing (NLP) is central to AI's ability to analyze and interpret textual content. NLP tools empower AI to detect harmful patterns and intent within written material, including comments, posts, and metadata. For instance, **sentiment analysis** identifies emotional tones in text, allowing AI to flag content with aggressive or harmful undertones. Additionally, NLP algorithms play a critical role in **hate speech detection**, recognizing discriminatory or violent language patterns that violate community guidelines (Gillespie, 2020; Kniazieva, 2023). AI systems also perform **toxicity classification**, where text is assessed for harmfulness, enabling platforms to determine appropriate actions, such as removal or user warnings (Gorwa et al., 2020). Moreover, NLP helps decode **emojis, slang, and informal language**, ensuring that AI systems account for evolving linguistic behaviors and user intent (Kniazieva, 2023).

Image and Video Moderation with Computer Vision: In addition to text, AI leverages computer vision technologies to analyze visual content, addressing the unique challenges posed by images and videos. Through **object detection and recognition**, AI can identify harmful visuals, such as violent imagery, hate symbols, or explicit material, ensuring prompt removal of prohibited content (Kniazieva, 2023). **Image classification** techniques further categorize images based on predefined rules, allowing platforms to enforce audience-specific content delivery. Deepfakes—AI-generated videos designed to mislead or deceive—are another growing concern. Advanced AI tools specifically detect such content, safeguarding platforms against the risks of misinformation (Kniazieva, 2023). AI also leverages Optical Character Recognition (OCR) to extract text hidden within visual content like images or videos. This technology ensures that potential policy violations, which might otherwise remain undetected, are identified effectively. By extending moderation capabilities to visual media, OCR plays a vital role in maintaining compliance across diverse content formats.

Audio Moderation with AI: AI offers advanced tools to enforce platform rules in voice-based interactions. Through speech-to-text transcription, spoken language is converted into text for analysis using Natural Language Processing (NLP) techniques, enabling the detection of harmful or inappropriate content (Mantri, 2021). Beyond simply transcribing, AI evaluates tone and emotion within audio files, identifying aggressive, abusive, or threatening language. These capabilities make moderating spoken violations as efficient as handling text-based content. Furthermore, AI can recognize specific sounds or music that infringe copyright or violate platform policies, ensuring content integrity across auditory formats.

Behavioral Analysis: AI's ability to analyze patterns in user behavior adds another layer to its moderation capabilities. Behavioral analysis tools enable platforms to monitor user interactions, network connections, and posting patterns to detect malicious activities. For instance, AI systems identify spam by recognizing repetitive content or the spread of harmful links. Additionally, AI detects ongoing harassment, isolating accounts that engage in abusive behavior or orchestrate coordinated attacks. Through network analysis, AI uncovers harmful activities conducted by interconnected groups, empowering platforms to proactively address organized harmful campaigns. These tools equip platforms with deeper insights into user behavior, enabling more precise and effective moderation strategies. (Mantri, 2021)

AI's contribution to content moderation is multifaceted, combining speed, scalability, and analytical accuracy to manage the vast volume of user-generated content. Through its core functions—proactive screening, real-time monitoring, prioritization, and threat detection—AI enables platforms to maintain safer online environments. Supported by advanced tools such as Natural Language Processing, computer vision, and behavioral analysis, AI can process diverse content formats while identifying emerging risks. However, as subsequent sections will explore, the limitations of AI underscore the importance of human collaboration, ensuring that contextual understanding, fairness, and ethical considerations remain central to content moderation efforts.

3.3 Case Studies

The integration of artificial intelligence (AI) with human oversight in content moderation represents a synergistic approach that leverages the unique strengths of both systems. AI brings efficiency and speed in processing vast datasets, while human moderators provide the necessary contextual understanding and ethical judgment required for nuanced cases. Leading platforms like **Meta**, **Reddit**, and **YouTube** have increasingly adopted this hybrid model to address the challenges of moderating diverse and extensive user-generated content. By examining their moderation strategies, successes, and limitations, the following case studies illustrate the practical application of AI-human collaboration in fostering safer online environments and safeguarding user expression.

3.3.1 Case Study 1: Meta

Meta, formerly known as Facebook, faces immense challenges as one of the largest social media platforms, serving over 2.9 billion users worldwide. Moderating this scale of content while balancing freedom of expression and the need to eliminate harmful material requires an integrated approach. Meta employs a hybrid moderation model where AI acts as the first filter, flagging potentially harmful content for human moderators to review. This strategy enables scalability while ensuring accuracy and nuance in decision-making, especially for ambiguous or culturally specific content (Singh, 2019).

In Meta's hybrid approach, AI systems rely on natural language processing (NLP) algorithms to identify harmful patterns, such as hate speech or violent language. For instance, these algorithms detect keywords and behavioral signals associated with inappropriate content. However, AI's inability to fully interpret context, such as satire or regional dialects, necessitates human oversight. In complex cases, content flagged by AI is escalated to human moderators who can account for intent, cultural norms, and linguistic nuances (Singh, 2019, pp. 22-24). This ensures that moderation decisions are more informed and fairer.

Meta's AI tools extend beyond textual analysis to address graphic and extreme content. Technologies like **PhotoDNA** employ hashing techniques to match content against databases of known harmful imagery, such as terrorist material, graphic violence, and child exploitation content. This proactive approach facilitates swift detection and removal, minimizing user exposure to traumatic material (Singh, 2019, pp. 12-13).

To address concerns around AI's transparency and accountability, Meta publishes the **Community Standards Enforcement Report (CSER)**. This report outlines AI's "proactivity rate"—a metric measuring the proportion of flagged content identified before user reports—and evaluates AI's accuracy in various categories, such as hate speech and graphic violence (Singh, 2019, p. 24). By offering these insights, Meta fosters trust and highlights its ongoing efforts to refine automated systems.

However, challenges persist within Meta's hybrid model. AI struggles with interpreting minority dialects, cultural expressions, or activist content, occasionally leading to errors and over-censorship. For example, legitimate activist content has sometimes been removed due to the limitations of algorithmic understanding, underscoring the risks of over-relying on automation (Singh, 2019, pp. 15-16).

In summary, Meta's hybrid strategy showcases how AI and human oversight can work together to address the scale and complexity of content moderation. While AI enhances efficiency and scalability, human moderators provide indispensable contextual interpretation. Meta's commitment to transparency, demonstrated through regular reporting, reflects an ongoing effort to balance platform safety with user freedom of expression.

3.3.2 Case Study 2: Reddit

Reddit stands apart from other platforms due to its **decentralized moderation structure**, which empowers individual subreddit communities to establish and enforce their own rules. With over 330 million monthly active users, Reddit combines this community-driven approach with AI tools like **AutoModerator** to assist volunteer moderators in managing content (Singh, 2019).

In Reddit's model, human moderators—or "mods"—play a pivotal role in maintaining the unique norms and cultures of their communities. AutoModerator, an AI-powered tool, supports this process by automating routine tasks, such as flagging or removing content that violates subreddit-specific rules. For example, AutoModerator can be configured to detect abusive language, spam, or links to malicious content, enabling human moderators to focus on complex or nuanced cases requiring judgment (Singh, 2019, pp. 25-26).

The adaptability of AutoModerator is one of its key strengths. It allows moderators to fine-tune its rules to align with the specific needs of each subreddit. By enabling the detection of language patterns, links, and behavior tailored to individual communities, AutoModerator fosters a moderation system that is scalable while remaining culturally sensitive. This flexibility ensures that Reddit's broader content policies coexist with the unique standards upheld by its various communities (Singh, 2019, pp. 26-27).

However, Reddit's decentralized model also presents challenges. While the platform publishes transparency reports detailing content removals by administrators and AutoModerator, the reports lack granularity regarding subreddit-specific actions. This opacity makes it difficult to assess AI's effectiveness and the impact of moderation decisions at a community level. Furthermore, AutoModerator's limited natural language processing capabilities hinder its ability to interpret nuanced or context-dependent language, occasionally leading to errors or inconsistent enforcement (Singh, 2019, pp. 27-28).

In conclusion, Reddit's AI-supported moderation model demonstrates the value of combining community-driven decision-making with automated tools. By empowering moderators with customizable AI assistance, Reddit achieves scalable and culturally sensitive moderation. However, addressing transparency gaps and enhancing AI's contextual understanding remain critical areas for improvement.

3.3.3 Case Study 3: YouTube

YouTube faces a unique content moderation challenge due to the platform's vast user base and the sheer volume of videos uploaded daily. To manage this scale effectively, YouTube employs a hybrid moderation system that integrates AI for rapid screening with human moderators for nuanced evaluations (Gillespie, 2018; Kniazieva, 2023).

AI serves as the frontline tool for YouTube's moderation processes, analyzing content across text, audio, and video formats. For instance, AI systems detect harmful language in video titles, descriptions, and comments through **text analysis** (Gillespie, 2018). Similarly, **computer vision** technologies identify inappropriate visuals, such as nudity, hate symbols, or violent imagery, while **audio analysis** tools convert speech into text for further NLP-based assessment (Kniazieva, 2023; Gorwa et al., 2020). Additionally, YouTube's **Content ID** system enforces copyright by matching uploaded videos against databases of protected material, enabling rights holders to act such as blocking, monetizing, or tracking content.

Despite AI's efficiency, YouTube relies heavily on human moderators to address its limitations. Human reviewers manage ambiguous cases where context, intent, or cultural nuances play a significant role—such as satire, parody, or regional dialects that AI systems may misinterpret. YouTube also incorporates user participation through reporting tools and its **Trusted Flaggers** program, creating an additional layer of accountability (Gillespie, 2018).

YouTube's hybrid approach demonstrates both its strengths and its challenges. While AI enables rapid, large-scale screening of content, its inability to interpret nuanced material underscores the necessity of human oversight. Transparency remains a key strength of YouTube's strategy, with the platform regularly publishing reports on moderation outcomes, including data on appeals and human-AI collaboration effectiveness (Gorwa et al., 2020).

In conclusion, YouTube's hybrid moderation system exemplifies the successful integration of AI and human judgment. AI efficiently manages content volume, while human moderators ensure context sensitivity and fairness. This collaboration highlights the importance of combining technological capabilities with human expertise to create safer, more inclusive online spaces.

3.3.4 Summary of Case Studies

The case studies of Meta, Reddit, and YouTube reveal how leading platforms leverage AI to enhance scalability and efficiency while incorporating human oversight to address limitations such as contextual understanding, transparency, and bias. These hybrid moderation systems demonstrate that the synergy between AI's analytical capabilities and human judgment is essential for creating effective, ethical, and culturally sensitive content moderation processes.

4 BENEFITS OF AI-HUMAN COLLABORATION IN CONTENT MODERATION

The hybrid model of content moderation, as demonstrated by platforms like **YouTube**, **Meta**, and **Reddit**, illustrates the powerful potential of combining AI's technological capabilities with human expertise. This collaborative approach addresses two key challenges: managing the overwhelming scale of user-generated content and navigating the complexities inherent in online communication. While AI excels in processing massive datasets, recognizing patterns, and performing repetitive tasks with unparalleled speed and precision, human moderators contribute their nuanced understanding of context, cultural sensitivity, and ethical judgment—qualities that

AI alone cannot replicate. Together, AI and human moderators form a system that is not only efficient but also adaptable, equitable, and ethical.

This section delves into the multifaceted benefits of AI-human collaboration, highlighting its impact on **speed and efficiency**, **accuracy**, **effectiveness**, and the protection and accountability of human moderators. These advantages ensure safer, fairer, and more responsive online ecosystems.

4.1 Speed and Efficiency

One of the most significant contributions of AI to content moderation is its ability to process and analyze vast amounts of data at extraordinary speeds. Platforms hosting millions of daily uploads—such as videos, comments, and posts—would be overwhelmed if left to human moderators alone. AI algorithms can quickly identify content that violates platform policies, such as explicit material or copyright infringement, enabling swift action without the need for constant manual oversight (L, 2024; Mantri, 2021).

By automating routine tasks, AI effectively **reduces the workload on human moderators**. For example, AI systems efficiently detect duplicate uploads, filter spam, and flag clear violations, such as violent imagery or hate speech. These repetitive, large-scale tasks, which would otherwise consume significant human resources, are streamlined through AI, allowing moderators to dedicate their efforts to complex cases that require greater judgment and context (Mantri, 2021; Mikalef & Gupta, 2021).

Additionally, AI's ability to operate **around the clock** ensures faster responses to harmful content. Unlike human moderators who are constrained by time and fatigue, AI systems function 24/7, continuously scanning and filtering live streams, comments, and uploads in real time. This minimizes the spread of harmful material, ensuring that platforms remain safer and more responsive to emerging threats (Gillespie, 2018; Vössing et al., 2022).

The combination of AI's scalability and speed, paired with human moderators' expertise, enables platforms to maintain better oversight of their ecosystems while optimizing resource utilization.

4.2 Improved Accuracy

AI-powered moderation systems significantly enhance accuracy in identifying harmful content by leveraging advanced pattern recognition capabilities. Trained on extensive datasets, AI can detect subtle cues that might elude human moderators, such as emerging slang or trends in hate speech, misinformation, and harassment.

This data-driven precision ensures that a broad range of violations is identified and addressed effectively (Kniazieva, 2023; Mantri, 2021; Saheb et al., 2024).

An important benefit of AI moderation is its **consistency in application**. Unlike human moderators, whose decisions may vary due to emotional states, cognitive biases, or fatigue, AI applies platform policies uniformly. By adhering strictly to predefined rules and criteria, AI reduces the risk of inconsistencies in content moderation, ensuring a fairer enforcement process across the platform (Hartmann, 2020).

Furthermore, AI minimizes the likelihood of **missed violations** by analyzing vast datasets at scale. Harmful content that might escape manual review due to volume or oversight can be efficiently flagged by AI, thereby improving the overall safety and integrity of the platform (L, 2024; Mantri, 2021).

However, it is the integration of AI with human moderators that truly enhances accuracy. While AI excels in detecting patterns and enforcing rules, human oversight is essential for reviewing borderline cases, correcting errors, and ensuring culturally and contextually informed decisions. Together, this collaboration achieves a moderation process that is precise, equitable, and responsive.

4.3 Enhanced Effectiveness

The effectiveness of content moderation relies on addressing both straightforward and nuanced cases—a balance that AI-human collaboration is uniquely equipped to achieve. AI excels at identifying and flagging explicit content or repeated violations of platform policies. However, it often struggles to grasp contextual subtleties, such as satire, parody, or culturally specific references, where the meaning depends heavily on intent or regional context (Gillespie, 2018, 2020; Molina & Sundar, 2022).

Human moderators are crucial in bridging these gaps. They offer the contextual understanding necessary to interpret ambiguous content, such as culturally specific humor or sarcasm, which AI might mistakenly classify as harmful. By recognizing intent, human moderators can make more accurate and equitable decisions (Molina & Sundar, 2022; Singh, 2019).

Beyond resolving ambiguity, human moderators bring adaptability to content moderation. Malicious actors continuously develop new tactics, such as coded language or shifting memes, to bypass AI detection. Human intervention ensures these evolving threats are addressed effectively. Human moderators can respond more quickly to these emerging trends, providing an adaptability that complements AI's structured learning processes (Singh, 2019; L, 2024). This model of **"conditional delegation"** ensures that AI handles routine, large-scale tasks while humans focus on complex cases requiring ethical judgment and contextual awareness. Together, this collaboration results in a more effective and nuanced moderation system, capable of addressing the evolving challenges of online content (Kniazieva, 2023; Lai et al., 2022).

4.4 Protecting Moderators and Maintaining Accountability

AI's role in content moderation also serves to protect the well-being of human moderators, shielding them from the psychological toll of reviewing harmful and graphic content. The constant exposure to violent imagery, hate speech, or disturbing material can lead to burnout, emotional distress, and long-term mental health challenges for moderators (Gillespie, 2020; Lai et al., 2022).

AI systems play a crucial role in easing the workload of human moderators by pre-screening and filtering out the most disturbing content before it reaches them. By managing a significant share of harmful material, AI minimizes the emotional toll on moderators, fostering a safer and more sustainable working environment (L, 2024).

Beyond reducing exposure, AI also prioritizes high-risk content for human review, allowing moderators to focus on critical or urgent cases. By streamlining resources toward areas that demand immediate attention, AI enhances the efficiency and effectiveness of human oversight (Singh, 2019).

This collaboration between AI and human moderators also strengthens accountability in moderation processes. While AI delivers speed and consistency, human reviewers ensure decisions are ethical and aligned with community standards. They serve as a safeguard against algorithmic errors, biases, or unjust enforcement, maintaining transparency and trust in moderation practices (Molina & Sundar, 2022; Tuncer & Ramirez, 2022).

Thus, by combining the efficiency of AI with the discernment of human judgment, platforms improve the quality of moderation while fostering trust and transparency within their communities. This partnership addresses the challenges of scale, accuracy, and complexity, all while protecting the well-being of moderators. With AI handling vast amounts of content swiftly and consistently, platforms can manage their operations with greater precision and care. Meanwhile, human moderators bring contextual awareness, adaptability, and ethical judgment to ensure that moderation decisions are fair, nuanced, and culturally informed.

Together, AI and human oversight create a balanced and effective moderation ecosystem—one that not only ensures safer and more inclusive online spaces but also fosters transparency, accountability, and trust among users.

5 CHALLENGES AND ETHICAL CONSIDERATIONS

While AI-driven content moderation has introduced transformative efficiencies in managing vast online ecosystems, it also presents significant challenges and ethical dilemmas. Striking a balance between scalability and fairness requires acknowledging the limitations of AI systems, addressing algorithmic biases, and navigating critical issues such as transparency, accountability, and privacy. The promising collaborative model of AI-human moderation is not without its complexities; it demands thoughtful implementation to mitigate risks while ensuring ethical responsibility.

This section explores the pressing challenges in AI-powered moderation, including false positives, algorithmic biases, and limitations in contextual understanding. It also delves into the broader ethical implications, such as privacy concerns, the need for diverse and representative training data, and the irreplaceable role of human oversight. Addressing these issues is essential for creating content moderation systems that are both effective and ethically sound.

5.1 Common Challenges

While AI systems have significantly enhanced the scalability and efficiency of content moderation, they continue to face critical challenges that limit their effectiveness. These challenges stem from AI's inability to fully understand human communication, its susceptibility to biases, and the rapidly evolving nature of online behaviors. Issues such as false positives, contextual misunderstandings, and algorithmic biases highlight the complexities of automated moderation systems. The following sections explore these challenges in detail, emphasizing the need for ongoing refinement and human oversight to address AI's limitations and ensure fairer outcomes:

5.1.1 False Positives and Limited Contextual Understanding

AI systems often struggle to accurately interpret the subtleties of human communication, leading to **false positives**, where benign content is incorrectly flagged as harmful. These errors arise primarily due to AI's limited ability to understand context, sarcasm, and cultural nuances, which are integral to human expression. For instance, AI may misconstrue satirical or sarcastic remarks as genuine policy violations due to its reliance on literal interpretations (Gillespie, 2018). Similarly, cultural idioms, humor, and region-specific expressions are often misinterpreted by AI systems trained on datasets from a single cultural context. This lack of adaptability undermines the system's ability to moderate fairly across diverse online communities (Gillespie, 2018).

Furthermore, the rapidly evolving nature of online language—through slang, coded communication, and emerging forms of harmful content—frequently outpaces AI's ability to adapt. While AI relies on historical data for training, the dynamic behaviors of online users can create significant gaps in its effectiveness (Gillespie, 2018). These shortcomings highlight the indispensable role of human moderators, who apply cultural and contextual understanding to ensure more accurate and nuanced decisions, particularly in cases that require interpretation beyond algorithmic capabilities (Gillespie, 2018).

5.1.2 Algorithmic Biases

Bias remains a persistent challenge in AI-powered content moderation, as AI systems inherently reflect the biases present in their training data. This often leads to **disproportionate and unfair outcomes**, where marginalized communities face over-censorship due to the misrepresentation of their language or cultural expressions in datasets (Saheb et al., 2024; Shin et al., 2022). For example, expressions commonly used within specific ethnic or cultural groups might be incorrectly flagged as harmful, perpetuating systemic inequalities in moderation practices.

Biases in AI can also **reinforce harmful stereotypes**, as the data used to train algorithms may include patterns that reflect societal prejudices. Without mechanisms to detect and rectify these biases, AI systems risk amplifying discrimination and undermining trust in moderation processes (Saheb et al., 2024; Shin et al., 2022). Compounding this issue is the **lack of transparency** in many AI systems, which makes it difficult to identify or address biased decision-making. The opaque nature of algorithms hinders accountability, as users and moderators may struggle to understand how content moderation decisions are made (Callari et al., 2024; Saheb et al., 2024).

Addressing algorithmic biases requires deliberate efforts to diversify training datasets and implement continuous evaluation mechanisms. Platforms must prioritize fairness and inclusivity to mitigate these biases and ensure that moderation systems serve all user groups equitably.

5.2 Ethical Implications

The deployment of AI in content moderation raises important ethical questions that extend beyond technical challenges. As AI systems increasingly rely on vast amounts of user data and automated decision-making, concerns surrounding **privacy**, **bias**, and **transparency** become paramount. Ethical content moderation requires a careful balance between leveraging AI's capabilities and safeguarding user rights, ensuring fairness, accountability, and inclusivity. The following subsections examine key ethical considerations, including privacy concerns, the need for diverse training data, and the indispensable role of human oversight in creating systems that are both effective and ethically sound:

5.2.1 Privacy Concerns

The reliance of AI moderation systems on vast quantities of user data raises significant privacy concerns. Platforms often collect and analyze personal data to train AI models and enforce moderation policies, creating questions about the scope, security, and retention of this data. It is imperative that platforms clearly communicate **what data is collected, why it is collected, and how it is used** to build trust and ensure transparency (Callari et al., 2024).

Equally critical is the implementation of robust **data security measures** to protect sensitive information. Strong encryption and restricted access controls are essential to prevent breaches or misuse of user data (Callari et al., 2024; Kniazieva, 2023). Additionally, platforms must establish clear **data retention policies** to limit the storage of personal information and minimize risks associated with prolonged data usage (Callari et al., 2024).

Transparency and user control further underpin ethical data practices. Users should be provided with insights into how AI systems are trained and how moderation decisions are made. Platforms must also offer mechanisms for users to contest AI decisions, ensuring fairness and accountability in content moderation (Callari et al., 2024; Kniazieva, 2023).

5.2.2 Need for Diverse Training Data

To reduce algorithmic biases and improve fairness, AI systems must be trained on datasets that represent the full spectrum of online communities. A critical requirement is the **representativeness** of training datasets, which should encompass varied demographics, languages, cultural contexts, and viewpoints. By incorporating diverse perspectives, AI systems can better understand and fairly moderate content across global platforms (Callari et al., 2024; Saheb et al., 2024).

Inclusive training data also plays a pivotal role in **mitigating bias**. AI systems trained on homogeneous datasets are more likely to perpetuate societal inequalities, as they fail to account for cultural and linguistic diversity. Ensuring that datasets reflect the complexity of human communication is essential to creating fairer and more effective moderation systems (Crawford, 2022; Kniazieva, 2023).

5.2.3 Human Oversight

Despite AI's advancements, human moderators remain irreplaceable in addressing the limitations of automated systems. Human oversight ensures that moderation practices align with ethical principles, community standards, and user expectations. For instance, human moderators excel at **contextual understanding**, interpreting subtle nuances such as satire, parody, and cultural references that AI systems might misclassify (Gillespie, 2018; Pflanzer et al., 2023).

Human involvement also provides **accountability** by reviewing AI decisions and ensuring that moderation practices are fair and transparent. Moderators can identify patterns of bias or inaccuracies in AI outputs, offering valuable feedback to refine and improve algorithms over time (Pflanzer et al., 2023). Additionally, human reviewers play a crucial role in providing **appeals and recourse** for users who believe their content was unfairly flagged or removed, creating a necessary check on automated systems (Bernard, 2023).

Human moderators also bring adaptability to content moderation. Unlike AI, which requires retraining to address new behaviors, humans can swiftly adjust strategies in response to evolving threats, emerging trends, or malicious tactics designed to bypass automated detection (Kniazieva, 2023; Molina & Sundar, 2022). This adaptability ensures that platforms remain agile in addressing dynamic online environments.

Experts widely advocate for a **"human-in-the-loop"** model, where AI supports human moderators rather than replacing them entirely. This collaborative approach leverages the speed and scalability of AI while ensuring that human judgment safeguards fairness, ethics, and accountability in moderation practices (Jiang et al., 2021; Lai et al., 2022).

Thus, the challenges and ethical considerations surrounding AI-powered content moderation underscore the complexities of maintaining safe and inclusive digital spaces. False positives, algorithmic biases, and privacy concerns remain significant obstacles that must be addressed through continuous refinement and oversight. Human moderators play a pivotal role in mitigating these challenges, ensuring that moderation decisions are nuanced, contextually informed, and aligned with ethical principles.

By embracing a collaborative AI-human approach, platforms can leverage the strengths of both systems to build trust, transparency, and fairness in content moderation. Addressing these challenges thoughtfully will enable platforms to create healthier online environments that balance scalability with ethical responsibility.

6 RECOMMENDATIONS FOR EFFECTIVE AI-HUMAN HYBRID MODERATION

A well-implemented AI-human hybrid moderation system demands thoughtful planning, ongoing refinement, and a strong commitment to ethical practices. By combining the strengths of artificial intelligence (AI) with the expertise of human moderators, platforms can create a robust and dynamic framework that effectively addresses the scale and complexity of content moderation. This balanced approach ensures efficiency, adaptability, and fairness while minimizing errors and ethical risks. To achieve this, platforms must establish clear operational guidelines, prioritize training and continuous improvement, maintain rigorous oversight, and emphasize transparency to foster trust among users, moderators, and stakeholders.

The following recommendations outline essential strategies for developing and sustaining a successful AI-human hybrid moderation system.

6.1 Establishing Clear Guidelines

The foundation of an effective hybrid moderation system lies in clearly defining the respective roles of AI and human moderators. While AI excels at handling large-scale tasks such as filtering vast volumes of content, detecting repetitive violations, and identifying specific patterns in harmful behavior, its limitations in understanding complex contexts necessitate human involvement. Tasks involving sarcasm, satire, or cultural nuances, for instance, require the ethical and contextual judgment that only human moderators can provide (Gillespie, 2020).

To minimize redundancy and ensure efficiency, platforms should focus on **role allocation**, assigning AI the responsibility of managing repetitive, rule-based filtering processes while reserving nuanced and ambiguous cases for human reviewers. Such delineation ensures that both systems operate in a complementary manner, leveraging their respective strengths. Additionally, platforms should establish **escalation protocols**—workflows in which AI identifies potentially complex cases and flags them for human intervention. This ensures that sensitive or context-dependent content receives the necessary scrutiny and ethical judgment required for accurate decision-making (Molina & Sundar, 2022).

By clearly defining responsibilities and creating escalation pathways, platforms can streamline content moderation processes while maximizing resource utilization.

6.2 Training and Continuous Improvement

The dynamic and ever-evolving nature of online content necessitates continuous updates to AI systems to maintain their effectiveness. AI moderation tools must be regularly trained on diverse and up-to-date datasets to reflect emerging trends, cultural behaviors, and evolving forms of harmful content.

A critical component of this process is **ongoing data integration**, where AI systems are fed with fresh datasets that encompass current linguistic patterns, cultural nuances, and new tactics employed by malicious actors. Such updates reduce algorithmic bias, improve adaptability, and enhance AI's ability to recognize emerging threats (Duan et al., 2019; Kniazieva, 2023). Platforms should also conduct regular **performance assessments** to evaluate AI's false positive and false negative rates—instances where harmless content is flagged, or harmful material is overlooked. By identifying performance gaps, platforms can adjust thresholds and retrain algorithms as needed to improve accuracy and reliability.

Moreover, safeguards must be implemented to **prevent algorithmic drift**, a phenomenon where AI's decision-making deviates from intended moderation goals over time. Continuous monitoring of AI systems ensures alignment with platform policies and ethical standards, maintaining consistent performance across all moderation activities.

A focus on training and continuous improvement creates a self-evolving moderation system, enabling AI to adapt to new challenges while minimizing errors and biases.

6.3 Feedback Mechanisms

Structured feedback loops between AI systems and human moderators are critical for enhancing AI's decision-making capabilities and ensuring ongoing improvements. A well-designed feedback system fosters collaboration, allowing AI to learn from human oversight and refine its performance over time.

Moderator feedback plays a central role in this process, enabling human reviewers to flag AI errors, such as misclassifications or missed nuances. These flagged cases serve as valuable input for retraining AI models, ensuring the system learns from real-world contexts and continuously improves its accuracy (Lai et al., 2022; Vössing et al., 2022). Platforms should also facilitate **two-way communication** between AI and moderators. AI can alert human reviewers about its decisions, while moderators provide corrective feedback to fine-tune the system's understanding of complex or ambiguous content. This iterative process creates a cycle of continuous improvement, enhancing both AI performance and human-AI collaboration.

Additionally, platforms should build **complex case databases**—repositories of challenging content identified by moderators. These databases can serve as training data for future AI updates, enabling the system to handle similar scenarios more effectively. By aligning AI's learning processes with real-world moderation challenges, platforms ensure that decision-making remains contextually informed and culturally sensitive.

6.4 Regular Oversight

To maintain the integrity of AI-human hybrid moderation systems, platforms must implement regular oversight through periodic audits, performance evaluations, and bias checks. Continuous monitoring ensures that moderation processes align with platform goals, ethical standards, and user expectations.

Platforms should conduct both **quantitative and qualitative reviews**, analyzing metrics such as false positive and false negative rates, user complaints, and moderator satisfaction to assess AI performance. By identifying areas of concern, platforms can make data-driven improvements to enhance the accuracy and fairness of moderation decisions. Additionally, **bias and drift checks** should be performed regularly to audit AI systems for algorithmic biases and deviations from intended moderation standards. Addressing these issues proactively ensures that AI systems remain fair, transparent, and aligned with ethical principles (Shin et al., 2022; Saheb et al., 2024).

Involving **independent reviewers**—such as third-party ethicists or external auditors—further strengthens oversight by providing impartial evaluations of AI systems. Independent reviews assess whether AI decision-making aligns with fairness, transparency, and accountability principles, building trust among users and stakeholders.

Through consistent oversight, platforms can ensure that AI systems operate ethically and effectively while adapting to emerging content moderation challenges.

6.5 Building Trust through Transparency

Transparency serves as a cornerstone of any successful content moderation strategy. Clear communication about how AI systems operate fosters trust among users, moderators, and other stakeholders, ensuring that moderation processes are understood, accountable, and fair.

Platforms should adopt **explainable AI (XAI)** tools that make AI decisions interpretable for human moderators and users. XAI enables stakeholders to understand why specific content was flagged, removed, or allowed, creating a sense of accountability and fairness (Ferreira & Monteiro, 2021; Molina & Sundar, 2022). Transparency reports further reinforce this trust by providing users with insights into AI's role in content moderation. These reports should include data on flagged content, error rates, appeals, and human-AI collaboration outcomes, building confidence in the moderation process.

Equally important is **moderator support** through education and training. Human moderators must be equipped with a clear understanding of AI's capabilities, limitations, and decision-making processes. Educating moderators on the effective use of AI tools is essential for fostering a seamless and informed collaboration between AI systems and human reviewers (Fui-Hoon Nah et al., 2023; Gillespie, 2020; Kniazieva, 2023; Saheb et al., 2024; Singh, 2019). By promoting transparency, platforms can strike a balance between efficiency and accountability, ensuring that moderation decisions uphold user rights while addressing harmful content effectively.

Building and maintaining a successful AI-human hybrid moderation system demands a combination of clear guidelines, continuous training, structured feedback, robust oversight, and unwavering transparency. Platforms must strategically allocate responsibilities, refine AI systems through ongoing updates and human feedback, and implement strong oversight mechanisms to leverage the strengths of both AI and human moderators.(Gillespie, 2018; Lai et al., 2022; Mikalef & Gupta, 2021; Ozanne et al., 2022; Shin et al., 2022)

Transparency is the cornerstone of trust, enabling users and stakeholders to understand and support the moderation process. By adopting these measures, platforms can establish a fair, adaptable, and ethically responsible moderation system, capable of meeting the ever-evolving challenges of online content governance. (L, 2024; Mantri, 2021; Shin et al., 2022; Singh, 2019)

7 FUTURE RESEARCH AREAS AND POLICY DIRECTIONS

The rapid integration of AI into content moderation has unlocked transformative possibilities for managing vast online ecosystems. However, this progress has also exposed challenges that require further exploration and policy innovation. The limitations of AI systems—particularly in contextual understanding, bias mitigation, and transparency—demand sustained research efforts and ethical frameworks to guide their development. Simultaneously, governments, industries, and civil society must collaborate to establish clear standards that ensure the responsible deployment of AI technologies.

This section examines key areas for future research, highlights the importance of developing ethical guidelines, and outlines the roles that governments and industries must play in creating a fair, transparent, and secure digital ecosystem.

7.1 Exploring Unsolved Problems

Despite significant advancements, AI-driven content moderation continues to face unresolved challenges that hinder its effectiveness and fairness. Limitations in contextual understanding, algorithmic biases, and language adaptability remain critical areas that demand further exploration. Addressing these challenges is essential to improving AI's ability to interpret nuanced communication, reduce biases, and adapt to the dynamic nature of online interactions. The following subsections highlight key research priorities, focusing on enhancing AI's contextual comprehension, mitigating bias, and improving the adaptability of language models:

7.1.1 Better Contextual Understanding

One of the most significant challenges facing AI-driven content moderation is its limited ability to interpret nuanced human language and cultural subtleties. AI systems often misclassify sarcasm, satire, or idiomatic expressions as harmful content due to their reliance on literal interpretations (Vössing et al., 2022; Saheb et al., 2024). Additionally, content that reflects cultural differences in humor, tone, or expression frequently eludes AI's understanding, resulting in moderation errors. Future research must focus on developing **context-aware AI models** capable of discerning these subtleties.

Advanced systems should also address the challenge of multi-layered communication, particularly in text, audio, and video formats. For instance, understanding visual memes or transcribed speech in videos often requires analyzing context beyond surface-level cues (Singh, 2019). By improving AI's contextual comprehension, platforms can reduce false positives and ensure culturally sensitive content moderation.

7.1.2 Improved Bias Mitigation

Algorithmic bias remains a persistent issue in AI systems, often reflecting disparities present in training data related to gender, ethnicity, or cultural representation. Biased AI models disproportionately flag or censor content from marginalized communities, perpetuating societal inequalities (Saheb et al., 2024; Singh, 2019). Future research must prioritize the creation of **diverse and representative datasets** that reflect a broad range of demographics, languages, and cultural norms.

Additionally, efforts to develop algorithms that minimize the amplification of societal prejudices are essential. Researchers should focus on designing metrics and evaluation techniques that identify, measure, and mitigate biases in AI systems at scale (Fui-Hoon Nah et al., 2023). Addressing these concerns will foster moderation processes that are both inclusive and equitable.

7.1.3 More Accurate Language Models

The adaptability of language models is crucial for improving AI's reliability in content moderation. Current models struggle to process the fluidity and variability of human language, particularly as online communication evolves. Regional dialects, emerging slang, and layered cultural expressions often challenge AI's ability to make accurate decisions (Singh, 2019).

Future research must enhance the adaptability of language models, enabling them to process linguistic complexities with greater precision. Advances in natural language processing (NLP) should focus on building systems capable of understanding subtle nuances, evolving slang, and layered meanings within diverse cultural contexts. Such improvements will strengthen AI's role in content moderation, making it more contextually aware and adaptable to global user behaviors.

7.2 Developing Ethical Guidelines

As AI becomes increasingly central to content moderation, the need for robust ethical guidelines has become paramount. Ensuring that AI systems operate fairly, transparently, and responsibly requires the establishment of comprehensive policies that address key challenges such as privacy, accountability, and bias. These guidelines must provide a framework for balancing technological efficiency with ethical principles, safeguarding user trust and platform integrity. The following subsections explore critical considerations for ethical AI implementation, including policy frameworks, fairness and privacy standards, and the importance of transparency and explainability:

7.2.1 Policy Frameworks for Ethical Challenges

As AI's role in content moderation grows, comprehensive regulatory frameworks are essential to address the ethical concerns surrounding fairness, accountability, and privacy. Policymakers and researchers must collaborate to establish guidelines that prioritize human safety, dignity, and trust in AI systems (Callari et al., 2024; Duan et al., 2019). These frameworks should ensure that AI tools are designed and implemented responsibly, balancing efficiency with ethical considerations.

Clear regulations on **data usage and consent** are critical. Platforms must develop transparent data policies that specify how user data is collected, processed, and stored, ensuring robust privacy protections. Ethical guidelines should emphasize minimizing risks while fostering trust between platforms and their users (Pflanzer et al., 2023).

7.2.2 Fairness, Privacy, and Safety

Ethical guidelines must also address fairness by promoting inclusivity and reducing algorithmic bias in AI systems. Platforms should commit to ongoing evaluations of fairness metrics, ensuring that moderation practices do not disproportionately affect marginalized communities (Saheb et al., 2024).

Privacy remains a cornerstone of ethical AI implementation. Transparent data collection practices, user consent mechanisms, and strict data retention policies are essential to safeguarding user information (Pflanzer et al., 2023). Additionally, robust safety protocols must be established to prevent misuse of AI systems, ensuring that flawed decisions do not harm individuals or infringe upon their rights.

7.2.3 Transparency and Explainability

Transparency is integral to building trust in AI-driven moderation systems. Ethical guidelines should mandate the adoption of **explainable AI (XAI)** techniques, which make AI decisions interpretable for users, moderators, and stakeholders. By providing clear explanations for why content was flagged or removed, platforms can foster a sense of accountability and fairness (Molina & Sundar, 2022).

Moreover, platforms must conduct regular **algorithmic audits** and publish public transparency reports detailing AI's performance, including error rates, decision rationales, and the role of human oversight. Such practices ensure that AI systems remain accountable and accessible, reinforcing user trust and platform integrity (Saheb et al., 2024).

7.3 Role of Governments and Industry

Effectively addressing the challenges posed by AI-driven content moderation requires collective action from multiple stakeholders, particularly governments, industries, and civil society. The global nature of online platforms necessitates collaboration among governments, industries, and civil society to establish ethical, fair, and adaptable content moderation systems that reflect societal values. While governments play a key role in regulation and fostering accountability, industries must prioritize the ethical design and deployment of AI systems.

7.3.1 Collaborative Efforts

Effectively addressing the challenges of AI in content moderation requires a multi-stakeholder approach. International cooperation is especially important in creating global standards that incorporate cultural differences, ethical principles, and fair labor practices (Gorwa, 2024).

Governments and industries should pursue co-regulation through voluntary codes of conduct that align with societal and ethical norms. These frameworks provide a foundation for content moderation practices that are both standardized and flexible enough to adapt to local contexts (Gorwa, 2024). Additionally, forming **specialized task forces**—comprising policymakers, technology experts, and civil society representatives—will facilitate the creation of best practices for AI-driven content moderation (Gorwa, 2024).

7.3.2 Specific Roles

Governments play a central role in addressing the ethical challenges of AI. By enacting comprehensive legislation, governments can regulate privacy protections, accountability measures, and fairness in AI systems. Funding and policy support should also incentivize the development of ethical AI technologies. Furthermore, governments must invest in research on AI ethics, explainability, and bias mitigation to advance responsible innovation (Callari et al., 2024).

Industries, meanwhile, must embed ethical considerations into AI design and deployment. This includes ensuring that AI systems account for diverse user groups, investing in bias mitigation techniques, and improving the inclusivity of training datasets (Saheb et al., 2024). Companies should also engage in open dialogue with regulators, researchers, and civil society organizations to build trust and transparency in content moderation practices.

By fostering collaboration between governments, industries, and civil society, stakeholders can develop robust, ethical, and accountable systems that address the challenges of AI-driven content moderation while ensuring fairness, privacy, and user trust.

Thus, the future of AI-powered content moderation hinges on continued research, ethical frameworks, and collaborative policymaking. Addressing unsolved challenges such as contextual understanding, bias mitigation, and language adaptability will enhance AI's reliability and fairness. Simultaneously, developing clear ethical guidelines and fostering transparency will ensure that AI systems remain accountable and aligned with societal values.

Governments, industries, and civil society must work together to establish global standards, co-regulatory frameworks, and best practices that guide the responsible development and deployment of AI technologies. By embracing these directions, platforms can create safer, fairer, and more transparent online ecosystems for all users.

8 CONCLUSION

To sum it up, integrating artificial intelligence (AI) into content moderation presents clear benefits, notably in scaling processes, enhancing consistency, and shielding human moderators from harmful content. AI excels at rapidly filtering large volumes of data, identifying patterns, and automating repetitive tasks, which alleviates human moderators' workload. This allows them to focus on complex cases requiring contextual understanding and nuanced judgment. However, realizing AI's potential in content moderation necessitates addressing its inherent challenges—particularly algorithmic biases, privacy concerns, and ethical dilemmas (Gillespie, 2020; Molina & Sundar, 2022; Saheb et al., 2024). These challenges underscore the necessity of implementing transparent systems and maintaining human oversight to ensure fairness and accountability.

Ultimately, a balanced, collaborative AI-human model is indispensable for effective content moderation. This hybrid approach, which combines AI's scalability and speed with human expertise in contextual evaluation, represents the most viable solution to address the complexities of online content. This model, often called "human-in-the-loop," highlights that neither AI nor human moderators alone can fully address the unique challenges posed by digital platforms. Rather, the synergy between both can mitigate AI's limitations, while improving efficiency and accuracy in handling a vast range of content types (Lai et al., 2022; Kniazieva, 2023).

Looking forward, it is essential to invest in the ethical development and deployment of AI solutions in content moderation. Regularly updating AI algorithms, refining policy frameworks, and instituting comprehensive review mechanisms will be critical. These steps will help ensure that AI systems evolve responsibly, in line with both technological advances and societal expectations. Additionally, platform operators and policymakers should foster transparency by regularly auditing AI models and making moderation processes clear to users. By committing to these actions, we can work toward a future where AI aids in maintaining a safer, fairer digital space that respects both user rights and platform standards (Jiang et al., 2021; Vössing et al., 2022).

Encouraging continued research and investment in ethical AI practices, combined with robust policy frameworks, is vital for the responsible deployment of AI in content moderation.

REFERENCES

Bernard, T. (2023, June 19). *Understanding User Perceptions of AI Content Moderation: Insights and Implications*. https://www.unitary.ai//articles/human-vs-machine-user-perceptions-of-trust-and-accountability-in-content-moderation

Callari, T. C., Vecellio Segate, R., Hubbard, E.-M., Daly, A., & Lohse, N. (2024). An ethical framework for human-robot collaboration for the future people-centric manufacturing: A collaborative endeavour with European subject-matter experts in ethics. *Technology in Society*, *78*, 102680. DOI: 10.1016/j.techsoc.2024.102680

Chandrasekharan, E., Gandhi, C., Mustelier, M., & Gilbert, E. (2019). Crossmod: A Cross-Community Learning-based System to Assist Reddit Moderators. *Proceedings of the ACM on Human-Computer Interaction*, *3*(CSCW), 1–30. DOI: 10.1145/3359276

Crawford, K. (2022). Atlas of AI: Power, Politics, and the Planetary Costs of Artificial Intelligence. *Perspectives on Science and Christian Faith*, *74*(1), 61–62. DOI: 10.56315/PSCF3-22Crawford

Duan, Y., Edwards, J. S., & Dwivedi, Y. K. (2019). Artificial intelligence for decision making in the era of Big Data – evolution, challenges and research agenda. *International Journal of Information Management*, *48*, 63–71. DOI: 10.1016/j.ijinfomgt.2019.01.021

Ferreira, J. J., & Monteiro, M. (2021). *The human-AI relationship in decision-making: AI explanation to support people on justifying their decisions* (No. arXiv:2102.05460). arXiv. https://doi.org//arXiv.2102.05460DOI: 10.48550

Fui-Hoon Nah, F., Zheng, R., Cai, J., Siau, K., & Chen, L. (2023). Generative AI and ChatGPT: Applications, challenges, and AI-human collaboration. *Journal of Information Technology Case and Application Research*, *25*(3), 277–304. DOI: 10.1080/15228053.2023.2233814

Gillespie, T. (2018). Custodians of the Internet: Platforms, Content Moderation, and the Hidden Decisions That Shape Social Media. In *Custodians of the Internet* (p. 288). Platforms, Content Moderation, and the Hidden Decisions That Shape Social Media., DOI: 10.12987/9780300235029

Gillespie, T. (2020). Content moderation, AI, and the question of scale. *Big Data & Society*, *7*(2), 205395172094323. DOI: 10.1177/2053951720943234

Gorwa, R., Binns, R., & Katzenbach, C. (2020). Algorithmic content moderation: Technical and political challenges in the automation of platform governance. *Big Data & Society*, *7*(1), 2053951719897945. DOI: 10.1177/2053951719897945

Gray, M. L., & Suri, S. (2019). *Ghost Work: How to Stop Silicon Valley from Building a New Global Underclass*. Houghton Mifflin Harcourt.

Hartmann, I. A. (2020). A new framework for online content moderation. *Computer Law & Security Review*, *36*, 105376. DOI: 10.1016/j.clsr.2019.105376

Huertas-García, Á., Martín, A., Huertas-Tato, J., & Camacho, D. (2023). Countering malicious content moderation evasion in online social networks: Simulation and detection of word camouflage. *Applied Soft Computing*, *145*, 110552. DOI: 10.1016/j.asoc.2023.110552

Jiang, J. A., Wade, K., Fiesler, C., & Brubaker, J. R. (2021). Supporting Serendipity: Opportunities and Challenges for Human-AI Collaboration in Qualitative Analysis. *Proc. ACM Hum.-Comput. Interact.*, *5*(CSCW1), 94:1-94:23. https://doi.org/DOI: 10.1145/3449168

Kniazieva, Y. (2023, March 30). *AI Content Moderation*. https://labelyourdata.com/articles/ai-content-moderation

L, F. (2024, February 27). *Understanding AI Content Moderation: Types & How it Works*. https://getstream.io/blog/ai-content-moderation/

Mantri, A. (2021). Real-Time Content Moderation Using Artificial Intelligence and Machine Learning. [IJSR]. *International Journal of Science and Research (Raipur, India)*, *10*(1), 1682–1684. DOI: 10.21275/SR24724150350

Mikalef, P., & Gupta, M. (2021). Artificial intelligence capability: Conceptualization, measurement calibration, and empirical study on its impact on organizational creativity and firm performance. *Information & Management*, *58*(3), 103434. DOI: 10.1016/j.im.2021.103434

Molina, M. D., & Sundar, S. S. (2022). When AI moderates online content: Effects of human collaboration and interactive transparency on user trust. *Journal of Computer-Mediated Communication*, *27*(4), zmac010. Advance online publication. DOI: 10.1093/jcmc/zmac010

Noble, S. U. (2018). *Algorithms of Oppression: How Search Engines Reinforce Racism*. New York University Press., DOI: 10.18574/nyu/9781479833641.001.0001

Ozanne, M., Bhandari, A., Bazarova, N. N., & DiFranzo, D. (2022). Shall AI moderators be made visible? Perception of accountability and trust in moderation systems on social media platforms. *Big Data & Society*, *9*(2), 20539517221115666. DOI: 10.1177/20539517221115666

Pflanzer, M., Traylor, Z., Lyons, J. B., Dubljević, V., & Nam, C. S. (2023). Ethics in human–AI teaming: Principles and perspectives. *AI and Ethics*, *3*(3), 917–935. DOI: 10.1007/s43681-022-00214-z

Ryan, M. (2020). In AI We Trust: Ethics, Artificial Intelligence, and Reliability. *Science and Engineering Ethics*, *26*(5), 2749–2767. DOI: 10.1007/s11948-020-00228-y PMID: 32524425

Saheb, T., Sidaoui, M., & Schmarzo, B. (2024). Convergence of artificial intelligence with social media: A bibliometric & qualitative analysis. *Telematics and Informatics Reports*, *14*, 100146. DOI: 10.1016/j.teler.2024.100146

Shin, D., Hameleers, M., Park, Y. J., Kim, J. N., Trielli, D., Diakopoulos, N., Helberger, N., Lewis, S. C., Westlund, O., & Baumann, S. (2022). Countering Algorithmic Bias and Disinformation and Effectively Harnessing the Power of AI in Media. *Journalism & Mass Communication Quarterly*, *99*(4), 887–907. DOI: 10.1177/10776990221129245

Singh, S. (2019, July 15). *Everything in Moderation*. New America. https://newamerica.org/oti/reports/everything-moderation-analysis-how-internet-platforms-are-using-artificial-intelligence-moderate-user-generated-content/

Tuncer, S., & Ramirez, A. (2022). Exploring the Role of Trust During Human-AI Collaboration in Managerial Decision-Making Processes. In Chen, J. Y. C., Fragomeni, G., Degen, H., & Ntoa, S. (Eds.), *HCI International 2022 – Late Breaking Papers: Interacting with eXtended Reality and Artificial Intelligence* (pp. 541–557). Springer Nature Switzerland., DOI: 10.1007/978-3-031-21707-4_39

Vössing, M., Kühl, N., Lind, M., & Satzger, G. (2022). Designing Transparency for Effective Human-AI Collaboration. *Information Systems Frontiers*, *24*(3), 877–895. DOI: 10.1007/s10796-022-10284-3

Compilation of References

Abdul, K. L., & Tan, M. N. (2018). Overcoming barriers to AI adoption in Mindanao campus journalism. *Journal of Communication Technology*, *5*(1), 34–48.

Abdulmajeed, M., & Fahmy, N. (2022, May). Meta-analysis of AI research in journalism: Challenges, opportunities and future research agenda for Arab journalism. In *European, Asian, Middle Eastern,North African Conference on Management & Information Systems* (pp. 213-225). Cham: Springer International Publishing.

Abuhamad, A. (2024). *Algorithmography: Intersections of Truth*. Authenticity and Representation of AI Generated Visual Content in Journalism.

Ahti, J. O. A. (2024). Systematic prioritization of AI initiatives: implementation factors and achievable value.

Aissani, R., Abdallah, R. A. Q., Taha, S., & Al Adwan, M. N. (2023, June). Artificial Intelligence Tools in media and journalism: Roles and concerns. In *2023 International Conference on Multimedia Computing, Networking and Applications (MCNA)* (pp. 19-26). IEEE. DOI: 10.1109/MCNA59361.2023.10185738

Alan, A., Al-Arnaout, Z., Topcu, A., Zaki, C., Shdefat, A., & Elbasi, E. (2022, November). How do default privacy settings on social media apps match people's actual preferences? In *2022 International Conference on Electrical and Computing Technologies and Applications (ICECTA)* (pp. 305-308). IEEE.

Al-Asmari, H. A., & Saleh, M. S. (2019, April). A conceptual framework for measuring personal privacy risks in facebook online social network. In *2019 International Conference on Computer and Information Sciences (ICCIS)* (pp. 1-6). IEEE.

Al-Halfawy, Aya, Ibrahim, Al-Ashry, & Walid, Mahmoud Hatab, Abdel-Hakam, ... & Amal. (2023). Trends of media students in Egyptian universities towards the use of artificial intelligence applications in the educational process. *Scientific Journal of Specific Educational Sciences*, *18*(18), 1013–1038.

Alowais, S. A., Alghamdi, S. S., Alsuhebany, N., Alqahtani, T., Alshaya, A. I., Almohareb, S. N., Aldairem, A., Alrashed, M., Bin Saleh, K., Badreldin, H. A., Al Yami, M. S., Al Harbi, S., & Albekairy, A. M. (2023). Revolutionizing healthcare: The role of artificial intelligence in clinical practice. *BMC Medical Education, 23*(1), 689. DOI: 10.1186/s12909-023-04698-z PMID: 37740191

America, P. E. N. (2020). *No excuse for abuse: What social media companies can do now to combat online harassment.* https://pen.org/report/no-excuse-for-abuse/

Amershi, S., Cakmak, M., Knox, W. B., & Kulesza, T. (2014). Power to the people: The role of humans in interactive machine learning. *AI Magazine, 35*(4), 105–120. DOI: 10.1609/aimag.v35i4.2513

Ariyo, O., & Zheng, J. (2022, December). A Study On Security and Privacy Risks of Self-Disclosure On Social Networking Sites During COVID-19 Pandemic. In *2022 IEEE International Conference on Big Data (Big Data)* (pp. 2828-2832). IEEE.

Aung, Z. M., Kyaw, T. Z., & Htay, T. (2021). Unpacking the ethics of AI-generated content in Myanmar campus journalism. *Media Ethics in Southeast Asia, 10*(4), 234–250.

Awani, A. (2024) How AI can help us spot its own fakes. https://www.astroawani.com/berita-dunia/how-ai-can-help-us-spot-its-own-fakes-473818

Awan, S. M., Waheed, U., Khalid, Y., Khan, M. A., Mansoor, Y., & Rehman, S. A. (2020, February). Violation of User's Privacy Rights by Facebook. In *2020 International Conference on Information Science and Communication Technology (ICISCT)* (pp. 1-4). IEEE.

Awasthi, M. (2022, December). Verifiable and practical compliance for data privacy laws. In *2022 IEEE 29th International Conference on High Performance Computing,Data and Analytics Workshop (HiPCW)* (pp. 59-60). IEEE.

Bankins, S., Formosa, P., Griep, Y., & Richards, D. (2022). AI decision making with dignity? Contrasting workers' justice perceptions of human and AI decision making in a human resource management context. *Information Systems Frontiers, 24*(3), 857–875. DOI: 10.1007/s10796-021-10223-8

Barrett, P. M. (2020). *Who moderates the moderators? The case for greater oversight of content moderation systems.* NYU Stern Center for Business and Human Rights.

Barrett, P. M. (2021). *Who moderates the social media giants?* NYU Stern School of Business, Center for Business and Human Rights.

Basta, Z. (2024). The Intersection of AI-Generated Content and Digital Capital: An Exploration of Factors Impacting AI-Detection and its Consequences. In.

Basumatary, B., & Kalita, H. K. (2022, March). Social media forensics-a holistic review. In *2022 9th International Conference on Computing for Sustainable Global Development (INDIACom)* (pp. 590-597). IEEE.

Benkler, Y. (2019). Don't let industry write the rules for AI. *Nature, 569*(7754), 161. DOI: 10.1038/d41586-019-01413-1 PMID: 31043715

Bernard, T. (2023, June 19). *Understanding User Perceptions of AI Content Moderation: Insights and Implications*. https://www.unitary.ai//articles/human-vs-machine-user-perceptions-of-trust-and-accountability-in-content-moderation

Binns, R., Veale, M., Van Kleek, M., & Shadbolt, N. (2018). "It's reducing a human being to a percentage": Perceptions of justice in algorithmic decisions. Proceedings of the 2018 CHI Conference on Human Factors in Computing Systems, 1–14. https://doi.org/DOI: 10.1145/3173574.3173951

Binns, R. (2018). Algorithmic accountability and public reason. *Philosophy & Technology, 31*(4), 543–556. DOI: 10.1007/s13347-017-0263-5 PMID: 30873342

Bird, J. J., & Lotfi, A. (2024). Cifake: Image classification and explainable identification of ai-generated synthetic images. *IEEE Access : Practical Innovations, Open Solutions, 12*, 15642–15650. DOI: 10.1109/ACCESS.2024.3356122

Blankenship, J. C. (2016). *Solo journalism and news routines: Using the hierarchical influences model to study the organizational and individual influences of solo journalism in local television news* (Doctoral dissertation, The University of North Carolina at Chapel Hill).

Boatwright, P., Basuroy, S., & Kamakura, W. (2007). Reviewing the reviewers: The impact of individual film critics on box office performance. *Quantitative Marketing and Economics, 5*(4), 401–425. DOI: 10.1007/s11129-007-9029-1

Bohle, P., & Tilley, A. J. (1989). The impact of night work on psychological well-being. *Ergonomics, 32*(9), 1089–1099. DOI: 10.1080/00140138908966876 PMID: 2806232

Bonawitz, K.. (2019). *Towards federated learning at scale: System design. Proceedings of Machine Learning Systems*. MLSYS.

Brandtzaeg, P. B., Følstad, A., & Chaparro Domínguez, M. Á. (2018). How journalists and social media users perceive online fact-checking and verification services. *Journalism Practice, 12*(9), 1109–1129. DOI: 10.1080/17512786.2017.1363657

Brigham, N. G., Wei, M., Kohno, T., & Redmiles, E. M. (2024). " Violation of my body:" Perceptions of AI-generated non-consensual (intimate) imagery. *arXiv preprint arXiv:2406.05520*.

Brundage, M., Avin, S., Clark, J., Eckersley, P., Garfinkel, B., & Amodei, D. (2018). *The malicious use of artificial intelligence: Forecasting, prevention, and mitigation*. ArXiv Preprint.

Buhmann, A., & Fieseler, C. (2021). Towards a deliberative framework for responsible innovation in artificial intelligence. *Technology in Society*, *64*, 101475. DOI: 10.1016/j.techsoc.2020.101475

Cai, J., Patel, A., Naderi, A., & Wohn, D. Y. (2024). Content moderation justice and fairness on social media: Comparisons across different contexts and platforms.

Callari, T. C., Vecellio Segate, R., Hubbard, E.-M., Daly, A., & Lohse, N. (2024). An ethical framework for human-robot collaboration for the future people-centric manufacturing: A collaborative endeavour with European subject-matter experts in ethics. *Technology in Society*, *78*, 102680. DOI: 10.1016/j.techsoc.2024.102680

Chancellor, S., & De Choudhury, M. (2022). "When AI Gets It Wrong": Examining the Psychological Toll of AI Misclassification on Mental Health Discourse. *CHI Conference on Human Factors in Computing Systems*.

Chandrasekharan, E., Gandhi, C., Mustelier, M. W., & Gilbert, E. (2019). Crossmod: A cross-community learning-based system to assist reddit moderators. *Proceedings of the ACM on human-computer interaction, 3*(CSCW), 1-30. DOI: 10.1145/3359276

Chen, A. (2014, October 23). The laborers who keep dick pics and beheadings out of your Facebook feed. *Wired*. https://www.wired.com/2014/10/content-moderation/

Cheng, S., Kim, S., & Pheng, L. S. (2019). Ethical considerations of AI in Cambodian journalism. *Ethics in Media Communication*, *26*(3), 201–215.

Chen, L., Wong, C., & Jiang, Z. (2020). Textual analysis of sentiment-based content regulation for hate speech moderation. *Social Media + Society*, *6*(3), 1–14. DOI: 10.1177/2056305120930846

Cherlin, A., & Reeder, L. G. (1975). The dimensions of psychological well-being: A critical review. *Sociological Methods & Research*, *4*(2), 189–214. DOI: 10.1177/004912417500400203

Chesney, R., & Citron, D. (2019). Deepfakes and the new disinformation war: The coming age of post-truth geopolitics. *Foreign Affairs*, *98*(1), 147–155.

Chibba, M., & Cavoukian, A. (2015, December). Privacy, consumer trust and big data: Privacy by design and the 3 C'S. In *2015 ITU Kaleidoscope: Trust in the Information Society (K-2015)* (pp. 1-5). IEEE.

Chida, Y., & Steptoe, A. (2008). Positive psychological well-being and mortality: A quantitative review of prospective observational studies. *Psychosomatic Medicine, 70*(7), 741–756. DOI: 10.1097/PSY.0b013e31818105ba PMID: 18725425

Cinelli, M., Quattrociocchi, W., Galeazzi, A., Valensise, C. M., Brugnoli, E., Schmidt, A. L., Zola, P., Zollo, F., & Scala, A. (2020). The COVID-19 social media infodemic. *Scientific Reports, 10*(1), 1–10. DOI: 10.1038/s41598-020-73510-5 PMID: 33024152

Citron, D. K. (2019). *Hate crimes in cyberspace*. Harvard University Press.

Cohan, A., Young, S., Yates, A., & Goharian, N. (2017). Triaging content severity in online mental health forums.

Cowie, R., & Cornelius, R. R. (2003). Describing the emotional states that are expressed in speech. *Speech Communication, 40*(1-2), 5–32. DOI: 10.1016/S0167-6393(02)00071-7

Crawford, K. (2021). *Atlas of AI: Power, Politics, and the Planetary Costs of Artificial Intelligence*. Yale University Press.

Crawford, K. (2022). Atlas of AI: Power, Politics, and the Planetary Costs of Artificial Intelligence. *Perspectives on Science and Christian Faith, 74*(1), 61–62. DOI: 10.56315/PSCF3-22Crawford

Crawford, K., & Paglen, T. (2021). *Atlas of AI: Power, politics, and the planetary costs of artificial intelligence*. Yale University Press.

Cunningham, S., & Craig, D. (2019). *Social media entertainment: The new intersection of Hollywood and Silicon Valley*. NYU Press.

D'amico, S., Dall'Olio, D., Sala, C., Dall'Olio, L., Sauta, E., Zampini, M., Asti, G., Lanino, L., Maggioni, G., Campagna, A., Ubezio, M., Russo, A., Bicchieri, M. E., Riva, E., Tentori, C. A., Travaglino, E., Morandini, P., Savevski, V., Santoro, A., & Della Porta, M. G. (2023). Synthetic data generation by artificial intelligence to accelerate research and precision medicine in hematology. *JCO Clinical Cancer Informatics, 7*(7), e2300021. DOI: 10.1200/CCI.23.00021 PMID: 37390377

Davidson, T., Bhattacharya, D., & Weber, I. (2019). Racial bias in hate speech detection. *Proceedings of the 2019 Workshop on Online Abuse and Harms,* 25–35.

De Gregorio, G., & Stremlau, N. (2023). Inequalities and content moderation. *Global Policy, 14*(5), 870–879. DOI: 10.1111/1758-5899.13243

De Souza, V. L. T., Marques, B. A. D., Batagelo, H. C., & Gois, J. P. (2023). A review on generative adversarial networks for image generation. *Computers & Graphics, 114*, 13–25. DOI: 10.1016/j.cag.2023.05.010

Deng, D., Rogers, T., & Naslund, J. A. (2023). The role of moderators in facilitating and encouraging peer-to-peer support in an online mental health community: A qualitative exploratory study. *JMIR Formative Research, 7*, e43541. DOI: 10.2196/43541 PMID: 36810998

Diakopoulos, N. (2020). Accountability, transparency, and algorithms. *The Oxford handbook of ethics of AI, 17*(4), 197.

Dias Oliva, T. (2020). Content moderation technologies: Applying human rights standards to protect freedom of expression. *Human Rights Law Review, 20*(4), 607–640. DOI: 10.1093/hrlr/ngaa032

Dinakar, K., Reichart, R., & Lieberman, H. (2012). Modelling the detection of textual cyberbullying. *The Workshop on Computational Approaches to Subjectivity and Sentiment Analysis*, 11-17.

Diseiye, O., Ukubeyinje, S. E., Oladokun, B. D., & Kakwagh, V. V. (2024). Emerging technologies: Leveraging digital literacy for self-sufficiency among library professionals. *Metaverse Basic and Applied Research, 3*, 59–59. DOI: 10.56294/mr202459

Divya, V., & Mirza, A. U. (2024). Transforming content creation: The influence of generative AI on a new frontier. *Exploring the frontiers of artificial intelligence and machine learning technologies, 143.*

Douek, E. (2020). The rise of content cartels. Knight First Amendment Institute. https://knightcolumbia.org

Duan, Y., Edwards, J. S., & Dwivedi, Y. K. (2019). Artificial intelligence for decision making in the era of Big Data – evolution, challenges and research agenda. *International Journal of Information Management, 48*, 63–71. DOI: 10.1016/j.ijinfomgt.2019.01.021

Elmendili, F., Chaoui, H., & Bouzekri El Idrissi, Y. E. (2019). Social Network's Security Related to Healthcare. *Intelligent Pervasive Computing Systems for Smarter Healthcare*, 91-113.

European Commission. (2018). General Data Protection Regulation (GDPR). Retrieved from https://gdpr-info.eu

European Commission. (2022). *Digital Services Act: Ensuring a safe and accountable online environment.* https://ec.europa.eu/info/business-economy-euro/banking-and-finance/digital-finance_en

Farahani, B., Firouzi, F., & Luecking, M. (2021). The convergence of IoT and distributed ledger technologies (DLT): Opportunities, challenges, and solutions. *Journal of Network and Computer Applications, 177*, 102936. DOI: 10.1016/j.jnca.2020.102936

Feinstein, A., Pavisian, B., & Storm, H. (2018). Moral injury in the context of humanitarian aid work: A review of current research. *European Journal of Psychotraumatology, 9*(1), 1462834.

Ferraz, T. P., Duarte, C. H. D., Ribeiro, M. F., Takayanagi, G. G. B., Alcoforado, A., Lopes, R. D., & Susi, M. (2024). Explainable AI to Mitigate the Lack of Transparency and Legitimacy in Internet Moderation. *Estudos Avançados, 38*, 381–405. DOI: 10.1590/s0103-4014.202438111.020

Ferreira, J. J., & Monteiro, M. (2021). *The human-AI relationship in decision-making: AI explanation to support people on justifying their decisions* (No. arXiv:2102.05460). arXiv. https://doi.org//arXiv.2102.05460DOI: 10.48550

Flemming, M. (2024) How Can We Tackle AI-Fueled Misinformation and Disinformation in Public Health? https://www.bu.edu/ceid/2024/04/25/how-can-we-tackle-ai-fueled-misinformation-and-disinformation-in-public-health/

Floridi, L., Cowls, J., Beltrametti, M., Chatila, R., Chazerand, P., Dignum, V., Luetge, C., Madelin, R., Pagallo, U., Rossi, F., Schafer, B., Valcke, P., & Vayena, E. (2018). AI4People—An ethical framework for a good AI society. *Minds and Machines, 28*(4), 689–707. DOI: 10.1007/s11023-018-9482-5 PMID: 30930541

Fui-Hoon Nah, F., Zheng, R., Cai, J., Siau, K., & Chen, L. (2023). *Generative AI and ChatGPT: Applications, challenges, and AI-human collaboration* (Vol. 25). Taylor & Francis.

Fui-Hoon Nah, F., Zheng, R., Cai, J., Siau, K., & Chen, L. (2023). Generative AI and ChatGPT: Applications, challenges, and AI-human collaboration. *Journal of Information Technology Case and Application Research, 25*(3), 277–304. DOI: 10.1080/15228053.2023.2233814

Ganesh, N. G., Venkatesh, N. M., & Prasad, D. V. V. (2022). A systematic literature review on forensics in cloud, IoT, AI & blockchain. *Illumination of Artificial Intelligence in Cybersecurity and Forensics*, 197-229.

Gao, L., Hao, J., & Huang, X. (2022). Multimodal AI for enhanced moderation systems. *Journal of AI Research*, *45*(3), 345–360.

Gilbert, C., & Gilbert, M. A. (2024). The Role of Artificial Intelligence (AI) in Combatting Deepfakes and Digital Misinformation. *International Research Journal of Advanced Engineering and Science (ISSN: 2455-9024)*, *9*(4), 170-181.

Gillespie, T. (2018). Custodians of the Internet: Platforms, Content Moderation, and the Hidden Decisions That Shape Social Media. In *Custodians of the Internet* (p. 288). Platforms, Content Moderation, and the Hidden Decisions That Shape Social Media., DOI: 10.12987/9780300235029

Gillespie, T. (2018). *Custodians of the internet: Platforms, content moderation, and the hidden decisions that shape social media*. Yale University Press.

Gillespie, T. (2018). *Custodians of the Internet: Platforms, content moderation, and the hidden decisions that shape social media*. Yale University Press.

Gillespie, T. (2020). Content moderation, AI, and the question of scale. *Big Data & Society*, *7*(2), 205395172094323. DOI: 10.1177/2053951720943234

Gillespie, T., & Karizat, N. (2021). Algorithmically Unjust: How Automated Moderation Contributes to the Silencing of Marginalized Voices. *Social Media + Society*, *7*(3).

Global Internet Forum to Counter Terrorism (GIFCT). (2021). *About GIFCT*. Retrieved from https://gifct.org

Gomez, H. I., & Rodriguez, J. M. (2020). Enhancing engagement through AI-driven chatbots: A study in Visayas campus journalism. *Journal of Interactive Media*, *15*(3), 112–129.

Gongane, V. U., Munot, M. V., & Anuse, A. D. (2022). Detection and moderation of detrimental content on social media platforms: Current status and future directions. *Social Network Analysis and Mining*, *12*(1), 129. DOI: 10.1007/s13278-022-00951-3 PMID: 36090695

Goni, A., & Tabassum, M. (2020). Artificial Intelligence (AI) in journalism: Is Bangladesh ready for it? A study on journalism students in Bangladesh. *Athens Journal of Mass Media and Communications*, *6*(4), 209–228. DOI: 10.30958/ajmmc.6-4-1

Gorwa, R. (2019). The platform governance triangle: Conceptualising the informal regulation of online content. *Internet Policy Review*, *8*(2), 1–22. DOI: 10.14763/2019.2.1407

Gorwa, R., Binns, R., & Katzenbach, C. (2020). Algorithmic content moderation: Technical and political challenges in the automation of platform governance. *Big Data & Society, 7*(1), 1–15. DOI: 10.1177/2053951719897945

Gray, M. L., & Suri, S. (2019). *Ghost Work: How to Stop Silicon Valley from Building a New Global Underclass*. Houghton Mifflin Harcourt.

Green, D. (2019). YouTube's moderation problems: Creators speak out. *The Guardian*. https://www.theguardian.com

Grossi, E., Tavano Blessi, G., Sacco, P. L., & Buscema, M. (2012). The interaction between culture, health and psychological well-being: Data mining from the Italian culture and well-being project. *Journal of Happiness Studies, 13*(1), 129–148. DOI: 10.1007/s10902-011-9254-x

Gruschka, N., Mavroeidis, V., Vishi, K., & Jensen, M. (2018, December). Privacy issues and data protection in big data: a case study analysis under GDPR. In *2018 IEEE International Conference on Big Data (Big Data)* (pp. 5027-5033). IEEE.

Guanah, J. S., Agbanu, V. N., & Obi, I. (2020). Artificial intelligence and journalism practice in Nigeria: Perception of journalists in Benin City, Edo State. *International review of humanities. Studies, 5*(2), 16.

Habgood-Coote, J. (2023). Deepfakes and the epistemic apocalypse. *Synthese, 201*(3), 103. DOI: 10.1007/s11229-023-04097-3

Habib, M. R. (2023). The role of social media in shaping the social capital of the new republic in light of the global challenges. *The Egyptian Journal of Media Research, 2023*(82), 383–432.

Hamel, C., Kelly, S., Thavorn, K., Rice, D., Wells, G., & Hutton, B. (2020). An evaluation of DistillerSR's machine learning-based prioritization tool for title/abstract screening–impact on reviewer-relevant outcomes. *BMC Medical Research Methodology, 20*(1), 1–14. DOI: 10.1186/s12874-020-01129-1 PMID: 33059590

Hamilton, N. A., Nelson, C. A., Stevens, N., & Kitzman, H. (2007). Sleep and psychological well-being. *Social Indicators Research, 82*(1), 147–163. DOI: 10.1007/s11205-006-9030-1

Hanusch, F., & Bruns, A. (2017). Journalistic branding on Twitter: A representative study of Australian journalists' profile descriptions. *Digital Journalism (Abingdon, England), 5*(1), 26–43. DOI: 10.1080/21670811.2016.1152161

Hartmann, I. A. (2020). A new framework for online content moderation. *Computer Law & Security Review, 36*, 105376. DOI: 10.1016/j.clsr.2019.105376

Hashemi, M. (2023). Geographical visualization of tweets, misinformation, and extremism during the USA 2020 presidential election using LSTM, NLP, and GIS. *Journal of Big Data*, *10*(1), 125. DOI: 10.1186/s40537-023-00797-2

Haupt, M., Freidank, J., & Haas, A. (2024). Consumer responses to human-AI collaboration at organizational frontlines: Strategies to escape algorithm aversion in content creation. *Review of Managerial Science*, •••, 1–37.

Haw, W. Y., Ho, E., Lim, Y. L., & Wong, J. W. (2013). *The effect of trailer, critics review, star power, and word of mouth toward decision making on movie consumption*. UTAR Institutional Repository.

Henderson, P., Hashimoto, T., & Lemley, M. (2023). Where's the Liability in harmful AI Speech? *J. Free Speech L.*, *3*, 589.

Hossain, L. (2021). *The extent to which Jordanian journalists are aware of the concept of robot journalism and its professional and ethical challenges*. Jordan Publishing Media Institute.

Hosseini, H., Kannan, S., & Mani, M. (2021). The limits of AI content moderation: A cautionary case study. *Proceedings of the AAAI/ACM Conference on AI, Ethics, and Society*, 173–179.

Hu, M., & Wu, X. (2018, June). Research on children's network privacy protection in mobile social media. In *2018 IEEE 20th International Conference on High Performance Computing and Communications; IEEE 16th International Conference on Smart City; IEEE 4th International Conference on Data Science and Systems (HPCC/SmartCity/DSS)* (pp. 1135-1138). IEEE.

Huang, M. H., & Rust, R. T. (2021). A strategic framework for artificial intelligence in marketing. *Journal of the Academy of Marketing Science*, *49*(1), 30–50. DOI: 10.1007/s11747-020-00749-9

Huang, Z., Wang, Y., & Zhang, L. (2023). Detecting deepfakes using AI: Challenges and advancements. *Journal of Artificial Intelligence Research*, *67*(4), 1123–1142.

Huertas-García, Á., Martín, A., Huertas-Tato, J., & Camacho, D. (2023). Countering malicious content moderation evasion in online social networks: Simulation and detection of word camouflage. *Applied Soft Computing*, *145*, 110552. DOI: 10.1016/j.asoc.2023.110552

Hutchens, J. (2023). *The Language of Deception: Weaponizing Next Generation AI*. John Wiley & Sons.

Iwaya, L. H., Iwaya, G. H., Fischer-Hübner, S., & Steil, A. V. (2022). Organisational privacy culture and climate: A scoping review. *IEEE Access : Practical Innovations, Open Solutions*, *10*, 73907–73930.

Jamal, S. (2024). *Applications of Predictive and Generative AI Algorithms: Regression Modeling*. Customized Large Language Models, and Text-to-Image Generative Diffusion Models.

Jamil, S. (2021). Artificial intelligence and journalistic practice: The crossroads of obstacles and opportunities for the Pakistani journalists. *Journalism Practice*, *15*(10), 1400–1422. DOI: 10.1080/17512786.2020.1788412

Jarrahi, M. H. (2018). Artificial intelligence and the future of work: Human-AI symbiosis in organizational decision making. *Business Horizons*, *61*(4), 577–586. DOI: 10.1016/j.bushor.2018.03.007

Jhaver, S., Bruckman, A., & Gilbert, E. (2019). Does transparency in moderation really matter? User behavior after content removal explanations on Reddit. *Proceedings of the ACM on Human-Computer Interaction, 3*(CSCW), 1–27.

Jiang, J. A., Wade, K., Fiesler, C., & Brubaker, J. R. (2021). Supporting Serendipity: Opportunities and Challenges for Human-AI Collaboration in Qualitative Analysis. *Proc. ACM Hum.-Comput. Interact., 5*(CSCW1), 94:1-94:23. https://doi.org/DOI: 10.1145/3449168

Jiang, N., Liu, X., Liu, H., Lim, E. T. K., Tan, C.-W., & Gu, J. (2023). Beyond AI-powered context-aware services: The role of human–AI collaboration. *Industrial Management & Data Systems*, *123*(11), 2771–2802. DOI: 10.1108/IMDS-03-2022-0152

Jigsaw. (2021). Perspective API: Technology to counter online toxicity. Retrieved from https://jigsaw.google.com

Jobin, A., Ienca, M., & Vayena, E. (2019). The health implications of AI and big data in medical research. *Lancet*, *394*(10210), 2134–2145.

John Den Saul, L. D., & Enciso, R. E. Exploring the Impact of Artificial Intelligence on Campus Journalism: A.

Kaye, D. (2022). Oversight Board Accountability Review. *Center for Human Rights & Policy*. https://www.ohchr.org

Kendon, T., Wu, L., & Aycock, J. (2023). AI-Generated Code Not Considered Harmful. Proceedings of the 25th Western Canadian Conference on Computing Education, Kivimaki, V. P. Open-Source Information for Intelligence Purposes: The Challenge of Disinformation. In *Routledge Handbook of Disinformation and National Security* (pp. 283-294). Routledge.

Khan, A., Gul, M. A., Uddin, M. I., Shah, S. A. A., Ahmad, S., Al Firdausi, M. D., & Zaindin, M. (2020). "Movie review summarization using supervised learning and graph-based ranking algorithm", Computational Intelligence and Neuroscience, 2020. *Article ID, 7526580*, 1–10.

Khan, A., Gul, M. A., Uddin, M. I., Shah, S. A. A., Ahmad, S., Al Firdausi, M. D., & Zaindin, M. (2020). "Summarizing Online Movie Reviews: A Machine Learning Approach to Big Data Analytics", Scientific Programming, 2020. *Article ID, 5812715*, 1–12.

Kim, E., Ding, M., Wang, X. S., & Lu, S. (2023). Does Topic Consistency Matter? A Study of Critic and User Reviews in the Movie Industry. *Journal of Marketing, 87*(3), 428–450. DOI: 10.1177/00222429221127927

Kim, J., Kim, J., & Oh, A. (2020). Detecting deepfake images in online spaces. *IEEE Transactions on Neural Networks and Learning Systems.*

Kleinheksel, A., Rockich-Winston, N., Tawfik, H., & Wyatt, T. R. (2020). Demystifying content analysis. *American Journal of Pharmaceutical Education, 84*(1), 7113. DOI: 10.5688/ajpe7113 PMID: 32292185

Klonic, K. (2021). The new governors: The people, rules, and processes governing online speech. *Harvard Law Review, 131*(6), 1598–1670.

Kniazieva, Y. (2023, March 30). *AI Content Moderation.* https://labelyourdata.com/articles/ai-content-moderation

Kolluri, N. L., & Murthy, D. (2021). CoVerifi: A COVID-19 news verification system. *Online Social Networks and Media, 22*, 100123. DOI: 10.1016/j.osnem.2021.100123 PMID: 33521412

Kondel, S., & Sing, N. (2019). A Paper on Movie Review by Implementing Movie Review App Using Android Technology. *JETIR, 6*(5), 1–5.

Kothari, A., & Cruikshank, S. A. (2022). Artificial intelligence and journalism: An Agenda for journalism research in Africa. *African Journalism Studies, 43*(1), 17–33. DOI: 10.1080/23743670.2021.1999840

Kowert, R. (2020). Toxic gaming: The impact of content moderation and the need for community-based approaches. *Cyberpsychology (Brno), 14*(4), 7.

Kučinskas, G. (2024). *Negative Effects of Revealing Ai Involvement in Products: Mediation by Authenticity and Risk, Moderation by Trust in Ai and Familiarity with Ai*. Moderation by Trust in Ai and Familiarity with Ai.

L, F. (2024, February 27). *Understanding AI Content Moderation: Types & How it Works*. https://getstream.io/blog/ai-content-moderation/

Lai, V., Chen, C., Liao, Q. V., Smith-Renner, A., & Tan, C. (2021). Towards a science of human-ai decision making: a survey of empirical studies. *arXiv preprint arXiv:2112.11471*.

Lai, V., Carton, S., Bhatnagar, R., Liao, Q. V., Zhang, Y., & Tan, C. (2022, April). Human-ai collaboration via conditional delegation: A case study of content moderation. In *Proceedings of the 2022 CHI Conference on Human Factors in Computing Systems* (pp. 1-18). DOI: 10.1145/3491102.3501999

Lal, K., & Saini, M. L. (2023). A study on deep fake identification techniques using deep learning. AIP Conference Proceedings, Lehtimäki, M.-L. (2024). Navigating Ethical and Practical Challenges in AI-Driven Visual Content Creation. DOI: 10.1063/5.0154828

Lee, S. K., Lindsey, N. J., & Kim, K. S. (2017). The effects of news consumption via social media and news information overload on perceptions of journalistic norms and practices. *Computers in Human Behavior, 75*, 254–263.

Li, C., & Callegari, A. (2024) Stop AI disinformation: Protecting truth in the digital world. https://www.weforum.org/agenda/2024/06/ai-combat-online-misinformation-disinformation/

Lipton, Z. C. (2018). The mythos of model interpretability. *Communications of the ACM, 61*(10), 36–43. DOI: 10.1145/3233231

Liu, C.-L., Hsaio, W.-H., Lee, C.-H., Lu, G.-C., & Jou, E. (2012). Movie Rating and Review Summarization in Mobile Environment. *IEEE Transactions on Systems, Man, and Cybernetics. Part C, Applications and Reviews, 42*(3), 345–358. DOI: 10.1109/TSMCC.2011.2136334

Llansó, E., Van Hoboken, J., Leerssen, P., & Harambam, J. (2020). Artificial intelligence, content moderation, and freedom of expression.

Llansó, E. J. (2020). No amount of "AI" in content moderation will solve filtering's prior-restraint problem. *Big Data & Society*, *7*(1), 2053951720920686. DOI: 10.1177/2053951720920686

Lloyd, T., Reagle, J., & Naaman, M. (2023). " There Has To Be a Lot That We're Missing": Moderating AI-Generated Content on Reddit. *arXiv preprint arXiv:2311.12702.*

Luchko, Y. I., & Dobrovichka, O. O. (2023). Application of cloud technologies in the educational process of higher education institutions.

Lykouris, T., & Weng, W. (2024). Learning to defer in content moderation: The human-ai interplay. *arXiv preprint arXiv:2402.12237.*

Lyu, S. (2024). *DeepFake the menace: mitigating the negative impacts of AI-generated content. Organizational Cybersecurity Journal: Practice.* Process and People.

Madaio, M., Stark, L., Wortman Vaughan, J., & Wallach, H. (2020). Co-designing checklists to understand organizational challenges and opportunities around fairness in AI. *Proceedings of the 2020 CHI Conference on Human Factors in Computing Systems*, 1–14. DOI: 10.1145/3313831.3376445

Mansour, M. (2024). The Moderation effect of AI Image Generator on the Relationship Between Evidences and Accurate Judgment. [IJTOP]. *International Journal of Theory of Organization and Practice*, *4*(1), 44–58.

Mantri, A. (2021). Real-Time Content Moderation Using Artificial Intelligence and Machine Learning. [IJSR]. *International Journal of Science and Research (Raipur, India)*, *10*(1), 1682–1684. DOI: 10.21275/SR24724150350

Manyika, J., Chui, M., Bughin, J., et al. (2017). Jobs lost, jobs gained: Workforce transitions in a time of automation. *McKinsey Global Institute Report.*

Marra, A., Righi, R., & Baletti, R. (2019). Collaborative frameworks for AI moderation. *Journal of Internet Policy*, *5*(2), 89–112.

Marsoof, A., Luco, A., Tan, H., & Joty, S. (2023). Content-filtering AI systems–limitations, challenges and regulatory approaches. *Information & Communications Technology Law*, *32*(1), 64–101. DOI: 10.1080/13600834.2022.2078395

Martínez-de-Morentin, I., Lareki, A., & Altuna, J. (2021). Risks Associated With Posting Content on the Social Media. *IEEE Revista Iberoamericana de Technologias del Aprendizaje*, *16*(1), 77–83. DOI: 10.1109/RITA.2021.3052655

Marzuki, W., Widiati, U., Rusdin, D., Darwin, , & Indrawati, I. (2023). The impact of AI writing tools on the content and organization of students' writing: EFL teachers' perspective. *Cogent Education, 10*(2), 2236469. DOI: 10.1080/2331186X.2023.2236469

Masood, M., Nawaz, M., Malik, K. M., Javed, A., Irtaza, A., & Malik, H. (2023). Deepfakes generation and detection: State-of-the-art, open challenges, countermeasures, and way forward. *Applied Intelligence, 53*(4), 3974–4026. DOI: 10.1007/s10489-022-03766-z

Matias, J. N. (2019). Preventing harassment and increasing group participation through social norms in 2,190 online science discussions. *Proceedings of the National Academy of Sciences of the United States of America, 116*(20), 9785–9789. DOI: 10.1073/pnas.1813486116 PMID: 31036646

Mcdonald, D. W. (2000). *Supporting nuance in groupware design: Moving from naturalistic expertise location to expertise recommendation*. University of California.

McGregor, S. C. (2019). Social media as public opinion: How journalists use social media to represent public opinion. *Journalism, 20*(8), 1070–1086. DOI: 10.1177/1464884919845458

Menczer, F., Crandall, D., Ahn, Y.-Y., & Kapadia, A. (2023). Addressing the harms of AI-generated inauthentic content. *Nature Machine Intelligence, 5*(7), 679–680. DOI: 10.1038/s42256-023-00690-w

MG, A. & Mahalakshmi, T. (2023). Movie Review Application [IJARSCT]. International Journal of Advanced Research in Science. *Tongxin Jishu, 3*(1), 50–55.

Mhlanga, D. (2023). Open AI in education, the responsible and ethical use of ChatGPT towards lifelong learning. In *FinTech and artificial intelligence for sustainable development: The role of smart technologies in achieving development goals* (pp. 387–409). Springer. DOI: 10.1007/978-3-031-37776-1_17

Mhlanga, M. X., Maiti, R. R., & Hammer, B. (2021, March). Privacy and Security Matters Related To Use Of Mobile Devices and Social Media. In *SoutheastCon 2021* (pp. 1–6). IEEE.

Mikalef, P., & Gupta, M. (2021). Artificial intelligence capability: Conceptualization, measurement calibration, and empirical study on its impact on organizational creativity and firm performance. *Information & Management, 58*(3), 103434. DOI: 10.1016/j.im.2021.103434

Miller, T. (2019). Explanation in artificial intelligence: Insights from the social sciences. *Artificial Intelligence, 267*, 1–38. DOI: 10.1016/j.artint.2018.07.007

Misra, G., & Such, J. M. (2016). How socially aware are social media privacy controls? *Computer*, *49*(3), 96–99.

Molina, M. D., & Sundar, S. S. (2024). Does distrust in humans predict greater trust in AI? Role of individual differences in user responses to content moderation. *new media & society, 26*(6), 3638-3656.

Molina, M. D., & Sundar, S. S. (2022). When AI moderates online content: Effects of human collaboration and interactive transparency on user trust. *Journal of Computer-Mediated Communication*, *27*(4), zmac010. Advance online publication. DOI: 10.1093/jcmc/zmac010

Morley, J., Floridi, L., Kinsey, L., & Elhalal, A. (2020). From what to how: An initial review of publicly available AI ethics tools, methods and research to translate principles into practices. *Science and Engineering Ethics*, *26*(4), 2141–2168. DOI: 10.1007/s11948-019-00165-5 PMID: 31828533

Mozilla Foundation. (2020). Creators and Moderation: A Stressful Relationship. https://foundation.mozilla.org

Mozur, P. (2018). A genocide was incited on Facebook, with posts from Myanmar's military. *The New York Times.* Retrieved from https://www.nytimes.com

Mundra, S., Reddy, J., Mundra, A., Mittal, N., Vidyarthi, A., & Gupta, D. (2023). *An Automated Data-driven Machine Intelligence Framework for Mining Knowledge To Classify Fake News Using NLP*. ACM Transactions on Asian and Low-Resource Language Information Processing. DOI: 10.1145/3607253

Mustaffa, N., Sannusi, S. N., Hasan, A. S. A., & Saad, M. Z. M. (2017). Journalism and news industry in Malaysia: new media, new challenges. *e-BANGI Journal, 12*.

Myers, C., & Feerrar, F. (2024) *AI and the spread of fake news sites: Experts explain how to counteract them*https://news.vt.edu/articles/2024/02/AI-generated-fake-news-experts.html

Nahmias, Y., & Perel, M. (2021). The oversight of content moderation by AI: Impact assessments and their limitations. *Harvard Journal on Legislation*, *58*, 145.

Napoli, P. M. (2019). *Social media and the public interest: Media regulation in the disinformation age*. Columbia University Press. DOI: 10.7312/napo18454

Nesi, J. (2020). The impact of social media on youth mental health: Challenges and opportunities. *North Carolina Medical Journal*, *81*(2), 116–121. DOI: 10.18043/ncm.81.2.116 PMID: 32132255

Newton, C. (2019). *The trauma floor: The secret lives of Facebook moderators in America*. The Verge.

Newton, C., & Witt, C. (2020). *The trauma floor: The secret lives of Facebook moderators*. The Verge.

Nguyen, A., Rai, A., & Maruping, L. (2024). Understanding the Unintended Effects of Human-Machine Moderation in Addressing Harassment within Online Communities. *Journal of Management Information Systems*, *41*(2), 341–366. DOI: 10.1080/07421222.2024.2340831

Nichele, E., Lavorgna, A., & Middleton, S. E. (2022). Identifying key challenges and needs in digital mental health moderation practices supporting users exhibiting risk behaviours to develop responsible AI tools: The case study of Kooth. *Frontiers in Digital Health*, *4*, 901169. DOI: 10.3389/fdgth.2022.901169 PMID: 36196212

Nishimura, M., Hashimoto, K., Oura, K., Nankaku, Y., & Tokuda, K. (2016). Singing Voice Synthesis Based on Deep Neural Networks. Interspeech, Pan, Z., Lau, S. L., Yang, X., Guo, N., & Wang, X. (2023). Automatic pavement crack segmentation using a generative adversarial network (GAN)-based convolutional neural network. *Results in Engineering*, *19*, 101267.

Noain Sánchez, A. (2022). Addressing the Impact of Artificial Intelligence on Journalism: The perception of experts, journalists and academics.

Noble, S. U. (2018). *Algorithms of oppression: How search engines reinforce racism*. NYU Press. DOI: 10.18574/nyu/9781479833641.001.0001

Ozanne, M., Bhandari, A., Bazarova, N. N., & DiFranzo, D. (2022). Shall AI moderators be made visible? Perception of accountability and trust in moderation systems on social media platforms. *Big Data & Society*, *9*(2), 20539517221115666. DOI: 10.1177/20539517221115666

Pang, J., Liu, A. X., & Golder, P. N. (2022). Critics' conformity to consumers in movie evaluation. *Journal of the Academy of Marketing Science*, *50*(4), 864–887. DOI: 10.1007/s11747-021-00816-9

Pappachan, P., Adi, N. S., & Firmansyah, G. (2024). Deep Learning-Based Forensics. *Digital Forensics and Cyber Crime Investigation: Recent Advances and Future Directions*, 211.

Pasquale, F. (2015). *The black box society: The secret algorithms that control money and information*. Harvard University Press. DOI: 10.4159/harvard.9780674736061

Paterson, T., & Hanley, L. (2020). Political warfare in the digital age: Cyber subversion, information operations and 'deep fakes'. *Australian Journal of International Affairs, 74*(4), 439–454. DOI: 10.1080/10357718.2020.1734772

Pennycook, G., & Rand, D. G. (2018). The Implied Truth Effect: Attaching warnings to a subset of fake news stories increases the perceived accuracy of stories without warnings. *Management Science, 66*(11), 4944–4957. DOI: 10.1287/mnsc.2019.3478

Pentheny, J. R. (2015). *The Influence of Movie Reviews on Consumers*. Honors Theses and Capstones.

Perry, A., Pyle, D., Lamont-Mills, A., du Plessis, C., & du Preez, J. (2021). Suicidal behaviours and moderator support in online health communities: A scoping review. *BMJ Open, 11*(1), e047905. DOI: 10.1136/bmjopen-2020-047905 PMID: 34193497

Pew Research Center. (2022). Social Media Engagement and User Trust. https://www.pewresearch.org

Pflanzer, M., Traylor, Z., Lyons, J. B., Dubljević, V., & Nam, C. S. (2023). Ethics in human–AI teaming: Principles and perspectives. *AI and Ethics, 3*(3), 917–935. DOI: 10.1007/s43681-022-00214-z

Picard, R. W. (2000). *Affective computing*. MIT Press. DOI: 10.7551/mitpress/1140.003.0008

Pillai, V. (2024). Enhancing Transparency and Understanding in AI Decision-Making Processes. *Iconic Research and Engineering Journals, 8*(1), 168–172.

Pirone, N. A. (2024). Determinants of Generative Artificial Intelligence Large Language Model Exploration Intent for Software Development.

Plevris, V. (2024). Addressing the Pitfalls of Image-Based Structural Health Monitoring: A Focus on False Positives, False Negatives, and Base Rate Bias. *arXiv preprint arXiv:2410.20384.*

Pokhrel, S., & Banjade, S. R.Shiv Raj Banjade. (2023). AI Content Generation Technology based on Open AI Language Model. *Journal of Artificial Intelligence and Capsule Networks, 5*(4), 534–548. DOI: 10.36548/jaicn.2023.4.006

Prates, M. O. R., Avelar, P. H., & Lamb, L. C. (2020). Assessing gender bias in machine translation. NeurIPS 2020.

Radwan, A. M., Abdel-Fattah, M. A., & Mohamed, W. AI-Driven Prioritization Techniques of Requirements in Agile Methodologies: A Systematic Literature.

Rafique, R., Gantassi, R., Amin, R., Frnda, J., Mustapha, A., & Alshehri, A. H. (2023). Deep fake detection and classification using error-level analysis and deep learning. *Scientific Reports*, *13*(1), 7422. DOI: 10.1038/s41598-023-34629-3 PMID: 37156887

Raji, I. D., & Buolamwini, J. (2019). Actionable auditing: Investigating the impact of publicly naming biased performance results of commercial AI products. *Proceedings of the 2019 AAAI/ACM Conference on AI, Ethics, and Society*, 429–435. DOI: 10.1145/3306618.3314244

Raji, I. D., Smart, A., White, R., Mitchell, M., Gebru, T., Hutchinson, B., & Barnes, P. (2020). Closing the AI accountability gap: Defining an end-to-end framework for internal algorithmic auditing. *Proceedings of the 2020 Conference on Fairness, Accountability, and Transparency*, 33–44. DOI: 10.1145/3351095.3372873

Raschke, P., Esau, K., & Meinel, C. (2019). Measuring the potential of online deliberation processes: Automated content analysis of argumentative quality. *Policy and Internet*, *11*(2), 208–227.

Reddy, V. S. S., & Reddy, N. (2024). AI-Powered Language Models Enhancing Natural Language Understanding And Generation. [IJAIML]. *International Journal of Artificial Intelligence and Machine Learning*, *3*(02), 101–115.

Reichwein, F. L. (2024). *Ethical and societal implications of generative AI-Models*. Technische Hochschule Ingolstadt.

Reinstein, D. A., & Snyder, C. M. (2005). The influence of expert reviews on consumer demand for experience goods: A case study of movie critics. *The Journal of Industrial Economics*, *53*(1), 27–51. DOI: 10.1111/j.0022-1821.2005.00244.x

Report, F. T. (2023). *Community Standards Enforcement Report*. Meta. https://transparency.fb.com

Report, T. T. (2023). *AI-driven content moderation: Challenges and achievements*. Retrieved from https://twitter.com/transparency

Report, T. T. (2022). https://transparency.twitter.com

Reyes, L. P., & Cruz, R. S. (2021). AI-assisted data analysis for investigative reporting: Exploring the potential in Northern Luzon. *Journal of Investigative Journalism*, *12*(4), 156–172.

Richards, N. M., & Hartzog, W. (2019). The pathologies of digital consent. *Washington University Law Review*, *96*(2), 1003–1071.

Roberts, S. T. (2019). *Behind the screen: Content moderation in the shadows of social media.* Yale University Press.

Romero Moreno, F. (2024). Generative AI and deepfakes: A human rights approach to tackling harmful content. *International Review of Law Computers & Technology, 38*(3), 1–30. DOI: 10.1080/13600869.2024.2324540

Rosen, G. (2020). Building transparency and oversight for Facebook's content decisions. *Facebook Newsroom.* Retrieved from https://about.fb.com/news

Rubin, V. L. (2022). Investigation in Law Enforcement, Journalism, and Sciences. In *Misinformation and Disinformation: Detecting Fakes with the Eye and AI* (pp. 123-156). Springer.

Ruini, C., Ottolini, F., Rafanelli, C., Tossani, E., Ryff, C. D., & Fava, G. A. (2003). The relationship of psychological well-being to distress and personality. *Psychotherapy and Psychosomatics, 72*(5), 268–275. DOI: 10.1159/000071898 PMID: 12920331

Ryan, M. (2020). In AI We Trust: Ethics, Artificial Intelligence, and Reliability. *Science and Engineering Ethics, 26*(5), 2749–2767. DOI: 10.1007/s11948-020-00228-y PMID: 32524425

Saheb, T., Sidaoui, M., & Schmarzo, B. (2024). Convergence of artificial intelligence with social media: A bibliometric & qualitative analysis. *Telematics and Informatics Reports, 14*, 100146. DOI: 10.1016/j.teler.2024.100146

Sander, B. (2019). Freedom of expression in the age of online platforms: The promise and pitfalls of a human rights-based approach to content moderation. *Fordham Int'l LJ, 43*, 939.

Santos, A. B., Lim, C. D., & Tan, E. F. (2019). AI powered news generation for increased efficiency: A case study in Metro Manila. *Journal of Medical Technology, 8*(2), 45–58.

Santos, M. A. (2017). Data-driven storytelling by AI-assisted student journalists in the Philippines. *Journal of Emerging Media Studies, 5*(2), 78–92.

Sap, M., Card, D., Gabriel, S., Choi, Y., & Smith, N. A. (2019). The risk of racial bias in hate speech detection. *Proceedings of the 57th Annual Meeting of the Association for Computational Linguistics*, 1668–1678. DOI: 10.18653/v1/P19-1163

Scherer, L. (2022). Building emotionally intelligent AI: A new frontier in human-centered design. *Journal of AI and Society, 37*(3), 85–102.

Scheuerman, M. K., Jiang, J. A., Fiesler, C., & Brubaker, J. R. (2021). A framework of severity for harmful content online

Schmidt, A., & Wiegand, M. (2017). A survey on hate speech detection using natural language processing. *Proceedings of the 5th International Workshop on Natural Language Processing for Social Media*. DOI: 10.18653/v1/W17-1101

Schroeder, R., Gurevych, I., & Eckert, K. (2021). *Multimodal approaches to content moderation*. Digital Platforms and Society Journal.

Sethu, S. G. (2020, July). Legal protection for data security: a comparative analysis of the laws and regulations of European Union, US, India and UAE. In *2020 11th International Conference on Computing, Communication and Networking Technologies (ICCCNT)* (pp. 1-5). IEEE.

Setiadi, D., Nurhayati, S., Ansori, A., Zubaidi, M., & Amir, R. (2023). Youth's digital literacy in the context of community empowerment in an emerging society 5.0. *Society*, *11*(1), 1–12. DOI: 10.33019/society.v11i1.491

Sezgin, E. (2023). Artificial intelligence in healthcare: Complementing, not replacing, doctors and healthcare providers. *Digital Health*, *9*, 20552076231186520. DOI: 10.1177/20552076231186520 PMID: 37426593

Shao, Y., Huang, C., Song, Y., Wang, M., Song, Y. H., & Shao, R. (2024). Using Augmentation-Based AI Tool at Work: A Daily Investigation of Learning-Based Benefit and Challenge. *Journal of Management*, •••, 01492063241266503. DOI: 10.1177/01492063241266503

Sharma, A., Kumar, V., & Poojari, A. (2024). *Prioritize Threat Alerts Based on False Positives Qualifiers Provided by Multiple AI Models Using Evolutionary Computation and Reinforcement Learning. Journal of The Institution of Engineers*. Series B. DOI: 10.1007/s40031-024-01175-z

Shin, D., Hameleers, M., Park, Y. J., Kim, J. N., Trielli, D., Diakopoulos, N., Helberger, N., Lewis, S. C., Westlund, O., & Baumann, S. (2022). Countering Algorithmic Bias and Disinformation and Effectively Harnessing the Power of AI in Media. *Journalism & Mass Communication Quarterly*, *99*(4), 887–907. DOI: 10.1177/10776990221129245

Shoaib, M. R., Wang, Z., Ahvanooey, M. T., & Zhao, J. (2023). Deepfakes, misinformation, and disinformation in the era of frontier AI, generative AI, and large AI models. *2023 International Conference on Computer and Applications (ICCA)*.

Siapera, E. (2022). AI content moderation, racism and (de) coloniality. *International Journal of Bullying Prevention : an Official Publication of the International Bullying Prevention Association*, *4*(1), 55–65. DOI: 10.1007/s42380-021-00105-7

Siddique, C. M., & D'Arcy, C. (1984). Adolescence, stress, and psychological well-being. *Journal of Youth and Adolescence, 13*(6), 459–473. DOI: 10.1007/BF02088593 PMID: 24306949

Simon, H., Baha, B. Y., & Garba, E. J. (2022). Trends in machine learning on automatic detection of hate speech on social media platforms: A systematic review. *FUW Trends in Science & Technology Journal, 7*(1), 001-016.

Singh, A. P. Safeguarding Authenticity in the Digital Realm: A Holistic Approach Integrating Content Provenance, Secure Watermarking, and Transparent Labeling to Combat Deepfakes.

Singh, S. (2019, July 15). *Everything in Moderation*. New America. https://newamerica.org/oti/reports/everything-moderation-analysis-how-internet-platforms-are-using-artificial-intelligence-moderate-user-generated-content/

Singhal, M., Ling, C., Paudel, P., Thota, P., Kumarswamy, N., Stringhini, G., & Nilizadeh, S. (2022). SoK: Content moderation in social media, from guidelines to enforcement, and research to practice.

Song, X., Mamidisetty, S., Blanco, E., & Hong, L. (2024). Assessing the Human Likeness of AI-Generated Counterspeech. *arXiv preprint arXiv:2410.11007.*

Stockinger, A., Schäfer, S., & Lecheler, S. (2023). Navigating the gray areas of content moderation: Professional moderators' perspectives on uncivil user comments and the role of (AI-based) technological tools. *new media & society*, 14614448231190901.

Subrahmanyam, S. (2021). The Psychodynamics of Apprehension in the Corporate World – A Hermeneutic Review of Literature. *Psychology and Education*, ISSN: 0033-3077, Volume-58 | Issue-3, 1684-1698.

Sulastri, R. (2023). Unveiling the Nuances of Human Interaction within Organizational Settings. *Advances in Human Resource Management Research, 1*(3), 150–163. DOI: 10.60079/ahrmr.v1i3.197

Sunyaev, A., & Sunyaev, A. (2020). Distributed ledger technology. *Internet computing: Principles of distributed systems and emerging internet-based technologies*, 265-299.

Sutton, R. S., & Barto, A. G. (2018). *Reinforcement learning: An introduction.* MIT Press.

Suzor, N. (2019). *Lawless: The Secret Rules That Govern Our Digital Lives*. Cambridge University Press. DOI: 10.1017/9781108666428

Suzor, N. P., West, S. M., Quodling, A., & York, J. (2019). What do we mean when we talk about transparency? *International Journal of Communication, 13*, 1526–1543.

Tabassam, S., Shah, H., Alghamdi, K., & Badshah, A. (2019, July). Social Netwoks and Digital Security. In *2019 International Conference on Electrical, Communication, and Computer Engineering (ICECCE)* (pp. 1-7). IEEE.

Taddei, S. (2021). AI and its ethical challenges. *AI & Society*, *36*(1), 101–115.

Taddeo, M., & Floridi, L. (2018). How AI can be a force for good. *Science*, *361*(6404), 751–752. DOI: 10.1126/science.aat5991 PMID: 30139858

Taibi, M. A. L. I. A., & Na, T. Y. (2020). The changes of media landscape in Malaysia: How citizen journalism poses threats to traditional media. *Jurnal Komunikasi: Malaysian Journal of Communication*, *36*(1), 396–380.

Talwar, A., Chaudhary, A., & Kumar, A. (2022, October). Encryption Policies of Social Media Apps and Its Effect on User's Privacy. In *2022 10th International Conference on Reliability, Infocom Technologies and Optimization (Trends and Future Directions)(ICRITO)* (pp. 1-4). IEEE.

Tan, R. M., Wong, L. S., & Ahmad, N. (2022). Audience reception of AI-generated news content in Malaysia. *Digital Journalism (Abingdon, England)*, *19*(5), 678–693.

Tejedor, S., & Vila, P. (2021). Exo journalism: a conceptual approach to a hybrid formula between journalism and artificial intelligence. *Journalism and media, 2*(4), 830-840.

The Chronicle of Higher Education, 2024. https://sponsored.chronicle.com/how-ai-is-being-used-to-fight-fake-news/index.html

TikTok Safety Center. (2023). *Adapting AI moderation for dynamic content*. Retrieved from https://www.tiktok.com/safety

Trujillo, A., & Cresci, S. (2022). One of many: Assessing user-level effects of moderation interventions on r/The_Donald.

Tuncer, S., & Ramirez, A. (2022). Exploring the Role of Trust During Human-AI Collaboration in Managerial Decision-Making Processes. In Chen, J. Y. C., Fragomeni, G., Degen, H., & Ntoa, S. (Eds.), *HCI International 2022 – Late Breaking Papers: Interacting with eXtended Reality and Artificial Intelligence* (pp. 541–557). Springer Nature Switzerland., DOI: 10.1007/978-3-031-21707-4_39

Turner, R. J. (1981). Social support as a contingency in psychological well-being. *Journal of Health and Social Behavior*, *22*(4), 357–367. DOI: 10.2307/2136677

Udupa, S., Maronikolakis, A., & Wisiorek, A. (2023). Ethical scaling for content moderation: Extreme speech and the (in) significance of artificial intelligence. *Big Data & Society*, *10*(1), 20539517231172424. DOI: 10.1177/20539517231172424

Vahed, S., Goanta, C., Ortolani, P., & Sanfey, A. G. (2024). Moral judgment of objectionable online content: Reporting decisions and punishment preferences on social media. *New Media & Society*. Advance online publication. DOI: 10.1177/14614448241244995 PMID: 38527036

Vallerand, R. J. (2012). The role of passion in sustainable psychological well-being. *Psychology of Well-Being: Theory. Psychology of Well-Being*, *2*(1), 1–21. DOI: 10.1186/2211-1522-2-1

Vázquez, C., Hervás, G., Rahona, J. J., & Gómez, D. (2009). Psychological well-being and health: Contributions of positive psychology. *Anuario de Psicología Clínica y de la Salud*, *5*, 15–27.

Vetagiri, A., Mogha, P., & Pakray, P. Multilate Classifier: A Novel Emsemble of Cnn-Bilstm with Resnet-Based Multimodal Classifier for Ai-Generated Hate Speech Detection. *Available atSSRN* 4951337. DOI: 10.2139/ssrn.4951337

Veturi, Y. A., Woof, W., Lazebnik, T., Moghul, I., Woodward-Court, P., Wagner, S. K., de Guimarães, T. A. C., Varela, M. D., Liefers, B., & Patel, P. J. (2023). SynthEye: Investigating the impact of synthetic data on artificial intelligence-assisted gene diagnosis of inherited retinal disease. *Ophthalmology Science*, *3*(2), 100258. DOI: 10.1016/j.xops.2022.100258 PMID: 36685715

Vidgen, B., Braun, R., & Hayes, G. (2021). Designing for digital governance: Challenges in automation and scaling content moderation at large platforms. *Communications of the ACM*, *64*(4), 24–27. DOI: 10.1145/3411789

Vössing, M., Kühl, N., Lind, M., & Satzger, G. (2022). Designing Transparency for Effective Human-AI Collaboration. *Information Systems Frontiers*, *24*(3), 877–895. DOI: 10.1007/s10796-022-10284-3

Wach, K., Duong, C. D., Ejdys, J., Kazlauskaitė, R., Korzynski, P., Mazurek, G., Paliszkiewicz, J., & Ziemba, E. (2023). The dark side of generative artificial intelligence: A critical analysis of controversies and risks of ChatGPT. *Entrepreneurial Business and Economics Review*, *11*(2), 7–30. DOI: 10.15678/EBER.2023.110201

Walczak, K., & Cellary, W. (2023). Challenges for higher education in the era of widespread access to Generative AI. *Economics and Business Review*, *9*(2), 71–100. DOI: 10.18559/ebr.2023.2.743

Wallentin, E. (2016). Demand for cinema and diverging tastes of critics and audiences. *Journal of Retailing and Consumer Services*, *33*, 72–81. DOI: 10.1016/j.jretconser.2016.08.002

Wang, X. S., & Zheng, J. (2024). Can Banning AI-generated Content Save User-Generated Q&A Platforms? *Jinyang, Can Banning AI-generated Content Save User-Generated Q&A Platforms*.

Wang, S. (2023). Factors related to user perceptions of artificial intelligence (AI)-based content moderation on social media. *Computers in Human Behavior*, *149*, 107971. DOI: 10.1016/j.chb.2023.107971

Wang, X., Luo, W., Bai, X., & Wang, Y. (2021, November). Research on big data security and privacy risk governance. In *2021 International Conference on Big Data, Artificial Intelligence and Risk Management (ICBAR)* (pp. 15-18). IEEE.

Wang, Y. (2023). Synthetic realities in the digital age: Navigating the opportunities and challenges of ai-generated content. *Authorea Preprints*.

Wardle, C., & Derakhshan, H. (2017). *Information disorder: Toward an interdisciplinary framework for research and policy making*. Council of Europe.

Warr, P., Cook, J., & Wall, T. (1979). Scales for the measurement of some work attitudes and aspects of psychological well-being. *Journal of Occupational Psychology*, *52*(2), 129–148. DOI: 10.1111/j.2044-8325.1979.tb00448.x

Waseem, Z., & Hovy, D. (2016). Hateful symbols or hateful people? Predictive features for hate speech detection on Twitter. *Proceedings of the NAACL Student Research Workshop*, 88–93. DOI: 10.18653/v1/N16-2013

West, S. M. (2021). Content moderation and the labor question. *Social Media + Society*, *7*(3), 1–12.

West, S. M., Whittaker, M., & Crawford, K. (2019). *Discriminating systems: Gender, race, and power in AI*. AI Now Institute.

Whittaker, M., Crawford, K., Dobbe, R., Fried, G., Kaziunas, E., Mathur, V., & Schwartz, O. (2018). *AI Now Report 2018*. AI Now Institute.

Wright, T. A., & Cropanzano, R. (2000). Psychological well-being and job satisfaction as predictors of job performance. *Journal of Occupational Health Psychology*, *5*(1), 84–94. DOI: 10.1037/1076-8998.5.1.84 PMID: 10658888

Wu, T. (2019). Will artificial intelligence eat the law? The rise of hybrid social-ordering systems. *Columbia Law Review*, *119*(7), 2001–2028.

Wu, Y. (2019). How age affects journalists' adoption of social media as an innovation: A multi-group SEM analysis. *Journalism Practice*, *13*(5), 537–557. DOI: 10.1080/17512786.2018.1511821

Xuan, G. (2023). Risks And Regulatory Framework of AI-Generated Content (AIGC) in the Judicial Field. *Journal of Education. Humanities and Social Sciences, 19*, 278–282.

Yang, Q., Liu, Y., Chen, T., & Tong, Y. (2019). Federated machine learning: Concept and applications. *ACM Transactions on Intelligent Systems and Technology, 10*(2), 1–19. DOI: 10.1145/3298981

Yeung, K., & Lodge, M. (2019). Algorithmic regulation: A critical interrogation. *Regulation & Governance, 13*(1), 1–16.

YouTube. (2019). Transparency Report. https://transparencyreport.google.com/youtube-policy

Zeng, J., Chan, C. H., & Fu, K. W. (2021). How false information spreads on social media: A systematic review. *Social Media + Society, 7*(2), 1–13.

Zhang, M., Xu, Y., & Wei, X. (2024). AI-centered vs. Human-centered: Exploring Users' Attitude toward AIGC in Varying Forms of Human-AI Collaboration.

Zhang, Y., Yang, X., Xu, X., Gao, Z., Huang, Y., Mu, S., Feng, S., Wang, D., Zhang, Y., & Song, K. (2024). Affective Computing in the Era of Large Language Models: A Survey from the NLP Perspective. *arXiv preprint arXiv:2408.04638.*

Zhou, J., Zhang, Y., Luo, Q., Parker, A. G., & De Choudhury, M. (2023). Synthetic lies: Understanding ai-generated misinformation and evaluating algorithmic and human solutions. *Proceedings of the 2023 CHI Conference on Human Factors in Computing Systems.*

Zhou, W., Zhao, H., & Tang, J. (2022). AI in the pandemic: Misinformation and its implications. *Computers in Human Behavior, 135*(C), 107635.

Zhu, W. (2022). *NLP measures for cyber environment safety: Detection, mitigation and intervention.* University of Illinois at Urbana-Champaign.

Zuckerberg, M. (2021). The challenges of governing content on digital platforms. *Journal of Digital Ethics, 5*(3), 67–81.

About the Contributors

Siddhartha Paul Tiwari (PhD, FRAS, FRAI) is an academic, technology expert, and researcher who has made significant contributions to the fields of education, mobile technology, digital strategies, and information and communications technology. He currently leads Google Asia Pacific's Mobile Policy for Southeast Asia, China, Japan, and Korea based out of Singapore. Prior to this, Dr. Tiwari oversaw Google's global learning and development initiatives from Tokyo. He is an Elected Fellow of the "Royal Anthropological Institute of Great Britain and Ireland" and the "Royal Asiatic Society" given his contributions to the field of technology and education. He has introduced over 30 postgraduate courses in collaboration with leading universities and institutions in Asia. He has been an invited speaker at TEDx, the G20 Summit, and the United Nations. Dr Tiwari has authored 50 research papers on technology management, emerging technologies, and technology and society, and has served as a pro bono visiting professor at institutions including INSEAD Singapore, the Indian Institute of Technology, Delhi, and the Lal Bahadur Shastri National Academy of Administration, Mussoorie.

Adi FahrudinAdi Fahrudin is a Professor in Social Work at the Faculty of Psychology, Universitas Bhayangkara Jakarta Raya, Indonesia (from 1 March 2022 until present). Prof Adi was early trained at Social Work Senior High School in Palembang, Indonesia, and became the best graduate (1986). He graduated and obtained a Doctorandus (Drs) in Social Work from the Bandung College of Social Welfare in 1991 (the best graduate), a Master of Social Science (Social Work) at the University of Science Malaysia in 1996, and then obtained a Ph.D. in Social Work from the same university in 1999. He also studied at the undergraduate level after his Ph.D. and obtained a Bachelor of Psychology (B.Psych) from PASIM University of Bandung (2010). In June 2022, Prof Adi was appointed as Director of the Institute for Research, Community Service and Publication. Since August 2023, he has been appointed Acting Dean of the Faculty of Psychology, Universitas

Bhayangkara Jakarta Raya. Before that, he was Professor in Social Work seconded to the Faculty of Social and Political Sciences, at the University of Muhammadiyah Jakarta (1 January 2012- 28 February 2022) and the Bandung Polytechnic of Social Welfare (1 March 1993 – December 2011). Prof Adi was also appointed as a Visiting Professor at the Japan University College of Social Work, Tokyo Japan (2018-2025). From 2015-2023, he was appointed as a Visiting Professor and Associate Research Fellow at The Psychology and Social Health Research Unit, Faculty of Psychology and Education, Universiti Malaysia Sabah. Previously he was appointed as a Visiting Professor in the Faculty of Applied Social Sciences, Universiti Sultan Zainal Abidin (UnisZa), Malaysia (2014-2015), and Visiting Associate Professor at Universiti Sains Malaysia (1997-1998). .

***

Saikat Gocchait is presently working with Symbiosis Institute of Telecom Management (constituent of Symbiosis International: Deemed University). Ph.D thesis was awarded with Coventry Bursary Award in 2010, Deusto International Tuning Academy (DITA) Scholarships from University of Deusto, Spain, and Taiwan Research Fellowship 2019 from Ministry of Foreign Affairs. Post Doctoral fellow from University of Extremadura, Spain.

Rashid Hashmi is a seasoned senior journalist with a rich and diverse experience spanning over 22 years in Broadcast, Digital, and Print Media. Prior to joining Sharda University, he held the position of Executive Editor and Senior Anchor at the renowned national news channel, 'India News'. Throughout his illustrious journalistic career, Rashid Hashmi has served in various capacities across prominent media platforms including Dainik Jagran Newspaper, ETV, Total TV, FM News, and India News. His expertise encompasses anchoring, debating, and ground zero reporting of numerous parliamentary and assembly elections, providing insightful coverage of pivotal political events. Rashid Hashmi is renowned for his engaging interviews with prominent personalities from the worlds of politics, sports, and Bollywood. His interviews have featured distinguished celebrities, political leaders, and sports icons, offering unique perspectives and valuable insights to viewers and readers alike. With a keen eye for detail and a commitment to journalistic integrity, Rashid Hashmi has earned widespread acclaim for his contribution to media discourse in India. His dynamic approach to storytelling and extensive experience across multiple media formats underline his versatility and depth as a journalist. Rashid Hashmi's tenure in the media industry reflects a dedication to delivering compelling and informative content while upholding the values of responsible journalism. His role in shaping public discourse through impactful reporting and incisive interviews underscores his standing as a respected figure in Indian journalism.

Hemlata Parmar is a luminary in the field of computer Science and Engineering. Her journey is defined by a constellation of achievements from prolific publications and patents to enlightening guest lectures. Yet, her brilliance is matched only by her unwavering commitment to human ethics. With a heart as vast as her intellect, she champions women's empowerment, bridging the gap with empathy and insight. In every endeavor, she embodies the perfect fusion of academic process and compassionate advocacy, inspiring generations to come.

Kus Hanna Rahmi, M.Psi, a clinical psychologist, is a lecturer at the Faculty of Psychology, Bhayangkara Jakarta Raya University. Born in Malang on October 26, 1977, she completed her Bachelor of Psychology (S1), then continued her Master of Professional Psychology (S2) and Doctor of Psychology (S3) at Persada Indonesia YAI University, Jakarta. As a practicing psychologist, Dr. Hanna actively provides clinical services at Rumah Sakit Muhammadiyah Taman Puring, South Jakarta, with a main focus on psychological interventions for adult individuals with various psychological problems. With more than 10 years of experience in clinical practice, she is committed to developing evidence-based intervention approaches. Much of her research and teaching relates to adult clinical interventions and therapeutic approaches. Currently, Dr. Hanna is developing the book "Trauma and Violence Psychological Review", as a contribution to deepen the understanding and treatment of trauma faced by individuals in the context of violence. Dr. Hanna is also active in providing training and seminars in various institutions and communities, as well as writing scientific articles in the field of clinical psychology. With high dedication to the profession and science of psychology, she continues to strive to advance the field of adult clinical psychology in Indonesia.

|**Sameer Saharan** is a dedicated researcher in Forensic Science, specializing in fingerprint analysis, cyber forensics, and DNA fingerprinting. He holds a Ph.D. in Forensic Science from Amity University, Haryana, and has authored several research papers and book chapters. With a passion for continuous learning, Dr. Saharan actively contributes to the advancement of forensic science through his expertise and knowledge. He is committed to nurturing the next generation of forensic scientists and making a positive impact in the field.

|**George Sedhom** is a multifaceted professional with a distinguished career in academia and the media industry. As an assistant professor of multimedia & new media technology at Galala University, he brings a wealth of applied experience to his role. His background in motion graphics design is particularly noteworthy, having

worked with various local and multinational television channels and networks. Dr. George's expertise extends to creating TV commercials and designing visual identities for diverse institutions. He has also made significant contributions to the pharmaceutical sector, providing visual solutions and branding identities. His versatility is further demonstrated by his extensive experience in higher education, having taught at multiple universities and institutes. Dr. George's research interests are broad and impactful, focusing on digital media, motion graphics, social media, media technology, education technology, visual effects, and 3D arts. He has published numerous research papers in these fields, contributing to the advancement of knowledge in multimedia and new media technology. Throughout his career, Dr. George has successfully bridged the gap between academic theory and practical application, making him a valuable asset in both educational and professional settings. His work continues to influence the fields of multimedia and new media technology, shaping the future of digital communication and visual arts.

Mridu Sharma is an Assistant Professor at Mody University of Science and Technology. Her research interests include Fingerprints, Toxicology, Ballistics, Cyber Forensics, Questioned Documents, Forensic Biology and Serology, Crime Scene Investigation, Forensic entomology, and anthropology.

Satya Subrahmanyam is a distinguished academic leader, researcher, and institutional strategist with over 27 years of experience in higher education, leadership, and research management. He holds two PhDs and a Postdoctoral qualification from the Polytechnic Institute of Leiria, Portugal. Currently serving as Professor and Dean (Research) at Holy Spirit University of Kaslik (USEK), Lebanon, he spearheads research initiatives that enhance academic excellence and institutional reputation. He played a pivotal role in the development of the Catholic University in Erbil, Kurdistan, where he established new departments, led research programs, and collaborated on international educational projects. As a founding member and Managing Partner of Vignan Institute of Technology and Management, India, he contributed to its transformation into a premier institution. With expertise in AI-driven business strategies, HR analytics, and leadership in technology adoption, he has published extensively, guided PhD research, and led training programs in corporate and academic settings.

Sharon Wilson is an Associate Professor at the Department of Mass Communication at Universiti Tunku Abdul Rahman (UTAR). She holds a PhD, in Communication from the National University of Malaysia (UKM). Her background is in journalism and much of her work has focused on media and crime working on online scams, gangs and serial rape. She currently chairs the Centre for Media and Communication Research (CMCR) at the university. Her research focuses on media, crime and society and woman and identity.

Index

Symbols

A

C

D

www.ingramcontent.com/pod-product-compliance
Lightning Source LLC
LaVergne TN
LVHW061545290926
849162LV00004B/914